Java Game Development with LibGDX

From Beginner to Professional

Second Edition

Lee Stemkoski

Apress®

Java Game Development with LibGDX: From Beginner to Professional

Lee Stemkoski
Garden City, New York, USA

ISBN-13 (pbk): 978-1-4842-3323-8   ISBN-13 (electronic): 978-1-4842-3324-5
https://doi.org/10.1007/978-1-4842-3324-5

Library of Congress Control Number: 2018931188

Cover image by Freepik (`www.freepik.com`)

Managing Director: Welmoed Spahr
Editorial Director: Todd Green
Acquisitions Editor: Steve Anglin
Development Editor: Matthew Moodie
Technical Reviewer: Garry Patchett
Coordinating Editor: Mark Powers
Copy Editor: April Rondeau

Distributed to the book trade worldwide by Springer Science+Business Media New York, 233 Spring Street, 6th Floor, New York, NY 10013. Phone 1-800-SPRINGER, fax (201) 348-4505, email orders-ny@springer-sbm.com, or visit `www.springeronline.com`. Apress Media, LLC is a California LLC and the sole member (owner) is Springer Science + Business Media Finance Inc (SSBM Finance Inc). SSBM Finance Inc is a **Delaware** corporation.

For information on translations, please email rights@apress.com, or visit `http://www.apress.com/rights-permissions`.

Apress titles may be purchased in bulk for academic, corporate, or promotional use. eBook versions and licenses are also available for most titles. For more information, reference our Print and eBook Bulk Sales web page at `http://www.apress.com/bulk-sales`.

Any source code or other supplementary material referenced by the author in this book is available to readers on GitHub via the book's product page, located at `www.apress.com/9781484233238`. For more detailed information, please visit `http://www.apress.com/source-code`.

Printed on acid-free paper

Contents

About the Author

Lee Stemkoski is a professor of computer science and mathematics. He earned his Ph.D. in mathematics from Dartmouth College in 2006. He has been teaching at the college level since, with an emphasis on Java programming, computer graphics, and video game development since 2010. Lee particularly enjoys playing classic games released for the Nintendo and Super Nintendo Entertainment System consoles. He has written another book, *Game Development with Construct 2*, in addition to many other scholarly articles and game development tutorials.

About the Technical Reviewer

Garry Patchett has worked in IT and engineering for more than 20 years designing products, creating software, and administering and documenting systems. With a master's degree in project management, he is a dedicated "systems nerd" whose interests vary from the technological to the philosophical. Garry is currently working freelance and is involved in various open source projects.

Acknowledgments

I would like to acknowledge the amazing editorial and support staff at Apress, for without their talent and dedication this book you are reading would not exist. In particular, I'd like to thank Mark Powers for his constant words of support and encouragement.

I'd also like to thank the technical reviewer, Garry Patchett, for his attention to both the programming and the pedagogical aspects of this book. From the very beginning, he intuitively understood who the target audience was and the level of detail and guidance they needed. Garry's many insightful comments and suggestions greatly improved the clarity of this book, and I am grateful for all the time and energy he put into helping to make this book the best that it could be.

Finally, a special thanks to my students, past and present, for their continuous and infectious enthusiasm. Your drive and devotion to game development is what inspired me to write this book.

Introduction

Welcome to *Java Game Development with LibGDX*!

In this book, you'll learn how to program games in Java using the LibGDX game development framework. The LibGDX libraries are both powerful and easy to use, and they will enable you to create a great variety of games quickly and efficiently. LibGDX is free and open source, can be used to make 2D and 3D games, and integrates easily with third-party libraries to support additional features.

I have taught courses in Java programming and video game development for many years, and I've often struggled to find game-programming books that I can recommend to my students without reservation, which led me to write this book you are currently reading. In particular, you will find that this book contains the following unique combination of features, chosen with the aspiring game developer (that's you!) in mind:

- This book recommends and explains how to use a simple Java development environment so that you can move on to programming games more quickly.

- By using the LibGDX framework, you won't have to "reinvent the wheel" for common programming tasks such as rendering graphics and playing audio. (An explanation of how to write such code from scratch would easily require fifty or more additional pages of reading.) LibGDX streamlines the development process and allows you to focus on game mechanics and design.

- This book contains *many* examples of video games that can be developed with LibGDX. The first part of the book will introduce you to the basic features provided by the framework. The second part will cover a variety of games to illustrate the power and flexibility of LibGDX. The third part of the book will introduce some advanced techniques to incorporate into previous and new game projects. I believe that working through many examples is fundamental to the learning process; you will observe programming patterns common to many games, see the benefits of writing reusable code in practice, have the opportunity to compare and contrast code from different projects, and gain experience by implementing additional features on your own.

- At the beginning of this book, I am assuming that you have only a basic familiarity with Java programming. (For more details about what background knowledge you need, please consult the appendix.) Throughout the first few chapters of this book, advanced programming concepts will be introduced and explained as they arise naturally and are needed in the context of game programming. By the time you reach the end of this book, you will have learned about many advanced Java programming topics that are also useful for software development in general.

Thank you for allowing me to be your guide as you begin your journey as a game programmer. I hope that you will find this book both informative and enjoyable, and that it enables and inspires you to create your own video games to share with the world.

Video Game Projects

As mentioned previously, this book is unique in the number and variety of games that are covered. In particular, you will learn how to create the following 12 video games in this book:

- *Starfish Collector*. In this game, you guide a turtle who is on a quest to collect starfish. This simple game is used to introduce the functionality of LibGDX and the extended framework you will create, and is revisited frequently throughout the book when introducing new features, such as user interfaces, cutscenes, audio, tilemaps, and gamepad controls.

- *Space Rocks*. This space-themed shoot-em-up game is inspired by the classic arcade game *Asteroids*, in which you control a spaceship and shoot lasers to destroy rocks that are flying around the screen.

- *The Missing Homework*. This is a visual novel–style game that is completely story driven. It presents to the player a series of choices that influence the progression of the story. In this game, you help a student to locate his misplaced homework, which is located somewhere in his school.

- *Rhythm Tapper*. This is a musical rhythm-based game in which the player presses a sequence of keys indicated by falling objects that overlap targets; the sequence is synchronized with music playing in the background.

- *Plane Dodger*. This endless side-scrolling action game is inspired by modern smartphone games such as *Flappy Bird* and *Jetpack Joyride*. In this game, you control a plane that dodges enemies flying past, while at the same time trying to collect stars to earn the highest score possible.

- *Rectangle Destroyer*. Inspired by arcade and early console games such as *Breakout* and *Arkanoid*, you move a paddle to bounce a ball into a wall of bricks to destroy them, earning points and powerups in the process.

- *Jigsaw Puzzle*. A drag-and-drop game where you move and arrange pieces of an image to reconstruct a larger picture.

- *52 Card Pickup*. A drag-and-drop solitaire card game in which you sort through a scattered pile of playing cards and arrange them into organized and ordered piles by rank and suit.

- *Jumping Jack*. This is a side-scrolling platform–style game inspired by arcade and console games such as *Donkey Kong* and *Super Mario Bros*. In this game, you help Jack the Koala collect coins and keys on his quest to reach the goal.

- *Treasure Quest*. This is a top-view adventure game inspired by classic console games such as *The Legend of Zelda*. In this game, you use your sword and arrows to defeat your enemies and collect coins to use at the item shop as you find your way to the treasure.

- *Maze Runman*. This maze-based game is inspired by arcade games such as *Pac-Man* and the early console game *Maze Craze*. In this game, you attempt to collect all the coins before being captured by a ghost that continuously follows you throughout a randomly created maze.

- *Starfish Collector 3D*. This game is a 3D remake of the *Starfish Collector* game introduced in the beginning of the book and introduces 3D game programming concepts.

Changes from the First Edition

There have been a great number of changes to the content and organization of the book based on feedback from readers, students, and teachers. The major changes are listed here:

- Reduced number of elementary examples; in particular, the games *Cheese Please* and *Balloon Buster* from the first edition have been removed.

- New functionality has been added to the BaseActor class to simplify gathering instances of a class into lists.

- Game entities are now typically written as extensions of the BaseActor class so as to increase encapsulation and reduce the amount of code required by the BaseScreen classes.

- The content of Chapter 4 ("Adding Polish to Your Game") of the first edition has been separated into Chapters 5 and 6 in the second edition, allowing for extended treatment of user-interface design and audio support. Each of these topics also has its own dedicated example game project.

- The material on the bitmap font–generating program Hiero has been replaced by bitmap font–generating classes, allowing the developer to more quickly generate custom fonts from true-type font (ttf) files in code. This circumvents the need to generate bitmap font images ahead of time, which should streamline the development process.

- The code for detecting the bounce angle for the ball in *Rectangle Destroyer* has been greatly simplified.

- The drag-and-drop–related code and tilemap-related code have been refactored into their own separate classes for easier reuse in other projects.

- Individual games have been reorganized into separate chapters and introduce many new game mechanics. In particular, Chapter 6 ("Additional Game Case Studies") of the first edition has been separated into Chapters 4, 7, 8, and 9 in the second edition. The games of Chapter 7 ("Integrating Third-Party Software") of the first edition have been separated into Chapters 11 and 12 in the second edition.

- Because of the importance of tilemaps, the corresponding material has been moved into its own chapter (Chapter 10) and is used to simplify previous game projects (*Starfish Collector* and *Rectangle Destroyer*) before moving on to move advanced games in the following chapters.

- The material on the physics engine Box2D has been eliminated to reduce complexity and unnecessary overhead in favor of using custom physics code.

- Advanced topics have been added (maze generation in Chapter 14 and shader programming in Chapter 15).

- The 3D demo from the first edition ("Pirate Cruiser") has been replaced by the game project *Starfish Collector 3D*.

- New appendices have been added containing advice and examples for game-design documentation and a complete JavaDoc-style listing of the extension classes developed in the book as a helpful reference.

PART I

■ ■ ■

Fundamental Concepts

In the following chapters, you will be introduced to the LibGDX library and build a custom framework on top of this library to simplify creating a variety of games. These chapters are the foundation for the rest of the book; future chapters will assume a working knowledge of the topics presented here.

Chapter 1: Getting Started with Java and LibGDX

This chapter will explain how to set up BlueJ, a Java development environment that has been chosen for its simplicity and user-friendliness. The standard first program (which prints "Hello, World!" to the text console) will be explained. Next, instructions for setting up the LibGDX software library will be given, and a visual "Hello, World!" program will be presented (which displays an image of the world in a window). Finally, some of the benefits of using LibGDX for game development will be explained in detail.

Chapter 2: The LibGDX Framework

This chapter will begin by discussing the overall structure of a video game program, including the stages that a game program progresses through and the tasks that must be accomplished at each stage. Many of the major features and classes of the LibGDX library will be introduced in the process of creating a basic game called *Starfish Collector*. This game is a recurring example throughout the book; features will be added to this project when introducing new topics.

Chapter 3: Extending the Framework

In this chapter, you'll start with a core LibGDX class that represents game entities and create an extension of this class to support animation, physics-based movement, improved collision detection, and the ability to manage multiple instances of an entity using lists.

Chapter 4: Shoot-em-up Games

This chapter will demonstrate the power of the framework you have created by using that framework to make an entirely new game: *Space Rocks*, a space-themed shoot-em-up game inspired by the classic arcade game *Asteroids*. Along the way, you will add to the framework, incorporating the ability to handle input for discrete actions such as shooting lasers (in contrast to continuous actions, such as movement).

Chapter 5: Text and User Interfaces

In this chapter, you will learn how to display text, create buttons that display an image or text, and design a user interface using tables. First, you will be introduced to these skills by adding these features to the *Starfish Collector* game from Chapter 3. Then, you will build on and strengthen these skills while learning how to create cutscenes (sometimes called in-game cinematics) that provide a narrative element to your games. In an optional final section, you will create a visual novel–style game called *The Missing Homework*, which focuses on a story and allows the player to make decisions about how the story proceeds.

Chapter 6: Audio

In this chapter, you will learn how to add audio elements—sound effects and background music—to your game. First, you will be introduced to these topics by adding these features to the *Starfish Collector*. Then, in an optional section, you will build on these skills with a musical rhythm-based game called *Rhythm Tapper*, in which the player presses a sequence of keys indicated visually that are synchronized with music playing in the background.

CHAPTER 1

■ ■ ■

Getting Started with Java and LibGDX

This chapter will explain how to set up a Java development environment and configure it to run with the LibGDX game development framework. You'll see a simple example of a "Hello, World!" program and explore it in enough detail to understand the different parts. Finally, you'll learn some of the advantages to be gained by working with the LibGDX library.

Choosing a Development Environment

Before diving into Java programming, you will need to set up an integrated development environment (IDE)—the software you will use for writing, debugging, and compiling code. There are many editors for writing your Java programs, each customized for different skill levels. BlueJ (`www.bluej.org`) and DrJava (`www.drjava.org`) are designed for beginners and educational use and are frequently used in introductory programming courses in schools and colleges. IntelliJ IDEA (`www.jetbrains.com/idea/`), NetBeans (`netbeans.org`), and Eclipse (`eclipse.org`) are advanced editors that are preferred by practicing professionals. For compiling and running Java code, you'll need the Java Development Kit (JDK), which is available directly from the Oracle Corporation or is bundled directly with some of the editors just listed.

Each editor has advantages and disadvantages. BlueJ and DrJava are user friendly and have simple, minimal user interfaces, but lack some of the advanced editors' features, such as autocompletion of fields, methods, and import statements. The advanced editors are faster, feature-packed, more powerful, highly customizable, and replete with various plug-ins, but they also have a steep learning curve and user interfaces that may be more daunting to beginners. Figure 1-1 illustrates this point with a side-by-side comparison of the Eclipse and BlueJ interfaces. The screenshots and descriptions of the BlueJ software in this chapter are from BlueJ version 4.1.0.

© Lee Stemkoski 2018
L. Stemkoski, *Java Game Development with LibGDX*, https://doi.org/10.1007/978-1-4842-3324-5_1

3

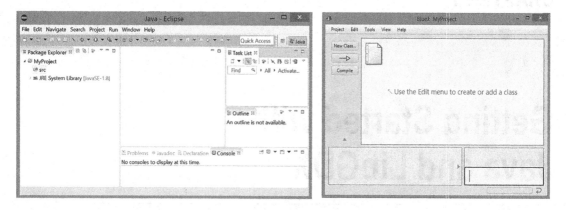

Figure 1-1. *User interfaces for Eclipse (left) and BlueJ (right)*

This chapter will cover how to set up BlueJ. I chose this particular IDE because it is quick and easy to set up and configure, which will enable you to start programming games even faster. However, if you are already familiar and comfortable with one of the more advanced editors, of course you should feel free to use it rather than BlueJ. A wealth of informational material is available for setting up Eclipse, NetBeans, and IntelliJ IDEA with LibGDX at the LibGDX wiki (https://github.com/libgdx/libgdx/wiki). If you choose to use one of these programs, then after your IDE is set up, skip ahead to the upcoming section "Creating a 'Hello, World!' Program for LibGDX."

Setting Up BlueJ

This section will cover how to set up the BlueJ IDE. Since it was designed for beginners, the number of steps is small and the process is straightforward, as you will see.

Downloading and Installing

BlueJ can be downloaded from www.bluej.org.

There are multiple download options available for a variety of operating systems. Furthermore, some of these downloads are bundled with the JDK, and some are not. The JDK includes tools for developing and debugging Java applications; in particular, it is necessary for compiling your code. If you have used your computer to develop Java applications before, you likely already have the JDK installed and can just select the stand-alone BlueJ installer. If you aren't sure, you should download and run the BlueJ combined installer.

Using BlueJ

When learning a new programming language or library, it is a well-established tradition in computer science to write a "Hello, World!" application as a first program. This section will cover the basics of using BlueJ to write this program:

1. Start up the BlueJ software. (The first time you run it, it may prompt you for the location of the directory where the JDK is stored, and it may also ask if you want to participate in helping to improve the software by providing information.)

2. When the main window appears, in the menu bar, select *Project*, then select *New Project*. BlueJ organizes your work into projects, which are stored as directories; all Java source code and compiled class files are stored in the project directory.

3. When prompted for a project name, navigate to a folder where you want to store your files, enter MyProject, and click the *OK* button. This creates a folder in the selected location with the same name.

After Step 3, your screen should look similar to Figure 1-2.

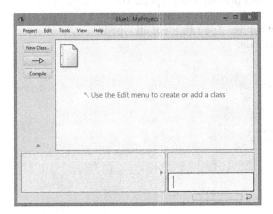

Figure 1-2. *The BlueJ project window*

4. Create a new class, either by clicking the *New Class* button or by selecting *Edit* and then selecting *New Class* from the menu bar.

5. When you are prompted to enter a name for the class, type HelloWorld and press the Enter key, or click the *OK* button. An orange rectangle appears with the name of your class at its top. The gray diagonal lines indicate that the code has not yet been compiled.

6. Either double-click the rectangle or right-click and select *Open Editor* to edit the file. You will see that some template code has been added. You should begin by deleting this code; the simplest way is to press Ctrl-A to select all the code, then press the Delete key. Then, enter the following code in its place:

```java
public class HelloWorld
{
    public static void main()
    {
        System.out.print("Hello, World!");
    }
}
```

After entering this code into BlueJ, it should appear similar to the screenshot in Figure 1-3. Don't worry about what this code does just yet. If there are any errors in the code, then that line number will be marked in red and the incorrect syntax will be underlined. If you hover the mouse pointer over the error, a popup will appear that provides a description of the error and sometimes a suggestion for how to fix it. Figure 1-4 illustrates what would happen if you accidentally typed pint instead of print in the preceding source code.

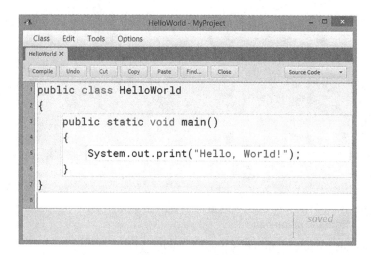

Figure 1-3. *A "Hello, World!" program displayed in the BlueJ code editor*

6

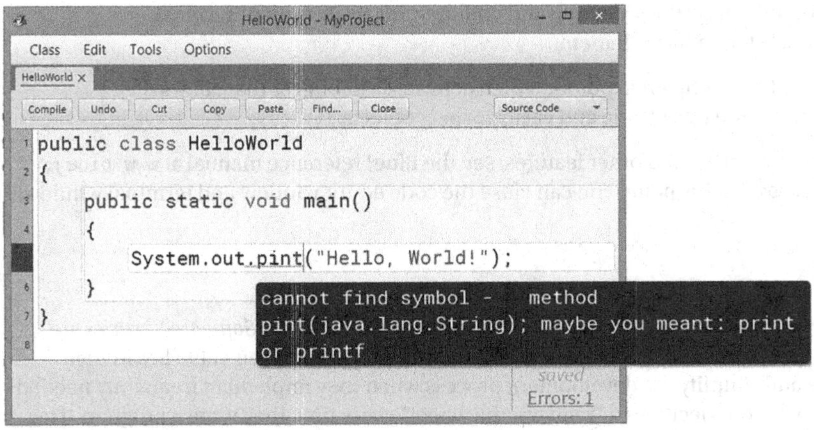

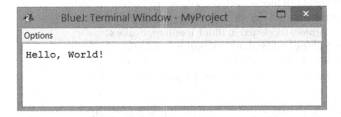

Figure 1-4. A syntax error caught by the BlueJ code editor

7. Click the *Compile* button to compile your code. (This action also automatically saves your code.) You should see the message "Class compiled – no syntax errors" in the status bar at the bottom of the window.

8. Return to the main BlueJ window. Right-click the orange rectangle representing the class (it contains the class name HelloWorld across the top), and select the method void main() from the list that appears. This runs the method that you have just written. A terminal window appears containing the text *Hello, World!*, as shown in Figure 1-5.

Figure 1-5. Text displayed by the "Hello, World!" program

Congratulations on running your first program using BlueJ!

BlueJ has a number of features that make programming easier. While entering the preceding code, you may have noticed the syntax highlighting (Java keywords and strings appear in different colors) and also that classes and methods appear surrounded by different background colors, which makes it easier to visually inspect your code. (Later, you'll notice that conditional statements and loops are similarly distinguished with background colors.) BlueJ contains additional features that you may find useful, such as the following:

- Automatic code formatting. Selecting *Auto-Layout* from the Edit menu of the source code editing window will adjust the whitespace in your code so that nested statements are aligned consistently.

- Listing available method names. After typing the name of a class or object, followed by a period, pressing Ctrl+Space will display a list of available method names.

- Shortcut keys for indenting/un-indenting and commenting/uncommenting blocks of code. These are listed in the Edit menu.

- A simple interface for adding breakpoints, which activates a debugger that allows you to step through code line by line and easily inspect objects.

For complete information on these and other features, see the BlueJ reference manual at www.bluej. org/doc/bluej-ref-manual.pdf. At this point, you can close the code editor window and terminal window.

Setting Up LibGDX

In this section, you'll configure BlueJ so that it can use the LibGDX software library. *Software libraries* are collections of prewritten code and methods that can be used by other programs. Their value lies in their reusability—they accelerate and simplify the development process when they implement frequently needed processes, saving programmers from needing to "reinvent the wheel" every time they write a program. The LibGDX libraries, for example, contain methods for displaying graphics, playing sounds, and getting input from the user. (Advanced functions are available as well, which will be discussed later in this chapter.)

In Java, libraries are stored in Java Archive (JAR) files. A JAR file contains many compiled Java files (similar to a ZIP file), stored in a standardized directory structure that the JDK can navigate. Your first step is to obtain the LibGDX JAR files that you will need for our project. The most up-to-date official information on obtaining these files is at https://github.com/libgdx/libgdx/wiki/Updating-LibGDX, which may be confusing for beginners. Alternatively, a simpler option is to use the versions of these files included on the download website for this book at apress.com.[1] The five JAR files you will need for all projects in this book are gdx.jar, gdx-sources.jar, gdx-natives.jar, gdx-backend-lwjgl.jar, and gdx-backend-lwjgl-natives.jar; they contain the core code for the LibGDX library.

Once these four JAR files have been obtained, BlueJ needs to be configured so that it recognizes and can use the contents of these files. There are two main ways to do so:

- The easiest way to make BlueJ aware of JAR files is to create a directory named +libs within the project directory, copy the JAR files into this directory, and then restart the BlueJ software. By default, when a project is opened in BlueJ, it automatically scans for the presence of a folder named +libs and takes its contents into account when compiling new code. Although this is the easiest method, you will need to recreate this directory and make copies of the JAR files for every new project, which is not the most efficient method.

- When there are JAR files that might be used in multiple projects, rather than creating redundant copies of these files in +libs directories for each of these projects, they can be copied to a special subdirectory, named userlib, in the folder where the BlueJ software is installed. The full path to the directory should be something similar to C:\Program Files\BlueJ\lib\userlib\; the exact name can be checked by selecting the menu option *Tools* ➤ *Preferences* in Windows, or *BlueJ* ➤ *Preferences* in OS X, and clicking the *Libraries* tab.

Once these steps are complete, BlueJ needs to be restarted, and then you'll be ready to write your first program in LibGDX.

---

[1]More recent versions of these files can be obtained from the website https://libgdx.badlogicgames.com/ nightlies/dist/. These are the nightly builds of the LibGDX libraries, which contain the most up-to-date code, but they are also under development and thus may contain a few bugs or glitches.

Creating a "Hello, World!" Program with LibGDX

Traditionally, a "Hello, World!" program displays a text message on the screen. Since our ultimate goal is to create video games—primarily visual programs—your first LibGDX program will draw a picture of the world in a window, as shown in Figure 1-6.

Figure 1-6. *A "Hello, World!" program created using LibGDX*

Here, you will begin to see some of the advantages of and start to understand what is meant by building upon the classes provided by the LibGDX libraries. Our first project contains two classes. The first class, called HelloWorldImage, makes use of the functionality of a LibGDX class called Game by extending it.

EXTENDING A CLASS

One of the central principles of software engineering is to design programs that avoid redundancy by creating reusable code. One way to accomplish this is by the object-oriented concept of inheritance: the creation of a new class based on an existing class.

For example, if we were designing a role-playing game, it would probably have many types of playable characters, such as warriors, ninjas, thieves, and wizards. If we were to design classes to represent each of these characters, they would have certain features in common: they each have a name, a certain number of health points (HP), and perhaps a method named attack that can be used when simulating combat.

Some features also may be unique to each character; for example, perhaps wizards also have a certain number of magic points (MP), and a method named castSpell that is called when they use magic. Because of the differences between these characters, we can't create a single class that represents all of them; at the same time, it feels redundant to keep entering the same fields over and over again in each of their separate classes. An elegant approach to this type of scenario is to create a base class that contains all the features common to these characters, and create other classes to extend this base class. The extending class has access to all the fields and methods of the base

---

class, and can also contain its own fields and methods as usual. We could implement this scenario with the following code:

```
public class Person
{
        String name;
        int HP;
        public void attack(Person other)
        {
                // insert code here...
        }
}
```

And then we can extend the Person class as follows:

```
public class Wizard extends Person
{
        int MP;
        public void castSpell( String spellName )
        {
                // insert code here...
        }
}
```

Then, if we were to create instances of these classes:

```
Person percy = new Person();
Wizard merlin = new Wizard();
```

Then, commands such as merlin.MP += 10 and merlin.castSpell("fireball") are valid, as well as commands involving fields and methods of the base class, such as merlin.HP -= 3 and merlin. attack(percy). However, the object called percy can use only the fields and methods of the Person class; code such as percy.HP += 5 will compile, but percy.castSpell("lightning") will result in an error when the file is compiled.

The concept of extending a class is not only useful for in-game entities, but also for framework-like elements. For example, it would be useful to have a Menu class that contains functionality common to all types of menus, such as opening and closing the menu. It might then be useful to create other classes that extend this one; for example, a class named SelectionMenu could be created, which is a Menu that specializes in displaying some sort of information and asks the player to make a selection from a set of options. An InformationMenu class might be a menu that displays some text-based information and simply closes when the player is finished reading it.

In BlueJ, the project named MyProject should still be open; if not, open the project. Create a new class in this project, called HelloWorldImage, and enter the source code that follows. Note that before the class itself, there are a number of import statements that indicate which of the LibGDX classes (from the JAR files you set up earlier) you'll be using in this program. Also note that this program uses an image with the filename world.png; this image is included in the source code for this chapter, in the folder MyProject (the source code is available from apress.com). You should copy this image into your MyProject folder. Alternatively, you could use an image of your own choosing instead; a size of 256 by 256 pixels is recommended for this program, and don't forget to change the filename in the following code accordingly if you do.

```java
import com.badlogic.gdx.Game;
import com.badlogic.gdx.Gdx;
import com.badlogic.gdx.files.FileHandle;
import com.badlogic.gdx.graphics.GL20;
import com.badlogic.gdx.graphics.g2d.SpriteBatch;
import com.badlogic.gdx.graphics.Texture;

public class HelloWorldImage extends Game
{
    private Texture texture;
    private SpriteBatch batch;

    public void create()
    {
        FileHandle worldFile = Gdx.files.internal("world.png");
        texture = new Texture(worldFile);
        batch = new SpriteBatch();
    }

    public void render()
    {
        Gdx.gl.glClearColor(1, 1, 1, 1);
        Gdx.gl.glClear(GL20.GL_COLOR_BUFFER_BIT);

        batch.begin();
        batch.draw( texture, 192, 112 );
        batch.end();
    }
}
```

The HelloWorldImage class contains two objects: a Texture and a SpriteBatch. A Texture is an object that stores image-related data: the dimensions (width and height) of an image and the color of each pixel. A SpriteBatch is an object that draws images to the screen.

The HelloWorldImage class also contains two methods: create and render.

The create method initializes the Texture and SpriteBatch objects. In particular, the Texture object requires an image file from which it will get its image data. For this purpose, you create a FileHandle: a LibGDX object that is used to access files stored on the computer. The Gdx class contains many useful static objects and methods (similar to Java's Math class); here, you use a method named internal to generate a FileHandle object that will be used by the Texture object. The internal method will search for the file in the BlueJ project directory, the same location where the compiled class files are stored.

After the create method is finished, the render method will be called by LibGDX approximately 60 times per second (since this is what the Game class does by default).[2] This method contains a pair of static method calls: one to select a particular background color (the values in this example correspond to the color white) and another to use that color to clear the window. After this, the SpriteBatch object is used to position and draw the texture to the window.

---

[2]Since neither the texture nor the coordinates are changing in this example, the fact that the render method is called repeatedly is irrelevant here. However, if you were to periodically change the image, you could generate an animation; if you were to gradually change the coordinates, you could simulate motion. You will see how to accomplish both of these variations in the following chapter.

Next, you'll create a second class that is used to start the program; it creates an instance of the HelloWorldImage class and activates its methods. Such a class is often called a *driver* class and requires you to write a *static* method.

STATIC METHODS AND DRIVER CLASSES

By default, the methods of a class are called by instances of that class. However, a method can also be declared to be *static*, meaning that it is called from the class directly (rather than an instance). Whether a method should be instance-based or class-based (static) depends on how the method is used and what data it requires.

An instance-based method usually depends on the internal data specific to that instance. For example, every String object has a method called charAt, which takes an integer as input and returns the character stored at that position in the String. If we create two String objects as follows:

```
String player1 = "Lee";
String player2 = "Dan";
```

then the expression player1.charAt(1) returns the character 'e', while player2.charAt(1) returns the character 'a'. The value returned by this method depends on the data stored in that instance, and thus charAt is most assuredly an instance-based method.

In object-oriented programming languages, most of the methods of a class will be instance-based because they either depend upon or potentially change the values of an instance's variables. There are, of course, situations where static methods are more natural. In general, any method that does not involve the internal state of an object could be declared as static (such as mathematical formulas—all the methods of Java's Math class are static).

A *driver* class (also sometimes referred to as a main, entry point, starter, or launcher class) is a class whose purpose is to drive the execution of another class, which often involves creating an instance of the class and calling one or more of its methods. The driver class typically requires only a single method to accomplish this task; this method is traditionally called main. Since it is the first method called by the program, the main method must be declared as static, because when a program starts, there are no instances available to run instance-based methods. If the main method were not static, we would have a problem similar to the philosophical conundrum: which came first, the chicken or the egg? Something has to be able to instantiate a class without itself being instantiated, and this is exactly what the static main method of a driver class does.

A standard "Hello, World!" program could be rewritten using a driver class as follows:

```
public class Greeter
{
        public void sayHello()
        {
                System.out.print("Hello!");
        }
}
```

```
public class Launcher
{
        public static void main()
        {
                Greeter greta = new Greeter();
                greta.sayHello();
        }
}
```

Next, in the same project, create a class called HelloLauncher that contains the following code:

```
import com.badlogic.gdx.backends.lwjgl.LwjglApplication;
public class HelloLauncher
{
    public static void main (String[] args)
    {
        HelloWorldImage myProgram = new HelloWorldImage();
        LwjglApplication launcher = new LwjglApplication( myProgram );
    }
}
```

As mentioned in the previous "Static Methods and Driver Classes" sidebar, this class first creates an instance of the HelloWorldImage class, called myProgram. Then, instead of running the methods of myProgram directly, the main method creates a LwjglApplication object, which sets up a window and manages the graphics and audio, keyboard and mouse input, and file access. The LwjglApplication object takes myProgram as input and then runs the create and render methods of myProgram as discussed previously.

The acronym LWJGL stands for the *Lightweight Java Game Library*, an open source Java library originally created by Caspian Rychlik-Prince to simplify game development in terms of accessing the desktop computer hardware resources. In LibGDX, LWJGL is used for the desktop backend to support all the major desktop operating systems, such as Windows, Linux, and Mac OS X.

Another benefit to having a driver class separate from the classes that contain the game functionality is the potential to create driver classes for other platforms, such as Android, which LibGDX also supports.

When you've entered all the code for both classes, return to the main window in BlueJ and click the *Compile* button. Then, right-click the orange rectangle for the HelloLauncher class, and in the list of methods that appears, select the method listed as void main(String[] args). A pop-up window appears, in which you could enter an array of strings as input if you needed to—but you don't. Click the *OK* button, and you should see a window as shown previously in Figure 1-6.

Congratulations on completing your first application using LibGDX!

■ **Note** Sometimes, your program will contain a runtime error, often caused by issues such as entering a filename incorrectly (which cannot be detected when the program is compiled). In this case, after fixing the error and running the program again, you may encounter a different error containing the message "No OpenGL context found in the current thread." This is due to the prior unexpected shutdown of the application and can usually be fixed in BlueJ by resetting the Java virtual machine, which can be done via the Tools menu or with a shortcut key combination (Ctrl-Shift-R on Windows).

Advantages to Using LibGDX

In addition to the ability to compile your game so that it can run on multiple platforms, there are many other advantages to using the LibGDX game development framework. LibGDX makes it easy to accomplish tasks such as these:

- Render 2D graphics, animations, bitmap-based fonts, and particle effects

- Stream music and play sound effects

- Process input from a keyboard, mouse, touchscreens, accelerometer, or game pad

- Organize user interfaces using a scene graph and fully skinnable UI control library

- Integrate third-party plug-ins, such as the Box2D physics engine (box2d.org), the Tiled map editor file format (mapeditor.org), and the Spine 2D animation software (esotericsoftware.com)

- Render 3D graphics with materials and lighting effects and load 3D models from common file formats such as OBJ and FBX

A complete list of LibGDX features can be found at the website: http://libgdx.badlogicgames.com/features.html.

Summary

In this chapter, you've set up BlueJ, an integrated development environment for Java programming, and configured BlueJ to use the LibGDX game development framework. Then, you created your first application with LibGDX: a "Hello, World!" program that displays an image of the world in a window. This program involved extending LibGDX's Game class and creating a driver class that runs the program on the desktop. Along the way, you learned about a few of the other classes involved in this program. Finally, you learned about some of the additional features of the LibGDX library, many of which will be discussed in detail in future chapters.

CHAPTER 2

The LibGDX Framework

This chapter will introduce many of the major features of the LibGDX library. It will illustrate how to use them in the process of creating a game called *Starfish Collector*, where you help the player's character, a turtle, swim around the ocean floor while looking for a starfish. A screenshot of this game in action appears in Figure 2-1. At first, you will create a basic, functional game. Following a motivational discussion of object-oriented design principles, you will rewrite parts of this project using some of the LibGDX classes to improve the organization of the code. Future chapters will revisit this example and use it as a basis to introduce new game-design principles and features of LibGDX.

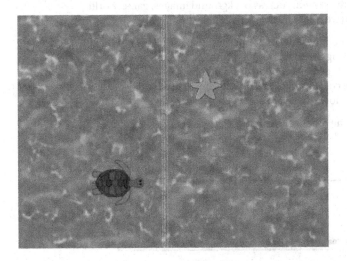

Figure 2-1. *The main screen for the game* Starfish Collector

© Lee Stemkoski 2018
L. Stemkoski, *Java Game Development with LibGDX*, https://doi.org/10.1007/978-1-4842-3324-5_2

The Life Cycle of a Video Game

Before jumping into the programming aspect of game development, it is important to understand the overall structure of a game program: the major stages that a game program progresses through and the tasks that a game program must perform in each stage. The stages are as follows:

- *Startup*: During this stage, any files needed (such as images or sounds) are loaded, game objects are created, and values are initialized.

- *The game loop*: A stage that repeats continuously while the game is running and that consists of the following three sub-stages:

- *Process input*: The program checks to see if the user has performed any action that sends data to the computer: pressing keyboard keys, moving the mouse or clicking mouse buttons, touching or swiping on a touchscreen, or pressing joysticks or buttons on a game pad.

- *Update*: Performs tasks that involve the state of the game world and the entities within it. This could include changing the positions of entities based on user input or physics simulations, performing collision detection to determine when two entities come in contact with each other and what action to perform in response, or selecting actions for nonplayer characters.

- *Render*: Draws all graphics on the screen, such as background images, game-world entities, and the user interface (which typically overlays the game world).

- *Shutdown*: This stage begins when the player provides input to the computer indicating that he is finished using the software (for example, by clicking a *Quit* button) and may involve removing images or data from memory, saving player data or the game state, signaling the computer to stop monitoring hardware devices for user input, and closing any windows that were created by the game.

The flowchart in Figure 2-2 illustrates the order in which these stages occur.

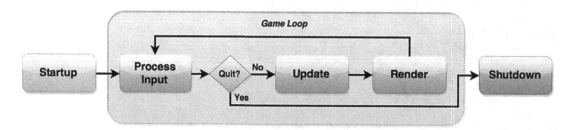

Figure 2-2. *The stages of a game program*

Some game developers may include additional stages in the game loop, such as the following:

- A *sleep* stage that pauses the execution of the program for a given amount of time. Many game developers aim to write programs that can run at 60 frames per second (FPS), meaning that the game loop will run once every 16.67 milliseconds.[1] If the game loop can run faster than this, the program can be instructed to pause for whatever amount of time remains in the 16.67-millisecond interval, thus freeing up the CPU for any other applications that may be running in the background. LibGDX automatically handles this for us, so we won't worry about including it here.

- An *audio* stage, where any background music is streamed or sound effects are played. In this book, we will consider playing audio as part of the update stage, and we will discuss how to accomplish this in a later chapter.

Most of these stages are handled by a corresponding method in LibGDX. For example, the startup stage is carried out by a method named create, the update and render stages are both handled by the render method,[2] and any shutdown actions are performed by a method named dispose.

In fact, when your driver class creates any kind of application (such as a LwjglApplication), the application will work correctly only if given an object that contains a certain set of methods (including create, render, and dispose); this is a necessary convention so that the application knows what to do during each stage of the game program's life cycle. You are able to enforce such requirements in Java programs by using interfaces.

INTERFACES

Informally, you can think of an *interface* as a kind of contract that other classes can promise to fulfill. As a simple example, let's say that you write a Player class, which contains a method named talkTo that is used to interact with objects in your environment. The talkTo method takes a single input, called creature, and in the code that follows, you have

```
creature.speak();
```

For the talkTo method to work correctly, whatever type of object that creature is an instance of, it *must* have a method named speak. Maybe sometimes creature is an instance of a Person class, while at other times creature is an instance of a Monster class. In general, you would like the talkTo method to be as inclusive as possible—any object with a speak method should be permitted as input. You can specify this behavior by using interfaces.

First, you create an interface as follows:

```
public interface Speaker
{
    public void speak();
}
```

---

[1] Running faster than this is usually unnecessary, because most computer display hardware is incapable of displaying images at a greater rate than this.

[2] A later section in this chapter will demonstrate how to organize code more intuitively so that the update and render stages are handled by separate methods.

At first glance, an interface appears similar to a class, except that the methods are only declared; they do not contain any actual code. All that is required is the *signature* of the method: the name, the output type, the input types (if any), and any modifiers, such as `public`. This information is followed by a semicolon instead of the familiar set of braces that encompass code. The classes that implement this interface will provide the code for their version of the `speak` function. It is important to emphasize that since `Speaker` is not a class, you *cannot* create an instance of a `Speaker` object; instead, you write other classes that include the methods as specified in the `Speaker` interface.

A class indicates that it meets the requirements of an interface (that it contains all the indicated fields and methods) by including the keyword `implements`, followed by the name of the interface, after the name of the class. Any class that implements the `Speaker` interface must provide the code for its version of the `speak` function. The following demonstrates with a class called `Person` and a class called `Monster`:

```
public class Person implements Speaker
{
    // additional code above
    public void speak()
    {   System.out.println( "Hello." );  }
    // additional code below
}
```

```
public class Monster implements Speaker
{
    // additional code above
    public void speak()
    {   System.out.println("Grrr!");  }
    // additional code below
}
```

Always remember: When implementing an interface, you *must* write methods for everything declared in the interface; otherwise, there will be a compile-time error. You could even write a method that contains no code between the braces, as shown next (for a class that represents a particularly untalkative piece of furniture). This can be convenient when you need to use only part of the functionality of the interface.

```
public class Chair implements Speaker
{
    // additional code above
    public void speak()  { }
    // additional code below
}
```

Finally, you write the method `talkTo` so that it takes a `Speaker` as input:

```
public class Player
{
        // additional code above
```

```
    public void talkTo(Speaker creature)
    {
            creature.speak();
    }

    // additional code below
}
```

Any class that implements the `Speaker` interface may be used as input for a `Player` object's `talkTo` method. For example, we present some code that creates instances of each of these classes, and then we describe the results in the accompanying comments:

```
Player dan = new Player();
Person chris = new Person();
Monster grez = new Monster();
Chair footstool = new Chair();
dan.talkTo(chris); // prints "Hello."
dan.talkTo(grez); // prints "Grrr!"
dan.talkTo(footstool); // does not print anything
```

An application in LibGDX requires user-created classes to implement the `ApplicationListener` interface so that it can handle all stages of a game program's life cycle. You may recall, however, that in our example from Chapter 1, the `HelloWorldImage` class did not implement the `ApplicationListener` class; it only extended the `Game` class. Why didn't this result in an error when the class was compiled? If you take a look "under the hood" (which, in the context of computer programming, typically means to inspect the source code[3]), you'll notice that the `Game` class itself implements the `ApplicationListener` class and includes "empty" versions of the functions; there is no code between the braces that define the body of each function. This enables you to write only variations of the interface methods that you need to use in the class that extends the `Game` class, which will then *override* the versions in the `Game` class; any interface method that you don't write will default to the empty version in the `Game` class. (In fact, the `ApplicationListener` interface requires a total of six methods: `create`, `render`, `resize`, `pause`, `resume`, and `dispose`; in our example, you wrote only two of these.)

Game Project: Starfish Collector

This section will introduce the game *Starfish Collector*, previously shown in Figure 2-1. Before starting to write the code for this game, it is helpful to precisely describe its features: the game mechanics and rules, how the player interacts with the software, the graphics that will be required, and so forth. Such a description is called a game-design document and is explained more fully in Appendix A of this book. Since this is the first game you will be creating with LibGDX, only the following minimal set of features will be created:

- The player will control a turtle, whose goal is to collect a single starfish.

- Movement is controlled by the arrow keys. The up arrow key moves the turtle toward the top of the screen, the right arrow key moves the turtle toward the right side of the screen, and so on. Multiple arrow keys can be pressed at the same time to move the turtle in diagonal directions. Movement speed is constant.

---

[3]The source code for LibGDX is currently hosted on GitHub at `https://github.com/libgdx/libgdx`.

- The turtle collects the starfish by coming into contact with it (when their graphics overlap). When this happens, the starfish disappears, and a message that reads "You Win" appears.

- The graphics required by this game include images of a turtle, a starfish, water, and a message that contains the text "You Win."

One version of the code that accomplishes these tasks is presented next. Some of the code and concepts will be familiar from the HelloWorldImage example, such as the Texture and SpriteBatch classes, the purpose of the create and render methods, and the role of the driver class. There are a few new additions as well. Since the coordinates of the turtle may change, you use variables to store these values. Most significantly, you introduce some code that makes our program interactive—you will process keyboard input from the user. Finally, you'll include a Boolean variable that keeps track of whether the player has won, which becomes true when the turtle reaches the starfish and affects when the "You Win" message is displayed on the screen.

In this section, as well as the sections that follow, you are invited to create a new project in BlueJ (after closing the previous project by selecting *Close* from the BlueJ Project menu) and enter the code that is presented, or, alternatively, to simply download the source code from the website for this book and run the code via the included BlueJ project files. The online source code also contains all the images that you will need, stored in the assets folder in each project, and referenced in the following code.

To begin, download the source code files for this chapter on the website for this book. Create a new project in BlueJ named Starfish Collector Ch2 (since there will be many versions of this project created throughout this book). In the project directory that is created by BlueJ, create a new folder called assets. Copy the image files from the downloaded project's assets folder into your new project's assets folder; keeping the source code separate from the images in this manner will help keep your files organized. Next, in your project directory, create a new folder named +libs. Copy the JAR files from the downloaded project's +libs folder into your new project's +libs folder. Restart BlueJ so that the JAR files newly added to the +libs folder are properly recognized by BlueJ.

In your BlueJ project, create a new class called StarfishCollectorAlpha. The source code for this class appears next. There are new import statements that enable you to create a variety of new objects, which are also explained in what follows:

```java
import com.badlogic.gdx.ApplicationListener;
import com.badlogic.gdx.Gdx;
import com.badlogic.gdx.Input.Keys;
import com.badlogic.gdx.graphics.GL20;
import com.badlogic.gdx.graphics.Texture;
import com.badlogic.gdx.graphics.g2d.SpriteBatch;
import com.badlogic.gdx.math.Rectangle;
import com.badlogic.gdx.Game;

public class StarfishCollectorAlpha extends Game
{
    private SpriteBatch batch;

    private Texture turtleTexture;
    private float turtleX;
    private float turtleY;
    private Rectangle turtleRectangle;

    private Texture starfishTexture;
    private float starfishX;
```

```java
private float starfishY;
private Rectangle starfishRectangle;

private Texture oceanTexture;
private Texture winMessageTexture;

private boolean win;

public void create()
{
    batch = new SpriteBatch();

    turtleTexture = new Texture( Gdx.files.internal("assets/turtle-1.png") );
    turtleX = 20;
    turtleY = 20;
    turtleRectangle = new Rectangle( turtleX, turtleY,
        turtleTexture.getWidth(), turtleTexture.getHeight() );

    starfishTexture = new Texture( Gdx.files.internal("assets/starfish.png") );
    starfishX = 380;
    starfishY = 380;
    starfishRectangle = new Rectangle( starfishX, starfishY,
        starfishTexture.getWidth(), starfishTexture.getHeight() );

    oceanTexture = new Texture( Gdx.files.internal("assets/water.jpg") );
    winMessageTexture = new Texture( Gdx.files.internal("assets/you-win.png") );

    win = false;
}

public void render()
{
    // check user input
    if (Gdx.input.isKeyPressed(Keys.LEFT))
        turtleX--;
    if (Gdx.input.isKeyPressed(Keys.RIGHT))
        turtleX++;
    if (Gdx.input.isKeyPressed(Keys.UP))
        turtleY++;
    if (Gdx.input.isKeyPressed(Keys.DOWN))
        turtleY--;

    // update turtle rectangle location
    turtleRectangle.setPosition(turtleX, turtleY);

    // check win condition: turtle must be overlapping starfish
    if (turtleRectangle.overlaps(starfishRectangle))
        win = true;

    // clear screen
    Gdx.gl.glClearColor(0,0,0, 1);
    Gdx.gl.glClear(GL20.GL_COLOR_BUFFER_BIT);
```

21

```
        // draw graphics
        batch.begin();
        batch.draw( oceanTexture, 0, 0 );
        if (!win)
            batch.draw( starfishTexture, starfishX, starfishY );
        batch.draw( turtleTexture, turtleX, turtleY );
        if (win)
            batch.draw( winMessageTexture, 180, 180 );
        batch.end();

    }
}
```

At this point, you can compile the code; if any error messages appear, double-check that the code you entered precisely matches the preceding code. You will also need a launcher-style class to create an instance of this class and run it. To accomplish this, create a new class named LauncherAlpha and enter the code as follows. Notice that additional parameters have been included in the LwglApplication constructor to set the title that is displayed and the size (the width and height, in pixels) of the window.

```
import com.badlogic.gdx.Game;
import com.badlogic.gdx.backends.lwjgl.LwjglApplication;

public class LauncherAlpha
{
    public static void main (String[] args)
    {
        Game myGame = new StarfishCollectorAlpha();
        LwjglApplication launcher =
            new LwjglApplication( myGame, "Starfish Collector", 800, 600 );
    }
}
```

At this point, the code can be compiled, after which the game can be run from the main BlueJ window by right-clicking the orange rectangle labeled LauncherAlpha, selecting the main method, and clicking the *OK* button in the window that appears (similar to the process for running the "Hello, World!" program from Chapter 1).

■ **Note**   When you are writing code, if there is a runtime error (such as an image file's failing to load due to a misspelled filename, even after fixing the error and running the program again), BlueJ may report another error containing a message such as "No OpenGL context found in the current thread." This is a highly technical error with a simple fix: in the BlueJ main window *Tools* menu, select the option *Reset Java Virtual Machine* and try to run the main method again. Provided that there are no additional runtime errors, your program should load as expected.

In the class StarfishCollectorAlpha, the create method initializes variables and loads textures. This program contains four images, which are stored as Texture objects: the turtle, the starfish, the water, and an image containing the words *You Win*. For brevity, instead of creating a new variable to store each of the FileHandle objects created by the internal method, you initialize them in the same line where you construct each new Texture object. The coordinates of the turtle's position are stored using floating-point numbers since you need to store decimal values, and the LibGDX game development framework uses float rather than double variables in its classes for a slight increase in program efficiency. Even though the coordinates of the starfish texture will not be changing, you still store them using variables so that future code involving these values is more readable. The oceanTexture and winMessageTexture objects do not require variables to store their coordinates, as their positions will not be changing, and their positions will be specified in the render method (discussed later in this section). Rectangle objects are also created that correspond to the turtle and starfish; these store the position and size of a rectangular area and are used because the Rectangle class contains a method named overlap that can be used to detect when the turtle has reached the starfish. The Boolean variable win indicates whether the player has won the game and is initialized to false.

The render method contains three main blocks of code that roughly correspond to the game loop sub-stages: process input, update, and render.

First, a sequence of commands use a method named isKeyPressed, belonging to (an object belonging to) the Gdx class, which determines whether a key on the keyboard is currently being pressed. The names of each key are represented using constant values from the Keys class. When one of the arrow keys is pressed, the corresponding x or y coordinate of the turtle is adjusted accordingly; x values increase toward the right side of the window, while y values increase toward the top of the window.[4] Note that if the user presses the left and right arrow keys at the same time, the effects of the addition and subtraction cancel each other out, and the position of the turtle will not change; a similar situation also applies when the user presses the up and down arrow keys at the same time. Also note that a sequence of if statements is used rather than a sequence of if-else if statements, enabling the program to respond appropriately if two keys are being pressed at the same time.

The second set of commands performs collision detection, determining whether the rectangular region corresponding to the turtleTexture image overlaps the rectangular region containing starfishTexture. The turtle's rectangle must be updated (using the setPosition method), since the position of the turtle may have changed. If the two rectangles overlap, then the Boolean variable win is set to true, which in turn affects which textures are drawn to the screen. As you test this game, you might notice that the starfish seem to disappear before the turtle actually reaches it. This is because rectangular shapes are being used to check for overlap; some of the transparent parts of the images may be overlapping, as shown in Figure 2-3. (This situation will be addressed and improved upon in the next chapter.)

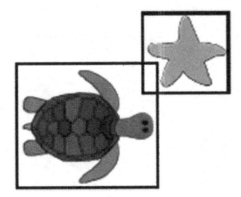

Figure 2-3. *Overlapping rectangles in transparent areas*

---

[4]The design choice to have y increase toward the top, while consistent with mathematical conventions, is the opposite of most computer science coordinate-system conventions, which place the origin point (0,0) at the top-left corner of a window so that the y value increases toward the bottom.

Finally, the third set of commands in the render method is where the actual rendering takes place. The glClear method draws a solid-colored rectangle on the screen using the color specified in the glClearColor method (in terms of red/green/blue/alpha values). The screen must be cleared in this manner during every rendering pass, effectively "erasing" the screen, because the images from previous render calls might be visible otherwise. The order of the draw method calls is particularly important: textures that are rendered later appear on top of those rendered earlier. Thus, you typically want to draw the background elements first, followed by the main in-game entities, and then the user interface elements last. The Batch class, used for drawing, optimizes graphics operations by sending multiple images at once to the computer's graphics processing unit (GPU).

Managing Game Entities with Actors and Stages

In the previous example—our first iteration of the *Starfish Collector* game—you saw that each game entity (such as the turtle and the starfish) has a lot of related information that you need to keep track of, such as textures and (x,y) coordinates. A central design principle in an object-oriented programming language like Java is to encapsulate related information in a single class. While you could create a Turtle class, a Starfish class, and so forth to manage this information, this approach would result in a lot of redundancy in your program, which is both inefficient and difficult to manage. Since another guiding principle in software engineering is to write reusable code, you want to implement a single class that contains the basic information common to all game entities, which you can then extend when necessary.

The LibGDX libraries provide a few different classes that can be used to manage the data associated with a game object; you will use the LibGDX class Actor as a foundation. This class stores data such as position, size (width and height), rotation, scaling factors, and more. However, it does not include a variable to store an image. This seeming "omission" in fact gives you greater flexibility in allowing you to specify how the object will be represented. You can extend the Actor class and include any additional information you need in your game, such as collision shapes, one or more images or animations, custom rendering methods, and more. The constructor for such an object should call the constructor of the class that it extends; this is accomplished by including the statement super(). For example, a game object that just requires a single Texture could use the following code:

```
public class TexturedActor extends Actor
{
    private Texture image;

    // constructor
    public TexturedActor()
    {  super();  }

    public void setTexture(Texture t)
    {  image = t;  }

    public Texture getTexture()
    {  return image;  }

    public void draw(Batch b)
    {
        b.draw( getTexture(), getX(), getY() );
    }
}
```

For a more complex example, your game might feature a character that has health points, and you might want to use different textures depending on how much health the character has. Such an object could be created with the following code:

```
public class HealthyActor extends Actor
{
    private int HP;
    private Texture healthyImage;
    private Texture damagedImage;
    private Texture deceasedImage;

    // omitted: constructor
    // omitted: methods to get/set preceding fields

    public void draw(Batch b)
    {
        if (HP > 50)
            b.draw( healthyImage, getX(), getY() );
        else if (HP > 0 && HP <= 50)
            b.draw( damagedImage, getX(), getY() );
        else    // in this case, HP <= 0
            b.draw( deceasedImage, getX(), getY() );
    }
}
```

There are a few additional features of the default Actor class that should be mentioned here. First, in addition to a draw method, the Actor class has an act method that can serve to update or modify the state of an Actor. Second, the Actor class was designed to be used in concert with a class called Stage (which you will be using in the near future). The main role of the Stage class is to store a list of Actor instances; it also contains methods (named act and draw) that call the act and draw methods of every Actor that has been added to it, which frees you from having to remember to draw every individual Actor instance yourself. The Stage class also creates and handles a Batch object, which reduces the amount of code that you need to write.

The next goal is to write an extension of the Actor class; this will require accessing and overriding methods already present in the Actor class.

OVERRIDING METHODS AND ACCESSING SUPERCLASS METHODS

When extending a class in Java, you may want to replace a method of the base class with a new version of the method. For example, consider a class that represents a person, with a method that simulates the person saying hello:

```
public class Person
{
    public void sayHello()
    { System.out.print("Hello."); }

    // other methods omitted
}
```

In your project, you may want to create extensions of this class, keeping the `sayHello` method, but changing the message that is printed. To do so, you only need to write a method with the same *signature*: the same method name, parameters, and output type. For example, you could write:

```
public class Shopkeeper extends Person
{
    public void sayHello()
    {  System.out.print("Greetings, travelers. Do you need any supplies?");  }
}
```

If you create an instance of a `Shopkeeper`, it will have access to all the fields and methods from the `Person` class (since `Shopkeeper` *extends* the `Person` class), but if a `Shopkeeper` instance calls the `sayHello` method, the version in the `Shopkeeper` class takes precedence and will be the one that is called. This technique is called *overriding* a method.

In some situations, however, you will want to build upon (and not replace) the code from the class that is being extended (sometimes called the *superclass*). For example, once again you might have a class that represents a person that stores a value (HP) corresponding to their health, as well as a method that restores it to its maximum value, as follows:

```
public class Person
{
    int HP;
    int maxHP;

    public void restore()
    {
        HP = maxHP;
    }
}
```

You might also have a class representing a wizard, which is a person that also has magical abilities and thus a value corresponding to the amount of magic (MP) they have available for use. It is natural to extend the `Person` class, and for a wizard the `restore` method should set both HP and MP to their maximum values. In this situation, you need the `Wizard` class to override the `restore` method of the `Person` class so as to add the magic-related functionality, while at the same time you want the `Wizard` class to be able to also run the `restore` method from the `Person` class to avoid your having to re-type the corresponding code. The way this is accomplished is by using the keyword `super`, which refers to the superclass. Within the context of the `Wizard` class, the expression `restore()` activates the method present in the `Wizard` class, while the expression `super.restore()` activates the method present in the `Person` class, as desired.

Making use of `super`, the `Wizard` class can be written as follows:

```
public class Wizard extends Person
{
    int MP;
    int maxMP;
```

```
    public void restore()
    {
        super.restore();
        MP = maxMP;
    }
}
```

As you write new classes that extend and build upon the functionality and methods of other classes, you will have the opportunity to use this technique repeatedly.

The extension of the Actor class that will be created for use in this chapter is called ActorBeta. It will be used to store a TextureRegion (which builds upon the functionality of the Texture class) and a Rectangle (used for detecting overlap between two objects). In the same BlueJ project, create a new class called ActorBeta with the following code:

```java
import com.badlogic.gdx.scenes.scene2d.Actor;
import com.badlogic.gdx.graphics.Texture;
import com.badlogic.gdx.graphics.g2d.Batch;
import com.badlogic.gdx.graphics.g2d.TextureRegion;
import com.badlogic.gdx.graphics.Color;
import com.badlogic.gdx.math.Rectangle;

/**
 *  Extend the Actor class to include graphics and collision detection.
 *  Actor class stores data such as position and rotation.
 */
public class ActorBeta extends Actor
{
    private TextureRegion textureRegion;
    private Rectangle rectangle;

    public ActorBeta()
    {
        super();
        textureRegion = new TextureRegion();
        rectangle = new Rectangle();
    }

    public void setTexture(Texture t)
    {
        textureRegion.setRegion(t);
        setSize( t.getWidth(), t.getHeight() );
        rectangle.setSize( t.getWidth(), t.getHeight() );
    }

    public Rectangle getRectangle()
    {
        rectangle.setPosition( getX(), getY() );
        return rectangle;
    }
```

```
public boolean overlaps(ActorBeta other)
{
    return this.getRectangle().overlaps( other.getRectangle() );
}

public void act(float dt)
{
    super.act(dt);
}

public void draw(Batch batch, float parentAlpha)
{
    super.draw( batch, parentAlpha );

    Color c = getColor(); // used to apply tint color effect

    batch.setColor(c.r, c.g, c.b, c.a);

    if ( isVisible() )
        batch.draw( textureRegion,
            getX(), getY(), getOriginX(), getOriginY(),
            getWidth(), getHeight(), getScaleX(), getScaleY(), getRotation() );
}
}
```

The following are some observations about this code:

- Instead of using a Texture, you are using a TextureRegion to store your image, which will enable greater flexibility when rendering an image. The main difference between these classes is that a TextureRegion can be used to store a Texture that contains multiple images or animation frames, and a TextureRegion also stores coordinates, called *(u,v) coordinates*, that determine which rectangular sub-area of the Texture is to be used.

- Within the constructor of the ActorBeta class, the statement super() activates the constructor of the superclass (Actor), which initializes the data structures used by that class.

- In the setTexture method, the sizes of the actor and the rectangle also need to be set (based on the width and height of the texture) so that the draw and overlaps methods work correctly.

- In the overlaps method, the keyword this is used to indicate the instance of the object calling the method. In this case, it is being used for clarity (to distinguish it from the instance named other that is a parameter for the method); using this is not strictly necessary and could be omitted if desired.

- Both the act and the draw methods begin by calling the corresponding superclass method (super.act and super.draw) so that their functionality is not lost, even though the methods are overridden in this class.

- In the draw method, if a color has been set (via the setColor method), it can be used to tint the image when it is rendered and must be passed along to the Batch object, which handles the actual rendering. (The default color is white, which has no effect on the image.) In addition, the Batch object can make use of the data stored in the actor object (such as position, rotation, and scaling factors) when rendering the image, although most of this functionality isn't used in this project.

- Occasionally, you will want to write even more specialized extensions of these classes. For this project, the turtle requires even more functionality than what is provided by the ActorBeta class. In particular, the turtle should move depending on which of the arrow keys are currently being pressed. In the interest of good object-oriented design practices (in particular, encapsulation), the corresponding code from the update method of the StarfishCollectorAlpha class will be moved to the act method of a new Turtle class. Also, notice the use of the moveBy method (inherited from the Actor class), which adjusts the position of the turtle in the same way as before, in terms of x and y coordinates.

Next, you will build upon the functionality of the ActorBeta class. Create a new class named Turtle with the following code:

```
import com.badlogic.gdx.Gdx;
import com.badlogic.gdx.Input.Keys;

public class Turtle extends ActorBeta
{
    public Turtle()
    {
        super();
    }

    public void act(float dt)
    {
        super.act(dt);

        if (Gdx.input.isKeyPressed(Keys.LEFT))
            this.moveBy(-1,0);
        if (Gdx.input.isKeyPressed(Keys.RIGHT))
            this.moveBy(1,0);
        if (Gdx.input.isKeyPressed(Keys.UP))
            this.moveBy(0,1);
        if (Gdx.input.isKeyPressed(Keys.DOWN))
            this.moveBy(0,-1);
    }
}
```

- After entering this code, you can compile it to check that everything was entered correctly. Next, you will create the new version of the *Starfish Collector* game source code. Create a new class named StarfishCollectorBeta; it will use the new ActorBeta class throughout. There are a few changes from the alpha version of the class. In particular:

  - A Stage object will be created, and Actor objects will be added to it. In addition, the act and draw methods of the Stage must be called (recall that calling the act and draw methods on a Stage results in the Stage object's calling the act and draw methods of all the Actor objects that have been added to it).

- The order in which actors are added to the Stage is important, just as the ordering of the draw statements was important when using the Batch object in the alpha version of this program. Actor objects that are added to the Stage first will be drawn first, thus appearing below those that are added later. For this reason, the background should be added first, and user interface elements (such as text displays) should be added last.

- The initial visibility of winMessage is set to false, because the player should not be able to see that particular image until later, after they have won the game.

- The act method requires an input: the amount of time (in seconds) that has elapsed since the previous iteration of the game loop. Since games in LibGDX run at 60 frames per second by default whenever possible, we have used 1/60 for this value. (In practice, the amount of time required for each iteration of the game loop could fluctuate, and there are methods available to obtain the exact value, but they are not necessary here.)

- When the turtle overlaps the starfish, the remove method is called on the starfish. This removes the starfish from the Stage object to which it was previously added. As a result, the starfish object's act and draw methods are no longer called at that point, causing the starfish graphic to disappear from the screen. (However, even though it is no longer visible, the starfish object remains in computer memory.)

The code for the StarfishCollectorBeta class is as follows:

```
import com.badlogic.gdx.ApplicationListener;
import com.badlogic.gdx.Game;
import com.badlogic.gdx.Gdx;
import com.badlogic.gdx.graphics.GL20;
import com.badlogic.gdx.graphics.Texture;
import com.badlogic.gdx.math.Rectangle;
import com.badlogic.gdx.scenes.scene2d.Stage;

public class StarfishCollectorBeta extends Game
{
    private Turtle turtle;
    private ActorBeta starfish;
    private ActorBeta ocean;
    private ActorBeta winMessage;

    private Stage mainStage;

    private boolean win;
```

```java
public void create()
{
    mainStage = new Stage();

    ocean = new ActorBeta();
    ocean.setTexture( new Texture( Gdx.files.internal("assets/water.jpg") )  );
    mainStage.addActor(ocean);

    starfish = new ActorBeta();
    starfish.setTexture( new Texture(Gdx.files.internal("assets/starfish.png")) );
    starfish.setPosition( 380,380 );
    mainStage.addActor( starfish );

    turtle = new Turtle();
    turtle.setTexture( new Texture(Gdx.files.internal("assets/turtle-1.png")) );
    turtle.setPosition( 20,20 );
    mainStage.addActor( turtle );

    winMessage = new ActorBeta();
    winMessage.setTexture( new Texture(Gdx.files.internal("assets/you-win.png")) );
    winMessage.setPosition( 180,180 );
    winMessage.setVisible( false );
    mainStage.addActor( winMessage );

    win = false;
}

public void render()
{
    // check user input
    mainStage.act(1/60f);

    // check win condition: turtle must be overlapping starfish
    if (turtle.overlaps(starfish))
    {
        starfish.remove();
        winMessage.setVisible(true);
    }

    // clear screen
    Gdx.gl.glClearColor(0,0,0, 1);
    Gdx.gl.glClear(GL20.GL_COLOR_BUFFER_BIT);

    // draw graphics
    mainStage.draw();
}
}
```

These changes make the code simpler to understand and will make it easier to incorporate additional elements in the future. At this point, you should compile the code you have written to verify that it is error-free. In order to run this game, create a new launcher class called LauncherBeta with the following code:

```
import com.badlogic.gdx.Game;
import com.badlogic.gdx.backends.lwjgl.LwjglApplication;

public class LauncherBeta
{
    public static void main (String[] args)
    {
        Game myGame = new StarfishCollectorBeta();
        LwjglApplication launcher =
            new LwjglApplication( myGame, "Starfish Collector", 800, 600 );
    }
}
```

In the rest of the chapter, you will reorganize this code in accordance with programming design principles.

Reorganizing the Game Flow

An important programming design practice is that each method should correspond to a single task. If a single method is handling multiple tasks, then it should be broken up into multiple methods. In the first section of this chapter, when the life cycle of a video game was discussed, you learned that in LibGDX, the render method is the method that is called repeatedly as the game is running, and therefore all the code related to the game loop is contained in that method. However, the game loop has multiple tasks: processing input, updating the state of the game world (such as determining what happens when two objects overlap), and drawing the graphics to the screen. These tasks should be separated into different methods if possible. Using the act method of the Actor class to process the input that affects each actor is a step in the right direction.

The next step is to separate the code used for updating and the code used for rendering into different methods. At the same time, you can also streamline future development projects by including commonly used code in a base class that can be extended when necessary, as you previously did with the Actor-derived classes. In particular, all future game projects will need to declare and initialize a Stage object and run its act and draw methods. You can use the method getDeltaTime to determine how much time has elapsed since the previous iteration of the game loop (which is typically 1/60 of a second, as discussed previously, but may fluctuate depending on the computer being used and the complexity of the program). Also, you typically clear the screen before redrawing the graphics in each iteration of the game loop.[5]

To accomplish these tasks, create a new class named GameBeta as shown next. However, there will be a few modifications made to this class later on in the chapter for reasons that will be explained.

```
import com.badlogic.gdx.Game;
import com.badlogic.gdx.Gdx;
import com.badlogic.gdx.graphics.GL20;
import com.badlogic.gdx.scenes.scene2d.Stage;
```

---

[5]Technically, if your program features a background graphic that covers the entire screen area, then this step is not necessary.

```java
public class GameBeta extends Game
{
    protected Stage mainStage;

    public void create()
    {
        mainStage = new Stage();
        initialize();
    }

    public void initialize() {  }

    public void render()
    {
        float dt = Gdx.graphics.getDeltaTime();

        // act method
        mainStage.act(dt);

        // defined by user
        update(dt);

        // clear the screen
        Gdx.gl.glClearColor(0,0,0,1);
        Gdx.gl.glClear(GL20.GL_COLOR_BUFFER_BIT);

        // draw the graphics
        mainStage.draw();
    }

    public void update(float dt) {  }
}
```

With this code in place, the StarfishCollectorBeta class could be changed to extend the GameBeta class. In the StarfishCollectorBeta class, the methods create and render would be changed to initialize and update (overriding the corresponding methods from the GameBeta class), and the redundant lines of code from the StarfishCollectorBeta class (those that also appear in the GameBeta class) would be removed.

However, before continuing on, there is one final topic that needs to be discussed to make this code more robust. In practice, any program that uses this class as a basis should be *required* to provide its own versions of the initialize and update methods. This brings to mind the concept of an interface (discussed earlier in this chapter), but an interface is not suitable in this situation because an interface can only declare the required method, and does not include any actual code. In this situation, there is code that would be helpful to reuse. What you need is a structure that combines elements of both an interface and a standard class that can be extended. Java provides exactly what is needed for this situation: *abstract* classes.

ABSTRACT CLASSES

Often in programming you will want to reduce redundant code by refactoring repeated features in a base class and then extending that class with specialized subclasses. In some situations, you will also know that all of the extending classes will need to implement a particular method—but they will all do it in a different way, so the code can't be written ahead of time in the base class, although the method needs to be declared in the base class.

For example, consider a fantasy-style role-playing game. Assume that the base class for player characters is named Person. This class will likely contain some standard fields and methods that all Person objects should have, such as a String called name that stores the name of the character, and get and set methods to access this information. You might want to create two classes, Wizard and Warrior, which extend the Person class. Assume that the user interface of this game is consistent for all types of characters and that it contains a *Sword* button that activates a method named useSword and a *Spell* button that activates a method named useSpell.

Although the Person class will declare these methods, their implementation will differ greatly in the Wizard and Warrior classes. Traditionally, warriors wield swords, and wizards do not; wizards cast magic spells, and warriors do not. Other types of characters might be imagined that can use both swords and spells, or characters that can use neither. Regardless, if the player clicks a button corresponding to an action that a character is unable to perform, a message should display onscreen explaining this; otherwise, the action should take place as expected.

In this situation, you will want to require extensions of the Person class in order to provide customized code to implement the methods useSword and useSpell, as an interface does; however, Person *cannot* be an interface, because it provides code for some of its methods, such as getting and setting the name field. In an interface, methods are only declared, not written.

The solution to this scenario is to create an *abstract* class. You declare the method as a class with the additional keyword abstract (similar to the way an interface is declared using the keyword interface), which indicates that some methods may be declared with the code being provided, and that other classes that extend this class must provide the code for such methods. Any such method is also declared using the modifier abstract, as shown in the example code that follows. Note that since not all of the code for this class is provided, you cannot create an instance of this class (again, similar to an interface).

```
public abstract class Person
{
    private String name;
    public void setName(String n)  { name = n; }
    public String getName()  { return name; }
    public abstract void useSword();
    public abstract void useSpell();
}
```

Any class that extends `Person` must provide an implementation of each method that was previously declared as abstract. For example:

```
public class Wizard extends Person
{
    public void useSword()
    {
        System.out.print("Wizards are unable to wield a sword...");
    }

    public void useSpell()
    {
        // insert code here to select a spell and its target
    }
}

public class Warrior extends Person
{
    public void useSword()
    {
        // insert code here to attack an enemy
    }

    public void useSpell()
    {
        System.out.print("Warriors are unable to use magic...");
    }
}
```

In this way, an abstract class combines the advantages of a standard class and an interface.

Using an abstract class will require any class that extends GameBeta to provide implementations of methods to initialize and update the game world. This also helps developers avoid potential mistakes such as misspelling the names of the methods that they are supposed to be overriding.

The changes that need to be made to the GameBeta class, presented previously, are as follows. Note in particular that the bodies of the `initialize` and `update` methods are removed, and there are semicolons added to the lines where these methods are declared.

```
// import statements remain the same

public abstract class GameBeta extends Game
{
    protected Stage mainStage;

    // create method remains the same

    public abstract void initialize();

    // render method remains the same

    public abstract void update(float dt);
}
```

With the GameBeta class serving as a base, the StarfishCollectorBeta class can be greatly simplified, as previously explained. The changes to the class are explained in the commented code that follows. Note that as you change the code in one class, other classes that depend on it will appear to have errors until the changes have been completed.

```java
// import statements remain the same

// this class now extends GameBeta rather than Game
public class StarfishCollectorBeta extends GameBeta
{
    // removed declaration of mainStage

    private Turtle turtle;
    private ActorBeta starfish;
    private ActorBeta ocean;
    private ActorBeta winMessage;

    private boolean win;

    // create method renamed to initialize
    public void initialize()
    {
        // removed initialization of mainStage
        // the rest of the method remains the same
    }

    // render method renamed to update; requires float parameter dt
    public void update(float dt)
    {
        // most code of the render method removed

        // check win condition: turtle must be overlapping starfish
        if (turtle.overlaps(starfish))
        {
            starfish.remove();
            winMessage.setVisible(true);
        }
    }
}
```

As you can see, this class now focuses on the game itself (the game objects and their interaction with each other) rather than framework issues (such as setting up and using the stage). You can now play the game by running the main method in the corresponding launcher class, as before.

Congratulations on creating your first game in LibGDX!

Summary and Next Steps

This chapter introduced many features of the LibGDX library. You began with an overview of the life cycle of a game program and learned how the stages of the life cycle are performed by methods with a particular naming convention, enforced by an interface. You learned how to process keyboard input by using the Gdx class and how to encapsulate game-entity data with the Actor class. You learned how the Stage class can be used to manage Actor instances, and how to extend the Actor class for greater functionality. You also learned how to reorganize the game flow and simplify future game development projects by extending the Game class.

To practice the skills you have developed in this chapter, you could try adding another object to the game: a shark that the turtle must avoid; if the turtle overlaps the shark, then the turtle should be removed from the stage, and a message that reads "Game Over" should be displayed on the screen. Graphics for this addition are provided in the assets folder for this project.

In the next chapter, you'll create a more polished version of the *Starfish Collector* game powered by a new extension of the Actor class (which will replace ActorBeta) that supports animation, physics-based movement, improved collision detection, and the ability to manage multiple actor instances with lists.

CHAPTER 3

■ ■ ■

Extending the Framework

In the previous chapter, you learned about some of the basic features and classes available in LibGDX and created a game called *Starfish Collector*. You also practiced good software development habits by gathering code that supports commonly needed functionality into a class named ActorBeta (which extends the LibGDX Actor class). However, the *Starfish Collector* game is still "rough around the edges"; some of the shortcomings of the version from the previous chapter include:

- There is a lack of animation.
- Movement is not smooth: speed is either zero or a constant value.
- Collisions are not precise.
- There are no barriers or obstacles.
- There is only a single object to collect.
- The game world is limited to the size of the window, and the turtle can move beyond the edges of the window.
- When the program is run, the game begins immediately.

To address these shortcomings, you will implement the following improvements in this chapter:

- Animations will be added: the turtle will appear to be swimming whenever it is moving (and it will face the direction of movement), the starfish will slowly rotate (to draw the player's attention), and a splash-like special effect will appear when the turtle collects the starfish.
- Realistic movement will be implemented by adding acceleration and deceleration.
- Collisions will be more precise by replacing rectangles with more precise polygon shapes.
- Solid-like barriers (rocks) will be added.
- Multiple instances of objects will be created.
- The game world will be enlarged beyond the size of the window.
- A start-menu screen will be displayed before the game begins.

A screenshot of the improved *Starfish Collector* game with these improvements added is shown in Figure 3-1.

© Lee Stemkoski 2018
L. Stemkoski, *Java Game Development with LibGDX*, https://doi.org/10.1007/978-1-4842-3324-5_3

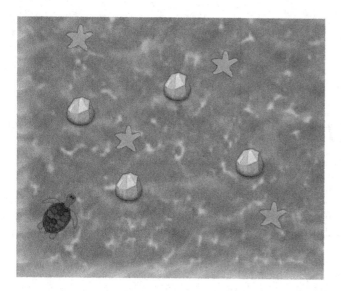

Figure 3-1. *The improved* Starfish Collector *game*

There are other obvious standard features missing that will be added in subsequent chapters, such as text and user interfaces (Chapter 5) and music and sound effects (Chapter 6). In addition, when advanced features (such as designing levels with tilemap editors and integrating gamepad controller support) are introduced much later on in this book, they will first be demonstrated in the context of the *Starfish Collector* game.

To incorporate all these changes, you will create a new class called BaseActor, which replaces the ActorBeta class from the previous chapter. The BaseActor class will be robust and feature-packed enough to be used in every game project in the remainder of this book, and for your own game projects as well. Over the course of this chapter, you will slowly rebuild and improve the *Starfish Collector* game, making use of the new BaseActor class throughout.

■ **Note**   The BaseActor class that you will create in this chapter will contain a lot of methods and functionality, not all of which will be needed for every game object. For example, not all game objects are animated, not all game objects move, and so forth. In general, object-oriented design principles would recommend that this functionality be split into separate classes. However, the decision was made to include all the actor-related functionality within a single class in order to simplify the class-dependency relationships and reduce the total number of classes required by future projects in this book.

To begin, download the source code files for this chapter on the website for this book. Create a new project in BlueJ named Starfish Collector Ch3 (to distinguish it from the version in the previous chapter). In the project directory that is created by BlueJ, create a new folder called assets. Copy all the image files from the downloaded project's assets folder into your new project's assets folder. Next (if you haven't previously added the LibGDX JAR files to the BlueJ userlib folder), in your project directory, create a new folder named +libs. Copy the JAR files from the downloaded project's +libs folder into your new project's +libs folder. Restart BlueJ so that the JAR files newly added to the +libs folder are properly recognized by BlueJ.

In your BlueJ project, create a new class named BaseActor. The first step is to write the constructor method. Since you will need to set the position of the actor and add it to a stage, you can supply this data via the constructor method and perform these actions automatically with the following code:

```
import com.badlogic.gdx.scenes.scene2d.Actor;
import com.badlogic.gdx.scenes.scene2d.Stage;

/**
 * Extend functionality of the LibGDX Actor class.
 */
public class BaseActor extends Actor
{
    public BaseActor(float x, float y, Stage s)
    {
        // call constructor from Actor class
        super();
        // perform additional initialization tasks
        setPosition(x,y);
        s.addActor(this);
    }
}
```

In the following sections, you will add support for animations, physics-based movement, improved collision detection and handling, and methods for working with collections of specific object types.

Animation

The first change you will implement in the BaseActor class is support for animation: creating the appearance of motion or change by altering an image that is being displayed. This section will discuss two types of animation: *value-based animation*, which uses a single image and continuously changes associated values (such as position or rotation), and *image-based animation*, which displays a sequence of images in rapid succession.

Value-Based Animations

Many visual effects can be achieved by continuously changing values associated with a game entity, such as the following:

- A movement effect can be created by changing the position-coordinate values.
- A spinning effect can be created by changing the rotation value.
- A growing or shrinking effect can be created by changing the scale factors.
- A color-cycling effect can be created by changing the color red/green/blue (RGB) component values.
- A fading in/out effect can be created by changing the alpha (transparency) value.

These effects can easily be added to your game by using LibGDX's Action class. An Action is an object that can be added to an Actor to automatically change the values of various fields (position, rotation, scale, color) over time. The code that processes actions is contained within the act method of the Actor class (and this is why you needed to call super.act(dt) in the previous chapter when writing the act method of the BaseActor class—to make sure that this code is executed). To create an Action, it is easiest to use the static methods available in the Actions class. There are dozens of methods available, only some of which will be discussed here.

For example, an Action named spin that rotates an actor by 180 degrees over the course of two seconds can be created and attached to an Actor named starfish with the following code:

```
Action spin = Actions.rotateBy( 180, 2 );
starfish.addAction( spin );
```

Similarly, an Action named shift that moves an actor 50 pixels horizontally (to the right) and 0 pixels vertically over the course of one second can be created with the following code:

```
Action shift = Actions.moveBy( 50, 0, 1 );
```

You can also create complex, compound visual effects by combining Action objects. If you add multiple actions to an Actor, they will run at the same time (often called *in parallel*). For example, if you add both the actions spin and shift to a single Actor, then during the first second, the Actor will rotate 90 degrees and move 50 pixels to the right, and during the next second, it will rotate an additional 90 degrees (but no longer move to the right, as that action will have already finished at that point). Alternatively, you may want a set of actions to run one after the other (often called *in sequence*). You can create an action that runs only after all of the previously added actions have completed by using the after method of the Actions class. This is demonstrated by the following example, in which the starfish actor will first rotate for two seconds and then move during the third second:

```
starfish.addAction( spin );
starfish.addAction( Actions.after( shift ) );
```

Finally, you may want an action to repeat a specific number of times or to repeat indefinitely. These behaviors are obtained by using the Actions class methods repeat and forever, respectively, as shown here:

```
Action spinTwice = Actions.repeat( spin, 2 );
Action spinForever = Actions.forever( spin );
```

This is just a sample of the methods available; for a complete listing of the types of predefined actions available, see the documentation for the LibGDX Actions class. Conveniently, this functionality is built into the Actor class, and since the BaseActor class extends the Actor class, no additions need to be made to the BaseActor class to be able to use the Action objects.

Image-Based Animations

As mentioned before, an image-based animation is created from images that are rapidly displayed in sequence to create the illusion of movement. In LibGDX, this can be accomplished using the Animation class. Creating an animation requires three pieces of information:

- An Array of images to be displayed
- The amount of time that each image should be displayed

- A value that indicates how the frames should be played—in the order given, in reverse order, from first to last to first again (*ping-pong order*)—and whether to repeat (loop) the animation

Animations can be created based on different classes that store image data, such as Texture and TextureRegion. For maximum flexibility, the Animation class is designed generically so that, when you declare an Animation object, you can also declare the type of data it will store.

GENERIC TYPES AND CLASSES

Data structures are a fundamental concept in computer programming, as they allow you to organize and use data efficiently. One of the most elementary and well-known data structure types is the array, which allows you to store a fixed number of values of a particular type. In the Java programming language, you indicate an array by first entering the data type being stored, followed by a set of square brackets; an array of strings is indicated by String[], while an array of floating-point decimal numbers is indicated by float[]. In general, given any class in Java, you can create an array whose elements are of that type. This makes arrays a very flexible and adaptable data structure.

Sometimes, you will design your own class to store a particular type of data. For example, storing the given name and family name of a person requires two strings, which could be stored using the following class:

```java
public class StringPair
{
    private String first;
    private String second;

    // constructor
    StringPair(String a, String b)
    {
        first = a;
        second = b;
    }

    // getter/setter methods
    public void setFirst(String s)  { first = s; }

    public String getFirst()  { return first; }

    public void setSecond(String s) { second = s; }

    public String getSecond()  { return second; }

    // standard methods
    public String toString()
    {
        return "[" + first + "," + second + "]";
    }
}
```

43

Similarly, to store the *x* and *y* coordinates of a point, you could use the following class:

```java
public class FloatPair
{
    private float first;
    private float second;

    // constructor
    FloatPair(float a, float b)
    {
        first = a;
        second = b;
    }

    // getter/setter methods
    public void setFirst(float x)  { first = x; }

    public float getFirst()  { return first; }

    public void setSecond(float x) { second = x; }

    public float getSecond()  { return second; }

    // standard methods
    public String toString()
    {
        return "[" + first + "," + second + "]";
    }
}
```

Comparing the code for each class, you will notice that it is nearly identical; the only substantial difference is the type of data being stored. In software development, it is highly desirable to reduce the amount of redundant code. Ideally, there should be a way to write a class that specifies the structure (such as the amount of data being stored and the methods used to access or modify it) and the type of data being stored when the object is created, just as is the case with arrays. As it happens, Java does in fact have such a capability. This is accomplished using generic programming.

In generic programming, you can write a class as usual, but instead of indicating specific types when declaring fields or method parameters, you instead use a type variable, traditionally indicated by a single uppercase letter (such as T or K). To indicate the presence of a type variable in a class, the name of the class must be followed by angle brackets (< and >). For example, a generic class that retains the structure of the StringPair and FloatPair classes could be written as follows:

```java
public class Pair<T>
{
    private T first;
    private T second;

    // constructor
    Pair(T a, T b)
```

```
    {
        first = a;
        second = b;
    }

    // getter/setter methods

    public void setFirst(T s)  { first = s; }

    public T getFirst()  { return first; }

    public void setSecond(T s) { second = s; }

    public T getSecond()   { return second; }

    // standard methods
    public String toString()
    {
        return "[" + first + "," + second + "]";
    }
}
```

Then, to create an instance of a `Pair` that could be used to store strings, for example, you would write:

```
Pair<String> personName = new Pair<String>("Kondas", "Kismet");
```

Similarly, you could create a `Pair` to store float numbers:

```
Pair<Float> coordinates = new Pair<Float>( 42.9001f, 337.14f );
```

Note that in the last example, the class name `Float` (with an uppercase F) must be used, rather than `float`, since `float` refers to a primitive data type, while `Float` refers to the corresponding class. Similarly, to store a pair of integer values, you must use `Pair<Integer>`, rather than `Pair<int>`.

The Animation class takes a generic type parameter that specifies which class is being used to store image data. You will use the `TextureRegion` class, as it provides the greatest number of options when rendering an image.

To support the animation-related methods that will be written in this section, add the following `import` statements to the `BaseActor` class:

```
import com.badlogic.gdx.Gdx;
import com.badlogic.gdx.utils.Array;
import com.badlogic.gdx.graphics.Color;
import com.badlogic.gdx.graphics.Texture;
import com.badlogic.gdx.graphics.Texture.TextureFilter;
import com.badlogic.gdx.graphics.g2d.TextureRegion;
import com.badlogic.gdx.graphics.g2d.Animation;
import com.badlogic.gdx.graphics.g2d.Animation.PlayMode;
import com.badlogic.gdx.graphics.g2d.Batch;
```

To store the animation and related data, add the following fields at the beginning of the BaseActor class:

```
private Animation<TextureRegion> animation;
private float elapsedTime;
private boolean animationPaused;
```

To initialize these variables, add the following code at the end of the constructor method:

```
animation = null;
elapsedTime = 0;
animationPaused = false;
```

Next, you will set up some methods that set values for these variables. The first of these methods is used to set the animation. Once an animation is set, the size (width and height) of the Actor will be able to be set, as well as the origin (the point around which the actor should be rotated, typically the center of the actor). The width and height of the actor will be set to the width and height of the first image of the animation (the images of an animation are also called *keyframes*). This is accomplished with the following method:

```
public void setAnimation(Animation<TextureRegion> anim)
{
    animation = anim;
    TextureRegion tr = animation.getKeyFrame(0);
    float w = tr.getRegionWidth();
    float h = tr.getRegionHeight();
    setSize( w, h );
    setOrigin( w/2, h/2 );
}
```

Changing the value of animationPaused is accomplished with the following method:

```
public void setAnimationPaused(boolean pause)
{
    animationPaused = pause;
}
```

The variable elapsedTime, which you will use to keep track of how long the animation has been playing and therefore which image should be displayed, does not need to be set directly. Instead, this value should be automatically updated; the correct place to do this is the act method of the Actor class, which is automatically called by the stage to which the actor belongs. The elapsed time needs be incremented by the amount of time that has passed since the previous iteration of the game loop (indicated by dt), provided that the game is not currently paused (indicated by animationPaused).

```
public void act(float dt)
{
    super.act( dt );

    if (!animationPaused)
        elapsedTime += dt;
}
```

You also need to override the Actor class draw method. In particular, you will determine the correct image of the animation to be drawn (once again using the getKeyFrame method and the elapsedTime variable) and draw it, taking into account the various properties stored in the Actor class (including position, size, scale, rotation, and origin). You can also tint the image by setting the color stored by the actor (the default color is white; tinting by white has no effect on the appearance of the image).

```java
public void draw(Batch batch, float parentAlpha)
{
    super.draw( batch, parentAlpha );

    // apply color tint effect
    Color c = getColor();
    batch.setColor(c.r, c.g, c.b, c.a);

    if ( animation != null && isVisible() )
        batch.draw( animation.getKeyFrame(elapsedTime),
            getX(), getY(), getOriginX(), getOriginY(),
            getWidth(), getHeight(), getScaleX(), getScaleY(), getRotation() );
}
```

The next task is to write code that loads image data and uses it to create Animation objects. There are two ways in which animation images may be stored. They could be stored as multiple files (one animation frame per file); this will be the case for the turtle in *Starfish Collector*, whose images are in the files turtle-1. png through turtle-6.png, illustrated by Figure 3-2.

turtle-1.png   turtle-2.png   turtle-3.png

turtle-4.png   turtle-5.png   turtle-6.png

Figure 3-2. *The six image files used for the turtle animation*

Alternatively, the images may be condensed into a single image—arranged in a rectangular grid—and stored as a single file, called a *spritesheet*. This will be the case for the whirlpool effect that will be displayed when the turtle collects a starfish, illustrated by Figure 3-3, which contains a single image file with ten sub-images arranged in a grid (two rows and five columns).

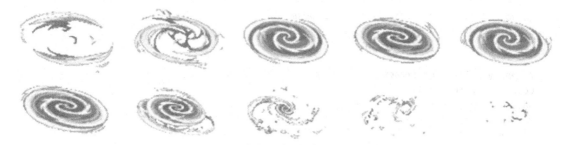

Figure 3-3. *A single image file containing the frames of the whirlpool animation*

In order to handle both of these possibilities, there will be two variations of the code that creates animations from image files. Furthermore, since the code will be highly reusable, it will be written as a pair of methods in the BaseActor class.

Recall that the data required by Animation objects include an array of images, the duration for which each frame will be displayed, and a value that indicates how the frames should be played. If the images are stored in separate files, you will specify the filenames with an array of strings, while if the images are stored in a spritesheet, you will specify the filename and number of rows and columns in the grid. For simplicity, you will assume that the animation frames either play from first to last one time (indicated by the constant value PlayMode.NORMAL) or repeat forever in a loop (indicated by PlayMode.LOOP); this can be specified with a Boolean variable indicating whether the animation loops or not.

A method for creating an animation from separate image files is provided next. Note that this method also sets the actor's animation if one has not yet been set (indicated by the value of animation being null). This method also returns the animation that was created, in case multiple animations are required by an actor (in which case, an extension of the BaseActor class should be created and the additional animations should be stored in additional variables).

```
public Animation<TextureRegion> loadAnimationFromFiles(String[] fileNames,
    float frameDuration, boolean loop)
{
    int fileCount = fileNames.length;
    Array<TextureRegion> textureArray = new Array<TextureRegion>();

    for (int n = 0; n < fileCount; n++)
    {
        String fileName = fileNames[n];
        Texture texture = new Texture( Gdx.files.internal(fileName) );
        texture.setFilter( TextureFilter.Linear, TextureFilter.Linear );
        textureArray.add( new TextureRegion( texture ) );
    }
```

```
Animation<TextureRegion> anim = new Animation<TextureRegion>(frameDuration, textureArray);

if (loop)
    anim.setPlayMode(Animation.PlayMode.LOOP);
else
    anim.setPlayMode(Animation.PlayMode.NORMAL);

if (animation == null)
    setAnimation(anim);

return anim;
}
```

Next is a similar method for creating an animation from a spritesheet. Conveniently, the TextureRegion class has a method named split that can be used to break up an image into a collection of sub-images. Using this method requires knowing the size of each sub-image, which is calculated in the following code based on the size of the original image and the number of rows and columns present in the spritesheet.

```
public Animation<TextureRegion> loadAnimationFromSheet(String fileName, int rows, int cols,
    float frameDuration, boolean loop)
{
    Texture texture = new Texture(Gdx.files.internal(fileName), true);
    texture.setFilter(TextureFilter.Linear, TextureFilter.Linear);
    int frameWidth = texture.getWidth() / cols;
    int frameHeight = texture.getHeight() / rows;

    TextureRegion[][] temp = TextureRegion.split(texture, frameWidth, frameHeight);

    Array<TextureRegion> textureArray = new Array<TextureRegion>();

    for (int r = 0; r < rows; r++)
        for (int c = 0; c < cols; c++)
            textureArray.add( temp[r][c] );

    Animation<TextureRegion> anim = new Animation<TextureRegion>(frameDuration,
    textureArray);

    if (loop)
        anim.setPlayMode(Animation.PlayMode.LOOP);
    else
        anim.setPlayMode(Animation.PlayMode.NORMAL);

    if (animation == null)
        setAnimation(anim);

    return anim;
}
```

Some game objects may be represented by a single image and do not require an animation. For consistency, however, you can display a still image using a one-frame animation; the frame duration and playback style do not matter in this case. For convenience, the following method will be used for this situation.

```
public Animation<TextureRegion> loadTexture(String fileName)
{
    String[] fileNames = new String[1];
    fileNames[0] = fileName;
    return loadAnimationFromFiles(fileNames, 1, true);
}
```

One more method you should include at this time will be used to check if the animation is finished, which is true if the animation is not looping and the elapsed time is greater than the time required to display all the images in the animation (the number of frames multiplied by the display time for each frame). This is calculated using the Animation class method isAnimationFinished; your method simply calls this method on the variable animation and automatically supplies the value elapsedTime.

```
public boolean isAnimationFinished()
{
    return animation.isAnimationFinished(elapsedTime);
}
```

At this point, you are ready to recreate part of the *Starfish Collector* game. First, you will create some classes that extend the BaseActor class: Turtle, Starfish, and Whirlpool. At a minimum, each of these classes needs a constructor, which will pass along the data for the initial position and stage to the BaseActor class constructor. In the extended classes, you can also set the texture or animation being used in the constructor method.

First is the code for the Turtle class, which features an animation using images from multiple files:

```
import com.badlogic.gdx.scenes.scene2d.Stage;

public class Turtle extends BaseActor
{
    public Turtle(float x, float y, Stage s)
    {
        super(x,y,s);

        String[] filenames =
            {"assets/turtle-1.png", "assets/turtle-2.png", "assets/turtle-3.png",
             "assets/turtle-4.png", "assets/turtle-5.png", "assets/turtle-6.png"};

        loadAnimationFromFiles(filenames, 0.1f, true);
    }
}
```

Next is the code for the Whirlpool class, which features an animation based on a spritesheet. Since this effect should disappear when the animation is finished, you should include an act method that checks if the animation is finished playing and, if so, calls the remove method to remove it from its stage (and thus the game).

```
import com.badlogic.gdx.scenes.scene2d.Stage;

public class Whirlpool extends BaseActor
{
    public Whirlpool(float x, float y, Stage s)
    {
        super(x,y,s);

        loadAnimationFromSheet("assets/whirlpool.png", 2, 5, 0.1f, false);
    }

    public void act(float dt)
    {
        super.act(dt);

        if ( isAnimationFinished() )
            remove();
    }
}
```

Next is the code for the Starfish class. There is only a single image used to display this object, so you will use the loadTexture method that you created for convenience. You will also add a value-based animation (a slow rotation of 30 degrees every ONE second) using the Action class, which will draw the player's attention to this object.

```
import com.badlogic.gdx.scenes.scene2d.Stage;
import com.badlogic.gdx.scenes.scene2d.Action;
import com.badlogic.gdx.scenes.scene2d.actions.Actions;

public class Starfish extends BaseActor
{
    public Starfish(float x, float y, Stage s)
    {
        super(x,y,s);

        loadTexture("assets/starfish.png");

        Action spin = Actions.rotateBy(30, 1);
        this.addAction( Actions.forever(spin) );
    }
}
```

Now that the classes for the game entities have been created, you can turn your attention to the game itself. At this point, the game will only display the objects and their animations; interactivity will not be added until the next section.

First, add the GameBeta class from the previous chapter to this project by creating a new class and copying the code from the previous project; the code you need is as follows:

```
import com.badlogic.gdx.Game;
import com.badlogic.gdx.Gdx;
import com.badlogic.gdx.graphics.GL20;
import com.badlogic.gdx.scenes.scene2d.Stage;
```

```
public abstract class GameBeta extends Game
{
    protected Stage mainStage;

    public void create()
    {
        mainStage = new Stage();
        initialize();
    }

    public abstract void initialize();

    public void render()
    {
        float dt = Gdx.graphics.getDeltaTime();
        mainStage.act(dt);
        update(dt);

        Gdx.gl.glClearColor(0,0,0,1);
        Gdx.gl.glClear(GL20.GL_COLOR_BUFFER_BIT);

        mainStage.draw();
    }

    public abstract void update (float dt);
}
```

Next, you will extend this class with a new class called StarfishCollector, which contains the following code. This class will be different from the version in the previous chapter. Note in particular that the background ocean image is simply implemented as a BaseActor object, and the image and size are set after it is initialized.

```
public class StarfishCollector extends GameBeta
{
    private Turtle turtle;
    private Starfish starfish;
    private BaseActor ocean;

    public void initialize()
    {
        ocean = new BaseActor(0,0, mainStage);
        ocean.loadTexture( "assets/water.jpg" );
        ocean.setSize(800,600);

        starfish = new Starfish(380,380, mainStage);

        turtle = new Turtle(20,20, mainStage);
    }
```

```
    public void update(float dt)
    {
        // code will be added later
    }
}
```

Finally, you need to write a Launcher class to run the game; it should be identical to the version from the previous chapter, as follows:

```
import com.badlogic.gdx.Game;
import com.badlogic.gdx.backends.lwjgl.LwjglApplication;

public class Launcher
{
    public static void main (String[] args)
    {
        Game myGame = new StarfishCollector();
        LwjglApplication launcher =
            new LwjglApplication( myGame, "Starfish Collector", 800, 600 );
    }
}
```

At this point, the main BlueJ window should contain seven orange rectangles, which correspond to the seven classes you have written. There will be arrows connecting various classes, indicating dependencies: an arrow with a dashed line indicates that one class is creating an instance of another class, while an arrow with a solid line indicates that one class extends the other. You can click and drag these rectangles around to make the dependencies easier to see, if you wish. One such arrangement is illustrated in Figure 3-4. You may notice that there is no line connecting the StarfishCollector class to the Whirlpool class; this is because no instance of the Whirlpool object has been created yet (this will be added later on in this chapter).

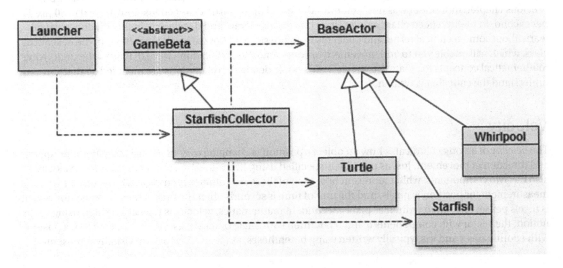

Figure 3-4. Relationships between the classes in an intermediate version of the Starfish Collector *game*

At this point, you may test your game by right-clicking on the rectangle labeled Launcher, selecting the method *void main(String[] args)* from the popup menu that appears, and clicking the *OK* button in the window that appears after that. The game will appear as shown in Figure 3-5; the turtle will seem to be swimming, and the starfish will be slowly rotating. You are not able to move the turtle yet; this functionality will be added in the next section.

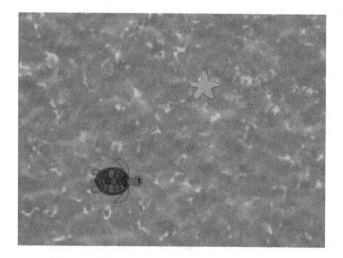

Figure 3-5. *The* Starfish Collector *game*

Physics and Movement

One of the issues raised at the beginning of this chapter was that in the version of *Starfish Collector* from the previous chapter, movement was not "smooth": the speed of the turtle changed instantly from 0 to 60 pixels per second. In reality, speed changes over time; objects accelerate and decelerate. In this section, you will learn about some technical terms and concepts from physics and how to implement them in the BaseActor class, which will enable you to add movement to your game. While you don't have to master the underlying mathematical concepts to create the games in this book, detailed explanations are included so that you can understand the code that is written.

Velocity

The *velocity* of an object indicates how an object's position is changing over time, including both the speed and direction of movement. Just as position is specified using two values[1]—x and y coordinates—velocity also has two components, which represent how each of these coordinates is changing. If the unit of measurement for position is pixels, and the unit of time is seconds, then the unit of measurement for velocity is pixels per second, often written as pixels/second. In mathematics, velocity is typically written using vector notion: the vector with components a and b is written with angle brackets, as < a , b >. In contrast, a position with coordinates x and y is typically written using parentheses, as (x , y). Vectors are visually represented

---

[1]Throughout this section, we are assuming that movement is on a flat, two-dimensional surface. If movement were occurring in three-dimensional space, then three values would be required to specify position and velocity.

as arrows; the vector <> is drawn with the end point located *a* units horizontally and *b* units vertically from the start point, as illustrated in Figure 3-6. The quantity *speed* can be viewed as the length (also called the *magnitude*) of this vector, denoted by *S* in the figure. The *direction* of the vector is quantified by the angle between the vector and a horizontal vector pointing to the right (along the direction of the positive x-axis); this angle is denoted by *A* in the figure. Given the values of *a* and *b*, the length and direction angle can be calculated using mathematics (using the Pythagorean Theorem and trigonometric functions, respectively), but thanks to the methods provided by the LibGDX Vector2 class (using the methods len and angle, respectively), you will not need to code these formulas yourself.

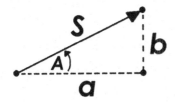

Figure 3-6. *Visual representation of the vector < a , b >, with length S and direction angle A*

Calculations involving position and velocity are relatively straightforward. For example, if an object's position is initially (7 , 5), and its velocity is < 2 , 3 >, then:

- After a one-second interval, the position will be (7 + 2 , 5 + 3) = (9 , 8).

- After a two-second interval, the position will be (9 + 2 , 8 + 3) = (11 , 11).

- After a three-second interval, the position will be (11 + 2, 11 + 3) = (13 , 14).

In general, if the initial position is *(x , y)* and the velocity is < *a , b* >, then after a *t*-second interval has passed, the formula for the position is *(x + t*a , y + t*b)*. This formula also works for fractional values of *t* as well.

To incorporate velocity data to the BaseActor class, add the following import statements:

```
import com.badlogic.gdx.math.Vector2;
import com.badlogic.gdx.math.MathUtils;
```

Then, add the following field to the class:

```
private Vector2 velocityVec;
```

You initialize this variable by adding the following statement to the constructor method:

```
velocityVec = new Vector2(0,0);
```

Next, you will add methods to set and get the speed and angle of motion of the Actor object. One subtle problem to consider is how the speed or angle should be set when the velocity vector is < 0 , 0 > (which corresponds to a speed of 0 and an undefined angle of motion). In this situation, setting the speed will cause the angle of motion to be zero degrees (along the direction of the positive x-axis), while setting the angle will have no effect (since if the speed of an object is 0, then it does not make sense to speak of it moving in any direction). The code for these methods is as follows:

```java
public void setSpeed(float speed)
{
    // if length is zero, then assume motion angle is zero degrees
    if (velocityVec.len() == 0)
        velocityVec.set(speed, 0);
    else
        velocityVec.setLength(speed);
}

public float getSpeed()
{
    return velocityVec.len();
}

public void setMotionAngle(float angle)
{
    velocityVec.setAngle(angle);
}

public float getMotionAngle()
{
    return velocityVec.angle();
}
```

The getMotionAngle method is particularly convenient for making an object face the direction in which it is moving, which can be accomplished with the code setRotation(getMotionAngle()) in the act method of an Actor. In some games, you may want to know when an Actor is moving (or not); for this purpose, include the following method in the BaseActor class as well:

```java
public boolean isMoving()
{
    return (getSpeed() > 0);
}
```

Acceleration

With a more formal understanding of the concept and terminology of velocity under our belt, it is time to turn to acceleration. Just as velocity represents how position is changing, *acceleration* represents how velocity is changing. It will be most helpful to keep this analogy in mind throughout what follows: acceleration is to velocity as velocity is to position.

If the units for velocity are pixels/second, then— since acceleration measures the change in this quantity over time—the units for acceleration are pixels/second per second, which could also be written as (pixels/second)/second, or pixels/second^2. Acceleration is also denoted using vector notion. The calculations for adjusting velocity based on acceleration are algebraically identical to the calculations for adjusting position based on velocity. In particular, if an object's initial velocity is $< a , b >$ and there is a constant acceleration of $< c , d >$, then after t seconds, the formula for the velocity at that time is $< a + t{*}c , b + t{*}d >$. These updated velocity values at each point in time will be used in turn to update the position of the object.

In the BaseActor class, for convenience, you will work with the acceleration vector by setting its magnitude (via a method named setAcceleration) and then accelerating in a specified direction (via a method named accelerateAtAngle that takes a direction angle as a parameter). To implement this, add the following fields:

```
private Vector2 accelerationVec;
private float acceleration;
```

Initialize these variables with the following statements in the constructor method:

```
accelerationVec = new Vector2(0,0);
acceleration = 0;
```

Next, add the following methods, as previously described:

```
public void setAcceleration(float acc)
{
    acceleration = acc;
}

public void accelerateAtAngle(float angle)
{
    accelerationVec.add( new Vector2(acceleration, 0).setAngle(angle) );
}
```

For convenience in later projects, now is a good time to add the following method, which accelerates an object in the direction it is currently facing:

```
public void accelerateForward()
{
    accelerateAtAngle( getRotation() );
}
```

Finally, there are some subtle behaviors to discuss and implement. When holding down an arrow key, the character that the player is controlling should typically accelerate in that direction. However, most objects cannot accelerate or speed up forever—there is a limit to how quickly they can move, a maximum speed, which will vary by object. Furthermore, when an arrow key is released, the moving character typically slows down and eventually stops. The rate at which an object will slow down, or *decelerate*, may vary depending on the context. For example, a car slows down more quickly on asphalt than on ice. However, some objects do not appear to decelerate at all, such as bullets or laser beams; their deceleration would be zero. These values (maximum speed and deceleration) will need to be stored and taken into account later. To this end, add the following fields to the BaseActor class:

```
private float maxSpeed;
private float deceleration;
```

Initialize these in the constructor as follows:

```
maxSpeed = 1000;
deceleration = 0;
```

Also add the following methods, used to set these values:

```
public void setMaxSpeed(float ms)
{
    maxSpeed = ms;
}

public void setDeceleration(float dec)
{
    deceleration = dec;
}
```

Movement

With these variables in place (velocityVec, accelerationVec, acceleration, maxSpeed, and deceleration) along with their accompanying methods, you are ready to write the method that will carry out the computations described throughout this section and update the position of the Actor object accordingly. This method will be called applyPhysics and will need to take the amount of elapsed time since the last update as a parameter. This method will handle the following tasks:

- Adjust the velocity vector based on the acceleration vector.

- If the object is not accelerating, it must apply the deceleration amount to the current speed.

- Make sure that the speed is not greater than the maximum speed value.

- Adjust the position of the Actor object based on the velocity vector.

- Reset the acceleration vector.

The code for this method is as follows:

```
public void applyPhysics(float dt)
{
    // apply acceleration
    velocityVec.add( accelerationVec.x * dt, accelerationVec.y * dt );

    float speed = getSpeed();

    // decrease speed (decelerate) when not accelerating
    if (accelerationVec.len() == 0)
        speed -= deceleration * dt;

    // keep speed within set bounds
    speed = MathUtils.clamp(speed, 0, maxSpeed);

    // update velocity
    setSpeed(speed);

    // apply velocity
    moveBy( velocityVec.x * dt, velocityVec.y * dt );

    // reset acceleration
    accelerationVec.set(0,0);
}
```

Now, with these methods added to the BaseActor class, you are ready to implement movement in the *Starfish Collector* game. The only additions will be to the Turtle class, since the turtle is the only object that will be moving. First, add the following import statements to the Turtle class:

```
import com.badlogic.gdx.Gdx;
import com.badlogic.gdx.Input.Keys;
```

Then, you need to initialize some of the physics-related parameters by adding the following code to the constructor method:

```
setAcceleration(400);
setMaxSpeed(100);
setDeceleration(400);
```

From this code, it is clear that the maximum speed of the turtle will be 100 pixels/second. The acceleration value of 400 means that the speed would increase by 400 pixels/second each second, but since the maximum speed is 100 pixels/second, the turtle will reach this speed in 100/400 = 0.25 seconds (when starting from rest).

Finally, you will add the act method, which will check if arrow keys are being pressed and, if so, accelerate the turtle in the corresponding direction. To actually update the position of the turtle, the applyPhysics method must be called. In addition, you will pause the animation whenever the turtle is not moving (and resume the animation when the turtle is moving), as well as rotate the turtle image to align with the angle of motion. These tasks are accomplished by the following code:

```
public void act(float dt)
{
    super.act( dt );

    if (Gdx.input.isKeyPressed(Keys.LEFT))
        accelerateAtAngle(180);
    if (Gdx.input.isKeyPressed(Keys.RIGHT))
        accelerateAtAngle(0);
    if (Gdx.input.isKeyPressed(Keys.UP))
        accelerateAtAngle(90);
    if (Gdx.input.isKeyPressed(Keys.DOWN))
        accelerateAtAngle(270);

    applyPhysics(dt);

    setAnimationPaused( !isMoving() );

    if ( getSpeed() > 0 )
        setRotation( getMotionAngle() );
}
```

This is a good point at which to test the code and verify that the turtle moves around the screen as expected. If you wish, you can experiment with the values set for acceleration, deceleration, and maximum speed and see what their effects are in the game.

At this point, when the turtle overlaps the starfish, nothing happens. This will be remedied in the next section, where collision polygons will be introduced, which allow you to determine when two objects overlap.

Collision Polygons

In the version of *Starfish Collector* created in the previous chapter, collisions between the turtle and starfish did not appear precise to the player. This is because rectangles were used to approximate the shapes of the objects, which included a large region of transparent pixels near the corners of each image. To improve this aspect of the game, in this section you will add the option to use a polygon instead of a rectangle to approximate the boundary of non-rectangular shapes. You will also learn how to check for collisions with polygon shapes using the `Intersector` class and how to simulate solid objects in your game.

Polygons Versus Rectangles

A `Polygon` is a data structure that defines a shape in terms of the coordinates of its vertices (corners); it is initialized with an array of `float` values that define the coordinates of the vertices, one after the other. (In contrast, the `Rectangle` class only requires a single vertex—the bottom-left corner—in addition to the width and height.) For example, if the vertices of a polygon are (x0,y0), (x1,y1), ... , (xN,yN), then the corresponding `Polygon` object would be initialized with the array $\{$`x0, y0, x1, y1, ... , xN, yN`$\}$. For instance, to create a polygon that is the same shape as a rectangle with bottom-left corner vertex (0,0), width w, and height h (as pictured in Figure 3-7), the vertices (in counter-clockwise order) are (0,0), (w,0), (w,h), and (0,h), and you would use the array $\{$`0, 0, w, 0, w, h, 0, h`$\}$.

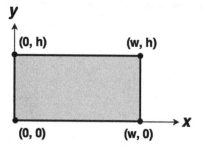

Figure 3-7. *The vertices of a rectangle with width w and height h*

In fact, a rectangular polygon will be used as the default shape for all game objects (a second option will be discussed later). An important reason to use the `Polygon` class rather than the `Rectangle` class is that a `Polygon` object can also rotated, which is useful for game entities that also rotate (such as the turtle in *Starfish Collector*).

To begin, add the following `import` statement to the `BaseActor` class:

```
import com.badlogic.gdx.math.Polygon;
```

Add the following field variable to the class:

```
private Polygon boundaryPolygon;
```

Next, add the following method, which creates a rectangular polygon as just described:

```
public void setBoundaryRectangle()
{
    float w = getWidth();
    float h = getHeight();
    float[] vertices = {0,0, w,0, w,h, 0,h};
    boundaryPolygon = new Polygon(vertices);
}
```

The best place to call this method so that this shape is automatically set as the default is as soon as the width and height are set, which typically happens in the setAnimation method. At the end of this method, add the following code:

```
if (boundaryPolygon == null)
    setBoundaryRectangle();
```

The next (and most complicated) task is to write a method to initialize a polygon shape that is "rounder" than a rectangle (to avoid the issue of overlapping corners that only contain transparent pixels). For this purpose, you will create a polygon that approximates the shape of an ellipse[2] contained within the rectangular region pictured in Figure 3-8. This method involves some mathematical equations to calculate the coordinates of the vertices. The trigonometric functions sine and cosine can be used to *parameterize* a circle or an ellipse, which means you can write functions for the x and y coordinates in terms of another variable, t. For example, if we let $x = \cos(t)$ and $y = \sin(t)$, then as the variable t takes on values ranging from 0 to 2 × pi (approximately 6.28),[3] the corresponding (x,y) points will trace out the shape of a circle with radius 1. You can adapt these equations to generate an ellipse that fits snugly within the given rectangular region, as illustrated in Figure 3-8. First, you must scale (multiply) x by $w/2$, and y by $h/2$, so the ellipse has the correct size. However, the resulting ellipse is centered at the origin, and you want the ellipse to be centered at $(w/2, h/2)$; therefore, add these values to the x and y equations, respectively. The final form of the equations are as follows:

```
x = w/2 * cos(t) + w/2
y = h/2 * sin(t) + h/2
```

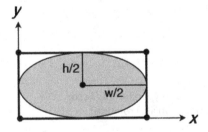

Figure 3-8. *Ellipse contained within a rectangle*

---

[2]Although LibGDX contains an Ellipse class, there are no classes or methods in LibGDX that perform collision detection with ellipse shapes; however, Polygon objects do have such functionality available.

[3]The interval extends from 0 to 6.28 because mathematical functions typically use radian measure for angles rather than degree measure. 6.28 radians roughly corresponds to 360 degrees, which represents a full rotation around the origin, which we need when calculating the values of points all the way around the ellipse.

The setBoundaryPolygon method contains a loop to generate a set of *n* equally spaced values for *t* in the interval [0, 6.28], then calculates the corresponding *x* and *y* coordinates and stores them in an array that will be used to initialize the polygon. If *n* = 4, the polygon will be a diamond shape; if *n* = 8, the polygon will be an octagon shape, and so forth. The larger the value of *n*, the smoother the shape will be. However, there is a trade-off: collision detection for general polygons is computationally intensive; large values of *n* can drastically slow down your program. For the games created in this book, a value of *n* = 8 should be sufficiently accurate. An ellipse alongside a polygon approximation with *n* = 8 is illustrated in Figure 3-9.

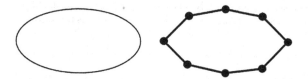

Figure 3-9. *An ellipse and an eight-sided polygon approximation of the ellipse*

The code for setBoundaryPolygon is provided next. It is important to remember to not call this method until *after* the size of the Actor object has been set (either manually from the setSize method or automatically from the setAnimation method), since this method requires values for the width and height to be set in order to work correctly.

```
public void setBoundaryPolygon(int numSides)
{
    float w = getWidth();
    float h = getHeight();

    float[] vertices = new float[2*numSides];
    for (int i = 0; i < numSides; i++)
    {
        float angle = i * 6.28f / numSides;
        // x-coordinate
        vertices[2*i] = w/2 * MathUtils.cos(angle) + w/2;
        // y-coordinate
        vertices[2*i+1] = h/2 * MathUtils.sin(angle) + h/2;
    }
    boundaryPolygon = new Polygon(vertices);
}
```

Next is a method named getBoundaryPolygon that returns the collision polygon for this Actor, adjusting it according to the Actor object's current parameters (such as position and rotation).

```
public Polygon getBoundaryPolygon()
{
    boundaryPolygon.setPosition( getX(), getY() );
    boundaryPolygon.setOrigin( getOriginX(), getOriginY() );
    boundaryPolygon.setRotation ( getRotation() );
    boundaryPolygon.setScale( getScaleX(), getScaleY() );
    return boundaryPolygon;
}
```

Detecting Collisions

Now that you've defined the collision polygons for the BaseActor class, there is still the matter of detecting when two polygons overlap. Unlike the Rectangle class, which has its own overlaps method, the Polygon class does not. Fortunately, another utility class provided by LibGDX, called Intersector, does have such a method. You will make use of this fact to create an overlaps method for the BaseActor class. First, you need to import the aforementioned class with the following statement:

```
import com.badlogic.gdx.math.Intersector;
```

Next, add the following method to the BaseActor class:

```
public boolean overlaps(BaseActor other)
{
    Polygon poly1 = this.getBoundaryPolygon();
    Polygon poly2 = other.getBoundaryPolygon();

    // initial test to improve performance
    if ( !poly1.getBoundingRectangle().overlaps(poly2.getBoundingRectangle()) )
        return false;

    return Intersector.overlapConvexPolygons( poly1, poly2 );
}
```

Checking if two polygons overlap requires a lot of computation. Therefore, to improve performance, this method contains a preliminary check to see if the rectangles surrounding the polygons intersect (which is a much simpler calculation). If these much larger rectangles do not intersect, then it would be impossible for the polygons to intersect, and so the method can immediately return false. Otherwise, there is a possibility that the polygons could intersect, in which case the method returns the result of this more precise test, which is performed by the static method overlapConvexPolygons from the Intersector class.

With this method available, you are ready to add interactivity to the *Starfish Collector* game. In the constructor methods of the Turtle and Starfish classes, add the following line of code (after the images have been loaded) so that each object uses an eight-sided collision polygon for improved accuracy:

```
setBoundaryPolygon(8);
```

Next, when the turtle overlaps the starfish, the following events should occur:

- The starfish should fade out and then be removed from the stage.

- A whirlpool effect should be created, centered on the starfish, and rendered semi-transparent so that the starfish can be seen beneath it.

- After the starfish fades, a "You Win" message should appear in the center of the screen, initially transparent and then slowly fading in.

Recall that the Actor method setPosition actually sets the bottom-left corner of an Actor object to a given location. In order to center an Actor at a given location, you would have shift it from this location by half its width along the *x* direction and half its width along the *y* direction. Since this calculation will be needed frequently in the future, add the following methods to the BaseActor class:

```
public void centerAtPosition(float x, float y)
{
    setPosition( x - getWidth()/2 , y - getHeight()/2 );
}
```

```
public void centerAtActor(BaseActor other)
{
    centerAtPosition( other.getX() + other.getWidth()/2 , other.getY() + other.getHeight()/2 );
}
```

The transparency of an Actor object can be changed by altering the alpha value of the color associated with it. To simplify this process now and for future projects, add the following method to the BaseActor class:

```
public void setOpacity(float opacity)
{
    this.getColor().a = opacity;
}
```

Using the methods just created together with Action objects, you can implement the items in the preceding list. To ensure that the starfish can only be "collected" once (and also to avoid actions' being repeatedly added unnecessarily), in the Starfish class add the following variable declaration:

```
private boolean collected;
```

In the constructor method, initialize this variable as follows:

```
collected = false;
```

Next, add the following two methods to the Starfish class: isCollected, which returns the value of the collected variable, and collect, which sets isCollected to true and applies an animated fading-out effect, after which it is removed from the stage.

```
public boolean isCollected()
{
    return collected;
}
```

```
public void collect()
{
    collected = true;
    clearActions();
    addAction( Actions.fadeOut(1) );
    addAction( Actions.after( Actions.removeActor() ) );
}
```

Next, you will return your attention to the StarfishCollector class. First, add the following import statement:

```
import com.badlogic.gdx.scenes.scene2d.actions.Actions;
```

Next, in the update method of the StarfishCollector class (which is currently empty), add the following code:

```
if (turtle.overlaps(starfish) && !starfish.isCollected() )
{
    starfish.collect();
```

```
Whirlpool whirl = new Whirlpool(0,0, mainStage);
whirl.centerAtActor( starfish );
whirl.setOpacity(0.25f);

BaseActor youWinMessage = new BaseActor(0,0,mainStage);
youWinMessage.loadTexture("assets/you-win.png");
youWinMessage.centerAtPosition(400,300);
youWinMessage.setOpacity(0);
youWinMessage.addAction( Actions.delay(1) );
youWinMessage.addAction( Actions.after( Actions.fadeIn(1) ) );
}
```

The first part of this block of code deals with the starfish: the `collect` method marks the starfish as having been collected and applies the effect previously described. The next part of the code creates a `Whirlpool` object, centers it at the location of the starfish, and makes it mostly transparent (as is the case with real water). Finally, a new `BaseActor` is created that contains an image of the text "You Win," is centered on the screen, and fades in after a delay of one second (corresponding to the one second during which the starfish is fading out). When you are finished adding this code, this is another good opportunity to run the program and verify that everything works as expected.

Simulating Solid Objects

Part of what makes a game fun is the challenge provided by obstacles that must be navigated or overcome as you strive to meet a goal. At this time, there are no obstacles at all in *Starfish Collector*; all you need to do to win the game is move the turtle in a straight line toward the starfish. Your next task will be to add the most basic of obstacles to this game: a solid object (a rock) that the turtle needs to swim around to reach the starfish. Granted, one rock by itself isn't much of a challenge, but once you have learned how to simulate solid objects in this section, and combine this with the knowledge you will gain in the following section (managing collections of objects), a whole new world of possibilities will open up (creating mazes, for example). Once again, the LibGDX framework greatly simplifies the development process.

Previously, you have seen that the `Intersector` class has the functionality to determine when two polygons overlap. In addition, this class can also be used to handle collision response, as you will soon see. In some situations, game objects should be permitted to overlap—this is how a player-controlled character typically collects items, for example. In other situations, however, it should be impossible for game objects to overlap, such as when one of them represents a solid object (like a wall). In each iteration of the game loop, after the character's new position is calculated (via a method such as `applyPhysics`), you need to check if the character is overlapping any solid objects. If so, you then need to adjust its position so that there is no longer any overlap with the solid object. There are many ways the adjustment can be implemented, such as the following:

- Return the character to their previous position (from before the `applyPhysics` method was run).

- Move the character by very small increments along the line from their current position to their previous position, stopping at the first point where there is no longer an overlap.

- Calculate the direction corresponding to the minimal distance the character needs to be moved so that there is no overlap, and move accordingly.

Of these three approaches, you will use the last one, because it is particularly simple to implement using the `Intersector` class. In the `Intersector` class, there is a variation of the `overlapConvexPolygons` method that takes three parameters. The first two parameters are the polygons being checked for overlap. The third parameter is a `MinimumTranslationVector` object, which is used to store the minimum distance and direction required to reposition the polygons as a `float` named `depth` and a `Vector2` named `normal`. If there is an overlap between the polygons, then the `Actor` calling the method will be moved according to the minimum translation vector, and there will no longer be an overlap between the two `Actor` objects. First, in the `BaseActor` class, add the following import statement:

```
import com.badlogic.gdx.math.Intersector.MinimumTranslationVector;
```

The method, named `preventOverlap`, is as follows:

```
public Vector2 preventOverlap(BaseActor other)
{
    Polygon poly1 = this.getBoundaryPolygon();
    Polygon poly2 = other.getBoundaryPolygon();

    // initial test to improve performance
    if ( !poly1.getBoundingRectangle().overlaps(poly2.getBoundingRectangle()) )
        return null;

    MinimumTranslationVector mtv = new MinimumTranslationVector();
    boolean polygonOverlap = Intersector.overlapConvexPolygons(poly1, poly2, mtv);

    if ( !polygonOverlap )
        return null;

    this.moveBy( mtv.normal.x * mtv.depth, mtv.normal.y * mtv.depth );
    return mtv.normal;
}
```

This method also returns the direction in which the `Actor` was moved (when an overlap exists). Although you will not make use of this information in this game, it will be helpful for future projects.

To add a rock as a solid obstacle in your game, first create a new class named `Rock` with the following code:

```
import com.badlogic.gdx.scenes.scene2d.Stage;

public class Rock extends BaseActor
{
    public Rock(float x, float y, Stage s)
    {
        super(x,y,s);
        loadTexture("assets/rock.png");
        setBoundaryPolygon(8);
    }
}
```

Then, in your `StarfishCollector` class, create a new field as follows:

```
private Rock rock;
```

Add the following line of code to the initialize method:

```
rock = new Rock(200,200, mainStage);
```

Finally, add the following line of code at the beginning of the update method:

```
turtle.preventOverlap(rock);
```

At this point, you can run your program and verify that the rock does indeed behave like a solid barrier. The game will currently appear as shown in Figure 3-10. Notice in particular that if the turtle swims directly at the rock, it will appear to slide around it; this is due to the shape of the collision polygons together with the use of the minimal translation vector to adjust the positions of the Actor objects.

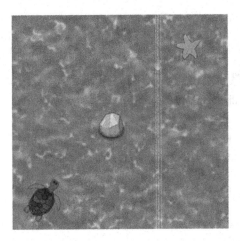

Figure 3-10. *The* Starfish Collector *game with a rock added*

As an entertaining and useful sidenote, if you switch the order of the objects in the preventOverlap method, instead writing rock.preventOverlap(turtle), then the rock will be the object that moves; it will appear as though the turtle is pushing the rock! This has the potential to be a useful game mechanic for a future game project.

Managing Collections of Actors

The next improvement to the *Starfish Collector* game will be adding multiple starfish and rock objects to the game. You certainly don't want to create a new variable for each individual instance, so you need a way to manage all these objects. You could create an array to store this data, but this would not work well for the starfish, since the number of starfish decreases as they are collected, and an array is used to store a fixed number of objects. A better data structure to use in this situation is a list.

```
                              LISTS
```

Data structures are specialized formats for storing, organizing, and accessing data. The first data structure typically encountered in Java programming is the *array*, which can store a fixed number of objects of a single type; the values stored in the array can be later accessed by an integer that refers to the position index within the array. While simple to understand, arrays have a few drawbacks, such as having a fixed size when they are created and needing to access the elements by index numbers. Java provides a number of alternative data structures, one of which is a list.

A *list* is a data structure used to store a collection of elements. There are many types of lists in the Java programming language, each of which implements the methods defined by the `List` interface. These methods include:

- `add`, which adds an element to the end of a list

- `remove`, which removes an element from a list (if it is in the list)

- `size`, which returns the number of elements in the list

- `contains`, which returns true if a list contains a specified element

There are many classes that implement the `List` interface; in this book, the `ArrayList` class will typically be used. When initializing an `ArrayList` (or any other type of list), the size of the list does not need to be specified. However, `ArrayList` is a generic class, and you should specify the type of data being stored in the list (using angle brackets). For example, consider the following code that creates an `ArrayList` to store `String` data and adds and removes some names:

```java
// initialize ArrayList to store String data
ArrayList<String> names = new ArrayList<String>();

// add data to list
names.add("Lee");
names.add("Dan");
names.add("Chris");

// names.size() returns 3
// names.contains("Lee") returns true

// remove "Lee" from list
names.remove("Lee");

// names.size() now returns 2
// names.contains("Lee") now returns false
```

Another advantage to using an `ArrayList` is that if you want to use a loop to perform some action with each of the elements, you can use a `for-each` loop (illustrated in the following code), which allows you to create an index variable that iterates through the *objects* stored in the `ArrayList`; this is in contrast to looping through a standard array, where your index variable must be an `int` that iterates over the *positions* of the objects stored in the array, and where retrieving the objects themselves requires an extra line of code. For example, consider the array-based code for looping through an array:

```
String[] nameArray;
// omitted: code to store values in array
for (int n = 0; n < nameArray.length; n++)
{
    String name = nameArray[n];
    // additional code here
}
```

This is equivalent to the following list-based code for looping through a list:

```
ArrayList<String> nameList;
// omitted: code to store values in list
for (Sting name : nameList)
{
    // additional code here
}
```

In many cases, the ArrayList version of the preceding code is more intuitive and easier to maintain. However, if you are iterating over a list in this way, you cannot add to nor remove from the list within the loop, as this will result in an exception (specifically, a ConcurrentModification exception.

In this book, you will use the ArrayList class to manage collections of actors. In theory, in the game class, you could create your own list for each type of actor (such as Starfish and Rock). In the interest of development efficiency, however, you will instead write a method in the BaseActor class to handle this task for you. As you may recall, each stage stores a list of actors. The general idea is to write a static[4] method that takes a Stage and a class name as parameters, extracts the list of actors from the stage, and creates a new list containing those actors that are instances of the class with the given name (or extensions of the class). To accomplish this task, add the following import statement to the BaseActor class:

```
import java.util.ArrayList;
```

Next, add the following method to the BaseActor class:

```
public static ArrayList<BaseActor> getList(Stage stage, String className)
{
    ArrayList<BaseActor> list = new ArrayList<BaseActor>();

    Class theClass = null;
    try
    { theClass = Class.forName(className);  }
    catch (Exception error)
    { error.printStackTrace();  }
```

---

[4]This method (and the one that follows) will be defined as static because there is no reason to call it from an instance of a BaseActor.

```
    for (Actor a : stage.getActors())
    {
        if ( theClass.isInstance( a ) )
            list.add( (BaseActor)a );
    }

    return list;
}
```

In the preceding code, the try-catch block is necessary in case the forName method fails to return a class (which may happen if a name is entered that does not correspond to a class in the project). The isInstance method checks whether a particular object is an instance of the given class (theClass) or of a class that extends the given class.

In some situations, it will also be convenient to know how many instances of a particular type of object are remaining at a given point in time. This can easily be calculated with the help of the previous method. Add the following method to the BaseActor class, which retrieves the corresponding list of objects and, rather than assigning it to a variable (which is unnecessary, as it does not need to be referenced again in this method), immediately calls the list's size method and returns this value.

```
public static int count(Stage stage, String className)
{
    return getList(stage, className).size();
}
```

Next, you will rewrite most of the StarfishCollector class to incorporate multiple starfish and rocks. You will be able to remove the Starfish and Rock variables, since the instances will be accessible via the newly added getList method. It may appear strange to simply call the constructor repeatedly and not store the results in variables, but remember, the BaseActor class constructor adds them to a Stage, so the instances are not lost. The changes mainly involve the introduction of for loops and rearranging code from the previous version, although the win condition is handled differently. Rewrite the StarfishCollector class as follows:

```
// same import statements as before

public class StarfishCollector extends GameBeta
{
    private Turtle turtle;
    private boolean win;

    public void initialize()
    {
        BaseActor ocean = new BaseActor(0,0, mainStage);
        ocean.loadTexture( "assets/water.jpg" );
        ocean.setSize(800,600);

        new Starfish(400,400, mainStage);
        new Starfish(500,100, mainStage);
        new Starfish(100,450, mainStage);
        new Starfish(200,250, mainStage);
```

```
    new Rock(200,150, mainStage);
    new Rock(100,300, mainStage);
    new Rock(300,350, mainStage);
    new Rock(450,200, mainStage);

    turtle = new Turtle(20,20, mainStage);

    win = false;
}

public void update(float dt)
{
    for (BaseActor rockActor : BaseActor.getList(mainStage, "Rock"))
        turtle.preventOverlap(rockActor);

    for (BaseActor starfishActor : BaseActor.getList(mainStage, "Starfish"))
    {
        Starfish starfish = (Starfish)starfishActor;
        if ( turtle.overlaps(starfish) && !starfish.collected )
        {
            starfish.collected = true;
            starfish.clearActions();
            starfish.addAction( Actions.fadeOut(1) );
            starfish.addAction( Actions.after( Actions.removeActor() ) );

            Whirlpool whirl = new Whirlpool(0,0, mainStage);
            whirl.centerAtActor( starfish );
            whirl.setOpacity(0.25f);
        }
    }

    if ( BaseActor.count(mainStage, "Starfish") == 0 && !win )
    {
        win = true;
        BaseActor youWinMessage = new BaseActor(0,0,mainStage);
        youWinMessage.loadTexture("assets/you-win.png");
        youWinMessage.centerAtPosition(400,300);
        youWinMessage.setOpacity(0);
        youWinMessage.addAction( Actions.delay(1) );
        youWinMessage.addAction( Actions.after( Actions.fadeIn(1) ) );
    }
}
}
```

When you are finished, you can run and test the game; it should appear as shown in Figure 3-11.

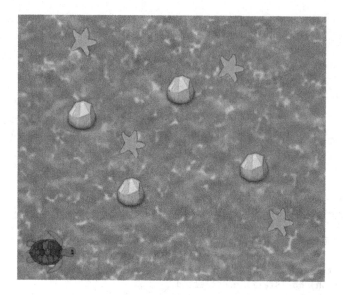

Figure 3-11. *The* Starfish Collector *game with multiple starfish and rocks added*

World Boundaries

The next improvements for the *Starfish Collector* game relate to the world itself. First, it is desirable to keep the turtle within the boundaries of the game world—the player should always be able to see the character they are controlling! The game world will be assumed to be rectangular in shape. It makes sense that the same boundaries should apply to all actors, so this data will be stored in a static Rectangle variable. In the BaseActor class, add the following import statement:

```
import com.badlogic.gdx.math.Rectangle;
```

Then, add the following field:

```
private static Rectangle worldBounds;
```

Next, add the following methods, which enable you to store the size of the game world, either directly from numerical values or based on an actor (such as an actor displaying the background image):

```
public static void setWorldBounds(float width, float height)
{
    worldBounds = new Rectangle( 0,0, width, height );
}

public static void setWorldBounds(BaseActor ba)
{
    setWorldBounds( ba.getWidth(), ba.getHeight() );
}
```

To keep an actor within the rectangular area defined by world bounds, you will need to perform four comparisons to check if any of the edges (left, right, top, and bottom) of the actor have passed beyond the corresponding edges of the screen, and, if so, the corresponding coordinate (x or y) is set to keep the actor on screen. This is accomplished with the following method:

```
public void boundToWorld()
{
    // check left edge
    if (getX() < 0)
        setX(0);
    // check right edge
    if (getX() + getWidth() > worldBounds.width)
        setX(worldBounds.width - getWidth());
    // check bottom edge
    if (getY() < 0)
        setY(0);
    // check top edge
    if (getY() + getHeight() > worldBounds.height)
        setY(worldBounds.height - getHeight());
}
```

Now, to establish the size of the game world in the *Starfish Collector* game, in the StarfishCollector class, add the following line of code to the initialize method, after the size of the ocean is set:

```
BaseActor.setWorldBounds(ocean);
```

To keep the turtle within the world boundaries, add the following line of code to the Turtle class at the end of the act method:

```
boundToWorld();
```

This is another good time to run the program and verify that the bounding works as intended—the turtle should be unable to move past the edge of the screen.

While on the topic of game-world boundaries, the next feature up for implementation is increasing the size of the game world so that it is larger than the size of the window. In this case, the player should only be able to see part of the game world at any point—an area that is the size of the window and centered on the player's character. The area of the game world that is seen is controlled by a Camera object, which is automatically set up by the Stage class (hence why you haven't needed to consider it until now). The main step in this process is to constantly update the position of the camera so that it is aligned with the character. However, care must be taken as the character approaches the edge of the game world. If the camera remains centered on the character even then, the camera will display part of the area beyond the game world, which will typically be rendered as solid black (or whatever color was initialized in the render method), as shown in Figure 3-12.

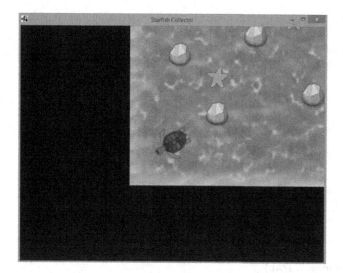

Figure 3-12. *Incorrect camera positioning causing the area beyond the game world to be rendered in black*

To avoid this issue, after centering the camera on the character, you may need to adjust the camera position so that its *x* coordinate is always at least half the viewing area's width away from the left and right edges of the game world (and similarly for the *y* coordinate). The region to which the camera position should be bound is illustrated by the area enclosed by the dashed lines in Figure 3-13. As long as the camera stays in this region, its viewing area will be completely contained within the game world.

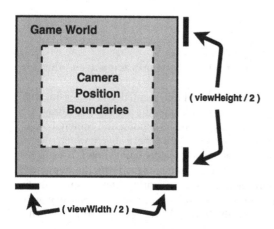

Figure 3-13. *Boundaries for the camera to keep the viewing area within the game world*

Next, add the following `import` statements to the `BaseActor` class:

```
import com.badlogic.gdx.graphics.Camera;
import com.badlogic.gdx.utils.viewport.Viewport;
```

Moving the camera as described earlier is accomplished with the following method, which should be added to the `BaseActor` class:

```
public void alignCamera()
{
    Camera cam = this.getStage().getCamera();
    Viewport v = this.getStage().getViewport();

    // center camera on actor
    cam.position.set( this.getX() + this.getOriginX(), this.getY() + this.getOriginY(), 0 );

    // bound camera to layout
    cam.position.x = MathUtils.clamp(cam.position.x,
        cam.viewportWidth/2,  worldBounds.width - cam.viewportWidth/2);
    cam.position.y = MathUtils.clamp(cam.position.y,
        cam.viewportHeight/2, worldBounds.height - cam.viewportHeight/2);
    cam.update();
}
```

To enlarge the game world, in the `StarfishCollector` class, instead of setting the size of the ocean to 800 by 600 pixels, you should change these numbers to 1200 and 900, which is significantly larger than the window size of 800 by 600. In addition, you may want to set the ocean's texture to be the image file `water-border.jpg` instead of `water.jpg`. This new texture features a sand-like border around the edge, which will only be visible on two edges of the screen when the game starts, giving the player a visual cue that the game world extends further in the other directions. Finally, in the `Turtle` class, at the end of the `act` method, add this single line of code:

```
alignCamera();
```

With these changes in place, you are ready to once again test your project and verify that the camera-scrolling feature works as expected.

However, if you play through to the end of the game, you will notice one problem: the "You Win" message does not remain fixed in the center of the screen. This is because it is part of the stage `mainStage`, whose camera is being adjusted to align with the turtle. This makes the message appear to be a physical entity in the game world, rather than part of the user interface (which should render above the game world, remain fixed in place, and always be visible to the player). The way to remedy this is to add a second `Stage` object to the framework, named `uiStage` (an abbreviation for user interface stage), which renders after (and therefore appears on top of) the stage containing the game-world entities, and whose attached `Camera` never changes position. Implementing this second stage mostly requires modifying the `GameBeta` class. In this class, add the following variable declaration:

```
protected Stage uiStage;
```

In the `create` method, add the following line of code after the corresponding line for the `mainStage` object:

```
uiStage = new Stage();
```

Finally, in the `render` method, add the following lines of code, each immediately after the corresponding lines for the `mainStage` object:

```
uiStage.act(dt);
uiStage.draw();
```

Now, return to the `StarfishCollector` class. The only change that needs to be made is replacing `mainStage` with `uiStage` when the `youWinMessage` object is created. This finishes the necessary changes; if you run the program and collect all the starfish, you will see that the "You Win" message remains centered on the screen, no matter what part of the game world the turtle swims to.

Multiple Screens

The last feature that will be added to *Starfish Collector* in this chapter is the ability to add multiple screens to the game, which can be used for menus and additional levels. Up to this point, all the game-related code has been contained in an extension of the Game class. For projects that require more than a single screen, the Game class also has the ability to pass control of the program to Screen objects, each of which has its own render method capable of handling the functionality of the game loop. In this section, you will refactor the code in the GameBeta class into two new abstract classes, BaseGame and BaseScreen, to support this functionality; these classes (along with BaseActor) will be the basis for all future game projects in this book. The BaseGame class is mainly responsible for storing a static reference to the Game object initialized by the Launcher class so that the Screen-derived classes can easily access and switch the currently active screen. The BaseScreen class will contain most of the code from the GameBeta class, along with some additional (empty) method declarations, as required by the Screen interface. The Launcher class will initialize a class that extends BaseGame, which in turn initializes the first screen to be displayed and sets it as the currently active screen. The different screens required by the game will extend the BaseScreen class; in this section, this will be the menu screen (named MenuScreen) and the screen where the gameplay occurs (named LevelScreen).

First is the code for the new BaseGame class:

```
import com.badlogic.gdx.Game;
public abstract class BaseGame extends Game
{
    private static BaseGame game;

    public BaseGame()
    {
        game = this;
    }

    public static void setActiveScreen(BaseScreen s)
    {
        game.setScreen(s);
    }
}
```

At this point, the BaseGame class will display an error until the BaseScreen class is created. Next is the code for the new BaseScreen class (most of which should appear familiar):

```
import com.badlogic.gdx.Gdx;
import com.badlogic.gdx.graphics.GL20;
import com.badlogic.gdx.scenes.scene2d.Stage;
import com.badlogic.gdx.Screen;

public abstract class BaseScreen implements Screen
{
    protected Stage mainStage;
    protected Stage uiStage;

    public BaseScreen()
    {
        mainStage = new Stage();
        uiStage = new Stage();

        initialize();
    }

    public abstract void initialize();

    public abstract void update(float dt);

    public void render(float dt)
    {
        uiStage.act(dt);
        mainStage.act(dt);

        update(dt);

        Gdx.gl.glClearColor(0,0,0,1);
        Gdx.gl.glClear(GL20.GL_COLOR_BUFFER_BIT);

        mainStage.draw();
        uiStage.draw();
    }

    // methods required by Screen interface
    public void resize(int width, int height) {  }

    public void pause()    {  }

    public void resume()  {  }

    public void dispose() {  }

    public void show()    {  }

    public void hide()    {  }
}
```

Now, create a new class named LevelScreen; except for the class declaration, this is identical to the StarfishCollector class from earlier, so you will simply copy the code from that class into this new class, as follows:

```
import com.badlogic.gdx.scenes.scene2d.Action;
import com.badlogic.gdx.scenes.scene2d.actions.Actions;

public class LevelScreen extends BaseScreen
{
    private Turtle turtle;
    private boolean win;

    public void initialize()
    {
        // code identical to StarfishCollector initialize method
    }

    public void update(float dt)
    {
        // code identical to StarfishCollector update method
    }
}
```

Now, create a class named MenuScreen, which features brand-new code. This screen will display the title of the game and a message that says "Press 'S' to start." When the player presses the S key (as detected in the update method), the game creates an instance of LevelScreen and transfers control to this instance.

```
import com.badlogic.gdx.Gdx;
import com.badlogic.gdx.Input.Keys;

public class MenuScreen extends BaseScreen
{
    public void initialize()
    {
        BaseActor ocean = new BaseActor(0,0, mainStage);
        ocean.loadTexture( "assets/water.jpg" );
        ocean.setSize(800,600);

        BaseActor title = new BaseActor(0,0, mainStage);
        title.loadTexture( "assets/starfish-collector.png" );
        title.centerAtPosition(400,300);
        title.moveBy(0,100);

        BaseActor start = new BaseActor(0,0, mainStage);
        start.loadTexture( "assets/message-start.png" );
        start.centerAtPosition(400,300);
        start.moveBy(0,-100);

    }
```

```
public void update(float dt)
{
    if (Gdx.input.isKeyPressed(Keys.S))
        StarfishGame.setActiveScreen( new LevelScreen() );
}
}
```

As before, until the referenced classes are created (in this case, the StarfishGame class), this class will display an error and cannot be compiled; this issue will be remedied shortly.

The menu screen that will appear once the game is run is shown in Figure 3-14.

Figure 3-14. *The menu screen for the* Starfish Collector *game*

You will specify which of the screens loads first by creating an extension of the BaseGame class, named StarfishGame, as follows:

```
public class StarfishGame extends BaseGame
{
    public void create()
    {
        setActiveScreen( new MenuScreen() );
    }
}
```

Finally, you need to change the code of the Launcher class so that the StarfishGame class is initialized and used when running the program.

```
import com.badlogic.gdx.Game;
import com.badlogic.gdx.backends.lwjgl.LwjglApplication;
```

```java
public class Launcher
{
    public static void main (String[] args)
    {
        Game myGame = new StarfishGame();
        LwjglApplication launcher =
            new LwjglApplication( myGame, "Starfish Collector", 800, 600 );
    }
}
```

There are now many classes being used in the *Starfish Collector* game. A screenshot of the main BlueJ window in Figure 3-15 shows how these classes are related (the rectangles corresponding to the classes have been arranged for clarity). In general, there are four main groups of classes involved in creating a game with this framework: the Launcher class, the BaseGame class and its extension, the BaseScreen class and its extensions, and the BaseActor class and its extensions.

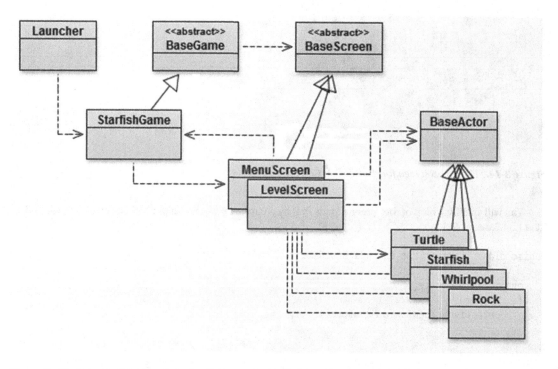

Figure 3-15. *Relationships between the classes in the final version of the* Starfish Collector *game*

At this point, you have finished adding all the improvements to the *Starfish Collector* game discussed at the beginning of this chapter. You should run your program to verify that everything works as expected, and be sure to take pride in all that you have accomplished. The foundation you have created here will serve you well in future chapters. Congratulations!

Summary and Next Steps

In this chapter, while improving the quality of the *Starfish Collector* game, you have in fact created a robust foundation that will enable you to rapidly develop a variety of games throughout the rest of this book. You implemented value-based and image-based animations, the latter from either individual image files or a single spritesheet. You simulated realistic motion by writing a set of methods to perform physics-based calculations. You improved the accuracy of collision detection and learned how to simulate solid objects. You added support for working with lists of actors. You wrote methods for working with a bounded, enlarged game world. Finally, you refactored the code to enable the addition of multiple screens to the game.

In order to practice your newfound skills and test your understanding of the framework, you should consider implementing additional features in the *Starfish Collector* game. For starters, you could add additional starfish and rocks throughout the enlarged level, perhaps laying out additional rocks to make collecting all the starfish more challenging. You could also consider adding enemies: sharks that are positioned around the level and cause the player to lose the game (and the turtle to be destroyed) on contact. Images of a shark and a "Game Over" message have been included with the assets for this chapter if you wish to try your hand at this addition. You may also want to consider adding a second level via a new class called LevelScreen2. For this addition, you would have to change the code in the LevelScreen class so that, after the player has collected all the starfish, a message appears (such as "Press 'C' to continue"), and so that, in the update method, when the C key is pressed, the game sets the active screen to a new instance of the LevelScreen2 class. Again, images that would be useful for this task have been included in the assets for this chapter.

You probably have additional ideas for game features to add, such as a time limit to collect all the starfish. Some of these ideas will be easier to implement after user interfaces and text displays are covered in more detail in Chapter 5. In addition, if you find determining the coordinates for the rocks and starfish to be overly time-consuming, take heart that this topic will be addressed in future chapters that discuss tilemaps and using third-party software to simplify level design.

In the next chapter, you will experience and appreciate first-hand the flexibility of the framework you have developed here as you use it to create an entirely new game, *Space Rocks*, a space-themed shoot-em-up game inspired by the classic arcade game *Asteroids*.

CHAPTER 4

■ ■ ■

Shoot-em-up games

In this chapter, you will create an entirely new game: *Space Rocks*, shown in Figure 4-1 and inspired by the classic arcade game *Asteroids*. You will make extensive use of the framework you created in the previous chapter (the BaseGame, BaseScreen, and BaseActor classes) and add a few new features along the way. The most significant addition will be the ability to handle discrete events: actions that should occur only once each time a key is pressed.

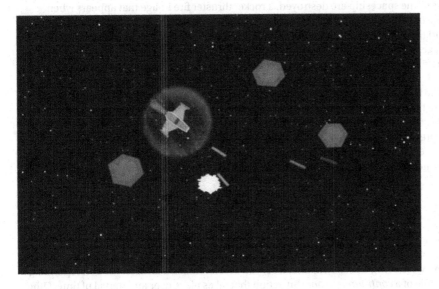

Figure 4-1. *The* Space Rocks *game*

Game Project: Space Rocks

When starting a new game project, before writing any code, it is important to plan out the features in detail. A *game design document* serves as the blueprint or master plan for creating a game: it describes the overall vision of a game, provides clarity and focus, and serves as a guide and a reference to the person or people working on the game. Game design documents are described in more detail in the appendix of this book. As each new game is introduced in this book, a detailed description will be given following the guidelines of such a document; what follows is the description of the *Space Rocks* game.

L. Stemkoski, *Java Game Development with LibGDX*, https://doi.org/10.1007/978-1-4842-3324-5_4

Space Rocks is a space-themed shoot-em-up game. The player controls a spaceship, whose goal is to shoot lasers and destroy rocks that are flying around the screen. The game world has a top-down perspective and features wraparound: when an object moves past the edge of the screen, it reappears on the opposite edge.

The spaceship can rotate to its left and right and accelerate in the direction it is facing. There is very little deceleration. The spaceship is able to shoot lasers, which travel in a straight line for one second, then fade out and disappear from the game if they haven't collided with a rock. If the laser hits a rock, then the laser and rock are both destroyed. The spaceship is surrounded by a shield. If the spaceship is hit by a rock while the shields are active, the rock is destroyed and the shields lose power. After shield power is reduced to 0, the shields disappear, and being hit by a rock destroys the spaceship and ends the game. The spaceship also has the ability to instantly and randomly teleport to a new location on the screen.

The player rotates left and right and accelerates forward with the arrow keys. Due to the small amount of deceleration, in order to stop suddenly the player will have to turn around and accelerate in the opposite direction. Lasers are fired using the spacebar key and can be fired as quickly as the player wishes. Teleportation is activated with the X key. While this can be used for quick escapes from an imminent collision, there is the possibility of teleporting onto a rock, and so the player may choose to use this ability sparingly.

The graphics required for this game include a starfield for the background and images for the spaceship, laser, and rock. There will be special effects used to provide visual user feedback. There will be an animated explosion for when rocks or the spaceship are destroyed, a rocket thruster fire image that appears when the player is accelerating, and an animated wormhole effect when the teleportation ability is used, which will appear at both the original and the new locations of the spaceship. If the player wins the game, a "Congratulations" message will appear; if the player loses, a "Game Over" message will appear.

To begin, create a new project in BlueJ named Space Rocks. Download the source code files for this chapter on the website for this book. In the project directory that is created by BlueJ, create a new folder called assets. Copy all the image files from the downloaded project's assets folder into your new project's assets folder. Next (if you haven't set up the BlueJ userlibs folder), in your project directory, create a new folder named +libs. Copy the JAR files from the downloaded project's +libs folder into your new project's +libs folder. From your previous BlueJ project, Starfish Collector Ch 3, copy the files BaseGame.java, BaseScreen.java, and BaseActor.java into the Space Rocks project directory. Restart BlueJ so that the Java source code and JAR files newly added to the +libs folder are properly recognized by BlueJ.

Discrete Input

In the game from the previous chapter, *Starfish Collector*, the only action performed by the turtle was movement. You handled this by checking at every possible moment (in the act method, which runs 60 times per second) if certain keys were being held down, and, if so, you accelerated the turtle in the corresponding direction. This is an example of a *continuous action*: an action that takes place over an interval of time. Other examples of continuous actions include walking, rotating, or sleeping. In contrast, a *discrete action* happens at a single instant in time. Examples include jumping, hitting an object, or shooting a projectile. With the keyboard, continuous actions typically involve holding a key down for a period of time, whereas discrete actions are triggered the instant a key is pressed. Mouse-based actions can also fall into either category: clicking on a button is a discrete action, while dragging a slider is a continuous action.

The main new feature that will be added to your custom framework classes is the ability to handle discrete input. Up to this point, you have been using a technique called *input polling*: repeatedly checking the status of an input device (such as a keyboard). In particular, you have been checking in the act or update methods (which typically run 60 times per second) whether particular keys were being held down or not. This is a fine way to handle continuous actions, but this approach will not work for discrete actions.

Fortunately, the LibGDX library provides a framework to handle discrete events as well. This involves writing functions that are automatically called when certain events occur (such as the initial press or release of a key or click of a mouse button). Any object can be assigned the responsibility of responding to discrete input events, but in order to do so correctly, it must contain a particular set of methods: those specified by the InputProcessor interface. There are a total of eight methods required by this interface:

- keyDown, keyUp, and keyTyped to handle keyboard events

- touchDown, touchUp, and touchDragged to handle both mouse and touchscreen events

- mouseMoved and scrolled to handle mouse events

The final question we need to address in this section is this: which object should bear the responsibility of responding to input events? On one hand, the Stage class already implements the InputProcessor interface; this is particularly helpful for a Stage that contains user-interface elements, because it enables button-like objects to activate methods when they are clicked. On the other hand, it would be convenient if the BaseScreen class implemented the InputProcessor interface so that when you write a class that extends BaseScreen, your class can include methods to handle discrete keyboard input. So, should the Stage class or the BaseScreen class be in charge of responding to input events? In practice, you want both objects to have the opportunity to do so. The way this arrangement will be implemented in your code is via the InputMultiplexer class. An InputMultiplexer object is itself an InputProcessor that contains a list of other InputProcessors. You can add the Stage and BaseScreen objects to an InputMultiplexer, and when input events occur, the InputMultiplexer will forward along the input data to each of these objects and give them the opportunity to respond accordingly.

First, you will modify the BaseGame class. Add the following import statements:

```
import com.badlogic.gdx.Gdx;
import com.badlogic.gdx.InputMultiplexer;
```

Next, you will add a create method to the BaseGame class, which is automatically called by LibGDX and will be used to initialize the InputMultiplexer object. (Adding InputProcessors will be handled later by the BaseScreen class.)

```
public void create()
{
    // prepare for multiple classes/stages to receive discrete input
    InputMultiplexer im = new InputMultiplexer();
    Gdx.input.setInputProcessor( im );
}
```

Now, you will turn your attention to the BaseScreen class. First, add the following import statements:

```
import com.badlogic.gdx.InputProcessor;
import com.badlogic.gdx.InputMultiplexer;
```

Next, you will change the declaration of the class to take into account that the InputProcessor methods will be implemented by this class. You can declare that multiple interfaces will be implemented[1] by listing them after the keyword implements and separating them with commas, as follows:

```
public abstract class BaseScreen implements Screen, InputProcessor
```

---

[1]Although you can implement multiple interfaces, you can only extend a single class at a time.

You will add empty methods for everything required by the InputProcessor interface; any methods that you actually plan to use, you can override in your extension of the BaseScreen class. You will notice that each of these methods returns a Boolean value. This value indicates whether this input data has been completely handled by this InputProcessor; if set to true, the input data will not be sent to any of the other InputProcessors stored in the InputMultiplexer. All the default values are set to false so that each InputProcessor will have the opportunity to process the data. The methods you need to add are as follows:

```
// methods required by InputProcessor interface

public boolean keyDown(int keycode)
{  return false;  }

public boolean keyUp(int keycode)
{  return false;  }

public boolean keyTyped(char c)
{  return false;  }

public boolean mouseMoved(int screenX, int screenY)
{  return false;  }

public boolean scrolled(int amount)
{  return false;  }

public boolean touchDown(int screenX, int screenY, int pointer, int button)
{  return false;  }

public boolean touchDragged(int screenX, int screenY, int pointer)
{  return false;  }

public boolean touchUp(int screenX, int screenY, int pointer, int button)
{  return false;  }
```

Finally, both of the Stage objects and the BaseScreen class itself should be added to the game's InputMultiplexer when this screen is displayed, and removed from the InputMultiplexer when a new screen is set. The best place to add this code is in the methods show and hide (previously required by the Screen interface), which are called when the screen appears and disappears in the game, respectively. First, change the show method as follows:

```
public void show()
{
    InputMultiplexer im = (InputMultiplexer)Gdx.input.getInputProcessor();
    im.addProcessor(this);
    im.addProcessor(uiStage);
    im.addProcessor(mainStage);
}
```

Then, change the hide method as follows:

```
public void hide()
{
    InputMultiplexer im = (InputMultiplexer)Gdx.input.getInputProcessor();
    im.removeProcessor(this);
    im.removeProcessor(uiStage);
    im.removeProcessor(mainStage);
}
```

At this point, you are ready to handle discrete input, and you can create the custom classes for the game entities in the *Space Rocks* game.

Spaceship Setup

In this section, you will add code for the spaceship and its related features and abilities: wrapping around the screen, thrusters that appear when the spaceship is accelerating, shields that surround the ship and protect it from rock collisions a number of times, and a teleporting ability that moves the ship to a random location on the screen.

First, create a new class named Spaceship with the following code:

```
import com.badlogic.gdx.scenes.scene2d.Stage;
import com.badlogic.gdx.Gdx;
import com.badlogic.gdx.Input.Keys;

public class Spaceship extends BaseActor
{
    public Spaceship(float x, float y, Stage s)
    {
        super(x,y,s);

        loadTexture( "assets/spaceship.png" );
        setBoundaryPolygon(8);

        setAcceleration(200);
        setMaxSpeed(100);
        setDeceleration(10);
    }

    public void act(float dt)
    {
        super.act( dt );

        float degreesPerSecond = 120; // rotation speed
        if (Gdx.input.isKeyPressed(Keys.LEFT))
            rotateBy(degreesPerSecond * dt);
        if (Gdx.input.isKeyPressed(Keys.RIGHT))
            rotateBy(-degreesPerSecond * dt);

        if (Gdx.input.isKeyPressed(Keys.UP))
            accelerateAtAngle( getRotation() );
```

```
        applyPhysics(dt);
    }
}
```

This class handles the standard tasks of loading an image, setting up a collision polygon, and specifying the physics setting. Note that the deceleration value is close to zero; this is meant to simulate the lack of friction or air resistance that slows down objects in outer space. Also notice in the act method that the left and right arrow keys are used to rotate the spaceship to its left and right (in contrast to moving the object to the screen's left and right, as was the case in the *Starfish Collector* game), and the up arrow key accelerates the spaceship forward; that is, in the direction it is currently facing.

The next characteristic movement feature is wrapping around the screen. Since many objects in the *Space Rocks* game share this feature, you will implement this feature by adding the following method to the BaseActor class:

```
public void wrapAroundWorld()
{
    if (getX() + getWidth() < 0)
        setX( worldBounds.width );

    if (getX() > worldBounds.width)
        setX( -getWidth());

    if (getY() + getHeight() < 0)
        setY( worldBounds.height );

    if (getY() > worldBounds.height)
        setY( -getHeight() );
}
```

Note that this method requires the worldBounds object to be set in order to work correctly. With this method in place, add the following line of code to the Spaceship class at the end of the act method:

```
wrapAroundWorld();
```

Next, you will begin to write the screen class, which will enable you to test the movement and wrap functionality. Create a new class named LevelScreen that contains the following code:

```
public class LevelScreen extends BaseScreen
{
    private Spaceship spaceship;

    public void initialize()
    {
        BaseActor space = new BaseActor(0,0, mainStage);
        space.loadTexture( "assets/space.png" );
        space.setSize(800,600);
        BaseActor.setWorldBounds(space);

        spaceship = new Spaceship(400,300, mainStage);
    }

    public void update(float dt)
    {    }
}
```

Before you can test your project, you will need to create two additional classes. First, create a class named SpaceGame with the following code:

```
public class SpaceGame extends BaseGame
{
    public void create()
    {
        super.create();
        setActiveScreen( new LevelScreen() );
    }
}
```

Next, create a class called Launcher containing the following code:

```
import com.badlogic.gdx.Game;
import com.badlogic.gdx.backends.lwjgl.LwjglApplication;

public class Launcher
{
    public static void main (String[] args)
    {
        Game myGame = new SpaceGame();
        LwjglApplication launcher = new LwjglApplication( myGame, "Space Rocks", 800, 600 );
    }
}
```

Now you are able to test your project so as to verify that the spaceship moves as expected. At this point, the game will appear as shown in Figure 4-2. If you feel that the movement is too slow or too fast, you should always feel free to adjust the corresponding parameters as desired.

Figure 4-2. *The* Space Rocks *game with starfield background image and spaceship added*

Next, you will add a thruster effect to the spaceship, which will appear whenever the player is holding down the key to accelerate the spaceship. This is an example of providing visual feedback to the player, an important game design principle that makes the overall game experience feel more responsive and polished. The trickiest aspect to implementing the thruster effect (and the shield effect that will be discussed following this) is keeping the position and rotation of the thrusters aligned relative to the spaceship. Effectively, you want to attach one actor to another and keep their relative positions in sync. Once again, the LibGDX framework provides this functionality.

LibGDX includes a class called Group that extends the Actor class and provides the ability to add additional actors to the group. Furthermore, when rendering these additional actors, their positions and rotations are determined with respect to the group itself, exactly as desired for this game and others to follow. To incorporate this functionality into your custom framework, in the BaseActor class, add the following import statement:

```
import com.badlogic.gdx.scenes.scene2d.Group;
```

Change the class declaration of the BaseActor class so that it extends the Group class instead of the Actor class, as follows:

```
public class BaseActor extends Group
```

Finally, so that the actors attached to the group render after (and therefore, appear on top of) the image corresponding to the group object itself, in the draw method, move the line of code

```
super.draw( batch, parentAlpha );
```

from the beginning of the method to the end of the method (after the batch.draw statement).

Next, create a new class named Thrusters with the following code:

```
import com.badlogic.gdx.scenes.scene2d.Stage;

public class Thrusters extends BaseActor
{
    public Thrusters(float x, float y, Stage s)
    {
        super(x,y,s);
        loadTexture("assets/fire.png");
    }
}
```

Now, in the Spaceship class, add the following field:

```
private Thrusters thrusters;
```

In the constructor method, initialize this object by adding the following code, which attaches the thrusters to the spaceship and adjusts their position relative to the spaceship so that they appear in the correct location, as shown in Figure 4-3.

```
thrusters = new Thrusters(0,0, s);
addActor(thrusters);
thrusters.setPosition(-thrusters.getWidth(), getHeight()/2 - thrusters.getHeight()/2 );
```

Finally, make the thrusters visible and invisible in the Spaceship class act method; change the code that checks whether the up arrow key is pressed to the following:

```
if (Gdx.input.isKeyPressed(Keys.UP))
{
    accelerateAtAngle( getRotation() );
    thrusters.setVisible(true);
}
else
{
    thrusters.setVisible(false);
}
```

This is another good point at which to test your code to verify that this feature is working as expected.

Next, you will add shields to the Spaceship object, which will enable the spaceship to withstand multiple collisions before being destroyed. Create a new class named Shield with the following code:

```
import com.badlogic.gdx.scenes.scene2d.Stage;
import com.badlogic.gdx.scenes.scene2d.Action;
import com.badlogic.gdx.scenes.scene2d.actions.Actions;

public class Shield extends BaseActor
{
    public Shield(float x, float y, Stage s)
    {
        super(x,y,s);
        loadTexture("assets/shields.png");

        Action pulse = Actions.sequence(
                Actions.scaleTo(1.05f, 1.05f, 1), Actions.scaleTo(0.95f, 0.95f, 1) );

        addAction( Actions.forever(pulse) );
    }
}
```

Note that a small pulsing effect (a value-based animation) has been added to the Shield object to make it more visually interesting. Next, you will add a Shield object to the Spaceship class, as you did with the Thrusters object. To measure how much power remains before the Shield object is destroyed, you will also add a variable named shieldPower. This will be used to change the opacity of the shields, which will serve as an approximate visual indicator of how much power the shields have remaining. In the BaseActor class, add the following field declarations:

```
private Shield shield;
public int shieldPower;
```

These variables are initialized in the constructor method, as follows:

```
shield = new Shield(0,0, s);
addActor(shield);
shield.centerAtPosition( getWidth()/2, getHeight()/2 );
shieldPower = 100;
```

Finally, the spaceship will update the shield opacity by adding the following code to the act method:

```
shield.setOpacity(shieldPower / 100f);
if (shieldPower <= 0)
    shield.setVisible(false);
```

If you wish, you can run the game to verify that the shields appear as expected.

Next, you will add the ability to teleport to a random location on the screen when the X key is pressed; this is the first discrete action that you will implement. First, you will set up a wormhole-like special effect that will appear both at the spaceship's original position and at the new position after the teleporting has taken place. The effect will fade out and remove itself from its stage shortly after it appears. Create a new class named Warp with the following code:

```
import com.badlogic.gdx.scenes.scene2d.Stage;
import com.badlogic.gdx.scenes.scene2d.Action;
import com.badlogic.gdx.scenes.scene2d.actions.Actions;

public class Warp extends BaseActor
{
    public Warp(float x, float y, Stage s)
    {
        super(x,y,s);

        loadAnimationFromSheet("assets/warp.png", 4, 8, 0.05f, true);

        addAction( Actions.delay(1) );
        addAction( Actions.after( Actions.fadeOut(0.5f) ) );
        addAction( Actions.after( Actions.removeActor() ) );
    }
}
```

Next, you will add a method to the Spaceship class that will be called by the LevelScreen class when the X key is pressed. (The code is organized in this way because the BaseScreen class was set up to handle discrete input, and the BaseActor class wasn't.) First, in the Spaceship class, add the following import statement:

```
import com.badlogic.gdx.math.MathUtils;
```

Next, add the following method, which uses the random method of the MathUtils class to generate random float numbers (up to the given parameter), which are used to set the position of the spaceship:

```
public void warp()
{
    if ( getStage() == null)
        return;

    Warp warp1 = new Warp(0,0, this.getStage());
    warp1.centerAtActor(this);
    setPosition(MathUtils.random(800), MathUtils.random(600));
    Warp warp2 = new Warp(0,0, this.getStage());
    warp2.centerAtActor(this);
}
```

The purpose of the conditional statement at the beginning of the warp method is to verify that the spaceship is still part of the game (indicated by being attached to a stage). If the getStage method returns null, then the spaceship has been removed from the game, and the method returns right away, effectively stopping the code that follows from executing.

Next, in the LevelScreen class, you will add the following keyDown method. This overrides the default keyDown method specified in the BaseScreen class. This method is activated once when a key is pressed. To determine which key is pressed, you will use the fields stored in the Keys class, so begin by adding the following import statement:

```
import com.badlogic.gdx.Input.Keys;
```

Next, add the following method:

```
// override default InputProcessor method
public boolean keyDown(int keycode)
{
    if ( keycode == Keys.X )
        spaceship.warp();

    return false;
}
```

Once again, feel free to run the code and check that the teleporting feature works as expected. With these effects added, the game will appear as shown in Figure 4-3. Next, you will add some of the game objects external to the spaceship: lasers, rocks, and explosions.

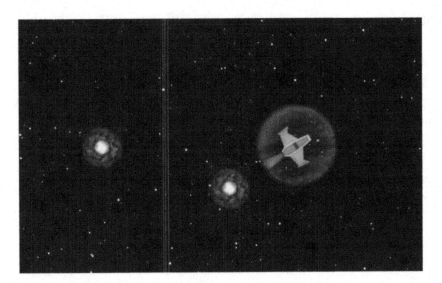

Figure 4-3. *The* Space Rocks *game with thrusters, shields, and warp effects added*

Lasers, Rocks, and Explosions

Next, you will add a laser that the spaceship will shoot. Similar to the spaceship, the laser wraps around the screen, and similar to the warp effect, the laser will automatically fade and remove itself from the game after a short delay. (Lasers that last forever would be overpowered in this game.) Unlike the spaceship, the laser travels at a constant speed, so rather than set an acceleration value, the speed of the laser object will be set directly, and the deceleration will be set to 0. Create a new class called Laser with the following code:

```
import com.badlogic.gdx.scenes.scene2d.Stage;
import com.badlogic.gdx.scenes.scene2d.Action;
import com.badlogic.gdx.scenes.scene2d.actions.Actions;

public class Laser extends BaseActor
{
    public Laser(float x, float y, Stage s)
    {
        super(x,y,s);

        loadTexture("assets/laser.png");

        addAction( Actions.delay(1) );
        addAction( Actions.after( Actions.fadeOut(0.5f) ) );
        addAction( Actions.after( Actions.removeActor() ) );

        setSpeed(400);
        setMaxSpeed(400);
        setDeceleration(0);
    }

    public void act(float dt)
    {
        super.act(dt);
        applyPhysics(dt);
        wrapAroundWorld();
    }
}
```

To shoot the lasers, you add the following method to the Spaceship class; similar to the warp method, it will be activated from the LevelScreen class in its keyDown method. In the Spaceship class, add the following code:

```
public void shoot()
{
    if ( getStage() == null )
        return;

    Laser laser = new Laser(0,0, this.getStage());
    laser.centerAtActor(this);
    laser.setRotation( this.getRotation() );
    laser.setMotionAngle( this.getRotation() );
}
```

In the keyDown method of the LevelScreen class, add the following code:

```
if ( keycode == Keys.SPACE )
    spaceship.shoot();
```

If you run the game at this point, you will be able to shoot lasers!

Next, you will add some rock objects to the game, giving you something to shoot at. Similar to the laser, they wrap around the screen and travel at a constant speed. Each rock will have a value-based animation (rotation) to add visual interest. To add some unpredictability to the game, you will randomize the rotation speed and movement speed by a small amount, again using the random function from the LibGDX MathUtils class. Create a new class named Rock with the following code:

```
import com.badlogic.gdx.scenes.scene2d.Stage;
import com.badlogic.gdx.scenes.scene2d.Action;
import com.badlogic.gdx.scenes.scene2d.actions.Actions;
import com.badlogic.gdx.math.MathUtils;

public class Rock extends BaseActor
{
    public Rock(float x, float y, Stage s)
    {
        super(x,y,s);

        loadTexture("assets/rock.png");

        float random = MathUtils.random(30);

        addAction( Actions.forever( Actions.rotateBy(30 + random, 1) ) );

        setSpeed(50 + random);
        setMaxSpeed(50 + random);
        setDeceleration(0);

        setMotionAngle( MathUtils.random(360) );
    }

    public void act(float dt)
    {
        super.act(dt);
        applyPhysics(dt);
        wrapAroundWorld();
    }
}
```

In order for the rocks to appear, you will have to create some in the initialize method of the LevelScreen class with the following code. Note that the rocks are positioned surrounding the spaceship at a distance. This gives the player a fair chance to move the spaceship out of the path of the rocks at the start of the game.

```
new Rock(600,500, mainStage);
new Rock(600,300, mainStage);
new Rock(600,100, mainStage);
new Rock(400,100, mainStage);
new Rock(200,100, mainStage);
new Rock(200,300, mainStage);
new Rock(200,500, mainStage);
new Rock(400,500, mainStage);
```

Before adding the code that governs how the spaceship, rocks, and lasers interact, you will add an explosion special effect, featuring an image-based animation, that will remove itself from the stage once the animation is finished. Create a new class named Explosion with the following code:

```
import com.badlogic.gdx.scenes.scene2d.Stage;

public class Explosion extends BaseActor
{
    public Explosion(float x, float y, Stage s)
    {
        super(x,y,s);

        loadAnimationFromSheet("assets/explosion.png", 6, 6, 0.03f, false);
    }

    public void act(float dt)
    {
        super.act(dt);

        if ( isAnimationFinished() )
            remove();
    }
}
```

Finally, you will handle the interaction between the rocks and the spaceship and lasers. In the update method of the LevelScreen class, add the following code:

```
for ( BaseActor rockActor : BaseActor.getList(mainStage, "Rock") )
    {
        if (rockActor.overlaps(spaceship))
        {
            if (spaceship.shieldPower <= 0)
            {
                Explosion boom = new Explosion(0,0, mainStage);
                boom.centerAtActor(spaceship);
                spaceship.remove();
                spaceship.setPosition(-1000,-1000);
            }
            else
            {
```

```
            spaceship.shieldPower -= 34;
            Explosion boom = new Explosion(0,0, mainStage);
            boom.centerAtActor(rockActor);
            rockActor.remove();
        }

    }

    for ( BaseActor laserActor : BaseActor.getList(mainStage, "Laser") )
    {
        if (laserActor.overlaps(rockActor))
        {
            Explosion boom = new Explosion(0,0, mainStage);
            boom.centerAtActor(rockActor);
            laserActor.remove();
            rockActor.remove();
        }
    }
}
```

Note that the shield power is reduced by 34 after each collision, which means that the shields can withstand three hits before the spaceship is in danger of being destroyed. Also note that even after the ship is removed from the stage, it still needs to be moved off-screen. Removing an object from its stage will stop its act and draw methods from being run, but the Spaceship object remains in the program memory, and collisions can still be detected at its final position when checked in the update method. (This issue could also be addressed by modifying the BaseActor method overlap to return false when either object's getStage method returns null, but that approach will not be used here.) Once again, you may wish to run the game and verify that everything works as expected; your game should now appear similar to Figure 4-1, shown at the beginning of this chapter.

Endgame Conditions

Determining when the game is over is relatively easy. If the spaceship collides with a rock when the shield power is less than or equal to zero, then the player loses the game. If there are no rocks remaining, then the player wins the game. In either scenario, a message should be displayed to communicate this information to the player and provide a sense of closure (otherwise, the player may be left wondering if there is something remaining to do). To this end, in the LevelScreen class, add the following field:

```
private boolean gameOver;
```

Set its value in the initialize method as follows:

```
gameOver = false;
```

When the player loses the game, an effect will be created to make the message fade in, so you need to add the following import statement:

```
import com.badlogic.gdx.scenes.scene2d.actions.Actions;
```

Next, to handle losing the game, add the following code in the update method, right after the code that removes the spaceship from the game:

```
BaseActor messageLose = new BaseActor(0,0, uiStage);
messageLose.loadTexture("assets/message-lose.png");
messageLose.centerAtPosition(400,300);
messageLose.setOpacity(0);
messageLose.addAction( Actions.fadeIn(1) );
gameOver = true;
```

Finally, to handle winning the game, add the following code at the end of the update method:

```
if ( !gameOver && BaseActor.count(mainStage, "Rock") == 0 )
{
    BaseActor messageWin = new BaseActor(0,0, uiStage);
    messageWin.loadTexture("assets/message-win.png");
    messageWin.centerAtPosition(400,300);
    messageWin.setOpacity(0);
    messageWin.addAction( Actions.fadeIn(1) );
    gameOver = true;
}
```

As usual, test your game to verify these changes work as expected. Attempt to win the game and then to lose the game to check that the corresponding messages appear on the screen.

Congratulations! You have finished implementing all the core mechanics of the *Space Rocks* game.

Summary and Next Steps

In this chapter, you extended the custom framework you have been creating to enable your game programs to respond to discrete inputs. Using this functionality, you created the space-themed shoot-em-up game *Space Rocks*, which featured a new style of movement, and discrete actions, such as shooting lasers and teleporting. Creating this second game also illustrates the flexibility of your game framework and provides excellent practice in using the features introduced in the previous chapter.

At this point, you may want to add a start menu screen that is displayed before the game begins, as you did in the previous chapter. You may also want to add or modify various features currently in the game. For example, after testing the gameplay, you will likely realize that the game is relatively easy: by spinning in place and shooting lasers as fast as you can, you will win relatively quickly. To address this issue, you could add more rocks, make the rocks smaller, make the rocks faster, or some combination of these features. Alternatively (or additionally), you may want to limit the rate at which the spaceship can fire lasers. The simplest way to implement this would be to add another condition in the Spaceship class shoot method that checks if the number of lasers on the stage exceeds a certain value, in which case it could return from the method immediately (before spawning a new laser object). In addition, you could take inspiration from the original *Asteroids* game, and when a rock collides with a laser have it spawn two smaller rocks; only if the rocks are "small enough" (if their width or height is less than some particular value) do they get destroyed forever without spawning additional rocks. In addition, to add to the challenge, you could add a new object: a UFO that spawns periodically off-screen and travels in a straight line to the opposite side, destroying the spaceship if it comes into contact with it. Finally, if all these additions make the game too challenging, you could add a "power-up" feature: a new object called PowerUp that has a random chance of spawning when a rock is destroyed, and if the player collects (collides with) it, the spaceship's shield power is restored to 100 percent.

In the next chapter, you will turn your attention to user-interface design and displaying text, a fundamental skill you will need to master for game development.

CHAPTER 5

Text and User Interfaces

In this chapter, you will learn how to display text, create buttons that display an image or text, and design a user interface using tables. First, you will be introduced to these skills by adding these features to the *Starfish Collector* game from Chapter 3, as shown in Figure 5-1. Then, you will build on and strengthen these skills while learning how to create cutscenes (sometimes called in-game cinematics) that provide a narrative element to your games; a cutscene for *Starfish Collector* is shown in Figure 5-2.

 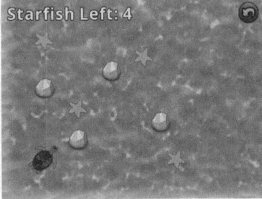

Figure 5-1. *The* Starfish Collector *game with an improved user interface*

© Lee Stemkoski 2018
L. Stemkoski, *Java Game Development with LibGDX*, https://doi.org/10.1007/978-1-4842-3324-5_5

Figure 5-2. *Cutscene for the* Starfish Collector *game*

In an optional final section, you will create a visual novel–style game, which focuses on a story and allows the player to make decisions about how the story proceeds; the game you will create is called *The Missing Homework* and is illustrated in Figure 5-3.

Figure 5-3. *Screenshot of the visual novel–style game* The Missing Homework

To begin, create a copy of your previous project from Chapter 3, the revised *Starfish Collector* game, and rename the copy of the project folder to Starfish Collector Ch 5 (to avoid confusion with the earlier version). Then, in the project folder, replace the files BaseGame.java, BaseScreen.java, and BaseActor.java with the versions you updated with new features and functionality in Chapter 4. To ensure the InputMultiplexer object introduced in Chapter 4 is initialized correctly, at the beginning of the StarfishGame class create method, add the following line of code:

```
super.create();
```

Next, download the source code files for this chapter on the website for this book, copy the files from the downloaded project's assets folder into your new project's assets folder, and do the same for the JAR files in the +libs folder (or the userlib folder, if you chose that option earlier). In both of these folders, the files used in previous projects have not been changed (so you can keep copies of the old files), but new files have been added that you will need. If BlueJ is currently running, close and restart so that the JAR files newly added to the +libs folder are properly recognized by BlueJ. At this point, you can compile and run the project to verify that everything is still working as before.

Displaying Text

In the LibGDX framework, text is displayed using Label objects. Labels are initialized with a String (containing the text to be displayed) and a LabelStyle object, which determines how the text will be rendered. Creating a LabelStyle object, in turn, requires a BitmapFont object. The sections that follow will show you how to create and use these objects.

To create a consistent design in your game, you will most likely want to create a single style that will be shared across multiple screens. For this reason, the best place to initialize these objects is in one of the Game-derived classes, rather than the Screen-derived classes. Since there is only one instance of a Game object for each project, you can simplify accessing this information by defining public static variables, and since this code will be useful for future projects, it will be added to the BaseGame class (rather than the StarfishGame class). To this end, in the BaseGame class, add the following import statements:

```
import com.badlogic.gdx.graphics.g2d.BitmapFont;
import com.badlogic.gdx.scenes.scene2d.ui.Label.LabelStyle;
```

In the class, add the following variable declaration:

```
public static LabelStyle labelStyle;
```

In the create method, add the following code to initialize the label style:

```
labelStyle = new LabelStyle();
labelStyle.font = new BitmapFont();
```

The default font created by the constructor is a size 15 Arial font, included in the LibGDX libraries. This will likely be too small for your applications, and thus the following sections will demonstrate how to create and incorporate custom fonts in your application.

Bitmap Fonts

The data for a computer-generated font is typically stored in one of two ways: either as a set of mathematical curves and formulas (these are called outline fonts or vector fonts and include standards such as TrueType font) or as a set of images. The latter is referred to as a bitmap font and is the format used by the LabelStyle class.

To create a BitmapFont object, you need two things: an image that contains all the characters you may want to represent in your application (Figure 5-4 contains an example) and an associated data file that lists the region (position and size) corresponding to each character. For example, the region in Figure 5-4 corresponding to the character A is located at x=319, y=134 and has width of 45 and a height of 41. When a bitmap font is used to display text, the image region corresponding to each character of the text is extracted, and these image regions are aligned side by side to produce the result seen onscreen.

Figure 5-4. *An image file (512 by 256 pixels) used to create a bitmap font*

There are two approaches that will be discussed for creating a bitmap font: using an external application to generate the necessary files prior to running your program, or using a special class to generate the required object at runtime. Each approach has its advantages and disadvantages. Using an external application lets you immediately see and adjust how the letters will appear when rendered, but running the application takes additional time and requires you to save additional files to your project's assets folder. The class-based approach makes it easier to change font parameters (only requiring changes to the code and avoiding having to save a new pair of files), but you will not see how the text appears until you run the program. Both approaches are fully explained in what follows. In the sample code for this chapter, the second of these approaches will ultimately be used, but in your own project, the final choice is up to you.

Using Hiero: A Bitmap Font Editor

An application named Hiero is provided by LibGDX and can be used to generate bitmap font data using fonts installed on your computer. The first version of Hiero was created by Kevin Glass for use with his Java game development library, Slick2D. Since then, Hiero has been ported to LibGDX by Nathan Sweet, one of the major contributors to the LibGDX libraries. Hiero is packaged as an executable JAR file; the current link to download it is posted on the LibGDX Wiki page,[1] as well as on the LibGDX Tools page,[2] which is accessible from the Downloads page of the main LibGDX website.

When you start Hiero, a variety of options are presented. Figure 5-5 contains a screenshot of the program in action. In the upper-left area, you may select a locally installed font; in the center region, you can enter the characters whose images you wish to generate (although leaving the default character set is recommended); in the upper-right area, you can select various effects to apply to the image (provided that *Rendering: Java* has been selected), including solid coloring, gradient coloring, outline, and drop shadow. Parameters for effects can be altered by clicking their values and entering or selecting a new value. The order in which the effects appear is important, as the effects are applied from top to bottom. When finished, select *Save BMFont files* from the File menu, and you'll have an FNT and PNG file ready to be used by the LibGDX BitmapFont class. The assets folder for this project contains the results of saving the bitmap font shown in

---

[1]Available at https://github.com/libgdx/libgdx/wiki/Hiero.
[2]Available at https://libgdx.badlogicgames.com/tools.html

this figure; the corresponding files are named cooper.fnt and cooper.png. To use this font in LibGDX, in the create method of the BaseGame class, you would change the line of code that sets the label-style object's font variable to the following:

```
labelStyle.font = new BitmapFont( Gdx.files.internal("myCustomFont.fnt") );
```

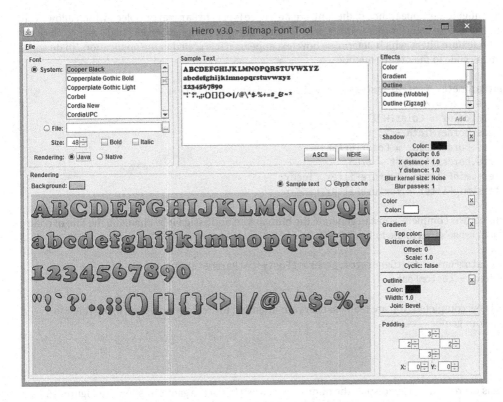

Figure 5-5. *The Hiero application for generating bitmap font data*

Using the FreeType Font Generator

Rather than create a bitmap font with an application, it is possible to use the FreeTypeFontGenerator class to create the bitmap font in code, eliminating the dependence on the external application. To create the font, you will need to include a TrueType Font file (extension TTF) in your assets folder as a basis for the bitmap font. TrueType fonts can easily be found online with an internet search.[3]

To begin, in the BaseGame class, add the following import statements:

```
import com.badlogic.gdx.graphics.Color;
import com.badlogic.gdx.graphics.Texture.TextureFilter;
import com.badlogic.gdx.graphics.g2d.freetype.FreeTypeFontGenerator;
import com.badlogic.gdx.graphics.g2d.freetype.FreeTypeFontGenerator.FreeTypeFontParameter;
```

---

[3]For example, three websites with freely available fonts include http://dafont.com, http://fontsquirrel.com, and http://1001freefonts.com.

Then, in the create method, initialize a FreeTypeFontGenerator object with a reference to the TTF file with the following code:

```
FreeTypeFontGenerator fontGenerator =
        new FreeTypeFontGenerator(Gdx.files.internal("assets/OpenSans.ttf"));
```

Next, to configure the appearance of the font, create a FreeTypeFontParameter object, which allows you to specify a font size, font color, border width, border color, straight or rounded border edges, and so forth. You can also set texture filters, which determine how text appears if it is scaled in the application. To do so, add the following code to the create method:

```
FreeTypeFontParameter fontParameters = new FreeTypeFontParameter();
fontParameters.size = 48;
fontParameters.color = Color.WHITE;
fontParameters.borderWidth = 2;
fontParameters.borderColor = Color.BLACK;
fontParameters.borderStraight = true;
fontParameters.minFilter = TextureFilter.Linear;
fontParameters.magFilter = TextureFilter.Linear;
```

Once this code is complete, you can generate the bitmap font and assign it by changing the line of code that sets the label style's font to the following:

```
BitmapFont customFont = fontGenerator.generateFont(fontParameters);
labelStyle.font = customFont;
```

With this task completed, you are ready to turn your attention to creating labels and using them to display text in your game.

Labels

The next goal is to create a label to display the number of starfish left in the game, as shown in Figure 5-6. With the BitmapFont and LabelStyle objects you created in the previous section, this is a straightforward process.

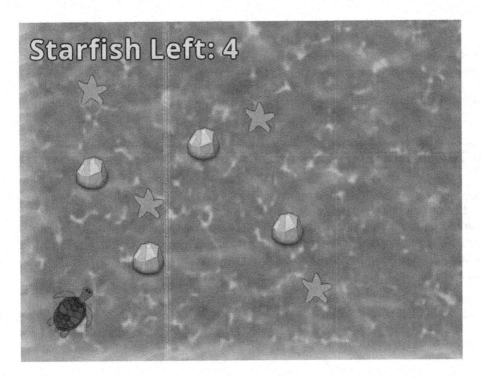

Figure 5-6. *Label displaying the number of starfish left to be collected*

First, in the LevelScreen class, add the following import statements:

```
import com.badlogic.gdx.graphics.Color;
import com.badlogic.gdx.scenes.scene2d.ui.Label;
```

Next, add the following variable declaration to the class:

```
private Label starfishLabel;
```

To initialize the label, add the following code to the initialize method, which will tint the label text a light blue color (in keeping with the aquatic theme),and position it near the upper-left corner of the user interface:

```
starfishLabel = new Label("Starfish Left:", BaseGame.labelStyle);
starfishLabel.setColor( Color.CYAN );
starfishLabel.setPosition( 20, 520 );
uiStage.addActor(starfishLabel);
```

Finally, in the update method, add the following code, which will set the label text to display the actual number of starfish left:

```
starfishLabel.setText("Starfish Left: " + BaseActor.count(mainStage, "Starfish"));
```

That's all there is to it! If you want to change the size of the text, you can either change the font size when configuring the FreeTypeFontParameter object in the BaseGame class or use the Label class method setFontScale, which applies a scaling factor to the text.

Buttons

A button is one of the most basic user-interface controls that gets input from a user. In this section, you will create two different types of buttons: one that only consists of an image to convey its functionality, and one that contains text that explains what it does. The most complex step in adding buttons to a project is specifying the code that will run when the button is clicked, which will be discussed before creating the buttons themselves.

FUNCTIONAL INTERFACES AND LAMBDA EXPRESSIONS

There are many situations in which it would be convenient to store a method in a variable. One common situation is to store the code that should activate when a button is clicked within the button object itself. However, in the Java programming language, methods cannot be stored in variables. As a substitute for this sort of functionality, developers will often create a *functional interface*: an interface that consists of a single method. When one needs to store a method, one implements the interface and specifies the function as required.

For example, consider a hypothetical Button class that requires the functionality just described. In this case, one could create the following interface:

```
public interface Function
{
    public void run();
}
```

Then, the Button class could be designed as follows:

```
public class Button
{
    private Function clickFunction;

    public void setFunction(Function f)
    {
        clickFunction = f;
    }

    public void click()
    {
        clickFunction.run();
    }
}
```

In theory, setting up the function could require quite a bit of code. One could create an entirely new class that implements the interface, then create an instance of the class and pass it as an argument to the Button class setFunction method. For example, to configure a button to exit a program, you would create the following class:

```
public class QuitFunction implements Function
{
    public void run()
    {
        System.exit(0);
    }
}
```

Then, in your application, you would write:

```
Button myButton = new Button();
myButton.setFunction( new QuitFunction() );
```

Incidentally, the instance of the QuitFunction class that is created is called an *anonymous instance*, since it is not assigned to a variable (which is fine, since it is stored by the Button class and would not be needed in the application code that follows).

An alternative to creating a separate class is to write the code for the QuitFunction class within the application class, since that is the only place it needs to be used. When arranging the code in this way, QuitFunction would be referred to as an *inner class* (basically, a class defined within another class). To take this idea one step further, since you only need to create a single instance of the class, you can combine these ideas and create an *anonymous inner class* by writing the class definition as the argument passed to the method, as follows:

```
myButton.setFunction(
    new Function()
    {
        public void run()
        {
            System.exit(0);
        }
    });
```

However, this is still a significant amount of code to write in order to effectively pass a method. For this reason, Java 8 introduced a new language feature called *lambda expressions*, which is condensed syntax for creating anonymous inner classes for functional interfaces. The arguments for the method are placed within a set of parentheses, which are then followed by a dash and greater-than symbol (->, which is meant to resemble an arrow), followed by a set of braces containing the code to be executed. For example, given the following interface:

```
public interface MathFunction
{
    public double calculate(double x);
}
```

Consider the lambda expression:

```
(double x) -> { return x*x; }
```

The lambda expression is equivalent to the following anonymous inner class:

```
new MathFunction
{
    public double calculate(double x)
    {
        return x*x;
    }
}
```

Note that, in particular, the lambda expression does not require you to specify the name of the interface or the function it contains (both of these are inferred from the context).

Returning to the previous button-based example, the quit functionality can be added to the button object with the following concise lambda expression:

```
myButton.setFunction(
    () -> { System.exit(0); }
);
```

Note that the parentheses are empty, as this method requires no parameters.

As you can see, using lambda expressions when possible will save a great deal of time when writing code.

Clicking a button is an example of a discrete event, and because of the functionality you added to the framework in the previous chapter, your program is prepared to respond to click events. Since the Stage class implements the InputProcessor interface, it will process mouse events (such as clicks). If the stage contains an actor at the position where the event occurs, and if the actor contains an EventListener object, the method contained in EventListener will be run. Since EventListener is a functional interface, you can (and will) use lambda expressions to specify the functionality in what follows.

With this preliminary material covered, you are now ready to create a button and add functionality to it.

Image-Based Buttons

First, you will create an image-based button that can be used to restart the level, as shown in Figure 5-7.

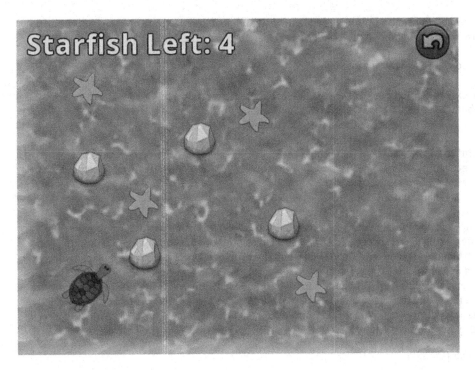

Figure 5-7. Starfish Collector *with a level restart button added in the upper-right corner*

Analogous to how a label requires a LabelStyle object that specifies a bitmap font, a button requires a ButtonStyle object that specifies a particular type of image. To begin, in the LevelScreen class, add the following import statements:

```
import com.badlogic.gdx.scenes.scene2d.ui.Button;
import com.badlogic.gdx.scenes.scene2d.ui.Button.ButtonStyle;
import com.badlogic.gdx.Gdx;
import com.badlogic.gdx.graphics.Texture;
import com.badlogic.gdx.graphics.g2d.TextureRegion;
import com.badlogic.gdx.scenes.scene2d.utils.TextureRegionDrawable;
import com.badlogic.gdx.scenes.scene2d.Event;
import com.badlogic.gdx.scenes.scene2d.InputEvent;
import com.badlogic.gdx.scenes.scene2d.InputEvent.Type;
```

Next, you need to create a ButtonStyle object, which has a field named up that is used to store the default image for the button. (Additional images may be stored that correspond to when the mouse hovers over the button or when the button is pressed; for more details, consult the LibGDX documentation.) LibGDX requires that images used in user-interface elements implement the Drawable interface; standard image-related classes (such as TextureRegion) have corresponding classes that also implement this interface. The following code creates the ButtonStyle object, creates and adds a TextureRegionDrawable image to it, and uses this to create a button, tinted light blue, and positioned in the upper-right corner. Add this code to the initialize method of the LevelScreen class:

```
ButtonStyle buttonStyle = new ButtonStyle();

Texture buttonTex = new Texture( Gdx.files.internal("assets/undo.png") );
TextureRegion buttonRegion =  new TextureRegion(buttonTex);
buttonStyle.up = new TextureRegionDrawable( buttonRegion );

Button restartButton = new Button( buttonStyle );
restartButton.setColor( Color.CYAN );
restartButton.setPosition(720,520);
uiStage.addActor(restartButton);
```

Finally, you need to add functionality to this button. You will do this using a lambda expression, as described at the beginning of this section. The first part of this code contains an important condition: you need to make sure that the event was an InputEvent, and then you need to cast the Event object to an InputEvent object and check the Type of the event to make sure it was a mouse-button click (rather than, say, a mouse-movement event). LibGDX handles mouse and touchscreen events in the same way, and so a mouse-click event is referred to as a touchdown event. If either of the conditions are not true, the method immediately exits and returns false. With this in mind, add the following code to the create method directly following the code you previously entered:

```
restartButton.addListener(
    (Event e) ->
    {
        if ( !(e instanceof InputEvent) ||
            !((InputEvent)e).getType().equals(Type.touchDown) )
            return false;

        StarfishGame.setActiveScreen( new LevelScreen() );
        return false;
    }
);
```

At this point, you should test your project to verify that the button works as expected.

Text-Based Buttons

Next, you'll add some text-based buttons to the menu screen, giving the user the ability to start or quit the game, as shown in Figure 5-8.

Figure 5-8. Starfish Collector *menu screen with buttons added*

Just as was the case with creating labels and image-based buttons, the first step in creating a text-based button is to create an associated style object that stores visual details. In this case, you need to create a TextButtonStyle object, where you will specify the bitmap font, font color, and background image.

The background image for the image-based button was a TextureRegionDrawable object. However, in a text-based button, one potential complication arises when the button's text is larger than the provided image, in which case the text will overflow past the borders of the button. To avoid this issue, you can use a special type of image called a *nine-patch* image, which is an image with nine defined sub-regions. When scaling a nine-patch image, the image is stretched along the border regions in the direction of its edges. A NinePatch object can be initialized using a Texture followed by four integers, as follows:

```
NinePatch np = new NinePatch( texture, left, right, top, bottom );
```

The integers represent distances, measured in pixels, from the correspondingly named edge of the image. They are used to divide the texture into nine regions, as illustrated in Figure 5-9.

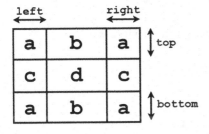

Figure 5-9. *Dividing a texture into nine regions*

When converted to a NinePatch object, the corners of the image (the regions labeled with a in Figure 5-9) will never be scaled; the b regions can scale horizontally, the c regions can scale vertically, and the central region d can scale in both directions. This is particularly useful for button-like images, so that the edges of the image do not appear distorted. Figure 5-10 illustrates a small image that is scaled using standard methods, and also scaled using nine-patch methods. Notice in particular that when using standard scaling, the border of the enlarged image appears thicker, while nine-patch scaling more closely preserves the appearance of the original border, as it only scales the border regions along the direction of the edges.

Figure 5-10. *A button-like image, scaled using standard methods and using nine-patch methods*

With this information in mind, you are ready to create a TextButtonStyle object. In the BaseGame class, add the following import statements:

```
import com.badlogic.gdx.scenes.scene2d.ui.TextButton.TextButtonStyle;
import com.badlogic.gdx.graphics.g2d.NinePatch;
import com.badlogic.gdx.scenes.scene2d.utils.NinePatchDrawable;
import com.badlogic.gdx.graphics.Texture;
```

Next, add the following variable declaration to the class:

```
public static TextButtonStyle textButtonStyle;
```

In the create method, add the following code to initialize and configure the TextButtonStyle object. Note that fontColor is set at this point, because calling the setColor method on the button itself only affects tint color used for the image, not the text.

```
textButtonStyle = new TextButtonStyle();
Texture    buttonTex   = new Texture( Gdx.files.internal("assets/button.png") );
NinePatch buttonPatch = new NinePatch(buttonTex, 24,24,24,24);
textButtonStyle.up       = new NinePatchDrawable( buttonPatch );
textButtonStyle.font        = customFont;
textButtonStyle.fontColor = Color.GRAY;
```

With the text button style set up, you are prepared to add text buttons to the menu screen. In the MenuScreen class, begin by adding the following import statements:

```
import com.badlogic.gdx.scenes.scene2d.ui.TextButton;
import com.badlogic.gdx.scenes.scene2d.Event;
import com.badlogic.gdx.scenes.scene2d.InputEvent;
import com.badlogic.gdx.scenes.scene2d.InputEvent.Type;
```

Next, remove the code in the initialize method that displays the image file named message-start.png (it is a message that reads "Press 'S' to start"). Then, still in the initialize method, add the following code to display two buttons, labeled "Start" and "Quit," as shown in Figure 5-8. Note that the TextButton objects are initialized using the text they will display and the style object from the BaseGame class, while the functionality is added using a lambda expression, similar to that of the image-based button that you added previously.

```
TextButton startButton = new TextButton( "Start", BaseGame.textButtonStyle );
startButton.setPosition(150,150);
uiStage.addActor(startButton);

startButton.addListener(
    (Event e) ->
    {
        if ( !(e instanceof InputEvent) ||
            !((InputEvent)e).getType().equals(Type.touchDown) )
            return false;

        StarfishGame.setActiveScreen( new LevelScreen() );
        return false;
    }
);

TextButton quitButton = new TextButton( "Quit", BaseGame.textButtonStyle );
quitButton.setPosition(500,150);
uiStage.addActor(quitButton);

quitButton.addListener(
    (Event e) ->
    {
        if ( !(e instanceof InputEvent) ||
            !((InputEvent)e).getType().equals(Type.touchDown) )
            return false;

        Gdx.app.exit();
        return false;
    }
);
```

Finally, in the interest of accessibility, you will create a keyDown method to enable the keyboard to perform the same functions as the buttons: pressing the Enter key will start the game, while pressing the Escape key will quit the game. (Although these keyboard controls are not listed on the menu screen, they are common enough that many players appreciate the addition of these keyboard-based controls.) Still in the MenuScreen class, add the following method:

```
public boolean keyDown(int keyCode)
{
    if (Gdx.input.isKeyPressed(Keys.ENTER))
        StarfishGame.setActiveScreen( new LevelScreen() );
    if (Gdx.input.isKeyPressed(Keys.ESCAPE))
        Gdx.app.exit();
    return false;
}
```

At this point, the text buttons are complete and functional; now is a good time to test your project and verify that everything works as expected.

Organizing Layouts with Tables

Determining the exact screen coordinates of where user-interface items such as labels and buttons should be displayed, taking into account the size of the items being placed to align them with each other, can be tedious. Fortunately, the LibGDX libraries provide a class named Table that greatly simplifies this process by automatically positioning and aligning these elements.

Table is a subclass of Actor, so it can be added to Stage objects; furthermore, Table is also a subclass of Group, so objects can be added to a Table as well. In particular, a Table consists of Cell objects, laid out in rows and columns, with each Cell containing an Actor. The add method creates a new Cell (containing an Actor, if one is specified) and adds it to the end of the current row. All tables contain a single row by default; to create a new row in the Table, positioned beneath the current row, we call the row method. For illustration purposes only (this will not be added to your code), to create a Table containing a two-by-two grid with Actor objects a, b, c, and d, as illustrated in Figure 5-11, you would write the following code:

```
Table t = new Table();
t.add(a);
t.add(b);
t.row();
t.add(c);
t.add(d);
```

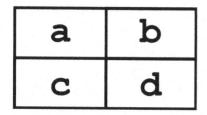

Figure 5-11. *A simple table with elements arranged as a two-by-two grid*

It is important to remember that, in general, individual table cells have the smallest size possible, while still being able to fit their contents. However, the width and height of the cells in each row and column will be enlarged to accommodate the largest element in that row or column. Furthermore, the add method returns the Cell object that is created, and which can be resized or formatted by calling any combination of the following methods on the result:

- width and height to set the size of the Cell (which in turn will affect the size of any UI components within the Cell)

- expandX and expandY to force a Cell to increase its size to fill the remaining table size in the horizontal or vertical direction, respectively

- padLeft, padRight, padBottom, padTop to add an amount of padding (in pixels) to the contents of the current Cell, or the pad method to apply padding in all directions

The contents of a table cell that has been enlarged beyond its default size will be center-aligned (both horizontally and vertically) within the cell by default, in which case you can use the Cell class methods left, right, bottom, and top to align the Actor within its cell. In addition, you can declare that a single cell span multiple columns using the Cell class method colspan, which takes as its argument the number of columns that the cell should fill.

With these methods at your disposal, arranging elements in a user interface becomes significantly easier and does not require calculating coordinates by hand. To begin, you will include some code in your custom framework that adds a table to each screen on the stage that you have been using for user-interface elements. In the BaseScreen class, add the import statement:

```
import com.badlogic.gdx.scenes.scene2d.ui.Table;
```

In the class, add the variable declaration:

```
protected Table uiTable;
```

In the BaseScreen constructor method, add the following code to initialize the table:

```
uiTable = new Table();
uiTable.setFillParent(true);
uiStage.addActor(uiTable);
```

Now, you will rewrite some code in the game-specific screen classes to utilize this newly added table. For example, consider the layout of the elements on the menu screen, represented abstractly on the right side of Figure 5-12, where the letter a represents the title graphic and the letters b and c represent the Start and Quit buttons, respectively.

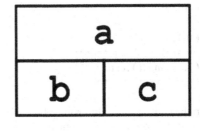

Figure 5-12. *Abstract layout for the menu-screen elements*

In the MenuScreen class, delete the code that is used to position the BaseActor variable named title, and also delete the code that is used to set the position of the text buttons and to add them to uiStage. Then, at the end of the initialize method, add the following code to implement the layout illustrated in Figure 5-12:

```
uiTable.add(title).colspan(2);
uiTable.row();
uiTable.add(startButton);
uiTable.add(quitButton);
```

If you run the program, you will see that the title graphic and buttons are arranged as expected. As a further example of the flexibility of this code, you will next use the table to simplify the user layout in the main game screen, represented abstractly on the right side of Figure 5-13, where the letter a represents the label and the letter b represents the Restart button. In order for these elements to appear along the left and right edges of the window, respectively, an empty cell will be added between them, and the expandX method will be used on it to "fill up" the row with the remaining window width. Similarly, to align the objects along the top edge of the window, the expandY method will be used on the empty cell so that the height of the table "fills up" the full height of the window. However, by default, objects are aligned in the center of their cells, and so the top method must be called on their cells in order to move the contents to the top. In addition, a small margin will be added using the pad method.

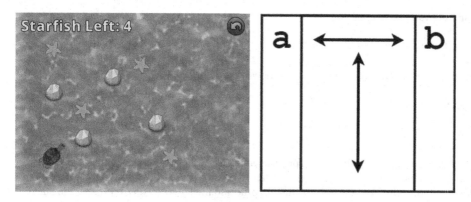

Figure 5-13. *Abstract layout for the level-screen elements*

In the LevelScreen class, remove the code that sets the positions of the label and the button, and also remove the code that adds these elements to uiStage. Then, add the following code at the end of the initialize method:

```
uiTable.pad(10);
uiTable.add(starfishLabel).top();
uiTable.add().expandX().expandY();
uiTable.add(restartButton).top();
```

If you run the code at this point, you will see that the user-interface elements are arranged as expected. Although you could theoretically continue to calculate screen coordinates for all these elements by hand, hopefully these examples have demonstrated that tables are an effective and efficient way to organize elements in your game project.

At this point in the chapter, you have learned the fundamentals of user interfaces: labels, buttons, and tables. The rest of the chapter includes advanced text-based mechanics (dialog boxes, signs, and cutscenes), which are interesting in their own right but are not necessary for the chapters that follow. Therefore, you can skip the rest of this chapter and proceed to the next, if you wish; otherwise, carry on!

Signs and Dialog Boxes

Many games feature signs that the player's character can read or non-player characters (NPCs) with whom the player can have a conversation. These types of game elements can serve a variety of purposes, such as

- an in-game tutorial or instructions;

- directions to locations in a large game environment (for example, a sign that reads "South - Item Shop"); or

- hints or guidance (for example, an NPC that says "I've heard rumors that there is a treasure hidden in the western part of the forest").

In this section, you will learn how to create dialog boxes to temporarily display the text corresponding to such an interaction, as shown in Figure 5-14.

Figure 5-14. *Turtle reading a sign in the* Starfish Collector *game*

In particular, you will eventually create a class called DialogBox that stores a background image and a label and has a set of methods that can be used to easily configure its appearance. You will position the dialog box on the screen using the Table class functionality you recently added to the BaseScreen class. The dialog box can be set to visible when text needs to be displayed and invisible when the player is finished reading. Signs will be added to the *Starfish Collector* game, which the turtle will be able to read. To keep the game controls as simple and as intuitive as possible, the sign-reading mechanic will be activated (and the dialog box will become visible and display the corresponding text) whenever the turtle is close to a sign. (Other games may require the player to press a particular key or button to read a sign.) To this end, a new method will be added to the BaseActor class that can be used to check whether two objects are "close."

To begin, in your BlueJ project, create a new class called DialogBox that contains the following code:

```
import com.badlogic.gdx.scenes.scene2d.Stage;
import com.badlogic.gdx.scenes.scene2d.ui.Label;
import com.badlogic.gdx.graphics.Color;
import com.badlogic.gdx.utils.Align;

public class DialogBox extends BaseActor
{
    private Label dialogLabel;
    private float padding = 16;

    public DialogBox(float x, float y, Stage s)
    {
        super(x,y,s);
        loadTexture("assets/dialog-translucent.png");
```

```
        dialogLabel = new Label(" ", BaseGame.labelStyle);
        dialogLabel.setWrap(true);
        dialogLabel.setAlignment( Align.topLeft );
        dialogLabel.setPosition( padding, padding );
        this.setDialogSize( getWidth(), getHeight() );
        this.addActor(dialogLabel);
    }

    public void setDialogSize(float width, float height)
    {
        this.setSize(width, height);
        dialogLabel.setWidth( width - 2 * padding );
        dialogLabel.setHeight( height - 2 * padding );
    }

    public void setText(String text)
    { dialogLabel.setText(text);  }

    public void setFontScale(float scale)
    { dialogLabel.setFontScale(scale);  }

    public void setFontColor(Color color)
    { dialogLabel.setColor(color);  }

    public void setBackgroundColor(Color color)
    { this.setColor(color);  }

    public void alignTopLeft()
    { dialogLabel.setAlignment( Align.topLeft );  }

    public void alignCenter()
    { dialogLabel.setAlignment( Align.center );  }
}
```

As expected, this class contains a label to display the text, with word wrap activated to enable the label to display multi-line text. Of particular interest is the setDialogSize method, which is needed to keep the size of the label and the background image in sync, while adding a small margin, whose size is specified by the padding variable. The remaining methods should be self-explanatory; they enable you to easily change the text displayed, change the color of the background image or the text, and scale and align the text (conversations containing English sentences are typically aligned to the top-left, while signs that display only the name of a place are typically aligned to the center).

Next, you will create the in-game signs. As usual, these objects will extend the BaseActor class, and, as you may expect, they will store text to be displayed by a DialogBox object. In addition, they will contain a Boolean variable that keeps track of whether the text of this sign is currently being viewed. (Later on, you will see that this information is very convenient when toggling the visibility of the dialog box.) To this end, create a new class named Sign that contains the following code:

```java
import com.badlogic.gdx.scenes.scene2d.Stage;

public class Sign extends BaseActor
{
    // the text to be displayed
    private String text;
    // used to determine if sign text is currently being displayed
    private boolean viewing;

    public Sign(float x, float y, Stage s)
    {
        super(x,y,s);
        loadTexture("assets/sign.png");
        text = " ";
        viewing = false;
    }

    public void setText(String t)
    {   text = t;   }

    public String getText()
    {   return text;   }

    public void setViewing(boolean v)
    {   viewing = v;   }

    public boolean isViewing()
    {   return viewing;   }
}
```

Next, you need a way to determine if two actors are "close." The way you will implement this is to temporarily enlarge the bounding polygon of one of the actors and then check for overlap. You can most easily enlarge the polygon by setting its scale (in both the x and y directions)[4]; the calculations that follow assume that the actor has not already been scaled in either direction. For example, if an actor has a width and height of 50 pixels, and you want to determine if another actor comes within 10 pixels, then you need to increase each of the dimensions by 20 pixels (10 pixels on each side), which amounts to a scaling factor of $(50 + 20)/50 = 1.4$. This calculation is accomplished by the following method, which you should add to the BaseActor class:

```java
public boolean isWithinDistance(float distance, BaseActor other)
{
    Polygon poly1 = this.getBoundaryPolygon();
    float scaleX = (this.getWidth() + 2 * distance) / this.getWidth();
    float scaleY = (this.getHeight() + 2 * distance) / this.getHeight();
    poly1.setScale(scaleX, scaleY);

    Polygon poly2 = other.getBoundaryPolygon();
```

---

[4]This calculation will not detect an exact distance from the original-boundary polygon in every direction (for example, at the corners of a rectangular polygon), but it will be close enough for all practical purposes.

119

```
// initial test to improve performance
if ( !poly1.getBoundingRectangle().overlaps(poly2.getBoundingRectangle()) )
    return false;

return Intersector.overlapConvexPolygons( poly1, poly2 );
}
```

Finally, you are ready to add signs and a dialog box to your game and implement the sign-reading mechanic. In the LevelScreen class, begin by adding the following variable declaration:

```
private DialogBox dialogBox;
```

Next, in the initialize method, add the following code to initialize and configure two signs, as well as the dialog box that will display the corresponding text (which is positioned in the user interface via the uiTable).

```
Sign sign1 = new Sign(20,400, mainStage);
sign1.setText("West Starfish Bay");

Sign sign2 = new Sign(600,300, mainStage);
sign2.setText("East Starfish Bay");

dialogBox = new DialogBox(0,0, uiStage);
dialogBox.setBackgroundColor( Color.TAN );
dialogBox.setFontColor( Color.BROWN );
dialogBox.setDialogSize(600, 100);
dialogBox.setFontScale(0.80f);
dialogBox.alignCenter();
dialogBox.setVisible(false);

uiTable.row();
uiTable.add(dialogBox).colspan(3);
```

Finally, in the update method, for each of the signs, you need to make sure the turtle does not overlap the signs (as they are solid objects in the game) as well as determine if the turtle is sufficiently near a sign (in this case, you'll assume that four pixels is sufficiently close). If the turtle is near a sign and the sign is not currently being viewed, then you will set the text of the dialog box according to the text stored in the sign, make the dialog box visible, and mark the sign as currently being viewed. You also need a way to make the dialog box invisible once the turtle has moved away from the sign currently being viewed. Therefore, there is a second condition in this loop, which checks if a sign is being viewed and the turtle is not nearby, in which case the dialog box becomes invisible and the sign is marked as no longer viewed. To implement this, add the following code to the update method:

```
for ( BaseActor signActor : BaseActor.getList(mainStage, "Sign") )
{
    Sign sign = (Sign)signActor;

    turtle.preventOverlap(sign);
    boolean nearby = turtle.isWithinDistance(4, sign);
```

```
if ( nearby && !sign.isViewing() )
{
    dialogBox.setText( sign.getText() );
    dialogBox.setVisible( true );
    sign.setViewing( true );
}

if (sign.isViewing() && !nearby)
{
    dialogBox.setText( " " );
    dialogBox.setVisible( false );
    sign.setViewing( false );
}
}
```

At this point, you have finished implementing the sign-reading mechanic; you should test your game to make sure everything works as expected. The same approach demonstrated here can be used to implement NPCs as well, just by replacing the sign graphic with the image of the character with whom you'd like to be able to speak.

Creating Cutscenes

In-game cinematics, also known as cutscenes, can be used to give your game a background story, character and plot development, and a resolution after the player achieves their goal. Analogous to a scene in a theatrical play that consists of actors performing actions and reciting dialogue, a cutscene will consist of Actor objects that have attached Action objects (displaying text in a DialogBox object being a special case of this). In this section, you will create the framework for displaying a cutscene and use it to create a scene for the *Starfish Collector* game, which will consist of the following parts:

- A background image of the seashore fades in.
- A turtle moves from off-stage (from beyond the left edge) to the center of the stage.
- A dialog box becomes visible.
- The dialog box displays the text "I want to be the very best . . . Starfish Collector!"
- The dialog box displays the text "I've got to collect them all!"
- The dialog box becomes invisible.
- The turtle moves to the right, beyond the right edge of the screen.
- The background image fades to black.

A sample image from this cutscene is shown in Figure 5-15.

Figure 5-15. *Cutscene for the* Starfish Collector *game*

Each one of these parts can be expressed with an Actor and an Action, and this information will be encapsulated in a class that you will soon create called SceneSegment. Another class that you will create, called Scene, will manage a collection of these objects (using an ArrayList). By having the Scene class extend the Actor class, you can write an act method that automatically advances through the scene segments as the corresponding actions are completed. (This will in turn require a method to determine when an Actor has completed its attached actions.)

To begin, create a new class called SceneSegment, containing the following code. This class will contain a method named start, which attaches the action to the actor. The isFinished method checks whether an actor has finished its actions by checking if there are zero actions attached to the actor; this works because actions are automatically removed from an actor once they have finished. Finally, the finish method calls the action's act method with a large value to complete any in-progress actions and then clears all actions from the actor in case any infinitely repeating actions were attached to the actor.

```
import com.badlogic.gdx.scenes.scene2d.Actor;
import com.badlogic.gdx.scenes.scene2d.Action;

public class SceneSegment
{
    private Actor actor;
    private Action action;

    public SceneSegment(Actor a1, Action a2)
    {
        actor = a1;
        action = a2;
    }
```

```
public void start()
{
    actor.clearActions();
    actor.addAction(action);
}

public boolean isFinished()
{
    return (actor.getActions().size == 0);
}

public void finish()
{
    // simulate 100000 seconds elapsed time to complete in-progress action
    if ( actor.hasActions() )
        actor.getActions().first().act(100000);

    // remove any remaining actions
    actor.clearActions();
}
}
```

Although DialogBox is an extension of BaseActor, displaying text doesn't fit into this framework until you create a custom Action that sets the text of a DialogBox. To do so, you will need to extend the Action class and override the act method, which is responsible for performing the corresponding action. The Action class contains a variable named target, which is a reference to the Actor to which the action has been added, which is important to know for writing the act method. The act method returns a Boolean that indicates whether or not the action has been completed. With this information, writing the custom Action class is relatively straightforward: it needs to store the text that will be displayed, and the act method needs to cast the Actor to a DialogBox so that it can use its setText method, at which point the action is complete, and so the act method should immediately return true. To implement this, create a class called SetTextAction that contains the following code:

```
import com.badlogic.gdx.scenes.scene2d.Stage;
import com.badlogic.gdx.scenes.scene2d.Action;

public class SetTextAction extends Action
{
    protected String textToDisplay;

    public SetTextAction(String t)
    {
        textToDisplay = t;
    }

    public boolean act(float dt)
    {
        DialogBox db = (DialogBox)target;
        db.setText( textToDisplay );
        return true;
    }
}
```

Next, you need a way to pause the scene after displaying text so as to give the player a chance to read the text. You also need an option to continue the scene when they are ready (indicated by pressing a key). This can be implemented by creating a DelayAction, set to repeat forever, and using it as part of a scene segment. Pressing a key will call the finish method of the segment, causing the scene to continue. To simplify creating this action (and others) when needed, you will next create a class analogous to the LibGDX Actions class, both of which contain static methods that create instances of various Action objects. To this end, create a new class called SceneActions with the following code:

```
import com.badlogic.gdx.scenes.scene2d.Stage;
import com.badlogic.gdx.scenes.scene2d.Action;
import com.badlogic.gdx.scenes.scene2d.actions.Actions;
import com.badlogic.gdx.graphics.g2d.Animation;

public class SceneActions extends Actions
{
    public static Action setText(String s)
    {
        return new SetTextAction(s);
    }

    public static Action pause()
    {
        return Actions.forever( Actions.delay(1) );
    }

}
```

While you're at it, it would be convenient to have the ability to move an actor to a particular area on the screen (left, center, right) or outside of the screen (to the left or right), as illustrated by Figure 5-16.

Figure 5-16. *Turtle positioned at positions (from left to right) outside-left, screen-left, screen-center, screen-right, and outside-right*

This can be accomplished in part with the MoveToAction and Align classes, but it also requires access to the size of the screen (or equivalently in this case, the size of the game world), which is stored in the worldBounds variable in the BaseActor class. To gain access to this information, add the following method to the BaseActor class:

```
public static Rectangle getWorldBounds()
{
    return worldBounds;
}
```

Next, returning to the SceneActions class, add this import statement:

```
import com.badlogic.gdx.utils.Align;
```

Then, add the following five static methods, whose functions are fully described by their method names:

```
public static Action moveToScreenLeft(float duration)
{
    return Actions.moveToAligned( 0, 0, Align.bottomLeft, duration );
}

public static Action moveToScreenRight(float duration)
{
    return Actions.moveToAligned( BaseActor.getWorldBounds().width, 0,
        Align.bottomRight, duration );
}

public static Action moveToScreenCenter(float duration)
{
    return Actions.moveToAligned( BaseActor.getWorldBounds().width / 2, 0,
        Align.bottom, duration);
}

public static Action moveToOutsideLeft(float duration)
{
    return Actions.moveToAligned( 0, 0, Align.bottomRight, duration );
}

public static Action moveToOutsideRight(float duration)
{
    return Actions.moveToAligned( BaseActor.getWorldBounds().width, 0,
        Align.bottomLeft, duration );
}
```

Now, you will design and implement the Scene class, which will manage a collection of SceneSegment objects. The class will use an ArrayList for this purpose, and will also store the index of the segment currently in process. Standard functionality that needs to be implemented includes adding segments and clearing the list of segments. A start method will set the index to 0 and call the start method of the first segment. In the Scene class act method, if the current segment is finished and it is not the last segment in the list, then the next segment should be loaded; these aspects will be implemented by the methods isSegmentFinished, isLastSegment, and loadNextSegment, respectively. Finally, for convenience, you will include a method that checks if a scene is finished, which can be useful for determining when to move on to the next part of the game. To implement all of this functionality, create a new class named Scene with the following code:

```
import com.badlogic.gdx.scenes.scene2d.Actor;
import java.util.ArrayList;

public class Scene extends Actor
{
    private ArrayList<SceneSegment> segmentList;
    private int index;
```

```java
    public Scene()
    {
        super();
        segmentList = new ArrayList<SceneSegment>();
        index = -1;
    }

    public void addSegment(SceneSegment segment)
    {
        segmentList.add(segment);
    }

    public void clearSegments()
    {
        segmentList.clear();
    }

    public void start()
    {
        index = 0;
        segmentList.get(index).start();
    }

    public void act(float dt)
    {
        if ( isSegmentFinished() && !isLastSegment() )
            loadNextSegment();
    }

    public boolean isSegmentFinished()
    {
        return segmentList.get(index).isFinished();
    }

    public boolean isLastSegment()
    {
        return (index >= segmentList.size() - 1);
    }

    public void loadNextSegment()
    {
        if ( isLastSegment() )
            return;

        segmentList.get(index).finish();
        index++;
        segmentList.get(index).start();
    }
```

```
    public boolean isSceneFinished()
    {
        return ( isLastSegment() && isSegmentFinished() );
    }
}
```

Now you are ready to create a cutscene for the *Starfish Collector* game. To begin, create a new class named StoryScreen with the following code:

```
import com.badlogic.gdx.Gdx;
import com.badlogic.gdx.Input.Keys;
import com.badlogic.gdx.scenes.scene2d.Action;
import com.badlogic.gdx.scenes.scene2d.actions.Actions;
import com.badlogic.gdx.graphics.Color;

public class StoryScreen extends BaseScreen
{
    Scene scene;
    BaseActor continueKey;

    public void initialize()
    {   }

    public void update(float dt)
    {   }

    public boolean keyDown(int keyCode)
    {    return false;   }
}
```

The continue key image will be a keyboard key (in this case, the letter "C") that appears after text is displayed as a visual cue to the player indicating that they should press that key to continue. This is what will enable the player to proceed to the next scene segment when a pause action is currently in progress. To this end, add the following code to the keyDown method (before the return statement):

```
if ( keyCode == Keys.C && continueKey.isVisible() )
    scene.loadNextSegment();
```

Next, in the initialize method, you will set up the actors that will be part of the scene. To do so, add the following code:

```
BaseActor background = new BaseActor(0,0, mainStage);
background.loadTexture( "assets/oceanside.png" );
background.setSize(800,600);
background.setOpacity(0);
BaseActor.setWorldBounds(background);

BaseActor turtle = new BaseActor(0,0, mainStage);
turtle.loadTexture( "assets/turtle-big.png" );
turtle.setPosition( -turtle.getWidth(), 0 );
```

127

```
DialogBox dialogBox = new DialogBox(0,0, uiStage);
dialogBox.setDialogSize(600, 200);
dialogBox.setBackgroundColor( new Color(0.6f, 0.6f, 0.8f, 1) );
dialogBox.setFontScale(0.75f);
dialogBox.setVisible(false);

uiTable.add(dialogBox).expandX().expandY().bottom();

continueKey = new BaseActor(0,0,uIStage);
continueKey.loadTexture("assets/key-C.png");
continueKey.setSize(32,32);
continueKey.setVisible(false);

dialogBox.addActor(continueKey);
continueKey.setPosition( dialogBox.getWidth() - continueKey.getWidth(), 0 );
```

Now, you are ready to create the sequence of scene segments that will be added to the scene. As previously described, after displaying text, the continue key image should be made visible, and a pause action should be added (the object to which this action is added is not important). After adding all segments to the scene, the scene's start method must be called. The complete scene, as described at the beginning of this section, is created by adding the following code to the end of the initialize method:

```
scene = new Scene();
mainStage.addActor(scene);

scene.addSegment( new SceneSegment( background, Actions.fadeIn(1) ));
scene.addSegment( new SceneSegment( turtle, SceneActions.moveToScreenCenter(2) ));
scene.addSegment( new SceneSegment( dialogBox, Actions.show() ));

scene.addSegment( new SceneSegment( dialogBox,
        SceneActions.setText("I want to be the very best . . . Starfish Collector!" ) ));

scene.addSegment( new SceneSegment( continueKey, Actions.show() ));
scene.addSegment( new SceneSegment( background, SceneActions.pause() ));
scene.addSegment( new SceneSegment( continueKey, Actions.hide() ));

scene.addSegment( new SceneSegment( dialogBox,
        SceneActions.setText("I've got to collect them all!" ) ));

scene.addSegment( new SceneSegment( continueKey, Actions.show() ));
scene.addSegment( new SceneSegment( background, SceneActions.pause() ));
scene.addSegment( new SceneSegment( continueKey, Actions.hide() ));

scene.addSegment( new SceneSegment( dialogBox, Actions.hide() ) );
scene.addSegment( new SceneSegment( turtle, SceneActions.moveToOutsideRight(1) ));
scene.addSegment( new SceneSegment( background, Actions.fadeOut(1) ));

scene.start();
```

When the scene is finished, the LevelScreen class should be loaded. To accomplish this task, add the following code to the update method:

```
if ( scene.isSceneFinished() )
    BaseGame.setActiveScreen( new LevelScreen() );
```

Finally, the StoryScreen class should be loaded from the MenuScreen class when clicking on the Start button or when pressing the Enter key. Therefore, in the MenuScreen class, replace both references to LevelScreen with StoryScreen (there is one reference in the lambda expression for the Start button and one reference in the keyDown method). When this is completed, test your program and enjoy the cutscene before diving into the action!

Game Project: Visual Novels

In this section, you will build upon the user-interface classes (such as TextButton and Table) and the cutscene framework to create a new game called *The Missing Homework*, as shown in Figure 5-17. This game can be classified in the genre of visual novel games, which are completely story driven and present a series of choices to the player that influence the progression of the story. While this is a good opportunity to practice and refine your skills at creating user-interface elements, it is not needed in the chapters that follow, so this project can be skipped if you are not interested in this style of game.

Figure 5-17. Screenshots from the game The Missing Homework

In the game *The Missing Homework*, a student named Kelsoe Kismet has misplaced his homework somewhere in his school. The player chooses the locations where Kelsoe will search until he arrives at the location of the homework. There are a total of four locations in the game, shown in Figure 5-18.

Figure 5-18. Locations in The Missing Homework: *hallway, classroom, science lab, and library*

The details of these locations are as follows:

- The hallway: This is where the character Kelsoe is introduced and the premise of the story is established. After the corresponding scene is finished, Kelsoe proceeds to the classroom.

- The classroom: After establishing that the homework is not at this location, the player may choose to proceed to the science lab or the library.

- The science lab: After establishing that the homework is not at this location, the player may choose to return to the classroom or proceed to the library.

- The library: After a brief search, Kelsoe discovers his missing homework, and the game ends.

The connections between these locations are illustrated by the diagram in Figure 5-19, where the circles represent branching points in the story corresponding to decisions that will be made by the player.

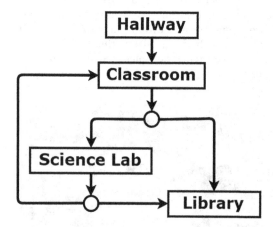

Figure 5-19. *Diagram of the locations in* The Missing Homework

To begin, create a new project in BlueJ named The Missing Homework. Download the files for this project from the book website and copy the assets folder and the +libs folder from the downloaded project into your local project. Also, in your local project folder, make copies of the following Java files from your Starfish Collector Ch 5 project: BaseGame.java, BaseScreen.java, and BaseActor.java, as well as the cutscene-related Java files DialogBox.java, Scene.java, SceneSegment.java, SetTextAction.java, and SceneActions.java. The project will need to be reopened in BlueJ to see the added classes.

Before starting to write any more code, it is important to establish the structure of this project. First, as always, there needs to be a custom launcher class and an extension of the BaseGame class. Similar to the *Starfish Collector* game with the cutscene added, there will be two extensions of the BaseScreen class: one containing a menu, the other containing the code to display the story. The latter will be a class named StoryScreen, which will contain four methods for initializing the scene segments corresponding to each of the locations described previously. (Note that the following classes will not compile until all classes have been created.) To begin, create a class named Launcher with the following code:

```
import com.badlogic.gdx.Game;
import com.badlogic.gdx.backends.lwjgl.LwjglApplication;

public class Launcher
{
    public static void main (String[] args)
    {
        Game myGame = new HomeworkGame();
        LwjglApplication launcher
            = new LwjglApplication( myGame, "The Missing Homework", 800, 600 );
    }
}
```

Next, create a class named HomeworkGame with the following code:

```
public class HomeworkGame extends BaseGame
{
    public void create()
    {
        super.create();
        setActiveScreen( new MenuScreen() );
    }
}
```

To reduce the size of the text in this game, in the BaseGame class, change the line of code that sets the font size (the variable fontParameters.size) so the font size is 24. Next, create a class named MenuScreen with the following code; it will produce the menu screen shown in Figure 5-20:

```
import com.badlogic.gdx.Gdx;
import com.badlogic.gdx.Input.Keys;
import com.badlogic.gdx.scenes.scene2d.ui.TextButton;
import com.badlogic.gdx.scenes.scene2d.Event;
import com.badlogic.gdx.scenes.scene2d.InputEvent;
import com.badlogic.gdx.scenes.scene2d.InputEvent.Type;

public class MenuScreen extends BaseScreen
{
    public void initialize()
    {
        BaseActor background = new BaseActor(0,0, mainStage);
        background.loadTexture( "assets/notebook.jpg" );
        background.setSize(800,600);

        BaseActor title = new BaseActor(0,0, mainStage);
        title.loadTexture( "assets/missing-homework.png" );

        TextButton startButton = new TextButton( "Start", BaseGame.textButtonStyle );
```

```java
        startButton.addListener(
            (Event e) ->
            {
                if ( !(e instanceof InputEvent) ||
                    !((InputEvent)e).getType().equals(Type.touchDown) )
                    return false;

                BaseGame.setActiveScreen( new StoryScreen() );
                return false;
            }
        );

        TextButton quitButton = new TextButton( "Quit", BaseGame.textButtonStyle );

        quitButton.addListener(
            (Event e) ->
            {
                if ( !(e instanceof InputEvent) ||
                    !((InputEvent)e).getType().equals(Type.touchDown) )
                    return false;

                Gdx.app.exit();
                return false;
            }
        );

        uiTable.add(title).colspan(2);
        uiTable.row();
        uiTable.add(startButton);
        uiTable.add(quitButton);
    }

    public void update(float dt)
    {    }

    public boolean keyDown(int keyCode)
    {
        if (Gdx.input.isKeyPressed(Keys.ENTER))
            BaseGame.setActiveScreen( new StoryScreen() );

        if (Gdx.input.isKeyPressed(Keys.ESCAPE))
            Gdx.app.exit();

        return false;
    }
}
```

Figure 5-20. *Menu screen for* The Missing Homework

Next, create a new class named StoryScreen that contains the following code:

```
import com.badlogic.gdx.Gdx;
import com.badlogic.gdx.Input.Keys;
import com.badlogic.gdx.scenes.scene2d.Action;
import com.badlogic.gdx.scenes.scene2d.actions.Actions;
import com.badlogic.gdx.graphics.Color;
import com.badlogic.gdx.scenes.scene2d.ui.TextButton;
import com.badlogic.gdx.scenes.scene2d.ui.Table;
import com.badlogic.gdx.scenes.scene2d.Event;
import com.badlogic.gdx.scenes.scene2d.InputEvent;
import com.badlogic.gdx.scenes.scene2d.InputEvent.Type;

public class StoryScreen extends BaseScreen
{
    public void initialize()
    {    }
    public void hallway()
    {    }
    public void classroom()
    {    }
    public void scienceLab()
    {    }
    public void library()
    {    }
    public void update(float dt)
    {    }
    public boolean keyDown(int keyCode)
    {   return false;  }
}
```

Since multiple background images will be used, and the main character expresses emotions using multiple images, you will create some classes that extend the BaseActor class to store this additional data. First, create a new class named Background with the following code:

```
import com.badlogic.gdx.scenes.scene2d.Stage;
import com.badlogic.gdx.graphics.g2d.Animation;

public class Background extends BaseActor
{
    public Animation hallway;
    public Animation classroom;
    public Animation scienceLab;
    public Animation library;

    public Background(float x, float y, Stage s)
    {
        super(x,y,s);
        hallway = loadTexture("assets/bg-hallway.jpg");
        classroom = loadTexture("assets/bg-classroom.jpg");
        scienceLab = loadTexture("assets/bg-science-lab.jpg");
        library = loadTexture("assets/bg-library.jpg");
        setSize(800,600);
    }
}
```

Next, create a new class named Kelsoe with the following code:

```
import com.badlogic.gdx.scenes.scene2d.Stage;
import com.badlogic.gdx.graphics.g2d.Animation;

public class Kelsoe extends BaseActor
{
    public Animation normal;
    public Animation sad;
    public Animation lookLeft;
    public Animation lookRight;

    public Kelsoe(float x, float y, Stage s)
    {
        super(x,y,s);
        normal = loadTexture("assets/kelsoe-normal.png");
        sad = loadTexture("assets/kelsoe-sad.png");
        lookLeft = loadTexture("assets/kelsoe-look-left.png");
        lookRight = loadTexture("assets/kelsoe-look-right.png");
    }
}
```

You will also need some special actions in this game (and in most visual novel–style games in general). To change the animation being displayed by a BaseActor, create a new class called SetAnimationAction with the following code. It is similar to the SetTextAction class in that it stores some extra data (in this case, an Animation) and casts the target actor in order to be able to use a method to set the animation.

```
import com.badlogic.gdx.scenes.scene2d.Action;
import com.badlogic.gdx.graphics.g2d.Animation;

public class SetAnimationAction extends Action
{
    protected Animation animationToDisplay;

    public SetAnimationAction(Animation a)
    {
        animationToDisplay = a;
    }

    public boolean act(float dt)
    {
        BaseActor ba = (BaseActor)target;
        ba.setAnimation( animationToDisplay );
        return true;
    }
}
```

To gradually display text in a DialogBox as if it were being typed out (a common effect in visual novels as a substitute for a speaking animation), create a new class named TypewriterAction that contains the following code. Note that this class extends SetTextAction (and thus has access to the String variable textToDisplay) and also keeps track of the time that has elapsed. According to the value stored in charactersPerSecond and the elapsed time, a substring of textToDisplay will be shown in the corresponding DialogBox.

```
import com.badlogic.gdx.scenes.scene2d.Stage;
import com.badlogic.gdx.scenes.scene2d.Action;

public class TypewriterAction extends SetTextAction
{
    private float elapsedTime;
    private float charactersPerSecond;

    public TypewriterAction(String t)
    {
        super(t);
        elapsedTime = 0;
        charactersPerSecond = 30;
    }

    public boolean act(float dt)
    {
        elapsedTime += dt;
        int numberOfCharacters = (int)(elapsedTime * charactersPerSecond);
        if (numberOfCharacters > textToDisplay.length())
            numberOfCharacters = textToDisplay.length();
        String partialText = textToDisplay.substring(0, numberOfCharacters);
        DialogBox db = (DialogBox)target;
        db.setText( partialText );
```

```
            // action is complete when all characters have been displayed
            return ( numberOfCharacters >= textToDisplay.length() );
    }
}
```

For consistency with your previous work and to simplify the creation of these two new actions, you will create a pair of corresponding static methods. In the SceneActions class, add the following two methods:

```
public static Action setAnimation(Animation a)
{
    return new SetAnimationAction(a);
}

public static Action typewriter(String s)
{
    return new TypewriterAction(s);
}
```

With these additions in place, you have all the Actors you will need for the game. Return to the StoryScreen class and add the following variables to the class:

```
Scene scene;
Background background;
Kelsoe kelsoe;
DialogBox dialogBox;
BaseActor continueKey;
Table buttonTable;
BaseActor theEnd;
```

Next, add the following code to the initialize method to initialize and configure these variables:

```
background = new Background(0,0, mainStage);
background.setOpacity(0);
BaseActor.setWorldBounds(background);

kelsoe = new Kelsoe(0,0, mainStage);

dialogBox = new DialogBox(0,0, uiStage);
dialogBox.setDialogSize(600, 150);
dialogBox.setBackgroundColor( new Color(0.2f, 0.2f, 0.2f, 1) );
dialogBox.setVisible(false);

continueKey = new BaseActor(0,0,uiStage);
continueKey.loadTexture("assets/key-C.png");
continueKey.setSize(32,32);
continueKey.setVisible(false);

dialogBox.addActor(continueKey);
continueKey.setPosition( dialogBox.getWidth() - continueKey.getWidth(), 0 );
```

```
buttonTable = new Table();
buttonTable.setVisible(false);

uiTable.add().expandY();
uiTable.row();
uiTable.add(buttonTable);
uiTable.row();
uiTable.add(dialogBox);

theEnd = new BaseActor(0,0,mainStage);
theEnd.loadTexture("assets/the-end.png");
theEnd.centerAtActor(background);
theEnd.setScale(2);
theEnd.setOpacity(0);

scene = new Scene();
mainStage.addActor(scene);
hallway();
```

In order to advance through the scene when the user presses a key (the C key), change the keyDown method to the following:

```
public boolean keyDown(int keyCode)
{
    if ( keyCode == Keys.C )
        scene.loadNextSegment();

    return false;
}
```

Before adding code to the methods corresponding to the various in-game locations, you will add another method to the StoryScreen class that will greatly reduce the amount of code you will have to write. Frequently, you need to display text, make the continue key visible, add a pause action, and then make the continue key invisible. For efficiency, add the following method to the StoryScreen class:

```
public void addTextSequence(String s)
{
    scene.addSegment( new SceneSegment( dialogBox, SceneActions.typewriter(s) ));
    scene.addSegment( new SceneSegment( continueKey, Actions.show() ));
    scene.addSegment( new SceneSegment( background, SceneActions.pause() ));
    scene.addSegment( new SceneSegment( continueKey, Actions.hide() ));
}
```

The first method you will implement is the hallway method. As you will notice, each of these location-specific methods begins by setting the correct background animation, fading in the background, moving Kelsoe to the center of the screen, and making the dialog box visible. Furthermore, these methods usually end with making the dialog box invisible, moving Kelsoe off-screen, and fading out the background. At the end of this method, to automatically progress to the next area, you need to call the classroom method. This can be accomplished with a RunnableAction, which takes a Runnable object as a parameter. Since Runnable is a functional interface, you will use a lambda expression for the parameter of this action. In particular, this expression will be () -> { classroom(); }, which indicates that there are no parameters and the classroom method should be called. Add the following code to the hallway method:

```
background.setAnimation( background.hallway );
dialogBox.setText("");
kelsoe.addAction( SceneActions.moveToOutsideLeft(0) );

scene.addSegment( new SceneSegment( background, Actions.fadeIn(1) ));
scene.addSegment( new SceneSegment( kelsoe, SceneActions.moveToScreenCenter(1) ));
scene.addSegment( new SceneSegment( dialogBox, Actions.show() ));

addTextSequence( "My name is Kelsoe Kismet. I am a student at Aureus Ludus Academy." );
addTextSequence( "I can be a little forgetful sometimes. Right now, I'm looking for my
        homework." );

scene.addSegment( new SceneSegment( dialogBox, Actions.hide() ));
scene.addSegment( new SceneSegment( kelsoe, SceneActions.moveToOutsideRight(1) ));
scene.addSegment( new SceneSegment( background, Actions.fadeOut(1) ));

scene.addSegment( new SceneSegment( background, Actions.run(() -> { classroom(); }) ));

scene.start();
```

Next, you will implement the classroom method. At the end of this method, two text buttons are created and added to the previously created button table. Within each of the buttons' lambda expressions, additional scene segments are added corresponding to the player's selection. Add the following code to the classroom method:

```
scene.clearSegments();
background.setAnimation( background.classroom );
dialogBox.setText("");
kelsoe.addAction( SceneActions.moveToOutsideLeft(0) );

scene.addSegment( new SceneSegment( background, Actions.fadeIn(1) ));
scene.addSegment( new SceneSegment( kelsoe, SceneActions.moveToScreenCenter(1) ));
scene.addSegment( new SceneSegment( dialogBox, Actions.show() ));

addTextSequence( "This is my classroom. My homework isn't here, though." );
addTextSequence( "Where should I look for my homework next?" );

scene.addSegment( new SceneSegment( buttonTable, Actions.show() ));

// set up options
TextButton scienceLabButton = new TextButton("Look in the Science Lab",
        BaseGame.textButtonStyle);
scienceLabButton.addListener(
    (Event e) ->
    {
        if ( !(e instanceof InputEvent) ||
            !((InputEvent)e).getType().equals(Type.touchDown) )
            return false;
```

```
        scene.addSegment( new SceneSegment( buttonTable, Actions.hide() ));
        addTextSequence( "That's a great idea. I'll check the science lab." );
        scene.addSegment( new SceneSegment( dialogBox, Actions.hide() ));
        scene.addSegment( new SceneSegment( kelsoe, SceneActions.moveToOutsideLeft(1) ));
        scene.addSegment( new SceneSegment( background, Actions.fadeOut(1) ));
        scene.addSegment( new SceneSegment( background, Actions.run(() -> { scienceLab(); }) ));

        return false;
    }
);

TextButton libraryButton = new TextButton("Look in the Library", BaseGame.textButtonStyle);
libraryButton.addListener(
    (Event e) ->
    {
        if ( !(e instanceof InputEvent) ||
            !((InputEvent)e).getType().equals(Type.touchDown) )
            return false;

        scene.addSegment( new SceneSegment( buttonTable, Actions.hide() ));
        addTextSequence( "That's a great idea. Maybe I left it in the library." );
        scene.addSegment( new SceneSegment( dialogBox, Actions.hide() ));
        scene.addSegment( new SceneSegment( kelsoe, SceneActions.moveToOutsideLeft(1) ));
        scene.addSegment( new SceneSegment( background, Actions.fadeOut(1) ));
        scene.addSegment( new SceneSegment( background, Actions.run(() -> { library(); }) ));

        return false;
    }
);

buttonTable.clearChildren();
buttonTable.add(scienceLabButton);
buttonTable.row();
buttonTable.add(libraryButton);

scene.start();
```

Next is the scienceLab method. This is similar to the previous method—once again, two text buttons will be displayed, in this case giving the player the choice to return to the classroom or proceed to the library. Add the following code to the scienceLab method:

```
scene.clearSegments();

background.setAnimation( background.scienceLab );
dialogBox.setText("");
kelsoe.addAction( SceneActions.moveToOutsideLeft(0) );

scene.addSegment( new SceneSegment( background, Actions.fadeIn(1) ));
scene.addSegment( new SceneSegment( kelsoe, SceneActions.moveToScreenCenter(1) ));
scene.addSegment( new SceneSegment( dialogBox, Actions.show() ));
```

```java
addTextSequence( "This is the science lab.");
scene.addSegment( new SceneSegment( kelsoe, SceneActions.setAnimation( kelsoe.sad ) ));
addTextSequence( "My homework isn't here, though." );
scene.addSegment( new SceneSegment( kelsoe, SceneActions.setAnimation( kelsoe.normal ) ));
addTextSequence( "Now where should I go?" );

scene.addSegment( new SceneSegment( buttonTable, Actions.show() ));

// set up options
TextButton classroomButton = new TextButton("Return to the Classroom",
        BaseGame.textButtonStyle);
classroomButton.addListener(
    (Event e) ->
    {
        if ( !(e instanceof InputEvent) ||
            !((InputEvent)e).getType().equals(Type.touchDown) )
            return false;

        scene.addSegment( new SceneSegment( buttonTable, Actions.hide() ));
        addTextSequence( "Maybe someone found it and put it in the classroom. I'll go
        check." );
        scene.addSegment( new SceneSegment( dialogBox, Actions.hide() ));
        scene.addSegment( new SceneSegment( kelsoe, SceneActions.moveToOutsideRight(1) ));
        scene.addSegment( new SceneSegment( background, Actions.fadeOut(1) ));
        scene.addSegment( new SceneSegment( background, Actions.run(() -> { classroom(); }) ));

        return false;
    }
);

TextButton libraryButton = new TextButton("Look in the Library", BaseGame.textButtonStyle);
libraryButton.addListener(
    (Event e) ->
    {
        if ( !(e instanceof InputEvent) ||
            !((InputEvent)e).getType().equals(Type.touchDown) )
            return false;

        scene.addSegment( new SceneSegment( buttonTable, Actions.hide() ));
        addTextSequence( "That's a great idea. Maybe I left it in the library." );
        scene.addSegment( new SceneSegment( dialogBox, Actions.hide() ));
        scene.addSegment( new SceneSegment( kelsoe, SceneActions.moveToOutsideRight(1) ));
        scene.addSegment( new SceneSegment( background, Actions.fadeOut(1) ));
        scene.addSegment( new SceneSegment( background, Actions.run(() -> { library(); }) ));

        return false;
    }
);
```

```
buttonTable.clearChildren();
buttonTable.add(classroomButton);
buttonTable.row();
buttonTable.add(libraryButton);

scene.start();
```

Finally, there is the `library` method. When the player arrives at this location, there will be some additional dialog, the story will end, and an image containing the words "The End" will fade in on the screen. Add the following code to the `library` method:

```
scene.clearSegments();

background.setAnimation( background.library );
dialogBox.setText("");
kelsoe.addAction( SceneActions.moveToOutsideLeft(0) );

scene.addSegment( new SceneSegment( background, Actions.fadeIn(1) ));
scene.addSegment( new SceneSegment( kelsoe, SceneActions.moveToScreenCenter(1) ));
scene.addSegment( new SceneSegment( dialogBox, Actions.show() ));

addTextSequence( "This is the library.");
addTextSequence( "Let me check the table where I was working earlier . . ." );
scene.addSegment( new SceneSegment( kelsoe, SceneActions.setAnimation( kelsoe.lookRight )
));
scene.addSegment( new SceneSegment( kelsoe, SceneActions.moveToScreenRight(2) ));
scene.addSegment( new SceneSegment( kelsoe, SceneActions.setAnimation( kelsoe.normal ) ));
addTextSequence( "Aha! Here it is!" );
scene.addSegment( new SceneSegment( kelsoe, SceneActions.moveToScreenCenter(0.5f) ));
addTextSequence( "Thanks for helping me find it!" );
scene.addSegment( new SceneSegment( dialogBox, Actions.hide() ));

scene.addSegment( new SceneSegment( theEnd, Actions.fadeIn(4) ));

scene.addSegment( new SceneSegment( background, Actions.delay(10) ));
scene.addSegment( new SceneSegment( background, Actions.run(
        () -> { BaseGame.setActiveScreen(new MenuScreen()); }) ));

scene.start();
```

At this point, you have finished the game *The Missing Homework*. Congratulations!

Summary and Next Steps

In this chapter, you learned how to create user-interface objects such as labels, image-based buttons, and text-based buttons. You created your own customized bitmap font for use in labels and text-based buttons and added some convenient default style objects to the `BaseGame` class. You specified the functionality of buttons using a lambda expression, which is a convenient shorthand notation for creating anonymous inner classes for functional interfaces. You learned how to efficiently arrange user-interface elements using tables and added table support to the `BaseScreen` class.

In the *Starfish Collector* game, you added a label to display the number of starfish remaining and a button to reset the level, and on the menu screen you added some text buttons to let the player start or quit the game. Next, you created the DialogBox class to conveniently display messages during gameplay, and you implemented a sign-reading mechanic with the help of a new method in the BaseActor class to determine when two objects are close to each other. Then, you created an entire framework for displaying cutscenes, including the new classes Scene, SceneSegment, SetTextAction, and SceneActions. Finally, you pushed the cutscene framework to its limits and created *The Missing Homework*, an entirely new game from the visual-novel genre.

At this point, there are many additions you could make to either game. In *Starfish Collector*, you could add a new game mechanic, such as a time limit for the turtle to collect all the starfish, in which case you would want to display the time remaining in another label and perhaps include a Pause button in your game. If you enjoyed creating the cutscene, you could add another class that plays a cutscene after the turtle collects all the starfish.

In *The Missing Homework*, simple additions would be more dialogue or locations. As a more substantial addition, you could add extra goals to complete during the game. For example, perhaps one location contains a key, and if the player collects the key, then another location will have an additional option (text button) that appears, such as "Unlock the door," leading to a previously inaccessible location.

In the next chapter, you will turn your attention to audio—background music and sound effects— another fundamental skill you will need to master for game development.

CHAPTER 6

■ ■ ■

Audio

In this chapter, you will learn how to add audio elements—sound effects and background music—to your game. First, you will be introduced to these topics by adding these features to the *Starfish Collector* game that you have been working on in previous chapters. Then, in an optional section, you will build on these skills with a musical rhythm-based game, called *Rhythm Tapper*, in which the player presses a sequence of keys indicated by falling objects overlapping targets, all of which is synchronized with music playing in the background. A screenshot of *Rhythm Tapper* is shown in Figure 6-1.

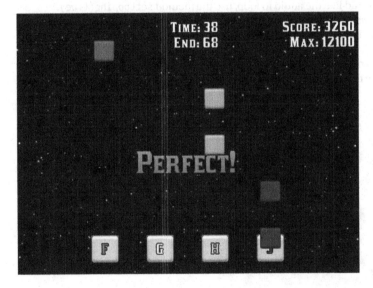

Figure 6-1. *Screenshot of the game Rhythm Tapper*

Sounds and Music

Incorporating audio into your game is a straightforward process, thanks to the built-in functionality of the LibGDX libraries. Supported file types include MP3, OGG, and WAV. LibGDX provides two interfaces for this purpose, Sound and Music, each of which can be created from the audio object of the Gdx class. The classes that implement the interfaces depend on the platform being used; conveniently, these details are handled for you by LibGDX.

The Sound interface is provided for sound effects: small audio files that are played when discrete game events occur, such as when an item is collected, a character jumps, or two objects collide. Sound effects are typically short (a few seconds or less), and the corresponding files should not be larger than 1 MB. (For larger audio clips, you should use the Music interface, explained next.) To create a Sound object from an audio file with the filename beep.wav, for example, you would write the following code:

```
Sound effect = Gdx.audio.newSound( Gdx.files.internal("beep.wav") );
```

After the sound has been created, it is played with the play method, which optionally takes a float parameter that determines how loudly the sound will be played (0 is silent, while 1 is full volume). A single sound effect can be played multiple times in rapid succession; the sounds will simply overlap each other in this case.

The Music interface is provided for longer audio sequences, such as background music or ambient sounds. Music objects are streamed from a file rather than being completely loaded into memory (the latter being the case with Sound objects), which is why files larger than 1 MB can be used in this case. To create a Music object from an audio file with the filename song.mp3, for example, you would write the following code:

```
Music song = Gdx.audio.newSound( Gdx.files.internal("song.mp3") );
```

The volume of a Music object can be set at any time using the setVolume method, which takes a float value just as Sound objects do. If you would like the audio to loop, use the method setLooping(true). To control playback, there are play, pause, and stop methods. To retrieve information about the current state of playback, you use the methods isPlaying, isLooping, and getPosition, the latter of which returns the current position in seconds.

Next, you'll see how to add music and sound effects to the *Starfish Collector* game created in the previous chapter, along with a button that can be used to mute and unmute the audio, as shown in Figure 6-2.

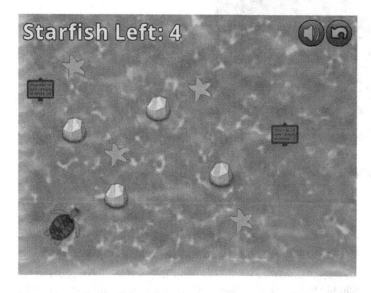

Figure 6-2. *The* Starfish Collector *game with audio and a mute button added*

To begin, create a copy of the project directory for *Starfish Collector* from the previous chapter and rename the folder to Starfish Collector Ch 6. Download the code from the book website and copy the three music files (which have the ogg extension) and the new image file (audio.png) from the downloaded project assets folder into your local project assets folder. Open your BlueJ project. First, in the BaseScreen class, you will add a method to simplify detecting touchdown events. Add the following import statements:

```
import com.badlogic.gdx.scenes.scene2d.Event;
import com.badlogic.gdx.scenes.scene2d.InputEvent;
import com.badlogic.gdx.scenes.scene2d.InputEvent.Type;
```

Next, add the following method, which will be used to check whether a mouse event corresponds to a button click (as opposed to a mouse movement event, for example):

```
public boolean isTouchDownEvent(Event e)
{
    return (e instanceof InputEvent) && ((InputEvent)e).getType().equals(Type.touchDown);
}
```

The remaining code in this section will be added to the LevelScreen class. First, add the following import statements:

```
import com.badlogic.gdx.audio.Sound;
import com.badlogic.gdx.audio.Music;
```

Then, in the class, declare the following variables:

```
private float audioVolume;
private Sound waterDrop;
private Music instrumental;
private Music oceanSurf;
```

At the end of the initialize method, add the following code to initialize these variables and begin the background music. The song "Master of the Feast" used in this application was created by Kevin MacLeod from incompetech.com.[1]

```
waterDrop    = Gdx.audio.newSound(Gdx.files.internal("assets/Water_Drop.ogg"));
instrumental = Gdx.audio.newMusic(Gdx.files.internal("assets/Master_of_the_Feast.ogg"));
oceanSurf    = Gdx.audio.newMusic(Gdx.files.internal("assets/Ocean_Waves.ogg"));

audioVolume = 1.00f;
instrumental.setLooping(true);
instrumental.setVolume(audioVolume);
instrumental.play();
oceanSurf.setLooping(true);
oceanSurf.setVolume(audioVolume);
oceanSurf.play();
```

---

[1]The website incompetech.com has a great selection of music freely available to download and released under the Creative Commons Attribution 3.0 license.

In the update method, the water-drop sound effect will be played whenever the turtle overlaps a starfish. Locate the line of code that reads starfish.collected = true, and after this line of code, add the following:

```
waterDrop.play(audioVolume);
```

According to the LibGDX documentation, when you are finished with a music object, you should call the Music class dispose method to free up memory (and stop the song from continuing to play). Therefore, in the initialize method, change the block of code that sets the listener for the Restart button to the following:

```
restartButton.addListener(
    (Event e) ->
    {
        if ( !isTouchDownEvent(e) )
            return false;

        instrumental.dispose();
        oceanSurf.dispose();

        StarfishGame.setActiveScreen( new LevelScreen() );
        return true;
    }
);
```

Finally, you will add a button to the user interface that can be used to mute and unmute the audio by changing the value of the audioVolume variable. In the initialize method, after the code that adds the listener to restartButton, add the following code. Note in particular the expression audioVolume = 1 - audioVolume, which is used to toggle the value of audioVolume between 0 and 1.

```
ButtonStyle buttonStyle2 = new ButtonStyle();

Texture buttonTex2 = new Texture( Gdx.files.internal("assets/audio.png") );
TextureRegion buttonRegion2 =  new TextureRegion(buttonTex2);
buttonStyle2.up = new TextureRegionDrawable( buttonRegion2 );

Button muteButton = new Button( buttonStyle2 );
muteButton.setColor( Color.CYAN );

muteButton.addListener(
    (Event e) ->
    {
        if ( !isTouchDownEvent(e) )
            return false;

        audioVolume = 1 - audioVolume;
        instrumental.setVolume( audioVolume );
        oceanSurf.setVolume( audioVolume );

        return true;
    }
);
```

Finally, to add this newly created button to the user interface, in the `initialize` method, locate the line of code that adds `restartButton` to `uiTable`, and right before this line of code, add the following:

```
uiTable.add(muteButton).top();
```

Also, now that `uiTable` contains four columns, one more modification must be made so that the other user-interface elements remain aligned as before. Locate the line of code that adds `dialogBox` to `uiTable` and change it to the following:

```
uiTable.add(dialogBox).colspan(4);
```

You have now successfully added audio and audio controls to your game! At this point in the chapter, you have learned the fundamentals of audio: the `Sound` and `Music` classes and their methods. The rest of this chapter includes advanced material and the creation of an audio-based game, which is not necessary for the chapters that follow. Therefore, you can skip the rest of this chapter and proceed to the next, if you wish; otherwise, feel free to continue.

Game Project: Rhythm Tapper

For the remainder of this chapter, you will creating a game called *Rhythm Tapper*, which can be classified in the genre of rhythm action video games, which includes classics such as the Konami arcade game *Dance Dance Revolution*, the Sony Playstation game *PaRappa the Rapper*, and the Umoni Studio mobile game *Piano Tiles*. Games in this genre require players to perform a sequence of actions (for this project, pressing a set of keys) with precise timing that is synchronized with music playing in the background. In *Rhythm Tapper*, the player will press the F, G, H, and J keys, which were chosen because they are in the center of the keyboard and are horizontally adjacent to each other, allowing the player to easily position a different finger above each of the keys at the same time. As seen in the game screenshot in Figure 6-1 at the beginning of this chapter, there are four squares (which we will call *target boxes*) at the bottom of the screen, each displaying one of these letters. Colored squares (which we will call *falling boxes*) spawn above the screen in line with these targets and fall down at a constant speed, typically overlapping the target box at the same time as a beat in the song. The player's goal is to press the corresponding key at the precise moment when the falling box overlaps and is perfectly centered on the target box. Each time a key is pressed, a number of points will be awarded based on how close the two boxes were (zero points when the boxes do not overlap at all), and a message will briefly flash on the screen to inform the player of how well they did (messages include "Perfect," "Great," "Good," "Almost," and "Miss").

The user interface will be displayed along the top edge of the screen. It will consist of a Start button that will begin the song when clicked, a label that will display the current time in the song and the ending time, and a label that will display the player's current score and the maximum possible score for this song. In addition, there will be many subtle value-based animation effects used throughout, such as a small pulse effect on the target boxes and a fading effect on the falling boxes when the corresponding key is pressed. There will also be a three-second countdown period between the time the Start button is pressed and the time the song begins to give the player a chance to get ready to press the keys; this countdown effect will be accompanied by numbers that appear and a blip-like sound effect that will occur at one-second intervals. Finally, a "Congratulations" message will appear after the song is finished.

The most difficult part of creating this rhythm game will be creating a file that stores the timing data required for creating the falling boxes: the key that the player should press and the song playback time at which the falling box should overlap the target box. Thus, before beginning work on the game application itself, the next section will discuss how to work with files in LibGDX, how to open a file-chooser dialog (to simplify the process of selecting files), the format of the file that stores timing data, and an application that can be used to help you create additional timing files.

To begin, create a new project in BlueJ named Rhythm Tapper. Download the files for this project from the book website and copy the assets folder and the +libs folder (if not using the BlueJ userlib folder) from the downloaded project into your local project. Also, in your local project folder, make copies of the following Java files from the downloaded project: BaseGame.java, BaseScreen.java, and BaseActor.java. For a new visual style, you will be using a new font file (Kirsty.ttf); you can change this font parameter in the BaseGama.java file. Also, change the font size to 32.

Working with Files

Java applications often use the File class to provide access to system files. LibGDX provides an alternative class for this purpose, called FileHandle, which handles the platform-specific details of file operations and provides additional functionality for

- reading from and writing to files;

- copying, moving, and deleting files;

- listing files and directories; and

- checking whether files and directories exist.

You have already been using FileHandle objects extensively, typically as anonymous instances passed as parameters to other methods, using the Gdx.files method internal, such as in the following example:

```
Texture tex = new Texture( Gdx.files.internal("assets/image.png") );
```

The internal method assumes that the file path is relative to the application. Another similar method, named external, assumes the path is relative to the root folder of the hardware device the application is running on. Alternatively, if you already have a File object, you can create an instance of the FileHandler class directly by using its constructor and the File object as parameters.

When working with text files using the standard Java libraries, you might use classes such as Scanner to read the contents of a file and PrintWriter to write to or append to an existing file. In the application you are going to build, since the files you will be reading and writing to only contain text, you will instead use the FileHandle methods readString and writeString. The readString method returns the entire contents of the file as a single string, which you can separate by line into an array of strings using the String class method split and indicating that the newline character "\n" indicates the next array element. As an example, if you wanted to split a FileHandle object named handle into an array of strings, one line per array element, you would use the following line of code:

```
String[] fileData = handle.readString().split("\n");
```

Writing string data to a file represented by a FileHandle object is similarly straightforward. The writeString method takes two parameters: a string (the data to be written) and a Boolean value that indicates whether the data should be appended to the file (when the value is true) or should be used to overwrite all the data currently in the file (when the value is false).

Browsing for Files

In the application you will build in the next subsection, it will simplify the process if you are able to select a music file to open or specify a filename and location to save to by using a standard file-chooser window rather than entering the path and filenames directly into the code, thus requiring you to change the code every time you want to work with a new file. Java has built-in functionality for creating such windows, while

LibGDX currently does not, so you will need to use the standard Java classes. There are two different Java frameworks available for creating applications with graphical user interfaces: *Swing* and *JavaFX*. Of these two, Swing has been around longer and is more well-known, but it is no longer being actively developed, and applications made with Swing appear less modern. In this section, you will be using the JavaFX classes. For example, Figure 6-3 shows the standard dialog windows for saving files with the Swing and JavaFX frameworks.

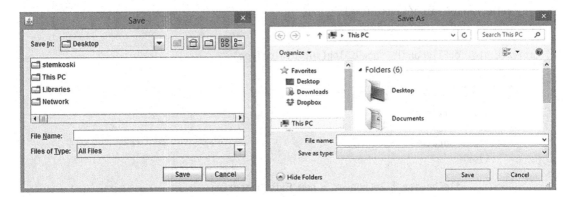

Figure 6-3. *Save dialog windows created with Swing (left) and JavaFX (right) frameworks*

In what follows, you will create a utility class called FileUtils that contains static methods to simplify creating these windows and converting the returned File object to a FileHandle object that can be used in LibGDX. One complication with integrating JavaFX classes into an application that is not purely built around JavaFX is that a number of background, framework-related classes must be initialized before you can use specific JavaFX classes themselves. (This is a common state of affairs; the LibGDX framework must also initialize platform-dependent objects, such as Gdx.files, Gdx.input, and Gdx.audio before you can start your game programs.) There are two ways to initialize the JavaFX toolkit that runs in the background: either by creating a JavaFX Application object (and running its start method) or by creating a JFXPanel object. In addition, JavaFX applications run on their own *thread*: a separate process that is run independently of others on the CPU. (When you run multiple applications on your computer or smartphone, each is running on a different thread, all of which are managed and scheduled by the CPU.) Therefore, the JavaFX classes and code need to be run not during the thread in which the LibGDX application is running, but during the thread in which the JavaFX application is running. This can be arranged using the JavaFX Platform class, which can schedule code to be run during the JavaFX thread via its runLater method. To accomplish these tasks, create a new class named FileUtils containing the following code, which will be explained more thoroughly after the code listing:

```
import javafx.embed.swing.JFXPanel;
import javafx.application.Platform;
import javafx.stage.FileChooser;
import java.io.File;
import com.badlogic.gdx.files.FileHandle;

public class FileUtils
{
    private static boolean finished;
    private static FileHandle fileHandle;
    private static int openDialog = 1;
    private static int saveDialog = 2;
```

```
    public static FileHandle showOpenDialog()
    {
        return showDialog(openDialog);
    }

    public static FileHandle showSaveDialog()
    {
        return showDialog(saveDialog);
    }

    private static FileHandle showDialog(int dialogType)
    {
        new JFXPanel();

        finished = false;

        Platform.runLater(
            () ->
            {
                FileChooser fileChooser = new FileChooser();
                File file;

                if (dialogType == openDialog)
                    file = fileChooser.showOpenDialog(null);
                else // dialogType == saveDialog
                    file = fileChooser.showSaveDialog(null);

                if (file != null)
                    fileHandle = new FileHandle(file);
                else
                    fileHandle = null;

                finished = true;
            }
        );

        while ( !finished )
        {
            // waiting for FileChooser window to close
        }

        return fileHandle;
    }
}
```

The heart of this class is the showDialog class, which begins by initializing a JFXPanel object solely for the purpose of initializing the JavaFX background processes; a variable is not used to store a reference to this object, since you will not need to use any of its methods at any point. The Platform.runLater method takes in a Runnable object (written here as a lambda expression) that contains code to be run on the JavaFX process thread. This code opens a FileChooser window, retrieves a File object, and in turn uses it to initialize a FileHandle object. However, some care must be taken: since this code is running on a separate thread, the CPU could return to the LibGDX thread and attempt to finish executing the showDialog method before the JavaFX code finishes executing. This is the reasoning behind the use of the Boolean variable finished: it is initialized to false by the showDialog method and is only set to true after the JavaFX code has completed running. A while loop in the showDialog method prevents the method from continuing until the file-chooser window is closed. As a result, if the user attempts to return to the LibGDX application window while the file-chooser window is still open, the LibGDX window title bar may say "not responding," but the application will return to normal after a file is selected. The other two methods in this class, showOpenDialog and showSaveDialog, are used to control which type of file chooser is opened by the showDialog method.

With this class prepared, you are ready to turn your attention to the data structure that will be used to store timing information for the falling boxes in the *Rhythm Tapper* game, and to the application you will create to record this data for later use in the game.

Recording Song Data

When creating a rhythm action game, one of the most difficult parts is to determine which keys should be pressed at which times as the music is playing. To accomplish this task, you will use a simple approach and record the keystrokes as the music is playing. (More precise approaches are possible, but are beyond the scope of this book.) The main drawback to this approach is that you must be capable of performing the sequence of keystrokes precisely, as the player's performance will be judged according to how closely it matches the recording you create.

You will use a simple text file to store this data; the first step is to determine what data needs to be stored. Based on this information, a class will be created to store the data, and associated methods will write the data to a file and read the data from a file. The information required for the application includes

- the name of the music file;

- the duration of the music file (which will be displayed in the rhythm game's user interface);

- a list of keyboard keys and associated times at which they should be pressed; and

- a variable to keep track of the current position in the list (for use when the song is playing in the rhythm game).

Since the keys and times should be stored in pairs, your data structure will also contain an inner class (a class defined within a class) to store these pairs. To begin, create a new class called SongData with the following code. Note that the inner class is called KeyTimePair, and the SongData class stores an ArrayList of these objects. KeyTimePair is declared here as an inner class because it will only be used within this class.

```
import java.util.ArrayList;
import com.badlogic.gdx.files.FileHandle;

public class SongData
{
    private String songName;
    private float songDuration;
    private ArrayList<KeyTimePair> keyTimeList;
    private int keyTimeIndex;

    public class KeyTimePair
    {
        private String key;
        private Float time;
```

```
        public KeyTimePair(String k, Float t)
        {
            key = k;
            time = t;
        }

        public String getKey()
        { return key; }

        public Float getTime()
        { return time; }
    }

    public SongData()
    {
        keyTimeList = new ArrayList<KeyTimePair>();
    }
}
```

Next, you need some standard set and get methods for the songName and songDuration variables, so add the following methods to the SongData class:

```
public void setSongName(String s)
{ songName = s; }

public String getSongName()
{ return songName; }

public void setSongDuration(float f)
{ songDuration = f; }

public float getSongDuration()
{ return songDuration; }
```

Next, you will need some methods to create and add key-time pairs to the list stored by the SongData class, to manipulate the variable that indexes the current position in the list, to retrieve pairs from the list, and to determine if the index variable has reached the end of the list. To accomplish these tasks, add the following methods to the SongData class:

```
public void addKeyTime(String k, Float t)
{ keyTimeList.add( new KeyTimePair(k,t) ); }

public void resetIndex()
{ keyTimeIndex = 0; }

public void advanceIndex()
{ keyTimeIndex++; }

public KeyTimePair getCurrentKeyTime()
{ return keyTimeList.get(keyTimeIndex); }
```

```
public int keyTimeCount()
{   return keyTimeList.size();   }

public boolean isFinished()
{   return keyTimeIndex >= keyTimeCount();   }
```

Finally, you need a pair of methods that write this data to and read this data from a text file. The first line of the text file will store the music filename, the second line will store the duration, and each of the remaining lines will store a key-time data pair, separated by a comma. When reading the file back in as a string, the numeric data will be converted to a float with the Float class parseFloat method. Add these methods to the SongData class:

```
public void writeToFile(FileHandle file)
{
    file.writeString( getSongName() + "\n", false );
    file.writeString( getSongDuration() + "\n", true );
    for ( KeyTimePair ktp : keyTimeList )
    {
        String data = ktp.getKey() + "," + ktp.getTime() + "\n";
        file.writeString( data, true );
    }
}

public void readFromFile(FileHandle file)
{
    String rawData = file.readString();
    String[] dataArray = rawData.split("\n");
    setSongName( dataArray[0] );
    setSongDuration( Float.parseFloat(dataArray[1]) );
    keyTimeList.clear();
    for (int i = 2; i < dataArray.length; i++)
    {
        String[] keyTimeData = dataArray[i].split(",");
        String key = keyTimeData[0];
        Float time = Float.parseFloat( keyTimeData[1] );
        keyTimeList.add( new KeyTimePair( key, time ) );
    }
}
```

Now, you are ready to create the application to record the sequence and timing of keypresses. (Alternatively, if you are not interested in producing your own song data files and you just want to use the provided example file [in the assets folder, called FunkyJunky.key], you may skip the rest of this section and proceed to the next section.) The utility application you will create will simply consist of three buttons: one to select the music file to play, one to start the recording process, and one to create (or select) a file to which the recorded song data should be saved. This simple application is shown in Figure 6-4.

Figure 6-4. *Screenshot of the keystroke-recording application*

Create a new class named RecorderScreen with the following code:

```java
import com.badlogic.gdx.Gdx;
import com.badlogic.gdx.Input.Keys;
import com.badlogic.gdx.scenes.scene2d.ui.TextButton;
import com.badlogic.gdx.scenes.scene2d.Event;
import com.badlogic.gdx.files.FileHandle;
import com.badlogic.gdx.audio.Music;

public class RecorderScreen extends BaseScreen
{
    Music music;
    SongData songData;
    float lastSongPosition;
    boolean recording;
    TextButton loadButton;
    TextButton recordButton;
    TextButton saveButton;

    public void initialize()
    {
        recording = false;

        loadButton = new TextButton( "Load Music File", BaseGame.textButtonStyle );
        loadButton.addListener(
            (Event e) ->
            {
                if ( !isTouchDownEvent(e) )
                    return false;

                FileHandle musicFile = FileUtils.showOpenDialog();

                if ( musicFile != null )
                {
                    music = Gdx.audio.newMusic(musicFile);
                    songData = new SongData();
```

```
                songData.setSongName( musicFile.name() );
            }

            return true;
        }
    );

    recordButton = new TextButton( "Record Keystrokes", BaseGame.textButtonStyle );
    recordButton.addListener(
        (Event e) ->
        {
            if ( !isTouchDownEvent(e) )
                return false;

            if ( !recording )
            {
                music.play();
                recording = true;
                lastSongPosition = 0;
            }

            return true;
        }
    );

    saveButton = new TextButton( "Save Keystroke File", BaseGame.textButtonStyle );
    saveButton.addListener(
        (Event e) ->
        {
            if ( !isTouchDownEvent(e) )
                return false;

            FileHandle textFile = FileUtils.showSaveDialog();

            if ( textFile != null )
                songData.writeToFile(textFile);

            return true;
        }
    );

    uiTable.add(loadButton);
    uiTable.row();
    uiTable.add(recordButton);
    uiTable.row();
    uiTable.add(saveButton);
}
```

```
    public void update(float dt)
    {
        if ( recording )
        {
            if ( music.isPlaying() )
                lastSongPosition = music.getPosition();
            else // song just finished
            {
                recording = false;
                songData.setSongDuration( lastSongPosition );
            }
        }
    }

    public boolean keyDown(int keycode)
    {
        if ( recording )
        {
            String key = Keys.toString(keycode);
            Float time = music.getPosition();
            songData.addKeyTime(key, time);
        }
        return false;
    }
}
```

The Boolean variable recording will be used to keep track of whether or not keypress data should still be added to the SongData object. Somewhat surprisingly, it is difficult to determine the length of a music file using Java, and so the lastSongPosition variable is used to keep track of the song position while the song is playing, and as soon as the song is finished playing, the value of lastSongPosition is written to the SongData object as the song's duration. As expected, the loadButton and saveButton objects make use of the methods provided by the FileUtils class that you wrote earlier.

To run this application, you need two more classes, as usual: one that extends the BaseGame class, and a launcher class. To this end, first create a new class called RecorderGame with the following code:

```
public class RecorderGame extends BaseGame
{
    public void create()
    {
        super.create();
        setActiveScreen( new RecorderScreen() );
    }
}
```

Next, for the launcher class, create a new class called RecorderLauncher with the following code:

```
import com.badlogic.gdx.backends.lwjgl.LwjglApplication;

public class RecorderLauncher
{
    public static void main (String[] args)
```

```
    {
        BaseGame myGame = new RecorderGame();
        LwjglApplication launcher = new LwjglApplication( myGame, "Recorder", 800, 600 );
    }
}
```

To use this class, run the main method of RecorderLauncher, then click the button labeled "Load Music File" and select a song. A sample MP3 is included in the assets folder, named FunkyJunky.mp3, created by Jason Shaw from audionautix.com,[2] but you can feel free to use your own music files if desired. Then, position your fingers over the F, G, H, and J keys and click the button labeled "Record Keystrokes." The music will immediately begin playing, at which point you should press the keys in time with the beat of the music you selected. This is likely the most difficult part of the process, as it requires you to be familiar with the music and have precise timing. When the song is finished, click the button labeled "Save Keystroke File," and in the file-chooser window that appears, select a location and enter a filename to save your file. You can enter whatever extension you like for this file. There is a sample file named FunkyJunky.key in the assets folder, which you can use later on in the game application; you will probably want to choose a different filename for your data file. When you are finished, make sure that both the music file and your data file are in the assets folder for your project for easy access by the game application you will develop next.

The Game Application

Now that you have a song data file to accompany a music file, you will turn your attention to creating the game application. To program this game efficiently, you will use a number of lists, which will store the different keys the player may press, the four target boxes that appear near the bottom of the screen, and a list of falling boxes that lie above each target box (and these lists of falling boxes will themselves be stored in a list).

Before starting the game itself, you will set up classes for the target boxes and the falling boxes. First, create a new class called TargetBox with the following code. Notice that the constructor also requires a string (the letter that will be displayed on the box) and a color (which will be used by the label displaying the letter).

```
import com.badlogic.gdx.scenes.scene2d.Stage;
import com.badlogic.gdx.graphics.Color;
import com.badlogic.gdx.scenes.scene2d.ui.Label;
import com.badlogic.gdx.utils.Align;

public class TargetBox extends BaseActor
{
    public TargetBox(float x, float y, Stage s, String letter, Color color)
    {
        super(x,y,s);
        loadTexture("assets/box.png");
        setSize(64,64);
```

---

[2]The website audionautix.com has a great selection of music freely available to download and released under the Creative Commons Attribution 3.0 license.

```
        // add a centered label containing letter with given color
        Label letterLabel = new Label(letter, BaseGame.labelStyle);
        letterLabel.setSize(64,64);
        letterLabel.setAlignment(Align.center);
        letterLabel.setColor( color );
        this.addActor(letterLabel);
    }
}
```

Next, create a new class called FallingBox with the following code. Note that the same image is being used by the TargetBox class, but the FallingBox class scales it down so that it will appear to fit within the TargetBox objects. Also notice that the act method has been implemented and applyPhysics has been called; this is because the falling boxes will have their speed and angle of motion set later so that they do in fact appear to be falling down.

```
import com.badlogic.gdx.scenes.scene2d.Stage;

public class FallingBox extends BaseActor
{
    public FallingBox(float x, float y, Stage s)
    {
        super(x,y,s);
        loadTexture("assets/box.png");
        setScale(0.75f, 0.75f);
    }

    public void act(float dt)
    {
        super.act(dt);
        applyPhysics(dt);
    }
}
```

Next, create a new class named RhythmScreen that contains the following code, which sets up the lists described in the beginning of this section, creates the four TargetBox instances, and arranges them near the bottom of the screen using a Table. The Java Collections class is used to reduce the amount of code required to add a set of values to the ArrayList objects.

```
import com.badlogic.gdx.graphics.Color;
import com.badlogic.gdx.scenes.scene2d.ui.Table;
import java.util.ArrayList;
import java.util.Collections;

public class RhythmScreen extends BaseScreen
{
    private ArrayList<String> keyList;
    private ArrayList<Color> colorList;
    private ArrayList<TargetBox> targetList;
    private ArrayList<ArrayList<FallingBox>> fallingLists;
```

```
    public void initialize()
    {
        BaseActor background = new BaseActor(0,0, mainStage);
        background.loadTexture( "assets/space.png" );
        background.setSize(800,600);
        BaseActor.setWorldBounds(background);

        keyList = new ArrayList<String>();
        String[] keyArray = {"F", "G", "H", "J"};
        Collections.addAll(keyList, keyArray);

        colorList = new ArrayList<Color>();
        Color[] colorArray = {Color.RED, Color.YELLOW, Color.GREEN, Color.BLUE};
        Collections.addAll(colorList, colorArray);

        Table targetTable = new Table();
        targetTable.setFillParent(true);
        targetTable.add().colspan(4).expandY();
        targetTable.row();
        mainStage.addActor(targetTable);

        targetList = new ArrayList<TargetBox>();
        for (int i = 0; i < 4; i++)
        {
            TargetBox tb = new TargetBox(0,0,mainStage, keyList.get(i), colorList.get(i));
            targetList.add(tb);
            targetTable.add(tb).pad(32);
        }

        fallingLists = new ArrayList< ArrayList<FallingBox> >();
        for (int i = 0; i < 4; i++)
        {
            fallingLists.add( new ArrayList<FallingBox>() );
        }
    }

    public void update(float dt)
    {   }

    public boolean keyDown(int keycode)
    {   return false;  }
}
```

In order to run this code, create a new class called RhythmGame that contains the following code:

```
public class RhythmGame extends BaseGame
{
    public void create()
    {
        super.create();
        setActiveScreen( new RhythmScreen() );
    }
}
```

Next, create a new class called RhythmLauncher that contains the following code:

```
import com.badlogic.gdx.backends.lwjgl.LwjglApplication;
public class RhythmLauncher
{
    public static void main (String[] args)
    {
        BaseGame myGame = new RhythmGame();
        LwjglApplication launcher = new LwjglApplication( myGame, "Rhythm Tapper", 800, 600
);
    }
}
```

At this point, test your application using the RhythmLauncher class, and you should see a screen similar to Figure 6-5, which consists of a dark background and four target boxes containing the letters F, G, H, and J in the colors red, yellow, green, and blue, respectively.

Figure 6-5. *Rhythm Tapper game with the target boxes added*

Synchronizing Game Objects and Audio

The next goal is to add the ability to play a music file and use the data stored in the associated text file to generate a sequence of FallingBox objects, which will overlap the corresponding TargetBox objects at the point in time specified by the song. This application will assume a "lead time" of three seconds: the song will start playing three seconds after a Start button is clicked, and FallingBox objects will be created above the top edge of the screen three seconds before the time specified by the song data file so that they overlap their target at the correct time. To coordinate the timing of these events, a float variable named advanceTimer will be created and incremented only after the song data is loaded; after three seconds have passed, the music will start to play, and from that point on, advanceTimer will be set to the music position plus three seconds. The advanceTimer variable will then be used to determine when to create the FallingBox objects.

To begin, add the following import statements to the RhythmScreen class:

```
import com.badlogic.gdx.Gdx;
import com.badlogic.gdx.audio.Music;
import com.badlogic.gdx.files.FileHandle;
import com.badlogic.gdx.scenes.scene2d.ui.TextButton;
import com.badlogic.gdx.scenes.scene2d.Event;
```

Next, add the following variables to the class:

```
private Music gameMusic;
private SongData songData;
private final float leadTime = 3;
private float advanceTimer;
private float spawnHeight;
private float noteSpeed;
```

Add the following code to the initialize method. Note that spawnHeight is set to 650 so that the falling boxes start above the top edge of the screen (which has a height of 600), and noteSpeed is calculated by dividing the total distance the falling boxes have to travel to reach the target boxes by the time they have to get there (leadTime). The following code uses a song data file (FunkyJunky.key) that has been provided for you, but if you created a different song data file, you can feel free to use it instead.

```
advanceTimer = 0;
spawnHeight = 650;
noteSpeed = ( spawnHeight - targetList.get(0).getY() ) / leadTime;

TextButton startButton = new TextButton( "Start", BaseGame.textButtonStyle );
startButton.addListener(
    (Event e) ->
    {
        if ( !isTouchDownEvent(e) )
            return false;

        FileHandle dataFileHandle = Gdx.files.internal("assets/FunkyJunky.key");
        songData = new SongData();
        songData.readFromFile( dataFileHandle );
        songData.resetIndex();

        FileHandle songFileHandle = Gdx.files.internal("assets/" + songData.getSongName());
        gameMusic = Gdx.audio.newMusic( songFileHandle );
        startButton.setVisible(false);
        return true;
    }
);

uiTable.add(startButton);
```

Next, add the following code to the update method. Note that if songData has not yet been loaded, then the update method returns right away. Otherwise, the value of advanceTimer is increased as previously described, and the music is played if advanceTimer becomes greater than three. If the value of advanceTimer increases past the next time stored by the songData object, then a FallingBox object is created and configured as necessary, and the internal songData index is advanced to the next position. A while loop is used rather than an if statement in case multiple FallingBox objects need to be created during this call to the update method.

```
if (songData == null)
    return;

if (advanceTimer < leadTime && advanceTimer + dt > leadTime)
    gameMusic.play();

if (advanceTimer < leadTime)
    advanceTimer += dt;
else
    advanceTimer = leadTime + gameMusic.getPosition();

 while ( !songData.isFinished()
        && advanceTimer >= songData.getCurrentKeyTime().getTime() )
{
    String key = songData.getCurrentKeyTime().getKey();
    int i = keyList.indexOf(key);

    FallingBox fb = new FallingBox(targetList.get(i).getX(), spawnHeight, mainStage);
    fb.setSpeed( noteSpeed );
    fb.setMotionAngle( 270 );
    fb.setColor( colorList.get(i) );

    fallingLists.get(i).add(fb);

    songData.advanceIndex();
}
```

At this point, if you run the program and click on the Start button, you should hear silence for three seconds, during which some falling boxes will appear, and then the music will begin and the falling boxes should align with the target boxes in time with the music as expected.

Adding Interactivity and Creating the User Interface

Next, you will add interactivity and the user interface. The user interface will consist of the Start button, a label showing the current song position and song duration, and another label showing the player's current score and the maximum possible score for this song. In addition, you will create an object that displays a message rating the player's performance (in terms of how close the falling box was to its target box when the corresponding key was pressed). To begin, create a new class called Message containing the following code:

```
import com.badlogic.gdx.scenes.scene2d.Stage;
import com.badlogic.gdx.graphics.g2d.Animation;
import com.badlogic.gdx.scenes.scene2d.Action;
import com.badlogic.gdx.scenes.scene2d.actions.Actions;
```

```
public class Message extends BaseActor
{
    public Animation perfect;
    public Animation great;
    public Animation good;
    public Animation almost;
    public Animation miss;

    public Message(float x, float y, Stage s)
    {
        super(x,y,s);

        perfect = loadTexture("assets/perfect.png");
        great = loadTexture("assets/great.png");
        good = loadTexture("assets/good.png");
        almost = loadTexture("assets/almost.png");
        miss = loadTexture("assets/miss.png");
    }

    public void pulseFade()
    {
        setOpacity(1);
        clearActions();
        Action pulseFade =
            Actions.sequence(
                Actions.scaleTo(1.1f,1.1f, 0.05f),
                Actions.scaleTo(1.0f,1.0f, 0.05f),
                Actions.delay(1),
                Actions.fadeOut(0.5f) );
        addAction(pulseFade);
    }
}
```

The method pulseFade in the Message class is included for multiple reasons. The scaling part of the generated action creates a short pulse effect that gets the player's attention, and it also helps the player identify if the same message has been displayed twice in a short interval. In addition, the fade part of the action makes sure that messages do not remain visible long after the corresponding key has been pressed.

Next, add the following import statements to the RhythmScreen class:

```
import com.badlogic.gdx.Gdx;
import com.badlogic.gdx.Input.Keys;
import com.badlogic.gdx.scenes.scene2d.ui.Label;
import com.badlogic.gdx.utils.Align;
```

Then, add the following variables to this class:

```
private Message message;
private Label scoreLabel;
private int score;
private int maxScore;
private Label timeLabel;
private float songDuration;
```

In the `initialize` method, directly before the code involving `uiTable`, add the following code, which will initialize the remaining user interface elements:

```
scoreLabel = new Label("Score: 0" + "\n" + "Max: 0", BaseGame.labelStyle);
scoreLabel.setAlignment(Align.right);
timeLabel = new Label("Time: 0" + "\n" + "End: 0", BaseGame.labelStyle);
timeLabel.setAlignment(Align.right);
message = new Message(0,0,uiStage);
message.setOpacity(0);
```

Some of the variables you have just added cannot be initialized until after the song data has been loaded, such as the maximum possible score. Once the song data has been loaded, the maximum score can be calculated by multiplying the number of points awarded for a perfect key press (in this game, 100 points) by the total number of key presses that will occur. Within the lambda expression for the Start button, add the following code directly before the `return` statement:

```
songDuration = songData.getSongDuration();
score = 0;
maxScore = 100 * songData.keyTimeCount();
scoreLabel.setText("Score: " + score + "\n" + "Max: " + maxScore);
timeLabel.setText("Time: " + 0 + "\n" + "End: " + (int)songDuration);
```

Finally, in the `initialize` method, to add the new labels and message object to the user interface, replace the code involving `uiTable` with the following:

```
uiTable.pad(10);
uiTable.add(startButton).width(200).left();
uiTable.add(timeLabel).width(150);
uiTable.add(scoreLabel).width(200).right();
uiTable.row();
uiTable.add(message).colspan(3).expandX().expandY();
```

To update the time label according to the current song position, add the following code to the `update` method:

```
if ( gameMusic.isPlaying() )
            timeLabel.setText( "Time: " + (int)gameMusic.getPosition() + "\n"
                    + "End: " + (int)songDuration );
```

Finally, you will add the interactivity in the keyDown method (since pressing a key is a discrete event). If songData has not been initialized, then this method will return immediately. Otherwise, if the key pressed corresponds to one of the previously specified keys (F, G, H, and J, stored in keyList), then the corresponding TargetBox and ArrayList of FallingBox objects will be retrieved. If the list of FallingBox objects is empty, then this keypress counts as a "miss" and the corresponding message will be displayed. Otherwise, the distance between the lowest FallingBox instance (which is the first in the list) and the TargetBox will be calculated, and points awarded according to how small the distance is:

- 0–8 pixels: "Perfect," worth 100 points

- 8–16 pixels: "Great," worth 80 points

- 16–24 pixels: "Good," worth 50 points

- 24–32 pixels: "Almost," worth 20 points

- greater than 32 pixels: considered a "Miss" and worth no points

After setting the correct message to be displayed and incrementing the score, the pulseFade method is called to animate the message, the text in the label displaying the score is updated, and the corresponding FallingBox object is removed from the list and from the game. All of this is accomplished by adding the following code to the keyDown method:

```
if (songData == null)
            return false;

String keyString = Keys.toString(keycode);
if ( keyList.contains(keyString) )
{
    int i = keyList.indexOf(keyString);
    TargetBox tb = targetList.get(i);
    ArrayList<FallingBox> fallingList = fallingLists.get(i);

    if ( fallingList.size() == 0 )
    {
        message.setAnimation(message.miss);
        message.pulseFade();
    }
    else
    {
        FallingBox fb = fallingList.get(0);
        float distance = Math.abs( fb.getY() - tb.getY() );

        if (distance < 8)
        {
            message.setAnimation(message.perfect);
            score += 100;
        }
        else if (distance < 16)
        {
            message.setAnimation(message.great);
            score += 80;
        }
        else if (distance < 24)
        {
            message.setAnimation(message.good);
            score += 50;
        }
        else if (distance < 32)
        {
            message.setAnimation(message.almost);
            score += 20;
        }
        else
        {
            message.setAnimation(message.miss);
        }
```

```
        message.pulseFade();
        scoreLabel.setText("Score: " + score + "\n" + "Max: " + maxScore);

        fallingList.remove(fb);
        fb.remove();
    }
}
```

One more case must be considered: what if a FallingBox passes below its corresponding TargetBox and the player doesn't press a key? The FallingBox needs to be automatically removed from the game at this point, and the "Miss" message should be displayed. To do so, add the following code to the end of the update method:

```
for (int i = 0; i < 4; i++)
{
    String key = keyList.get(i);
    ArrayList<FallingBox> fallingList = fallingLists.get(i);
    if ( fallingList.size() > 0 )
    {
        FallingBox fb = fallingList.get(0);
        TargetBox tb = targetList.get(i);
        if ( fb.getY() < tb.getY() && !fb.overlaps(tb) )
        {
            message.setAnimation(message.miss);
            message.pulseFade();
            fallingList.remove(fb);
            fb.remove(); // remove from stage immediately
        }
    }
}
```

This is another excellent point at which you should test your game. All the core mechanics have been implemented; you can play a complete game and see how close you can get to the maximum possible score.

Finishing Touches

At this point, there are a few finishing touches you can add to improve the player's experience. Perhaps most significantly, the player may feel as though the song begins rather suddenly; you will address this by adding a countdown that is indicated both visually and audibly. Also, when the song is finished, it is a good idea to display a message indicating that the game is over to provide the player a stronger sense of closure. Finally, some subtle visual effects will be added: a pulse effect on the target boxes when the corresponding key is pressed, and a brightening and fading effect will be applied to the falling boxes when they disappear.

First, the new actions will be added to the game objects. In the FallingBox class, add the following import statements:

```
import com.badlogic.gdx.scenes.scene2d.Action;
import com.badlogic.gdx.scenes.scene2d.actions.Actions;
import com.badlogic.gdx.graphics.Color;
```

Next, add the following method:

```
public void flashOut()
{
    float duration = 0.25f;
    Action flashOut =
        Actions.parallel(
            Actions.scaleTo(1.5f,1.5f, duration),
            Actions.color(Color.WHITE, duration),
            Actions.fadeOut(duration) );

    addAction( flashOut );
    addAction( Actions.after( Actions.removeActor() ) );
}
```

In the TargetBox class, add the following import statements:

```
import com.badlogic.gdx.scenes.scene2d.Action;
import com.badlogic.gdx.scenes.scene2d.actions.Actions;
```

Then, add the following method:

```
public void pulse()
{
    Action pulse =
        Actions.sequence(
            Actions.scaleTo(1.2f,1.2f, 0.05f),
            Actions.scaleTo(1.0f,1.0f, 0.05f) );
    addAction(pulse);
}
```

Next, you will activate these methods in the game. In the RhythmScreen class, there are two parts of the code where falling boxes disappear, indicated by the code fb.remove(): one near the end of the update method, and one near the end of the keyDown method. In both of these locations, replace the line of code fb.remove() with the following two lines of code to apply the fading effect:

```
fb.setSpeed(0);
fb.flashOut();
```

Also in the keyDown method, after the line that gets the TargetBox from targetList, add the following line of code to apply the pulsing effect:

```
tb.pulse();
```

Next, you will implement the countdown and end-of-game message functionality in the Message class. To begin, in the Message class, add the following import statements:

```
import com.badlogic.gdx.Gdx;
import com.badlogic.gdx.audio.Sound;
```

Next, add the following variables:

```
private Animation countdown3;
private Animation countdown2;
private Animation countdown1;
private Animation countdownGo;
private Animation congratulations;
private Sound blip;
private Sound tone;
```

In the Message class constructor method, you initialize these newly added variables by adding the following code:

```
countdown3 = loadTexture("assets/countdown-3.png");
countdown2 = loadTexture("assets/countdown-2.png");
countdown1 = loadTexture("assets/countdown-1.png");
countdownGo = loadTexture("assets/countdown-go.png");
congratulations = loadTexture("assets/congratulations.png");
blip = Gdx.audio.newSound(Gdx.files.internal("assets/blip.wav"));
tone = Gdx.audio.newSound(Gdx.files.internal("assets/tone.wav"));
```

Finally, in the Message class, add the following two methods. In the countdown method, you will see that the Actions.run method and lambda expressions are used extensively to switch animations and play sounds at precise times.

```
public void displayCountdown()
{
    Action countdown =
        Actions.sequence(
            Actions.run( () -> setAnimation(countdown3) ),
            Actions.run( () -> blip.play() ),
            Actions.alpha(1),
            Actions.scaleTo(1.1f,1.1f, 0.05f), Actions.scaleTo(1.0f,1.0f, 0.05f),
            Actions.delay(0.5f), Actions.fadeOut(0.4f);
            Actions.run( () -> setAnimation(countdown2) ),
            Actions.run( () -> blip.play() ),
            Actions.alpha(1),
            Actions.scaleTo(1.1f,1.1f, 0.05f), Actions.scaleTo(1.0f,1.0f, 0.05f),
            Actions.delay(0.5f), Actions.fadeOut(0.4f),
            Actions.run( () -> setAnimation(countdown1) ),
            Actions.run( () -> blip.play() ),
            Actions.alpha(1),
            Actions.scaleTo(1.1f,1.1f, 0.05f), Actions.scaleTo(1.0f,1.0f, 0.05f),
            Actions.delay(0.5f), Actions.fadeOut(0.4f),
            Actions.run( () -> setAnimation(countdownGo) ),
            Actions.run( () -> tone.play() ),
            Actions.alpha(1),
            Actions.fadeOut(1) );

    addAction(countdown);
}
```

```
public void displayCongratulations()
{
    setOpacity(0);
    setAnimation(congratulations);
    setScale(2);
    addAction( Actions.fadeIn(4) );
}
```

With these methods added, you can now activate them at the appropriate times during the game. In the RhythmScreen class initialize method, within the lambda expression for the Start button, add the following code directly before the return statement:

```
message.displayCountdown();
```

At the end of the update method, add the following code:

```
if ( songData.isFinished() && !gameMusic.isPlaying() )
{
    message.displayCongratulations();
    songData = null;
}
```

Once you have reached this point, congratulations on finishing the *Rhythm Tapper* game!

Summary and Next Steps

In this chapter, you learned how to add music and sound effects to your games. You began by adding audio to the *Starfish Collector* game, along with a button that can be used to mute and unmute the audio. Then, you created an entirely new audio-based game called *Rhythm Tapper* from the rhythm action genre. Along the way, you also learned how to write to and read from text files in LibGDX.

At this point, there are still many audio-based features you could add to your projects. In *Starfish Collector*, you could add a sound effect (such as a trumpet fanfare) that plays after all the starfish have been collected. You might also consider adding background music to the menu screen or cutscene. In *Rhythm Tapper*, adding an applause sound effect at the end of the game would be particularly appropriate. In addition, you could consider displaying additional information at the end of the game, such as a table that displays the number of times each of the various messages ("Perfect," "Great," etc.) appeared during the song, or you could display the percentage of possible points the player earned (calculated from their score divided by the maximum possible score). To practice your audio coding skills, you could add music and sound effects to the *Space Rocks* game from Chapter 4, which would greatly improve the overall quality of that project.

Having finished this chapter, you have learned all the fundamentals of LibGDX and created a powerful and versatile custom framework that can be used to create a great variety of games. In the next set of chapters, you will learn how to implement new game mechanics while working on projects that feature genres such as side-scrolling games, bouncing and collision games, drag-and-drop games, platform games, and adventure games.

PART II

■ ■ ■

Intermediate Examples

With the solid foundation in the fundamental concepts and classes in LibGDX and the custom framework you developed and refined in Part I, you are now prepared to create a variety of video games of different genres, each featuring different mechanics. The chapters in this part are independent of each other and may be read in any order, except for Chapters 11 and 12, as they rely on tilemaps, which are introduced in Chapter 10.

Chapter 7: Side-Scrolling Games

In this chapter, you will create a side-scrolling action game called *Plane Dodger* inspired by modern smartphone games such as *Flappy Bird* and *Jetpack Joyride*. Along the way, you will learn how to create an endless scrolling background effect, simulate gravity using acceleration settings, and implement a difficulty ramp that increases the challenge to the player as time passes.

Chapter 8: Bouncing and Collision Games

In this chapter, you will create a ball-bouncing, brick-breaking game called *Rectangle Destroyer* inspired by arcade and early console games such as *Breakout* and *Arkanoid*. New features that will be implemented in this game include moving an object using the mouse, simulating objects bouncing off of other objects, and creating power-up items that the player can collect.

Chapter 9: Drag-and-Drop Games

In this chapter, you will learn how to add drag-and-drop functionality to your games; you will then create a new class containing the related code. To demonstrate the flexibility of this new class, you will create two new games that make use of it. The first will be a jigsaw-puzzle game that consists of an image that has been broken into pieces and must be rearranged correctly on a grid. The second will be a solitaire card game called *52 Card Pickup* where a standard deck of playing cards must be organized into piles.

Chapter 10: Tilemaps

This chapter will explain how to use Tiled, a general-purpose map-editing software program that can be used for multiple aspects of the level design process. Then, you will create a class that allows you to import the data from tilemap files into the custom framework you have developed. This knowledge will be used to improve two previous game projects: for the *Starfish Collector* game you will design a maze-like level (using rocks for walls) and add some scenery, while for the *Rectangle Destroyer* game you will design a colorful layout of bricks. The topics learned in this chapter are needed for the following two chapters.

Chapter 11: Platform Games

In this chapter, you will learn how to create the platform game *Jumping Jack*, which is inspired by arcade and console games such as *Donkey Kong* and *Super Mario Bros*. New concepts introduced in this chapter include game entities with multiple animations, platform physics, using extra actors as "sensors" to monitor the area around an object for overlap and collision, jump-through platforms, and key-and-lock mechanics.

Chapter 12: Adventure Games

This chapter features the most ambitious game project in the entire book: a combat-based adventure game named *Treasure Quest* inspired by classic console games such as *The Legend of Zelda*. This game uses new features such as enemy combat with two different types of weapons (a sword and an arrow), non-player characters (NPCs) with messages that depend on the state of the game (such as the number of enemies remaining), and an item-shop mechanic.

CHAPTER 7

Side-Scrolling Games

In this chapter, you will create a side-scrolling action game called *Plane Dodger*, shown in Figure 7-1, inspired by modern smartphone games such as *Flappy Bird* and *Jetpack Joyride*. Along the way, you will create an endless scrolling background effect, simulate gravity using acceleration settings, and implement a difficulty ramp that increases the challenge difficulty as time passes.

Figure 7-1. *The* Plane Dodger *game*

Game Project: Plane Dodger

Plane Dodger is an endless side-scrolling action game in which the player controls a plane that moves up and down with the goal of dodging enemy planes that fly across the screen and, whenever possible, collecting stars that appear. If the player's plane collides with an enemy plane, the game is over. Dodging enemy planes and collecting stars both award points to the player, and so the longer the player survives, the higher their score will be. Stars appear at regular intervals beyond the right edge of the screen at random heights and slowly move from right to left. If the player adjusts their plane's vertical position so that it collides with the star, the star disappears and the player earns a point. Enemy planes also appear beyond the right edge of the screen at random heights and move from left to right. At first, enemy planes appear with the same frequency and travel at the same speed as the stars, but as time passes, the enemy planes appear with

© Lee Stemkoski 2018
L. Stemkoski, *Java Game Development with LibGDX*, https://doi.org/10.1007/978-1-4842-3324-5_7

increasing frequency and travel at greater speeds. Every time an enemy plane passes beyond the left edge of the screen, the player earns a point. At first, collecting stars is an easy source of extra points, but as the enemy planes move faster, the risk may no longer be worth the reward.

The player presses the spacebar key to give their plane a small boost of speed upward. This is a discrete action; there is one boost of speed per key press. To move upward quickly requires the player to rapidly press the spacebar key. The force of gravity is always pulling the plane downward and will eventually pull the plane down to the ground. Colliding with the ground or the top edge of the screen has no effect on the plane; these only serve as lower and upper boundaries for the plane's vertical position. The player's plane cannot actually move left or right; the appearance of flying to the right is simulated by the scrolling background. The user interface contains only a single text display (the total number of points) along the top edge in the center of the screen. When the player loses the game, a "Game Over" message appears in the center of the screen.

This game uses a vibrant, colorful, cartoonish art style and has driving, fast-paced background music to help establish an energetic, excited mood. The interaction of objects is enhanced by visual and audio effects. When the plane collides with a star, a sparkling visual effect will appear, accompanied by a light, quiet tinkling sound. When the plane collides with an enemy, an explosion will appear, accompanied by a deep, rumbling, explosion-like sound.

Beginning this project requires the same steps as in previous projects: creating a new project, creating an assets folder and a +libs folder (the latter not being necessary if you have set up the userlib directory), copying the custom framework files you created in the first part of this book (BaseGame.java, BaseScreen.java, BaseActor.java), and copying the graphics and audio for this project into your assets folder. To simplify this process, a BlueJ project named Framework has been created for your convenience, which contains these items (except for the project-specific assets) and can be used as a starting point for this project and future projects, although using the code you have previously developed is perfectly acceptable as well. Therefore, to begin this project,

- download the source code files for this chapter;

- make a copy of the downloaded Framework folder (and its contents) and rename it to Plane Dodger;

- copy all the contents of the downloaded Plane Dodger project assets folder into your newly created Plane Dodger assets folder; and

- open the BlueJ project in your Plane Dodger folder.

You will notice that a few additional classes have been provided for your convenience, including a launcher class, with the following code:

```
import com.badlogic.gdx.Game;
import com.badlogic.gdx.backends.lwjgl.LwjglApplication;

public class Launcher
{
    public static void main (String[] args)
    {
        Game myGame = new CustomGame();
        LwjglApplication launcher = new LwjglApplication( myGame, "Game Title", 800, 600 );
    }
}
```

An extension of the BaseGame class, called CustomGame, is also included and contains the following code:

```
public class CustomGame extends BaseGame
{
    public void create()
    {
        super.create();
        setActiveScreen( new LevelScreen() );
    }
}
```

An extension of the BaseScreen class, called LevelScreen, is also included and contains the following code:

```
public class LevelScreen extends BaseScreen
{
    public void initialize()
    {

    }

    public void update(float dt)
    {

    }
}
```

This project can be run immediately (by running the main method of the Launcher class, as was the case with previous projects), but all it will display at this point is a black screen, since no content has been added.

To begin your *Plane Dodger* game project, in the CustomGame class, change the name of the class to PlaneDodgerGame (this will also cause BlueJ to rename the source code file to PlaneDodgerGame.java). Then, in the Launcher class, change the contents of the main method to the following:

```
Game myGame = new PlaneDodgerGame();
LwjglApplication launcher = new LwjglApplication( myGame, "Plane Dodger", 800, 600 );
```

At this point, you are ready to begin creating the classes for the game-specific objects and the code for the gameplay itself.

Infinite Scrolling

First, background elements will be set up to provide an "infinite" scrolling effect. This requires a *seamless texture* an image that can be placed side by side with itself without creating a noticeable boundary. Two copies of such an image will be used, each of which is at least as large as the screen. The setup is illustrated in Figure 7-2; the rectangles with dashed-line boundaries contain the seamless texture, while the rectangle with the solid-line boundary represents the game screen. The left edge of image 2 is adjacent to the right edge of image 1, and they both move to the left at the same rate. When the right edge of image 1 moves completely past the left edge of the screen, image 1 will be repositioned to the opposite side; the left edge of image 1 will become adjacent to the right edge of image 2. This process continues indefinitely.

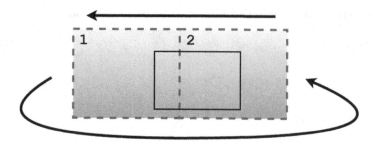

Figure 7-2. *Positioning seamless textures to produce an infinite scrolling effect*

First, you will create a sky object, which scrolls slowly to the left. The act method of this object will check if the right edge of the image has passed beyond the left edge of the screen. If so, it will shift the image to the right so that its left edge becomes aligned with the right edge of the other image, which requires moving in the x-direction by twice the width of the image. To accomplish these tasks, create a new class named Sky containing the following code:

```
import com.badlogic.gdx.scenes.scene2d.Stage;

public class Sky extends BaseActor
{
    public Sky(float x, float y, Stage s)
    {
        super(x,y,s);
        loadTexture("assets/sky.png");
        setSpeed(25);
        setMotionAngle(180);
    }

    public void act(float dt)
    {
        super.act(dt);
        applyPhysics(dt);

        // if moved completely past left edge of screen:
        //    shift right, past other instance.
        if ( getX() + getWidth() < 0 )
        {
            moveBy( 2 * getWidth(), 0 );
        }
    }
}
```

Next, you will repeat this process to create a ground object that appears to scroll forever in the same way. The code will be nearly identical, except for the image used and the speed of the object. The difference in the speeds is motivated by the following observation: if you have ever watched the scenery go by while travelling in a car or a train, you may have noticed that the more distant objects appear to change position more slowly than the closer objects. This effect, called *parallax*, provides an easy way to add an illusion of depth in a 2D game. Since the ground should appear closer to the player than the background images of the sky, the ground should be moving at a faster rate. To set up the ground object, create a new class named Ground with the following code:

```java
import com.badlogic.gdx.scenes.scene2d.Stage;

public class Ground extends BaseActor
{
    public Ground(float x, float y, Stage s)
    {
        super(x,y,s);
        loadTexture("assets/ground.png");
        setSpeed(100);
        setMotionAngle(180);
    }

    public void act(float dt)
    {
        super.act(dt);
        applyPhysics(dt);

        // if moved completely past left edge of screen:
        //   shift right, past other instance.
        if ( getX() + getWidth() < 0 )
        {
            moveBy( 2 * getWidth(), 0 );
        }
    }
}
```

To initialize two instances of each of these objects in the actual game, in the LevelScreen class, add the following code to the initialize method. (Note that these objects do not need to be stored in variables, since they can be easily accessed by the getList method of the BaseActor class at a later time.)

```java
new Sky(0,0, mainStage);
new Sky(800,0, mainStage);
new Ground(0,0, mainStage);
new Ground(800,0, mainStage);
```

This is a good point at which to test your project and verify that the scrolling works as expected; both the sky and the ground should appear to scroll to the left forever, and the ground should be moving faster than the sky, creating the illusion that the ground is closer to the player than the sky is.

The Player Plane and Simulating Gravity

Next, you will set up the plane that is controlled by the player. The plane will use an image-based animation that makes the propeller appear to be spinning. You also need to set a maximum speed and a collision polygon that is more accurate than the default rectangle. To do so, create a class named Plane with the following code:

```
import com.badlogic.gdx.scenes.scene2d.Stage;

public class Plane extends BaseActor
{
    public Plane(float x, float y, Stage s)
    {
        super(x,y,s);
        String[] filenames =
            {"assets/planeGreen0.png", "assets/planeGreen1.png",
                "assets/planeGreen2.png", "assets/planeGreen1.png"};

        loadAnimationFromFiles(filenames, 0.1f, true);

        setMaxSpeed(800);
        setBoundaryPolygon(8);
    }
}
```

No matter what the player does, the force of gravity should always be pulling the plane downward. This can be simulated by accelerating the plane at an angle of 270 degrees (which points downward). The larger the value used for acceleration, the faster the plane will fall, and the "heavier" the plane will appear to be to the player. The best place to include this code is in an act method for the Plane class, since it is automatically called in each iteration of the game loop. There are a few other tasks that are best handled in the act method:

- The plane should not fall through the ground object. This can be accomplished by checking if the plane overlaps with any of the ground objects and, if so, repositioning the plane (via the preventOverlap method) and setting the plane speed to 0. This last step is necessary, for otherwise the plane would continue to accelerate and build up speed, and eventually would build up enough speed that it could pass though the ground in a single iteration of the game loop, which would make it appear as though the plane had suddenly disappeared, which the player would consider to be a glitch (an event that should be impossible according to the mechanics of the game world).

- The plane should not be able to pass beyond the top edge of the screen. This can be accomplished by setting the world bounds in the game, and if the top edge of the plane passes beyond the top edge of the world bounds, calling the boundToWorld method and setting the plane speed to 0. In this case, the speed adjustment is necessary, because otherwise the residual speed would make the plane appear to float or stick to the top edge of the screen until the simulated gravity pulled it downward.

To handle all of these tasks, in the `Plane` class, add the following act method:

```
public void act(float dt)
{
    super.act(dt);

    // simulate force of gravity
    setAcceleration(800);
    accelerateAtAngle(270);
    applyPhysics(dt);

    // stop plane from passing through the ground
    for (BaseActor g : BaseActor.getList(this.getStage(), "Ground"))
    {
        if ( this.overlaps(g) )
        {
            setSpeed(0);
            preventOverlap(g);
        }
    }

    // stop plane from moving past top of screen
    if ( getY() + getHeight() > getWorldBounds().height )
    {
        setSpeed(0);
        boundToWorld();
    }
}
```

Finally, you need to add a way for the player to control the vertical movement of the plane. As described earlier in the chapter, the plane movement will be discrete: with each tap of the spacebar key, the plane will get a little boost of speed. Similar to the organization of the code implementing the discrete actions in the *Space Rocks* game, you will create a method in the `Plane` class that gives a boost of vertical speed to the plane, and this method will be called by the keyDown method in the `LevelScreen` class.

First, in the `Plane` class, add the following method:

```
public void boost()
{
    setSpeed(300);
    setMotionAngle(90);
}
```

Next, you will turn your attention to the `LevelScreen` class and set up the plane, the world bounds, and a keyDown method to handle discrete input. Since the plane object will be referenced in multiple methods, it will be assigned to a variable in the class for convenience. First, add the following import statement to the `LevelScreen` class:

```
import com.badlogic.gdx.Input.Keys;
```

Next, add the following variable declaration:

```
Plane plane;
```

In the `initialize` method, add the following code:

```
plane = new Plane(100, 500, mainStage);
BaseActor.setWorldBounds(800,600);
```

Finally, add the following method to the `LevelScreen` class:

```
public boolean keyDown(int keyCode)
{
    if (keyCode == Keys.SPACE)
        plane.boost();

    return true;
}
```

Now is another good time to test your game. Due to the scrolling backgrounds, it seems as though the plane is moving forward, but as you know, its x-coordinate never changes. Pressing the spacebar key should give the plane a small upward boost, and the plane should not be able to pass through the ground or beyond the top edge of the screen.

Collectibles and Obstacles

Next, you will add an objective and an obstacle to the *Plane Dodger* game. The first addition will be collectible stars that spawn regularly past the right side of the screen, then move to the left side; if the player collects a star (by colliding with it), they earn a point.

The second addition will be enemy planes, which spawn in a similar fashion. If the player's plane dodges (does not collide with) an enemy plane, they earn a point. If the player does collide with an enemy plane, then the game is over, and a message to that effect will appear on the screen. Additional variables will be used to set the speed and spawn frequency of the enemy planes, and their values will be slowly changed over time to gradually increase the difficulty level of the game. The score will be simply displayed as a number in the top-center of the screen, as illustrated in Figure 7-1.

Stars

The first addition to this project will be the star object. Create a class called `Star` that contains the following code. Since there is no image-based animation for the star, a value-based animation—a pulsing effect—is applied in the constructor for this object. Also note that in the `act` method, the star is removed from the game if it passes completely beyond the left edge of the screen; this is to reduce the amount of memory used by the game, which improves performance (the display rate might be less than 60 frames per second if there were hundreds of extra stars floating around off-screen).

```
import com.badlogic.gdx.scenes.scene2d.Stage;
import com.badlogic.gdx.scenes.scene2d.Action;
import com.badlogic.gdx.scenes.scene2d.actions.Actions;

public class Star extends BaseActor
{
    public Star(float x, float y, Stage s)
    {
        super(x,y,s);
        loadTexture("assets/star.png");
```

```
        Action pulse = Actions.sequence(
                Actions.scaleTo(1.2f,1.2f, 0.5f),
                Actions.scaleTo(1.0f,1.0f, 0.5f) );
        addAction( Actions.forever(pulse) );

        setSpeed(100);
        setMotionAngle(180);
    }

    public void act(float dt)
    {
        super.act(dt);
        applyPhysics(dt);

        // remove after moving past left edge of screen
        if ( getX() + getWidth() < 0 )
            remove();
    }
}
```

Next, you need to set up the spawning mechanic in the code for the game itself. This will require the use of a float variable (called starTimer) to keep track of the amount of time that has passed since the previous star was created. For readability, there will be a variable (called starSpawnInterval) that stores how frequently the stars will appear; the value of this variable will not change during the course of the game. At the same time, a variable needs to be created to store the player's score, and a label needs to be added to display the score. To implement these features, in the LevelScreen class, begin by adding the following import statements:

```
import com.badlogic.gdx.scenes.scene2d.ui.Label;
import com.badlogic.gdx.math.MathUtils;
```

Next, add the following variable declarations to the class:

```
float starTimer;
float starSpawnInterval;
int score;
Label scoreLabel;
```

Next, to initialize these variables (and in the case of the label, position it on the user interface), in the initialize method, add the following code:

```
starTimer = 0;
starSpawnInterval = 4;
score = 0;
scoreLabel = new Label( Integer.toString(score), BaseGame.labelStyle );
uiTable.pad(10);
uiTable.add(scoreLabel);
uiTable.row();
uiTable.add().expandY();
```

Next, in the update method, you need to spawn the stars regularly as discussed (and reset the value of starTimer after each new star is created) and check for collisions between the player's plane and the star objects (updating the score and label if that occurs). To accomplish these tasks, in the update method, add the following code:

```
starTimer += dt;
if (starTimer > starSpawnInterval)
{
    new Star( 800, MathUtils.random(100,500), mainStage );
    starTimer = 0;
}

for (BaseActor star : BaseActor.getList(mainStage, "Star"))
{
    if (plane.overlaps(star))
    {
        star.remove();
        score++;
        scoreLabel.setText( Integer.toString(score) );
    }
}
```

This is another excellent point at which to test your game. Collect stars and watch your score increase! However, the player would quickly lose interest without any obstacles to provide a challenge, which you will add next.

The Enemy Planes

In many ways, the enemy planes are similar to the stars, in that they spawn regularly and move similarly, should be removed from the game once they move past the left edge, have the power to affect the player's score, and something happens when the player collides with them. To begin, create a new class named Enemy with the following code:

```
import com.badlogic.gdx.scenes.scene2d.Stage;

public class Enemy extends BaseActor
{
    public Enemy(float x, float y, Stage s)
    {
        super(x,y,s);
        String[] filenames =
            {"assets/planeRed0.png", "assets/planeRed1.png",
                "assets/planeRed2.png", "assets/planeRed1.png"};

        loadAnimationFromFiles(filenames, 0.1f, true);

        setSpeed(100);
        setMotionAngle(180);
        setBoundaryPolygon(8);
    }
```

```
public void act(float dt)
{
    super.act(dt);
    applyPhysics(dt);
}
}
```

One difference you may notice between this class and the Star class is that in the Enemy class the act method does not contain code to remove the enemy from the game once it moves past the left edge of the screen. This is because you also want to increase the player's score when this happens, which requires that this action take place in the LevelScreen class. At this point, turn your attention to the LevelScreen class. First, add the following import statement, which is needed to load the "Game Over" message image (since it is not important enough to warrant its own class):

```
import com.badlogic.gdx.Gdx;
```

Next, add the following variable declarations:

```
float enemyTimer;
float enemySpawnInterval;
float enemySpeed;
boolean gameOver;
BaseActor gameOverMessage;
```

At the end of the initialize method, add the following code to initialize these variables:

```
enemyTimer = 0;
enemySpeed = 100;
enemySpawnInterval = 3;

gameOver = false;
gameOverMessage = new BaseActor(0,0,uiStage);
gameOverMessage.loadTexture("assets/game-over.png");
gameOverMessage.setVisible(false);
```

In addition, to place the "Game Over" message into the user interface, locate the line of code containing the statement uiTable.add().expandY() and change it to the following:

```
uiTable.add(gameOverMessage).expandY();
```

Next, at the end of the update method, add the following code, which will spawn enemy planes and check for collisions and movement off-screen, as previously described. Notice that after an enemy spawns, in addition to the value of the enemyTimer variable resetting, the enemy spawn interval is reduced and the enemy speed is increased, which increases the challenge. (Later on, you may wish to adjust the amount by which these variables are changed.) Also, a pair of conditional statements serves to check that the values of these variables do not get too small or too large, which could make the game ridiculously difficult. (For example, if the spawn rate were to become less than 0.016, then enemies would spawn every frame, resulting in a nearly continuous stream of enemies that would be impossible to dodge.)

```
enemyTimer += dt;
if (enemyTimer > enemySpawnInterval)
{
    Enemy enemy = new Enemy( 800, MathUtils.random(100,500), mainStage );
    enemy.setSpeed(enemySpeed);

    enemyTimer = 0;
    enemySpawnInterval -= 0.10f;
    enemySpeed += 10;

    if (enemySpawnInterval < 0.5f)
        enemySpawnInterval = 0.5f;

    if (enemySpeed > 400)
        enemySpeed = 400;
}

for (BaseActor enemy : BaseActor.getList(mainStage, "Enemy"))
{
    if (plane.overlaps(enemy))
    {
        plane.remove();
        gameOver = true;
        gameOverMessage.setVisible(true);
    }

    if (enemy.getX() + enemy.getWidth() < 0)
    {
        score++;
        scoreLabel.setText( Integer.toString(score) );
        enemy.remove();
    }
}
```

Finally, the purpose of the Boolean variable gameOver is to stop the stars and enemy planes from spawning and points from being awarded once the game is over. This can be accomplished by skipping the previously written code in the update method once gameOver becomes true, which you accomplish by adding the following statement to the beginning of the update method:

```
if (gameOver)
    return;
```

Once again, you have reached a good point at which to test your game. Make sure that you earn a point each time the enemy plane goes off-screen to the left and that the "Game Over" message appears (and objects stop spawning) once the player's plane collides with an enemy plane. Before considering this game to be complete, you will add a few finishing touches: special effects and audio.

Finishing Touches

Although the game mechanics have been completely implemented, some additional consideration should be paid to aesthetics. In this section, you will add some background music to help set the mood of the game, as well as visual and audio feedback (special effects and sound effects) when the player's plane collides with another object. When the plane collides with a star, a sparkling visual effect will appear, accompanied by a light, quiet tinkling sound. When the plane collides with an enemy, an explosion will appear, accompanied by a deep, rumbling, explosion-like sound. The background music is a driving instrumental piece named "Prelude and Action,"[1] and was selected to add a sense of tension and excitement to the game.

To begin adding these features, you will first create classes for the visual effects. First, create a class named Sparkle with the following code:

```
import com.badlogic.gdx.scenes.scene2d.Stage;

public class Sparkle extends BaseActor
{
    public Sparkle(float x, float y, Stage s)
    {
        super(x,y,s);

        loadAnimationFromSheet("assets/sparkle.png", 8,8, 0.02f, false);
    }

    public void act(float dt)
    {
        super.act(dt);

        if ( isAnimationFinished() )
            remove();
    }
}
```

Next, create a class named Explosion with the following code:

```
import com.badlogic.gdx.scenes.scene2d.Stage;

public class Explosion extends BaseActor
{
    public Explosion(float x, float y, Stage s)
    {
        super(x,y,s);
        loadAnimationFromSheet("assets/explosion.png", 6,6, 0.02f, false);
    }

    public void act(float dt)
    {
        super.act(dt);
```

---

[1]"Prelude and Action" was written by Kevin McLeod from http://incompetech.com and released under the Creative Commons Attribution 3.0 license.

```
        if ( isAnimationFinished() )
            remove();
    }
}
```

Next, in the LevelScreen class, add the following two import statements to enable the use of audio in your game:

```
import com.badlogic.gdx.audio.Sound;
import com.badlogic.gdx.audio.Music;
```

Next, add the following variable declarations:

```
Music backgroundMusic;
Sound sparkleSound;
Sound explosionSound;
```

To initialize these objects, add the following code at the end of the initialize method:

```
backgroundMusic = Gdx.audio.newMusic(Gdx.files.internal("assets/Prelude-and-Action.mp3"));
sparkleSound    = Gdx.audio.newSound(Gdx.files.internal("assets/sparkle.mp3"));
explosionSound  = Gdx.audio.newSound(Gdx.files.internal("assets/explosion.wav"));

backgroundMusic.setLooping(true);
backgroundMusic.setVolume(1.00f);
backgroundMusic.play();
```

To add the new features corresponding to a collision with a star, in the update method, locate the block of code following the conditional statement if (plane.overlaps(star)), and add the following:

```
Sparkle sp = new Sparkle(0,0,mainStage);
sp.centerAtActor(star);
sparkleSound.play();
```

To add the new features corresponding to a collision with an enemy plane, also in the update method, locate the block of code following the conditional statement if (plane.overlaps(enemy)), and add the following:

```
Explosion ex = new Explosion(0,0,mainStage);
ex.centerAtActor(plane);
ex.setScale(3);
explosionSound.play();
backgroundMusic.stop();
```

With these additions, the new aesthetic features have been completely added. Even though the total amount of code required to implement these features is small, the impact they have on the player's experience will be large. Once again, run your project to make sure the code works as expected. Enjoy your game!

Summary and Next Steps

In this chapter, you created the side-scrolling action game *Plane Dodger*. Using the custom framework classes developed in the first part of this book, you learned how to implement some new mechanics, such as an infinite scrolling background, parallax, gravity, and difficulty ramps.

There are still many features you could add to improve the quality of this game. Some of the easier additions include adding a start menu that is displayed before the game begins, and a button that appears after the game ends to allow the player to return to the start menu. You may also want to store the highest score achieved by the player in a variable and display it on the start menu. An ambitious addition would be to store the high score in a text file, using the skills you developed in Chapter 6, so that the high score is preserved even if the player exits the application and restarts it later. For variety, you could also consider changing the movement pattern of the enemy planes, perhaps changing their y-coordinate as they move across the screen in the pattern of a sine wave, for example. To improve the visual and audio feedback, you could add an animated exhaust-like visual effect to the player's plane that appears each time the player activates the vertical boost (similar in spirit to the appearance of the thrusters in the *Space Rocks* game), accompanied by a sound effect. You could also add an engine-like sound effect for each enemy plane that passes by. For a completely different gameplay feeling, you could consider moving the player's plane continuously rather than discretely by removing the boost method functionality and checking for keyboard input in the update method (accelerating the player's plane upward in that case). To lengthen the gameplay sessions, you could allow the player to be hit a fixed number of times by the enemy's plane before being destroyed (similar in spirit to the purpose of the shields in the *Space Rocks* game).

In the next chapter, you will once again explore the possibilities of this custom framework by creating a brick-breaking game called *Rectangle Destroyer*, where you will learn how to implement new mechanics such as bouncing and power-ups.

CHAPTER 8

■ ■ ■

Bouncing and Collision Games

In this chapter, you will create a ball-bouncing, brick-breaking game called *Rectangle Destroyer*, shown in Figure 8-1, inspired by arcade and early console games such as *Breakout* and *Arkanoid*. New features that will be implemented in this game include bouncing off of objects and power-up items.

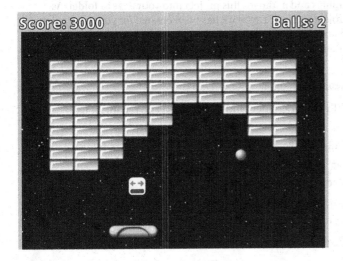

Figure 8-1. *The* Rectangle Destroyer *Game*

Game Project: Rectangle Destroyer

Rectangle Destroyer is an action game in which the player controls a paddle that moves from side to side along the bottom of the screen and uses it to bounce a ball toward the rectangular brick-like objects above to destroy them. Destroying each brick awards points to the player, and if all the bricks are destroyed, the player wins the game. If the ball falls past the bottom edge of the screen, the ball is lost. If there are any balls in reserve (the player begins with three in reserve), a new ball will be spawned above the paddle. When the ball collides with the paddle, the angle at which it bounces off is determined by the point of collision: hitting the left side of the paddle causes the ball to bounce to the left, hitting the right side causes the ball to bounce to the right, and hitting the center causes the ball to bounce straight up.

Occasionally, a destroyed brick will release an item that will drift toward the bottom of the screen. Items can have various effects on gameplay, such as changing the size of the paddle or altering the speed of the ball. The effect of the item is indicated by its image. If the paddle collects the item (by colliding with it), then the item's effect is activated. There are some items that make the game more difficult, such as the paddle-shrinking item, which the player may wish to avoid. Occasionally, collecting a beneficial item also includes the risk of missing the ball as it falls toward the bottom of the screen; the player must make decisions carefully.

The player controls the paddle by moving the mouse left and right. At the start of the game, and every time the ball is respawned, the ball will be locked to the top of the paddle and will be released when the player clicks a mouse button.

The user interface contains a few text displays. Along the top of the screen, the player's score and the number of balls in reserve are displayed. In the center of the screen, text will appear informing the player that they should click a mouse button to start the game, and a message will appear when the player has won or lost the game.

The game has a simple line-art style and has upbeat background music to match the pace of the game. Short sound effects are played when game-world objects interact: when the ball bounces off of the paddle, bricks, or walls, and when items appear and are collected.

Beginning this project requires the same steps as in previous projects: creating a new project, creating an assets folder and a +libs folder (the latter not being necessary if you have set up the userlib directory), copying the custom framework files you created in the first part of this book (BaseGame.java, BaseScreen.java, BaseActor.java), and copying the graphics and audio for this project into your assets folder. As described in the previous chapter, a BlueJ project named Framework has been created for your convenience that contains these items (except for the project-specific assets), as well as a launcher class and extensions of the BaseGame and BaseScreen classes. For efficiency, these files will be used as a starting point. To begin this project:

- Download the source code files for this chapter.

- Make a copy of the downloaded Framework folder (and its contents) and rename it to Rectangle Destroyer.

- Copy all the contents of the downloaded Rectangle Destroyer project assets folder into your newly created Rectangle Destroyer assets folder

- Open the BlueJ project in your Rectangle Destroyer folder.

- In the CustomGame class, change the name of the class to RectangleGame (BlueJ will then rename the source code file to RectangleGame.java).

- In the Launcher class, change the contents of the main method to the following:

```
Game myGame = new RectangleGame();
LwjglApplication launcher = new LwjglApplication(
        myGame, "Rectangle Destroyer", 800, 600 );
```

At this point, you are ready to begin creating the classes for the game-specific objects and the code for the gameplay itself.

Creating the Game Objects

Over the course of this section, you will create classes for the four main game objects: the paddle, the walls, the bricks, and the ball. After creating each class, you'll add code to the screen class that adds the objects to the game and enables them to interact with each other.

Paddle

First, you will create a class that represents the paddle object controlled by the player, which will be the simplest object to set up. Create a new class called `Paddle` that contains the following code:

```
import com.badlogic.gdx.scenes.scene2d.Stage;

public class Paddle extends BaseActor
{
    public Paddle(float x, float y, Stage s)
    {
        super(x,y,s);
        loadTexture("assets/paddle.png");
    }
}
```

Then, in the `LevelScreen` class, add the following `import` statement (which will enable you to get the position of the mouse later):

```
import com.badlogic.gdx.Gdx;
```

Then, add the following variable declaration to the class:

```
Paddle paddle;
```

In the `initialize` method, set up a background image and the paddle by adding the following code:

```
BaseActor background = new BaseActor(0,0, mainStage);
background.loadTexture("assets/space.png");
BaseActor.setWorldBounds(background);
paddle = new Paddle(320, 32, mainStage);
```

Then, in the `update` method, add the following code, which will keep the paddle horizontally aligned with the mouse (by adjusting its x-coordinate), while also keeping the paddle completely on the screen. (If the mouse is off-screen, however, this code will have no effect.)

```
float mouseX = Gdx.input.getX();
paddle.setX( mouseX - paddle.getWidth()/2 );
paddle.boundToWorld();
```

This is a good point at which to test your game (by running the `main` method from the `Launcher` class); you should be able to control the position of the paddle by moving the mouse; at this point, your game should appear as shown in Figure 8-2.

Figure 8-2. The game with the background image and paddle added

Walls

Next, you will create a class for the wall objects. Walls will be positioned along the left, right, and top edges of the screen, and the ball will bounce off of them. Since walls may have different sizes, the constructor of the Wall class will also take the width and the height of the wall as parameters. To this end, create a new class called Wall that contains the following code:

```
import com.badlogic.gdx.scenes.scene2d.Stage;
import com.badlogic.gdx.graphics.Color;

public class Wall extends BaseActor
{
    public Wall(float x, float y, float width, float height, Stage s)
    {
        super(x,y,s);
        loadTexture("assets/white-square.png");
        setSize(width, height);
        setColor( Color.GRAY );
        setBoundaryRectangle();
    }
}
```

If desired, the color can be set to something other than Color.GRAY. Note that since the boundary polygon is set to match the size of the texture that is loaded, changing the object size with the setSize method should be followed by calling the setBoundaryRectangle method to update this data as well.

Next, in the initialize method of the LevelScreen class, add the following code:

```
new Wall(  0,0, 20,600, mainStage); // left wall
new Wall(780,0, 20,600, mainStage); // right wall
new Wall(0,550, 800,50, mainStage); // top wall
```

192

Variables to store the Wall objects are not needed, since a list of Brick objects can be easily obtained later on using the getList method of the BaseActor class. Note in particular that the top wall has a large height; this will be to provide space for labels in the user interface, implemented later in this chapter. If desired, you can test the program again at this point to visually inspect that the walls are placed correctly.

Bricks

Next, you will add the rectangular bricks to the game. Create a new class called Brick that contains the following code:

```
import com.badlogic.gdx.scenes.scene2d.Stage;

public class Brick extends BaseActor
{
    public Brick(float x, float y, Stage s)
    {
        super(x,y,s);
        loadTexture("assets/brick-gray.png");
    }
}
```

If desired, you can use the setColor method in the constructor to tint the bricks to a particular color.

Next, you will set up a rectangular grid of bricks on the main screen. The easiest way to do this is with a nested for loop. The coordinates of each brick can be calculated in terms of the row and column position and width and height of each brick. To determine the width and height of the bricks, a single Brick object is created and removed after its size is stored. To position the grid of bricks near the center of the screen, margins are also calculated and taken into account. To implement this, in the initialize method of the LevelScreen class, add the following code:

```
Brick tempBrick = new Brick(0,0,mainStage);
float brickWidth = tempBrick.getWidth();
float brickHeight = tempBrick.getHeight();
tempBrick.remove();

int totalRows = 10;
int totalCols = 10;
float marginX = (800 - totalCols * brickWidth) / 2;
float marginY = (600 - totalRows * brickHeight) - 120;

for (int rowNum = 0; rowNum < totalRows; rowNum++)
{
    for (int colNum = 0; colNum < totalCols; colNum++)
    {
        float x = marginX + brickWidth  * colNum;
        float y = marginY + brickHeight * rowNum;
        new Brick( x, y, mainStage );
    }
}
```

Once again, you can test the project at this point to verify that the bricks appear as desired. The preceding code produces the arrangement shown in Figure 8-3; you can adjust the number of bricks in each row and column if desired by changing the values of totalRows and totalCols, or even add some spacing between the bricks by adding a small value to brickHeight and brickWidth.

***Figure 8-3.** Adding a rectangular grid of bricks*

Some games in this genre will add visual interest by creating a pixel art–style picture out of bricks of different colors. While technically possible at this point, it is not really worth the effort involved. Designing and loading a pattern of colored bricks with the assistance of a third-party program for tilemap editing will be the topic of a future chapter.

Ball

Next, you will implement the ball object. The ball will make use of the physics functionality in the BaseActor class: it will travel at a constant velocity. A small amount of gravitational force will be simulated so that the ball never gets "stuck" at a given vertical position, moving directly from the left wall to the right wall and back again. At the beginning of the game, the ball also needs to be stationary until the user clicks a mouse button. For this reason, the Ball class will include a Boolean variable called paused (and associated methods setPaused and isPaused) that controls whether the physics will be applied in the act method. To begin, create a new class called Ball with the following code:

```
import com.badlogic.gdx.scenes.scene2d.Stage;
import com.badlogic.gdx.math.Vector2;

public class Ball extends BaseActor
{
    public boolean paused;

    public Ball(float x, float y, Stage s)
    {
        super(x,y,s);
        loadTexture("assets/ball.png");
```

```
            setSpeed(400);
            setMotionAngle(90);
            setBoundaryPolygon(12);
            setPaused(true);
        }

        public boolean isPaused()
        {
            return paused;
        }

        public void setPaused(boolean b)
        {
            paused = b;
        }

        public void act(float dt)
        {
            super.act(dt);

            if ( !isPaused() )
            {
                // simulate gravity
                setAcceleration(10);
                accelerateAtAngle(270);
                applyPhysics(dt);
            }
        }
    }
}
```

In addition, the ball needs to "bounce" off of the bricks and the walls. This is accomplished with the help of the vector returned by the preventOverlap method in the BaseActor class, which represents the direction in which the actor was moved so that the actors involved no longer overlap. By comparing the x and y components of the vector, you can estimate whether the overlap was mostly along the x-direction (in which case, the ball should bounce horizontally) or the y-direction (in which case, the ball should bounce vertically). Bouncing in either direction involves reversing the velocity in that direction, which is accomplished by multiplying the corresponding component by -1. For this reason, change the velocityVec field in the BaseActor class to

```
protected Vector2 velocityVec;
```

After making this change, the Ball class can access and modify this variable. To implement this, in the Ball class, add the following method:

```
public void bounceOff(BaseActor other)
{
    Vector2 v = this.preventOverlap(other);
    if ( Math.abs(v.x) >= Math.abs(v.y) ) // horizontal bounce
        this.velocityVec.x *= -1;
    else // vertical bounce
        this.velocityVec.y *= -1;
}
```

To add a ball to the game, in the LevelScreen class, add the following variable declaration:

```
Ball ball;
```

In the initialize method, add the following line of code:

```
ball = new Ball(0,0, mainStage);
```

To lock the ball into place above the center of the paddle when the ball is paused, add the following block of code to the update method:

```
if ( ball.isPaused() )
{
    ball.setX( paddle.getX() + paddle.getWidth()/2  - ball.getWidth()/2 );
    ball.setY( paddle.getY() + paddle.getHeight()/2 + ball.getHeight()/2 );
}
```

Finally, to release the ball when the user clicks the mouse button, add the following method to the LevelScreen class:

```
public boolean touchDown(int screenX, int screenY, int pointer, int button)
{
    if ( ball.isPaused() )
    {
        ball.setPaused(false);
    }
    return false;
}
```

At this point, you can test the game once again. The ball should appear centered above the paddle as it moves back and forth, and if you click a mouse button, the ball will fly straight up toward (and past) the top edge of the screen. In the next section, you will add code to make the ball bounce off of the various game objects.

Bouncing Around

In this section, you will add the code that enables the ball to bounce off the walls, the bricks, and the paddle. The simplest of these is bouncing off the walls. In the update method of the LevelScreen class, add the following code:

```
for (BaseActor wall : BaseActor.getList(mainStage, "Wall"))
{
    if ( ball.overlaps(wall) )
    {
        ball.bounceOff(wall);
    }
}
```

Only slightly more difficult is bouncing off bricks, as these will also be destroyed when hit. In the update method of the LevelScreen class, add the following code:

```
for (BaseActor brick : BaseActor.getList(mainStage, "Brick"))
{
    if ( ball.overlaps(brick) )
    {
        ball.bounceOff(brick);
        brick.remove();
    }
}
```

Finally, you will add the code that enables the ball to bounce off the paddle. As described at the beginning of this chapter, the angle of bounce is dependent on the part of the paddle that is hit, and so the Ball class bounceOff method will not be used here. Instead, you determine the *x*-coordinate of the center of the ball and calculate how far along the paddle it lies, as a percentage: 0.00 represents the leftmost point, 0.50 represents the exact center, and 1.00 represents the rightmost point. The percentage is then used to (linearly) interpolate the angle of bounce using the MathUtils class lerp method: a percentage of 0.00 will correspond to an angle of 150 degrees (which points toward the left), a percentage of 1.00 will correspond to an angle of 30 degrees (which points towards the right), and percentages in between are interpolated correspondingly using a linear function (the equation of the line connecting these two data points). To implement this, add the following import statement to the LevelScreen class:

```
import com.badlogic.gdx.math.MathUtils;
```

Then, in the update method, add the following code.

```
if ( ball.overlaps(paddle) )
{
    float ballCenterX = ball.getX() + ball.getWidth()/2;
    float paddlePercentHit = (ballCenterX - paddle.getX()) / paddle.getWidth();
    float bounceAngle = MathUtils.lerp( 150, 30, paddlePercentHit );
    ball.setMotionAngle( bounceAngle );
}
```

At this point, you should test the game and verify that the ball bounces off the walls, bricks, and paddle as expected. It is important to note that there are two possible strange behaviors that may arise in gameplay. First, if the walls are too thin and the ball is moving too quickly, it is possible for the ball to pass through the wall in a single iteration of the game loop. If this happens while you are playtesting, you may want to cap the speed of the ball or increase the size of the walls. Also, the ball may appear to pass through bricks instead of bouncing off of them; this can happen if the ball happens to overlap two bricks at the same time; the bounceOff method is called twice, and reversing the velocity twice (for the same component) will result in the ball continuing in the same direction. There seems to be no simple or elegant approach to eliminating this behavior, but it happens infrequently in practice, so it will not be addressed here.

User Interface

Next, you will implement a simple user interface for this game: three labels, two of which will appear near the top edge of the screen and display the number of points earned and the number of balls in reserve, as shown in Figure 8-1. A third label will appear in the center of the screen and contain the message "Click to start" while the ball is paused, and messages for winning and losing the game. To begin, in the LevelScreen class, add the following import statements:

```
import com.badlogic.gdx.scenes.scene2d.ui.Label;
import com.badlogic.gdx.graphics.Color;
```

Add the following variable declarations to the class:

```
int score;
int balls;
Label scoreLabel;
Label ballsLabel;
Label messageLabel;
```

To set up these variables, in the initialize method add the following code:

```
score = 0;
balls = 3;
scoreLabel = new Label( "Score: " + score, BaseGame.labelStyle );
ballsLabel = new Label( "Balls: " + balls, BaseGame.labelStyle );
messageLabel = new Label("click to start", BaseGame.labelStyle );
messageLabel.setColor( Color.CYAN );
```

To arrange the labels using uiTable, you will create a two-row, three-column table, the center column being empty to separate scoreLabel and ballsLabel. The second row will span all three columns and contain messageLabel so that it appears near the center of the screen. This is accomplished by adding the following code to the initialize method:

```
uiTable.pad(5);
uiTable.add(scoreLabel);
uiTable.add().expandX();
uiTable.add(ballsLabel);
uiTable.row();
uiTable.add(messageLabel).colspan(3).expandY();
```

First of all, the messageLabel should disappear when the player clicks a button. In the touchDown method, in the block of code that checks if the ball is paused, add the following line of code at the end of, but inside, the if statement:

```
messageLabel.setVisible(false);
```

Next, you will earn points when a brick is destroyed. In the update method, in the block of code that checks if the ball overlaps a brick (after brick.remove()), add the following two lines of code:

```
score += 100;
scoreLabel.setText("Score: " + score);
```

If all the bricks are destroyed, a "You win!" message should be displayed. This is accomplished by adding the following code to the update method:

```
if ( BaseActor.count(mainStage, "Brick") == 0)
{
    messageLabel.setText("You win!");
    messageLabel.setColor( Color.LIME );
    messageLabel.setVisible(true);
}
```

Next, you will set up the reserve ball and respawn mechanic. If the ball moves past the bottom edge of the screen, then it should be removed from the game. If there are any balls left, a new ball should be spawned, the number of balls should be decreased, and the message label should display "Click to start" again. If there are not any balls left, then a "Game Over" message should be displayed. Note that the condition also checks that there are bricks remaining, because these messages should not be displayed if the player has already won the game. Add the following code to the update method:

```
if ( ball.getY() < -50 && BaseActor.count(mainStage, "Brick") > 0 )
{
    ball.remove();

    if (balls > 0)
    {
        balls -= 1;
        ballsLabel.setText("Balls: " + balls);
        ball = new Ball(0,0,mainStage);

        messageLabel.setText("Click to start");
        messageLabel.setColor( Color.CYAN );
        messageLabel.setVisible(true);
    }
    else
    {
        messageLabel.setText("Game Over");
        messageLabel.setColor( Color.RED );
        messageLabel.setVisible(true);
    }
}
```

At this point, your game is ready for testing again! Make sure that the score and ball labels change as expected and that the correct text appears in the message label at the correct times.

Items

To add interest and variability to the gameplay, you will next implement items. To keep track of the different types of items, you will use an enumerated type.

ENUMERATED TYPES

An *enumerated type* is a special data type you can define that consists of a set of fixed values. This is particularly useful when you want a variable to store only a certain set of values.

For example, if you want to represent a compass direction, you could create an integer variable and a set of predefined constants, as follows:

```
final int NORTH = 0;
final int SOUTH = 1;
final int EAST = 2;
final int WEST = 3;
int direction;
```

Later on, you could write code such as:

```
direction = NORTH;
```

However, this code suffers from the drawback that *any* integer value could be assigned to the direction variable, including values that do not make sense, such as:

```
direction = 4;
```

Enumerated types eliminate this problem entirely. The same functionality just described could be implemented much more robustly. Using the enum keyword, you can define an enumerated type (named Direction) and corresponding variable as follows:

```
enum Direction { NORTH, SOUTH, EAST, WEST };
Direction direction;
```

In this example, Direction is now a user-defined data type, and direction is a variable of that type. The syntax for using the values of an enumerated type is similar to that for accessing static fields defined in a class. For example, to set the value of direction to the Direction value NORTH, you would enter:

```
direction = Direction.NORTH;
```

Finally, you can compare the value of an enumerated type variable using == or the equals method, and you can obtain an array containing the values with the values method.

In this section, you will create four different types of items: two that affect the size of the paddle (one expanding it, the other shrinking it) and two that affect the speed of the ball (one increasing it, the other decreasing it). The type will be specified with an enum (called Type). Each type of item will have a corresponding image, as shown in Figure 8-4.

Figure 8-4. *Item images (paddle expand, paddle shrink, ball speed up, ball speed down)*

When items are created, the following will happen:

- A random type will be selected.

- There will be an animated effect that causes the item to grow from a point to its full size.

- The item will move toward the bottom of the screen at a constant speed.

- If the item moves past the bottom edge of the screen, it will be removed from the game.

To implement these features, create a new class named Item containing the following code. Observe that in the constructor, after changing the size of the image, the origin coordinates and the boundary shape need to be updated as well.

```
import com.badlogic.gdx.scenes.scene2d.Stage;
import com.badlogic.gdx.math.MathUtils;
import com.badlogic.gdx.scenes.scene2d.actions.Actions;

public class Item extends BaseActor
{
    public enum Type { PADDLE_EXPAND, PADDLE_SHRINK,
                       BALL_SPEED_UP, BALL_SPEED_DOWN };

    private Type type;

    public Item(float x, float y, Stage s)
    {
        super(x,y,s);
        setRandomType();

        setSpeed(100);
        setMotionAngle(270);

        setSize(50,50);
        setOrigin(25,25);
        setBoundaryRectangle();

        setScale(0,0);
        addAction( Actions.scaleTo(1,1, 0.25f) );
    }
```

```
    public void setType(Type t)
    {
        type = t;

        if (t == Type.PADDLE_EXPAND)
            loadTexture("assets/items/paddle-expand.png");
        else if (t == Type.PADDLE_SHRINK)
            loadTexture("assets/items/paddle-shrink.png");
        else if (t == Type.BALL_SPEED_UP)
            loadTexture("assets/items/ball-speed-up.png");
        else if (t == Type.BALL_SPEED_DOWN)
            loadTexture("assets/items/ball-speed-down.png");
        else
            loadTexture("assets/items/item-blank.png");
    }

    public void setRandomType()
    {
        int randomIndex = MathUtils.random(0, Type.values().length - 1);
        Type randomType = Type.values()[randomIndex];
        setType(randomType);
    }

    public Type getType()
    {
        return type;
    }

    public void act(float dt)
    {
        super.act(dt);
        applyPhysics(dt);

        if (getY() < -50)
            remove();
    }
}
```

Items should be spawned occasionally when bricks are destroyed. To implement this, in the LevelScreen class update method, locate the block of code that is run if the ball overlaps a brick and add the following. (You can adjust the value of spawnProbability as desired to make items appear more or less frequently.)

```
float spawnProbability = 20;
if ( MathUtils.random(0, 100) < spawnProbability )
{
    Item i = new Item(0,0,mainStage);
    i.centerAtActor(brick);

}
```

To implement the item effects when the paddle overlaps the item, add the following code to the update method. Note that the BaseActor objects retrieved by the getList method must be cast to Item objects in order to be able to access the getType method. Also note that after changing the size of the paddle, its boundary shape must be updated as well.

```
for (BaseActor item : BaseActor.getList(mainStage, "Item"))
{
    if ( paddle.overlaps(item) )
    {
        Item realItem = (Item)item;

        if (realItem.getType() == Item.Type.PADDLE_EXPAND)
            paddle.setWidth( paddle.getWidth() * 1.25f );
        else if (realItem.getType() == Item.Type.PADDLE_SHRINK)
            paddle.setWidth( paddle.getWidth() * 0.80f );
        else if (realItem.getType() == Item.Type.BALL_SPEED_UP)
            ball.setSpeed( ball.getSpeed() * 1.50f );
        else if (realItem.getType() == Item.Type.BALL_SPEED_DOWN)
            ball.setSpeed( ball.getSpeed() * 0.90f );

        paddle.setBoundaryRectangle();
        item.remove();
    }
}
```

Once again, it is a good opportunity to test your code, this time making sure that all the powerups work as expected. For testing purposes, you may want to temporarily increase the value of spawnProbability so that items spawn more frequently, giving you more opportunities to test the items, or you may want to set the item type after they are spawned if there is one item type in particular you would like to test.

Sounds and Music

Finally, you will add some sounds and music to the game to help set the mood and to accentuate the interactions between the objects. In particular, there will be sound effects when the ball hits a wall, when the ball hits a brick, when the ball hits the paddle, when an item is spawned, and when an item is collected. The background music is called "Rollin at 5"[1] and is an upbeat, jazzy piece appropriate to the pacing of this game. To begin, add the following import statements to the LevelScreen class:

```
import com.badlogic.gdx.audio.Sound;
import com.badlogic.gdx.audio.Music;
```

---

[1]"Rollin at 5" was written by Kevin McLeod from http://incompetech.com and released under the Creative Commons Attribution 3.0 license.

Next, add the following variable declarations to the same class:

```
Sound bounceSound;
Sound brickBumpSound;
Sound wallBumpSound;
Sound itemAppearSound;
Sound itemCollectSound;
Music backgroundMusic;
```

In the `initialize` method, add the following code:

```
bounceSound      = Gdx.audio.newSound(Gdx.files.internal("assets/boing.wav"));
brickBumpSound   = Gdx.audio.newSound(Gdx.files.internal("assets/bump.wav"));
wallBumpSound    = Gdx.audio.newSound(Gdx.files.internal("assets/bump-low.wav"));
itemAppearSound  = Gdx.audio.newSound(Gdx.files.internal("assets/swoosh.wav"));
itemCollectSound = Gdx.audio.newSound(Gdx.files.internal("assets/pop.wav"));

backgroundMusic = Gdx.audio.newMusic(Gdx.files.internal("assets/Rollin-at-5.mp3"));
backgroundMusic.setLooping(true);
backgroundMusic.setVolume(0.50f);
backgroundMusic.play();
```

Next, you will add the lines of code that play the sound effects at the appropriate moments, all of which occur in the `update` method. In the block of code following the conditional statement that checks if the ball overlaps the wall, directly after the line of code that makes the ball bounce off the wall, add the code:

```
wallBumpSound.play();
```

In the block of code following the conditional statement that checks if the ball overlaps a brick, directly after the line of code that makes the ball bounce off the brick, add the code:

```
brickBumpSound.play();
```

After the line of code that spawns a new `Item` object, add the code:

```
itemAppearSound.play();
```

In the block of code following the conditional statement that checks if the ball overlaps the paddle, directly after the line of code that sets the angle of motion after the ball, add the code:

```
bounceSound.play();
```

Finally, in the block of code following the conditional statement that checks if the paddle overlaps an item, directly after the line of code that removes the item from the stage, add the code:

```
itemCollectSound.play();
```

Test your project to verify that the music and sounds play as expected.
Congratulations—you have finished creating the *Rectangle Destroyer* game!

Summary and Next Steps

In this chapter, you created the ball-bouncing, brick-breaking action game *Rectangle Destroyer*. You learned how to simulate bouncing and how to use enumerated types in the process of creating collectible items that affect the gameplay.

As always, there are many features you could add to improve the quality of this game, such as a start menu that is displayed before the game begins. You could add more sounds corresponding to game-object interaction, such as a sound when the ball is lost, when the player wins the game, and when the player loses the game. You could add some solid, moving objects in the brick area that knock the ball around. Most of all, you may want to consider creating some additional powerups. Some ideas for extra item effects are:

- bonus points added to score

- an extra reserve ball

- change the size of the ball (smaller or larger)

- destroy a random brick

- stop the paddle from moving for 1–3 seconds

In the next chapter, you will learn how to implement a completely different game mechanic: drag-and-drop functionality, a key aspect of card-based and puzzle-based games.

CHAPTER 9

■ ■ ■

Drag-and-Drop Games

In this chapter, you will learn how to add drag-and-drop functionality to your games: the ability to click on an object and, while the mouse button is held down, have the selected object move along with the mouse until the button is released. Since this functionality is useful in many contexts, you will create an extension of the BaseActor class, called DragAndDropActor, containing the related code. To demonstrate the flexibility of this new class, you will create two new games that make use of this class. The first will be a jigsaw-puzzle game, shown in Figure 9-1, which consists of an image that has been broken into pieces and must be rearranged correctly on a grid. The second will be a solitaire card game called *52 Card Pickup*, shown in Figure 9-2, where a standard deck of playing cards must be correctly arranged in a set of piles.

Figure 9-1. *A jigsaw-puzzle game*

© Lee Stemkoski 2018
L. Stemkoski, *Java Game Development with LibGDX*, https://doi.org/10.1007/978-1-4842-3324-5_9

Figure 9-2. *A solitaire card game*

Beginning this project requires the same steps as in previous projects: creating a new project, creating an assets folder and a +libs folder (the latter not being necessary if you have set up the userlib directory), copying the custom framework files you created in the first part of this book (BaseGame.java, BaseScreen. java, BaseActor.java), and copying the graphics and audio for this project into your assets folder. As described in the previous chapter, a BlueJ project named Framework has been created for your convenience that contains these items (except for the project-specific assets), as well as a launcher class and extensions of the BaseGame and BaseScreen classes. For efficiency, these files will be used as a starting point. To begin the first project:

- Download the source code files for this chapter.

- Make a copy of the downloaded Framework folder (and its contents) and rename it to Jigsaw Puzzle (as usual, you do not need the +libs folder if using the userlibs folder to store JAR files).

- Copy all the contents of the downloaded Jigsaw Puzzle project assets folder into your newly created Jigsaw Puzzle assets folder.

- Open the BlueJ project in your Jigsaw Puzzle folder.

- In the CustomGame class, change the name of the class to JigsawPuzzleGame (BlueJ will then rename the source code file to JigsawPuzzleGame.java).

- In the Launcher class, change the contents of the main method to the following:

```
Game myGame = new JigsawPuzzleGame ();
LwjglApplication launcher = new LwjglApplication(
        myGame, "Jigsaw Puzzle Game", 800, 600 );
```

In the next section, you will create classes that encapsulate the drag-and-drop functionality for both this game project and the next. Unfortunately, there will be no way to test the functionality of the drag-and-drop actor classes until the game projects themselves are well under way.

Drag-and-Drop Functionality

The first step in developing the new DragAndDropActor class is to consider what functionality is required. Most importantly, this class will need to be able to respond to user input. When originally creating the BaseScreen class, you implemented the InputProcessor interface, which allowed the game to respond to mouse and touch input via methods such as touchDown, touchDragged, and touchUp. Similarly, the Actor class (and, by extension, the Group class, which is what the BaseActor class is based on) contains a method named addListener, which allows you to attach an InputListener object to the actor with implementations of the same methods as the InputProcessor class. The touch methods have the following method signatures:

```
public void touchDown(InputEvent event, float x, float y, int pointer, int button)

public void touchDragged(InputEvent event, float x, float y, int pointer)

public void touchUp(InputEvent event, float x, float y, int pointer, int button)
```

The most important point to note regarding the touch methods is that the float parameters x and y of these methods store the coordinates of the mouse *relative* to the object being clicked—they represent offsets, not absolute positions. For example, if an object has a width of 200 pixels and a height of 300 pixels, clicking in the center of this object would set the value of x to 100 and value of y to 150, regardless of where the object is located on the screen. For this reason, to calculate how much to move the actor by in the touchDragged method, you need to store the original x and y offsets received from the touchDown method.

With this knowledge, you are now ready to begin writing some code. To begin, create a new class named DragAndDropActor containing the following code. Note that a reference to the actor itself needs to be stored in the variable self in order to access the class variables grabOffsetX and grabOffsetY within the context of the InputListener methods. The keyword this is a reference to the object whose method is being invoked. In the InputListener, this would refer to the InputListener itself, whereas you need to refer to the DragAndDropActor, thus necessitating the use of the extra variable self.

```
import com.badlogic.gdx.scenes.scene2d.Stage;
import com.badlogic.gdx.scenes.scene2d.InputListener;
import com.badlogic.gdx.scenes.scene2d.InputEvent;

/**
 *  Enables drag-and-drop functionality for actors.
 */
public class DragAndDropActor extends BaseActor
{
    private DragAndDropActor self;

    private float grabOffsetX;
    private float grabOffsetY;

    public DragAndDropActor(float x, float y, Stage s)
    {
        super(x,y,s);

        self = this;
```

```java
        addListener(
            new InputListener()
            {
                public boolean touchDown(InputEvent event, float offsetX, float offsetY,
                                        int pointer, int button)
                {
                    self.grabOffsetX = offsetX;
                    self.grabOffsetY = offsetY;

                    self.toFront();

                    return true;
                }

                public void touchDragged(InputEvent event, float offsetX, float offsetY,
                                        int pointer)
                {
                    float deltaX = offsetX - self.grabOffsetX;
                    float deltaY = offsetY - self.grabOffsetY;

                    self.moveBy(deltaX, deltaY);
                }

                public void touchUp(InputEvent event, float offsetX, float offsetY,
                                    int pointer, int button)
                {
                    // will add code later
                }
            }
        );
    }

    public void act(float dt)
    {
        super.act(dt);
    }
}
```

As it stands, the preceding code allows an object to be dragged across the screen. However, you will often want such an object to interact with another type of object on which it is dropped. For example, in the jigsaw-puzzle game, you will want to drop puzzle pieces on particular board areas, while in the card game you will want to drop cards on particular piles. To this end, you will create another class that represents an object that can be targeted by a DragAndDropActor. You will also include a Boolean variable that can be used to indicate whether the object can be targeted. This can be important for games in which you eventually want to disable the drop-target functionality for particular targets. For example, in the jigsaw-puzzle game, once you have dropped a puzzle piece on a certain area, you will not want to be able to drop a second piece onto the same area. Create a new class named DropTargetActor containing the following code:

```
import com.badlogic.gdx.scenes.scene2d.Stage;

public class DropTargetActor extends BaseActor
{
    private boolean targetable;

    public DropTargetActor(float x, float y, Stage s)
    {
        super(x,y,s);
        targetable = true;
    }

    public void setTargetable(boolean t)
    {
        targetable = t;
    }

    public boolean isTargetable()
    {
        return targetable;
    }
}
```

Next, you will return to the DragAndDropActor class to add functionality for interacting with DropTargetActor objects. In the touchUp method of the InputListener, you will identify the DropTargetActor that the DragAndDropActor was dropped upon (if any), storing it in a variable for later access. The main part of this method involves a for loop over the set of DropTargetActor objects attached to the stage that are both targetable and overlap the actor being dragged. However, a bit of extra code is required to handle the case where the dragged actor overlaps two or more drop targets. In this case, you will want to select the target that is *closest* to the dragged actor. To do so, in the loop you will keep track of the distance from the dragged actor to the candidate drop target, and if this distance is smaller than the closest distance encountered thus far, the candidate will be set as the new drop target.

In the DragAndDropActor class, add the following import statement:

```
import com.badlogic.gdx.math.Vector2;
```

Add the following variable declaration to the class:

```
private DropTargetActor dropTarget;
```

In the touchUp method of the InputListener, add the following code:

```
self.setDropTarget(null);

// keep track of distance to closest object
float closestDistance = Float.MAX_VALUE;
```

211

```
for ( BaseActor actor : BaseActor.getList(self.getStage(), "DropTargetActor") )
{
    DropTargetActor target = (DropTargetActor)actor;

    if ( target.isTargetable() && self.overlaps(target) )
    {
        float currentDistance =
            Vector2.dst(self.getX(),self.getY(), target.getX(),target.getY());

        // check if this target is even closer
        if (currentDistance < closestDistance)
        {
            self.setDropTarget(target);
            closestDistance = currentDistance;
        }
    }
}
```

Also, to work with the dropTarget variable, add the following methods to the DragAndDropActor class:

```
public boolean hasDropTarget()
{   return (dropTarget != null);   }

public void setDropTarget(DropTargetActor dt)
{   dropTarget = dt;   }

public DropTargetActor getDropTarget()
{   return dropTarget;   }
```

There are a few minor additions left for the DragAndDropActor class. First, you will add the ability to disable the drag functionality. This is useful if you want to lock an object in position. For example, in the solitaire card game, once a card is moved to the correct pile, you don't want to move it off the pile. To do this, add the following variable declaration to the DragAndDropActor class:

```
private boolean draggable;
```

Initialize this value in the class constructor by adding the following line of code:

```
draggable = true;
```

Add the following methods to work with the draggable variable:

```
public void setDraggable(boolean d)
{   draggable = d;   }

public boolean isDraggable()
{   return draggable;   }
```

In the beginning of the touchDown method of the InputListener, add the following code, which will cancel the drag action and stop the touchDragged and touchUp methods from being activated by returning false when draggable has been set to false.

```
if ( !self.isDraggable() )
    return false;
```

The next additions will be some convenience methods that automatically move this actor to the center of another actor, or move the actor to its original position (at the moment when the drag began). For example, in the solitaire card game, when dropping a card onto the correct pile, you will want to center it on that pile. Conversely, when dropping a card onto an incorrect pile, you will want to return it to its original position so that the pile is not obscured. To accomplish this, begin by adding the following import statements to the DragAndDropActor class. The Interpolation class is used to modify the actor movement, smoothing out the transition at the beginning and end of the action.

```
import com.badlogic.gdx.math.Interpolation;
import com.badlogic.gdx.scenes.scene2d.actions.Actions;
```

Add the following variable declarations to the class:

```
private float startPositionX;
private float startPositionY;
```

In the touchDown method of the InputListener, add the following code after the values of grabOffsetX and grabOffsetY are set:

```
self.startPositionX = self.getX();
self.startPositionY = self.getY();
```

Finally, add the following methods to the class. The Interpolation object is used to slow down the movement at the beginning and end of the motion, which makes it appear more natural.

```
public void moveToActor(BaseActor other)
{
    float x = other.getX() + (other.getWidth()  - this.getWidth()) / 2;
    float y = other.getY() + (other.getHeight() - this.getHeight()) / 2;
    addAction( Actions.moveTo(x,y, 0.50f, Interpolation.pow3) );
}

public void moveToStart()
{
    addAction( Actions.moveTo(startPositionX, startPositionY, 0.50f, Interpolation.pow3) );
}
```

The next addition is a subtle visual effect that adds to the sense of immersion. When dragging an object, the player often imagines the object being raised above the play area, and when dropping the object, the player imagines the object being lowered back down to the play area. Objects that are closer to the player should appear slightly larger; this can be accomplished by adding an action to scale the image to a larger size when the drag begins and then scale the image to its original size when the drag ends. To accomplish this, in the touchDown method, right before the last line of code, add the following:

```
self.addAction( Actions.scaleTo(1.1f, 1.1f, 0.25f) );
```

213

Then, at the end of the touchUp method, add the following:

```
self.addAction( Actions.scaleTo(1.00f, 1.00f, 0.25f) );
```

The final addition will simplify the use of the DragAndDropActor class in your actual games. In games that make use of the DragAndDropActor and the DropTargetActor classes, you will typically extend these classes with custom classes representing the specific entities in your game. To add extra functionality to when the drag starts and when the object is dropped, you will add two extra functions to the DragAndDropActor class, named onDragStart and onDrop, which are called at the end of the touchDown and touchUp methods, respectively. In this class, the methods will contain no code; they are meant to be overridden by the extending classes. In the DragAndDropActor class, add the following two methods:

```
public void onDragStart()
{    }

public void onDrop()
{    }
```

Then, in the touchDown method, right before the last statement, add the following line of code:

```
self.onDragStart();
```

Finally, at the end of the touchUp method, add the following line of code:

```
self.onDrop();
```

With these additions, the DragAndDropActor class is complete, and you are ready to begin creating the game-specific objects for the *Jigsaw Puzzle* game.

Game Project: Jigsaw Puzzle

In the *Jigsaw Puzzle* game, an image will be broken up into smaller pieces, which must then be dragged and dropped onto the correct location on a grid of squares. The pieces are randomly positioned on the left side of the screen, while the areas on which they should be dropped are positioned on the right side of the screen. Once a piece is dropped onto a square area, it will automatically align itself to the area, and no other pieces may be dropped on that particular area, although the piece may be repositioned, thus freeing up the area once again.

There are only two game-specific objects that need to be created for this project: a class named PuzzlePiece, which represents the individual pieces and will extend DragAndDropActor, and a class named PuzzleArea, which represents the grid squares on which pieces will be dropped and will extend DropTargetActor. When the puzzle pieces are initialized, a row and column value will be stored that indicates its location in the original image. The puzzle-area objects will also store a row and column value, indicating their position in the grid of area objects. When the puzzle piece and puzzle area row and column values are equal, the piece will be considered to be in the correct position, and when all the pieces are in the correct position, the player will have won the game, and a "You win" message will appear on the screen.

To begin, create a new class called PuzzleArea that contains the following code, which provides the functionality previously described:

```
import com.badlogic.gdx.scenes.scene2d.Stage;

public class PuzzleArea extends DropTargetActor
{
    private int row;
    private int col;

    public PuzzleArea(float x, float y, Stage s)
    {
        super(x,y,s);
        loadTexture("assets/border.jpg");
    }

    public void setRow(int r)
    {   row = r;   }

    public void setCol(int c)
    {   col = c;   }

    public int getRow()
    {   return row;   }

    public int getCol()
    {   return col;   }
}
```

Next, you will set up the class for the puzzle pieces. In addition to variables that store its correct row and column values, there will also be a variable that stores the area upon which the piece is currently positioned (if any) and a method to check if the piece is currently placed correctly. Create a new class called PuzzlePiece containing the following code:

```
import com.badlogic.gdx.scenes.scene2d.Stage;

public class PuzzlePiece extends DragAndDropActor
{
    private int row;
    private int col;

    private PuzzleArea puzzleArea;

    public PuzzlePiece(float x, float y, Stage s)
    {
        super(x,y,s);
    }

    public void setRow(int r)
    {   row = r;   }
```

215

```java
    public void setCol(int c)
    {  col = c;  }

    public int getRow()
    {  return row;  }

    public int getCol()
    {  return col;  }

    public void setPuzzleArea(PuzzleArea pa)
    {  puzzleArea = pa;  }

    public PuzzleArea getPuzzleArea()
    {  return puzzleArea;  }

    public void clearPuzzleArea()
    {  puzzleArea = null;  }

    public boolean hasPuzzleArea()
    {  return puzzleArea != null;  }

    public boolean isCorrectlyPlaced()
    {
        return hasPuzzleArea()
        && this.getRow() == puzzleArea.getRow()
        && this.getCol() == puzzleArea.getCol();
    }
}
```

In addition, a majority of the game logic will be handled in this class by overriding the onDragStart and onDrop methods from the DragAndDropActor class. In particular, when the piece is dropped, if there is an available (targetable) puzzle area underneath it, the piece will be moved to that area, the piece's corresponding puzzle-area variable will be set, and that particular area will not be targetable. Also, when a piece is dragged, if there was a corresponding puzzle area set, that area becomes targetable again, and the piece's corresponding puzzle-area variable will be cleared. To accomplish these tasks, add the following two methods to the PuzzlePiece class:

```java
// override methods from DragAndDropActor class
public void onDragStart()
{
    if ( hasPuzzleArea() )
    {
        PuzzleArea pa = getPuzzleArea();
        pa.setTargetable(true);
        clearPuzzleArea();
    }
}
```

```
public void onDrop()
{
    if ( hasDropTarget() )
    {
        PuzzleArea pa = (PuzzleArea)getDropTarget();
        moveToActor(pa);
        setPuzzleArea(pa);
        pa.setTargetable(false);
    }
}
```

With these classes in place, you are ready to turn your attention to the LevelScreen class. To begin, you will load an image, split it into smaller regions (as shown in Figure 9-3), and load these images into PuzzlePiece objects randomly positioned on the left side of the screen.

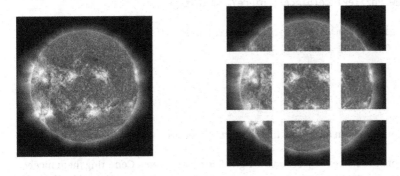

Figure 9-3. *Image split into smaller images for puzzle pieces*

In the LevelScreen class, add the following import statements:

```
import com.badlogic.gdx.Gdx;
import com.badlogic.gdx.graphics.Texture;
import com.badlogic.gdx.graphics.g2d.TextureRegion;
import com.badlogic.gdx.math.MathUtils;
import com.badlogic.gdx.graphics.g2d.Animation;
```

Then, in the initialize method, add the following code. Note in particular the use of the TextureRegion class split method, which is perfectly suited to the needs of this game, as it takes an image and creates a two-dimensional array of sub-images. Without this method, the creation of the puzzle-piece images would be much more difficult. Also note that since BaseActor objects use animations, the TextureRegion objects must be loaded into Animation objects in order to be used by the BaseActor class.

```
BaseActor background = new BaseActor(0,0, mainStage);
background.loadTexture("assets/background.jpg");

int numberRows = 3;
int numberCols = 3;
```

```
Texture texture = new Texture(Gdx.files.internal("assets/sun.jpg"), true);
int imageWidth   = texture.getWidth();
int imageHeight  = texture.getHeight();
int pieceWidth   = imageWidth  / numberCols;
int pieceHeight  = imageHeight / numberRows;

TextureRegion[][] temp = TextureRegion.split(texture, pieceWidth, pieceHeight);

for (int r = 0; r < numberRows; r++)
{
    for (int c = 0; c < numberCols; c++)
    {
        // create puzzle piece at random location on left half of screen
        int pieceX = MathUtils.random(0, 400 - pieceWidth);
        int pieceY = MathUtils.random(0, 600 - pieceHeight);
        PuzzlePiece pp = new PuzzlePiece(pieceX, pieceY, mainStage);

        Animation<TextureRegion> anim = new Animation<TextureRegion>(1, temp[r][c]);
        pp.setAnimation( anim );
        pp.setRow(r);
        pp.setCol(c);
    }
}
```

At this point, you can test your program and verify that the puzzle pieces can be dragged and dropped around the screen.

Next, you will set up a grid of PuzzleArea objects on the right side of the screen. Centering them nicely requires a bit of calculation to determine the margins to use, as seen next. In the innermost for loop in the initialize method, add the following code:

```
int marginX = (400 - imageWidth)/2;
int marginY = (600 - imageHeight)/2;

int areaX = (400 + marginX) + pieceWidth * c;
int areaY = (600 - marginY - pieceHeight) - pieceHeight * r;

PuzzleArea pa = new PuzzleArea(areaX, areaY, mainStage);
pa.setSize(pieceWidth, pieceHeight);
pa.setBoundaryRectangle();
pa.setRow(r);
pa.setCol(c);
```

Finally, you will set up a label to display a "You win" message once all the pieces are in their correct positions. In the LevelScreen class, add the following import statements:

```
import com.badlogic.gdx.scenes.scene2d.ui.Label;
import com.badlogic.gdx.graphics.Color;
```

Next, add the following variable declaration to the class:

```
private Label messageLabel;
```

218

To set up the label and position it in the lower central area of the screen, add the following code to the end of the `initialize` method:

```
messageLabel = new Label("...", BaseGame.labelStyle);
messageLabel.setColor( Color.CYAN );
uiTable.add(messageLabel).expandX().expandY().bottom().pad(50);
messageLabel.setVisible(false);
```

Finally, the place you will check whether the puzzle has been solved correctly is in the `update` method. One way to handle this logic is to begin by assuming that the puzzle is solved, then check all the pieces; if *any* are not correctly placed, then the puzzle is *not* solved. To implement this, in the `update` method, add the following code:

```
boolean solved = true;
for (BaseActor actor : BaseActor.getList(mainStage, "PuzzlePiece"))
{
    PuzzlePiece pp = (PuzzlePiece)actor;

    if ( !pp.isCorrectlyPlaced() )
        solved = false;
}

if (solved)
{
    messageLabel.setText("You win!");
    messageLabel.setVisible(true);
}
else
{
    messageLabel.setText("...");
    messageLabel.setVisible(false);
}
```

With this addition, the *Jigsaw Puzzle* game is complete! Test the program and make sure that after placing the pieces in the correct areas, the "You win!" message appears. Feel free to split the image into a different number of regions, or use an entirely different image altogether (although the image should be small enough that it fits within the right half of the window; 400 pixels by 600 pixels is the largest size that will fit).
- To demonstrate the versatility of the drag-and-drop classes you have created, you will now create a second game using these classes where the player will drag and drop playing cards instead of puzzle pieces.

Game Project: 52 Card Pickup

In the solitaire card game *52 Card Pickup*, the 52 cards of a standard deck of playing cards are scattered around randomly; the goal is to arrange the cards into piles. There are four different piles corresponding to the four card suits: Clubs, Hearts, Spades, and Diamonds. In each pile, the cards must be arranged by rank: starting with the Ace (A), followed by 2, 3, 4, 5, 6, 7, 8, 9, 10, Jack (J), Queen (Q), and King (K). If a card is dropped onto the correct pile (meaning that it has the same suit and the rank following the top card on the pile), then it will automatically align itself to the pile. Otherwise, the card will be returned to its original position so as to not obscure the card currently on top of the pile. Once all cards have been added to the correct piles, a "You win!" message will appear on the screen.

Once again, there are only two game-specific objects that need to be created for this project: a class named Card, which represents the individual playing cards and will extend DragAndDropActor, and a class named Pile, which will be the areas on which cards will be dropped and will extend DropTargetActor.

Beginning this project requires the same steps as before: creating a new project, creating an assets folder and a +libs folder (the latter not being necessary if you have set up the userlib directory), copying the custom framework files from a previous project (or from the BlueJ project named Framework), and copying the graphics and audio for this project into your assets folder. To begin this project:

- Download the source code files for this chapter (if you haven't already).

- Make a copy of the downloaded Framework folder (and its contents) and rename it to 52 Card Pickup.

- Copy all the contents of the downloaded 52 Card Pickup project assets folder into your newly created 52 Card Pickup assets folder.

- Open the BlueJ project in your 52 Card Pickup folder.

- In the CustomGame class, change the name of the class to PickupGame (BlueJ will then rename the source code file to PickupGame.java).

- In the Launcher class, change the contents of the main method to the following:

```
Game myGame = new PickupGame();
LwjglApplication launcher = new LwjglApplication(
        myGame, "52 Card Pickup", 800, 600 );
```

In addition, you will need to copy your recently created classes, DragAndDropActor and DropTargetActor, into this project.

Once your project files are set up, the first step will be to create a class to represent the card objects. To simplify comparison, the rank and suit of each card will be stored as an integer variable, but the Card class will contain the names of the ranks and suits as well for convenience. If you examine the contents of the assets folder for this project, you will see that the naming convention for the card images is the word *card*, followed by the suit name, followed by the rank name (although single letters are used for Ace, Jack, Queen, and King). When the rank and suit values are set, the corresponding names will be determined and used to load the corresponding image into the actor. Create a new class named Card that contains the following code:

```java
import com.badlogic.gdx.scenes.scene2d.Stage;

public class Card extends DragAndDropActor
{
    public static String[] rankNames = {"A", "2", "3", "4", "5", "6",
                                    "7", "8", "9", "10", "J", "Q", "K"};
    public static String[] suitNames = {"Clubs", "Hearts", "Spades", "Diamonds"};

    private int rankValue;
    private int suitValue;

    public Card(float x, float y, Stage s)
    {
        super(x,y,s);
    }

    public void setRankValue(int r)
    {   rankValue = r;  }
```

```
    public int getRankValue()
    {   return rankValue;   }

    public String getRankName()
    {   return rankNames[ getRankValue() ];   }

    public void setSuitValue(int s)
    {   suitValue = s;   }

    public int getSuitValue()
    {   return suitValue;   }

    public String getSuitName()
    {   return suitNames[ getSuitValue() ];   }

    public void setRankSuitValues(int r, int s)
    {
        setRankValue(r);
        setSuitValue(s);
        String imageFileName = "assets/card" + getSuitName() + getRankName() + ".png";
        loadTexture(imageFileName);
        setSize(80,100);
        setBoundaryRectangle();
    }

    public void act(float dt)
    {
        super.act(dt);
        boundToWorld();
    }
}
```

Next, you will create a class to represent the piles to which the cards will be added in ascending order of rank and matching suit. In addition to being the drop target for the cards, each pile will store a list of cards that have been added to the pile. An ArrayList will be used for this purpose, and a few methods will be created to add a card to the "top" of the pile (array index 0), to access the card in that position, and to determine the size of the list (which will be used when checking if the player has won the game). To this end, create a new class called Pile with the following code:

```
import com.badlogic.gdx.scenes.scene2d.Stage;
import java.util.ArrayList;

public class Pile extends DropTargetActor
{
    private ArrayList<Card> cardList;

    public Pile(float x, float y, Stage s)
    {
        super(x,y,s);
        cardList = new ArrayList<Card>();
        loadTexture("assets/pile.png");
```

```
        setSize(100,120);
        setBoundaryRectangle();
    }

    public void addCard(Card c)
    {
        cardList.add(0, c);
    }

    public Card getTopCard()
    {
        return cardList.get(0);
    }

    public int getSize()
    {
        return cardList.size();
    }
}
```

Now that the Pile class has been created, you can write the code for the interaction between Card and Pile objects. In particular, when a Card object is dropped onto the correct Pile object (as described in the beginning of this section), it will be added to the pile's list and moved to align with the pile. If a Card is dropped onto an incorrect Pile object, it will be moved back to its original position. To implement this, in the Card class, add the following method (which overrides the onDrop method in the DragAndDropActor class):

```
public void onDrop()
{
    if ( hasDropTarget() )
    {
        Pile pile = (Pile)getDropTarget();
        Card topCard = pile.getTopCard();

        if (this.getRankValue() == topCard.getRankValue() + 1
         && this.getSuitValue() == topCard.getSuitValue() )
        {
            moveToActor(pile);
            pile.addCard(this);
        }
        else
        {
            // avoid blocking view of pile when incorrect
            moveToStart();
        }
    }
}
```

At this point, the Card and Pile classes are complete, and it is time to turn your attention to the LevelScreen class. First, you will initialize the 52 card objects at random positions on the lower part of the screen. In the LevelScreen class, add the following import statement:

```
import com.badlogic.gdx.math.MathUtils;
```

Next, in the `initialize` method, add the following code:

```
BaseActor background = new BaseActor(0,0, mainStage);
background.loadTexture("assets/felt.jpg");
BaseActor.setWorldBounds(background);

for (int r = 0; r < Card.rankNames.length; r++)
{
    for (int s = 0; s < Card.suitNames.length; s++)
    {
        int x = MathUtils.random(0,800);
        int y = MathUtils.random(0,300);
        Card c = new Card(x,y, mainStage);
        c.setRankSuitValues(r,s);
    }
}
```

At this point, you can test your program, and you should see all 52 cards on the bottom area of the screen. However, you may notice that the low-rank cards (Ace, 2, 3, etc.) are usually buried underneath the high-rank cards (Jack, Queen, King), as shown in Figure 9-4.

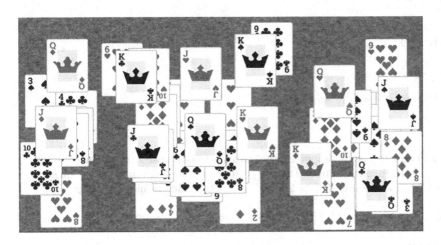

Figure 9-4. *High-rank cards appearing on top of low-rank cards*

This is happening because the high-rank cards are initialized and added to the stage later, and thus they render later and appear "on top." This would make it difficult for the player to locate the cards they need and could lead to frustration. To remedy this situation, you can alter the rendering order (also known as *z-order*) of the cards. After each card is initialized, you will send it to the back of the stage; thus, the high-rank cards will appear under the low-rank cards. To accomplish this, at the end of the inner `for` loop from the code you just added, add the following code:

```
c.toBack();
```

However, if you were to run your program at this point, it would seem that all the cards have disappeared! The reason for this is that the cards are being instructed to render before every other actor that has been added to the stage—including the background image! To remedy this, after the for loops in the initialize method, add the following code:

```
background.toBack();
```

Now, if you test your program, you will see that all the cards appear as desired, with the low-rank cards appearing on top.

Next, you will set up the four piles to which the cards will be added. The piles themselves will be stored in an ArrayList to provide a simpler way to associate a number (and thus, a suit) with each Pile object. First, in the LevelScreen class, add the following import statement.

```
import java.util.ArrayList;
```

Next, add the following variable declaration to the class:

```
private ArrayList<Pile> pileList;
```

At the end of the initialize method, add the following code to create four Pile objects, arranged along the top edge of the screen:

```
pileList = new ArrayList<Pile>();
for (int i = 0; i < 4; i++)
{
    int pileX = 120 + 150 * i;
    int pileY = 450;
    Pile pile = new Pile(pileX, pileY, mainStage);
    pileList.add(pile);
}
```

If you were to run the code at this point, dropping a card on a pile would cause an error, since the pile lists do not yet contain any cards. To remedy this and to help get the player started, you will place the Ace (rank 0) cards on the piles. To do so, at the end of the initialize method, add the following code:

```
for ( BaseActor actor : BaseActor.getList(mainStage, "Card") )
{
    Card card = (Card)actor;
    if ( card.getRankValue() == 0 )
    {
        Pile pile = pileList.get( card.getSuitValue() );
        card.toFront();
        card.moveToActor(pile);
        pile.addCard(card);
        card.setDraggable(false);
    }
}
```

At this point, you may test your game, and you will find that it is playable. To provide a sense of closure for the player at the end of the game, you will now add a label that displays a "You win!" message once each of the piles contains all 13 cards of the corresponding suit in the correct order. In the LevelScreen class, add the following import statements:

```
import com.badlogic.gdx.scenes.scene2d.ui.Label;
import com.badlogic.gdx.graphics.Color;
```

Then, add the following variable declaration to the same class:

```
private Label messageLabel;
```

At the end of the initialize method, add the following code (which is identical to the corresponding code from the *Jigsaw Puzzle* game project):

```
messageLabel = new Label("...", BaseGame.labelStyle);
messageLabel.setColor( Color.CYAN );
uiTable.add(messageLabel).expandX().expandY().bottom().pad(50);
messageLabel.setVisible(false);
```

Finally, to determine if the player has won the game, you will use a logical approach similar to the *Jigsaw Puzzle* game: in the update method, begin by assuming the player has won the game, then check all the piles; if *any* pile contains less than 13 cards, then the cards have *not* all been correctly placed. To implement this, in the update method, add the following code:

```
boolean complete = true;
for (Pile pile : pileList)
{
    if ( pile.getSize() < 13 )
        complete = false;
}

if (complete)
{
    messageLabel.setText("You win!");
    messageLabel.setVisible(true);
}
```

With this addition, the *52 Card Pickup* game is complete! Test the program and make sure that after placing all the cards on the correct piles, the "You win!" message appears.

Summary and Next Steps

In this chapter, you created a pair of classes, DragAndDropActor and DropTargetActor, which implement drag-and-drop functionality. You implemented the corresponding methods using the methods touchDown, touchDragged, and touchUp within an InputListener object. You then demonstrated the flexibility of these classes by creating two games: a jigsaw-puzzle game and a solitaire card game.

As usual, many potential features could be added to these games. Both games would benefit from some subtle sound effects corresponding to when the pieces/cards appear to be lifted and dropped, similar to the sound of a piece of paper being slid off the top of a pile. You might also consider playing an effect when a puzzle piece is dropped onto an available area, making it sound like it has clicked into place. Similarly, you might consider a metallic tinging sound when a card is dropped onto the correct pile, or in the case of a card dropped onto an incorrect pile, a soft whooshing sound to accompany the card's movement back to its original position. Some sample sound files have been included for your convenience in the `Jigsaw Puzzle` project `assets` folder. If you choose to implement sound effects, the simplest approach is to add the `Sound` objects to the `PuzzlePiece` class and play the sounds in the `onDragStart` and `onDrop` methods.

To give players a measure of their performance in these games, you might want to include a label that displays the amount of time the player has spent playing; beating one's own fastest time is a motivating goal for some players. Alternatively, to create a sense of tension or urgency, you could instead create a time limit and display a timer counting down to 0, at which point the player loses the game.

You might have observed that the puzzle game is not very challenging as it is. An obvious way to increase the difficulty would be to divide the image into more pieces. An alternative and potentially more interesting way to increase the difficulty would be to add the ability to rotate the individual pieces by increments of 90 degrees. Pieces could be initialized with a random amount of rotation (0, 90, 180, or 270 degrees) in addition to having a random initial position on the left side of the screen. The `PuzzlePiece` class would need to store the current amount of rotation, and when checking whether a piece is placed correctly, you would add the condition that the angle of rotation is equal to 0 degrees. The player controls for rotating pieces would require a bit of planning. One approach could be to consider the index of the mouse button being pressed: the left mouse button could be used when dragging pieces, while clicking the right mouse button could rotate the piece 90 degrees clockwise. Another approach would be to use a double-click to indicate a rotation; this can be accomplished by replacing the `InputListener` object with a `ClickListener` object (an extension of the `InputListener` class) that contains additional mouse- and touch-related methods, including `getTapCount`, which can be used to check for double-clicks or double taps. If you choose to add rotation functionality, you will definitely want to consider adding a menu screen with control instructions, since you shouldn't expect the player to be able to guess your control scheme.

Similarly, the solitaire card game *52 Pickup* is not challenging; rather, it is mostly an exercise in patience. Using the skills you have developed creating that game, a worthwhile project would be to create a similar game that involves more player choice and strategy. One recommendation is to create a solitaire version of the game *Crazy Eights* (similar to the commercial game *UNO*). The setup and rules for this game are as follows:

- At the beginning of the game, eight random cards are lined up along the bottom of the screen. This set of cards is referred to as your hand.

- A pile, called the discard pile, containing a single card is placed in the center of the screen.

- The remaining cards are positioned off-screen (for simplicity) and are referred to as the deck.

- At any time, a card from your hand may be placed on the discard pile if it has the same rank or the same suit. In addition, the cards with rank 8 are called wild cards: they can be placed on the discard pile at any time, and when they are on top of the discard pile, any card may be placed on it.

- When a card from the hand is successfully placed on the discard pile, the player earns a point, and a random card is selected from the deck and moved on screen to replace the card from the hand.

- If all cards from the deck and the hand are placed on the discard pile (or in other words, if the player earns 51 points), then the player wins the game.

In the next chapter, you will revisit some previous projects (*Starfish Collector* and *Rectangle Destroyer*) and learn how to use some third-party software to simplify the level-design process.

CHAPTER 10

Tilemaps

In some of the games previously developed in this book, one challenging aspect has been the placement of objects: calculating the positions where the actors will appear on the main stage. In this chapter, you will learn how to use Tiled, a general-purpose map-editing software program that can be used for multiple aspects of the level-design process. In particular, you will learn how to use Tiled while improving the design of two previous games: *Starfish Collector* and *Rectangle Destroyer*. For the *Starfish Collector* game, you will design a maze-like level (using rocks for walls) and add some scenery, as shown in Figure 10-1. For the *Rectangle Destroyer* game, you will design a colorful layout of bricks, as shown in Figure 10-2. The gameplay for both these games remains identical to what it was before; the only code-related changes will be the addition of a class to import the map data files you create with Tiled, and the `initialize` method for these games will be simplified.

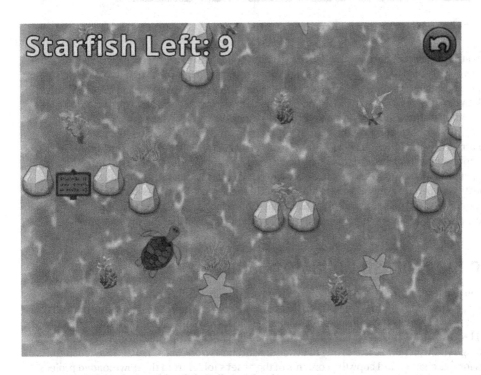

Figure 10-1. *The redesigned* Starfish Collector *level*

© Lee Stemkoski 2018
L. Stemkoski, *Java Game Development with LibGDX*, https://doi.org/10.1007/978-1-4842-3324-5_10

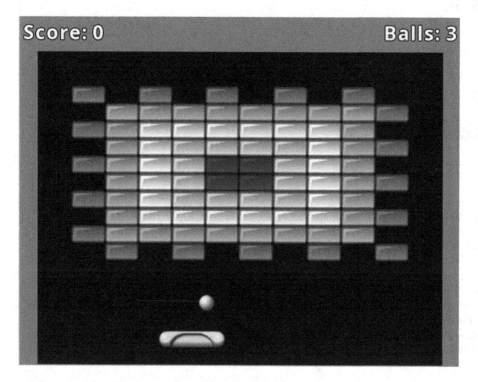

Figure 10-2. *The redesigned brick layout for* Rectangle Destroyer

Tiled was created in 2008 by Thorbjørn Lindeijer and is still under active development, with new features and improvements being added regularly. The software is open source and free (although donations to support development would be greatly appreciated by the developer), and it is available for Windows, MacOS, and Linux systems. A link to download the software is provided on the website http://www.mapeditor.org/.

One of the primary features of Tiled is to take a *tileset* (a spritesheet consisting of rectangular images, or *tiles*, that represent possible features of the game-world terrain) and enable the user to create a *tilemap* (a selection and arrangement of tiles that corresponds to an image of the game world). In addition, Tiled can also be used to associate text-based data with individual tiles or geometric shapes, which can be useful for instantiating game-world entities. Levels can be designed for games with a top-down perspective or a side-view perspective, depending on the images and tilesets being used. Tiled stores map files using *XML* (eXtensible Markup Language), a text-based file format that is both human-readable and machine-readable; LibGDX has many classes available to help parse these data files, as you will learn in the sections that follow.

Revisiting the Starfish Collector Game

In this section, you will learn how to use Tiled in the context of designing and creating a tilemap for *Starfish Collector*. To begin, make a copy of the Starfish Collector project from Chapter 5 (which introduced user interfaces and included Sign objects in the game) and change the name of the folder (and thus the project) to Starfish Collector Ch 10. In theory, copying your Starfish Collector project from Chapter 6 is also acceptable, although you won't make use of any of the audio additions from that chapter. Download the source code files for this chapter and copy the contents of the assets folder from the downloaded project into the assets folder of your new project; new files include a background image named large-water.jpg that is 1024 by 1024 pixels, a spritesheet called `ocean-plants.png` that is a 2 by 2 grid of images of ocean plants, each of which is 64 by 64 pixels, and the image `starfish.png`, which has been resized to 64-by-64 pixels to align easily with the tilemap that will be created. Also, download and install the Tiled software from the website previously mentioned.

Creating the Tilemap

After downloading and installing Tiled, run the program. When the program starts, from the File menu, select *New*, then *New Map*, and a small window will appear, as shown in Figure 10-3, that allows you to configure the general map settings. In the area labeled *Map size*, change the *Width* and *Height* settings to 32 tiles and change the Tile size *Width* and *Height* settings to 32 px. This will create a map that is 1024 by 1024 pixels large, which will be indicated underneath the map size settings. The other parameters should be left at their default settings, as seen in Figure 10-3. Click on the button labeled *Save As . . .* and navigate to your project's `assets` directory. Save the file with the name `map.tmx` (you can replace the existing file in the folder). It is very important that your tilemap file is saved to the same directory that contains the images you use, because the tilemap file stores the location of the image files relative to the tilemap file itself, and moving the tilemap file to a new folder later will result in the image files' failing to load.

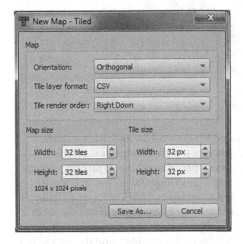

Figure 10-3. *Tiled settings window for creating a new map*

At this point, the main editor window will appear, as shown in Figure 10-4. In order to see the full grid of squares in the central area, you may need to zoom out (one or more times), which can be accessed from the View menu. In the top-right region of this window, you will see a list of layers, which includes a single *Tile Layer* (named `Tile Layer 1`) by default, which is used to create an image from tilesets.

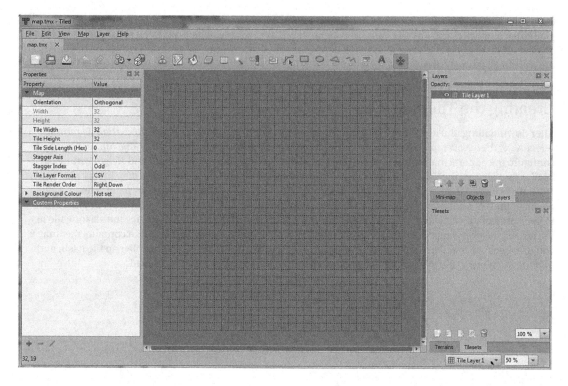

Figure 10-4. *The main window for the Tiled map-editor software*

The other types of layers you can add include an *Image layer*, which is useful for displaying a single background image, and an *Object layer*, which is useful for adding tiles or geometric objects that have custom text-based data associated with them. You will use all of these types of layers in this project, so from the Layer menu, select *New* and then *Image layer*, and, similarly, add a new Object layer (you may leave the names set to their defaults). In the top-right panel, you will see a list of layers, with Tile Layer 1 at the bottom. The order of the layers is important; the layers are rendered in order from the bottom of the list to the top of the list. You will want Image Layer 1 to render first, since it represents the background. To lower the position of this layer in the list, click on *Image Layer 1* so that it is highlighted in blue, and then in the row of icons underneath the list, click the picture of the arrow pointing down; the list of layers should be ordered as shown in Figure 10-5. (Alternatively, you could have selected *Tile Layer 1* and clicked on the icon with the arrow pointing up.)

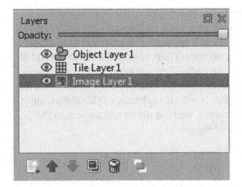

Figure 10-5. *Reordered layers for the* Starfish Collector *map*

Next, you will add the background image. In the list of layers, make sure that Image Layer 1 is currently selected. On the left region of the window is a panel titled Properties containing two columns of data: the left column lists property names, while the right column lists the corresponding values. In the row with the property named Image, click on the area to the right in the value column, and a button labeled "..." will appear. Click this button and select the image large-water.jpg from your assets directory. When you are finished, the name of the image file should appear in the value column, and the image itself will be displayed in the central area, as shown in Figure 10-6.

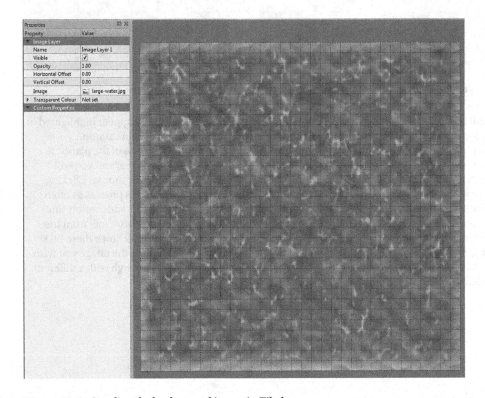

Figure 10-6. *Loading the background image in Tiled*

Next, you are going to create a tileset from a spritesheet. The panel in the lower-right region of the window displays tilesets. In the row of icons along the bottom of this area, click on the first icon (which looks like a rectangle with a glowing star), and a window titled New Tileset will appear. Click on the button labeled *Browse* and select the image ocean-plants.png from the assets directory. Then, change both the tile width and tile height values to 64 px, since the individual images within the spritesheet are each that large. Finally, check the box next to the words "Embed in map"; this is very important, since LibGDX currently only has the functionality to process a single tmx file. The button labeled *Save As . . .* will then change to *OK*; the window will appear as shown on the left side of Figure 10-7. Click the *OK* button, and the tileset will appear in the lower-right region of the Tiled window, as shown on the right side of Figure 10-7.

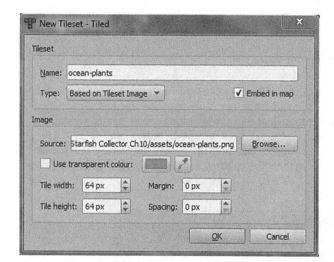
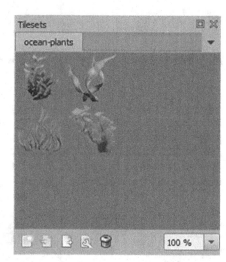

Figure 10-7. *Settings for the New Tileset window (left), and the resulting tileset (right)*

Next, you will set up the tile layer. In the Layers panel, select *Tile Layer 1*; it should appear highlighted in blue. Across the top of the window are a set of icons; click on the icon that looks like an ink stamp (or press the B key). This activates the *Stamp Brush* tool. In the Tileset panel, click on one of the plants; it should appear highlighted in a blue rectangle. Then, move your mouse to the central area, and you will see a translucent copy of the image aligned to the nearest grid location underneath your mouse. Clicking the mouse button will place (or "stamp") a copy of the image at that location. Repeat this process as often as you like to create additional instances of various plant images around the screen; this adds variety and visual interest to the level. If you wish to remove a tile image from the map, select the *Eraser* tool from the set of icons across the top (or press the E key) and click on the image you wish to remove. Since these tiles occupy multiple grid squares, you need to click on the lower-left grid square containing the image you wish to remove. When you are finished, your picture may appear similar to Figure 10-8, although with a different arrangement of plants.

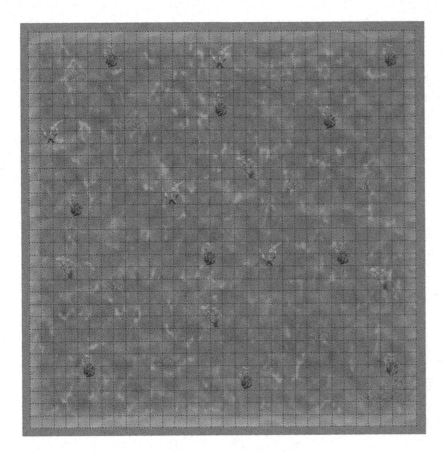

Figure 10-8. *The* Starfish Collector *tilemap with additions from the ocean plant tileset*

Finally, you will add some object data to this level that will be used to create instances of the Rock, Starfish, and Sign classes. The first step is to create some additional tilesets to represent each type of object, although each of these will consist only of a single image. You will follow the same process as before: to begin, in the Tileset panel (in the lower-right region of the window), click on the icon to create a new tileset. In the New Tileset window that appears, click *Browse*, select the image starfish.png from the assets directory, change both the tile width and tile height values to 64 px, check the box for "Embed in map," and click the *OK* button. Repeat this process for the image rock.png and again for the image sign.png. When you are finished, the names of the different tilesets (ocean-plants, starfish, rock, sign) will appear in tabs across the top of the Tileset panel, and you can then switch between these tilesets by clicking on the tabs.

Next, you will add some custom properties to these new tilesets. In particular, you need to store the name of the Java class that will be instantiated for these objects, as well as any additional data required (in the case of the signs, the message to be displayed). To begin, click on the tab for the starfish tileset. In the row of icons at the bottom of the Tileset panel, click on the image that looks like a wrench on top of a rectangle (hovering the mouse over this icon will display the tooltip *Edit Tileset*). Then, in the main window, a new tab will appear with the tileset (the image of the starfish) in the central area. The new tab should contain the text map.tmx#starfish, which indicates that you are editing the starfish tileset embedded in the tilemap file map.tmx. Click on the image of the starfish, and the Properties panel on the left will appear as shown in Figure 10-9.

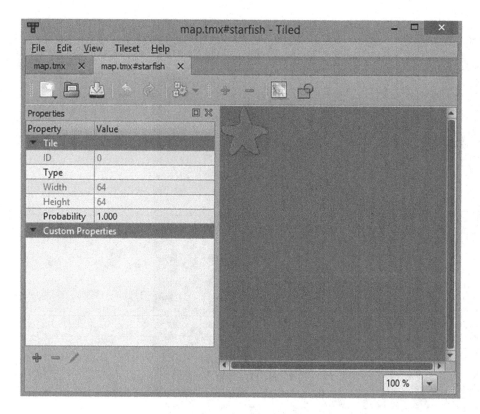

Figure 10-9. *The tilesest editor*

At the bottom of the Properties panel is an area to display custom properties, which is currently empty. This is where you will enter the custom data needed by your game. Click on the plus icon at the bottom of the Properties panel to add a new property. In the small window that appears, enter the name and then press the *OK* button. A new row will appear in the Custom Properties area, and in the text field in the value column, enter Starfish. This is all the data you need to enter for this object, as the Starfish class doesn't require anything further. Click on the tab at the top of the window labeled map.tmx to return to the tilemap.

Then, in the Tileset panel, select the rock tileset and click on the icon to edit the tileset. A new tab will appear, labeled map.tmx#rock. Here, click on the image of the rock, and in the Properties panel, click on the plus icon to create a new custom property called Name, but this time enter Rock for the value. Return to the tilemap and proceed as before, editing the sign tileset and creating a custom property called Name with a value of Sign. However, before you return to the tilemap, you need to create a second custom property that stores the text to be displayed by the sign. This property should be called message and should contain the value Hello, world! (This is a default value for this property, which will be changed later when placing instances of this tile on the map.) When you are finished, click on the tab to return to the tilemap.

Now, you will use these tilesets to add object data to your map. Since you have returned to the main tilemap editor, the Layers panel will be displayed in the upper-right region of the window. Click on the layer named *Object Layer 1* so that it is highlighted in blue. In the row of icons across the top of the window, the icons for the tools used when editing the tile layer will appear grayed out (meaning that they cannot be used when editing an object layer), and a different set of tool icons to the right will become colored (meaning that they are available for use). Click on the icon with an image like a photograph (or press T) to activate the *Insert Tile* tool. Then, in the Tileset panel, click the tab for the rock tileset, click the image of the rock so that it is highlighted in blue, and then click on the map to add instances of the rock to the map (similar to the

Stamp Brush tool you used when editing the tile layer). To align object tiles with the grid, you may want to activate the *Snap to Grid* setting in the View menu if it isn't already activated. To delete a tile you have added, right-click on the tile and, in the pop-up menu that appears, select *Remove Object*. When placing rocks, keep in mind that for maneuvering the turtle, its width requires four grid squares (128 pixels). After adding some rocks, repeat this process to add some starfish (making sure that they are accessible by the turtle) and at least two sign objects. One possible map arrangement is shown in Figure 10-10.

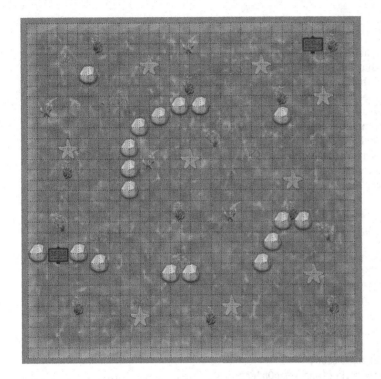

Figure 10-10. *The tilemap with object tiles added*

Next, you will override the default messages for the instances of the sign tiles you have placed. Press S to activate the *Select Objects* tool (or click on the icon whose picture includes a rectangle whose border is a dashed line). Click on one of the signs that you placed, and it will be outlined with a moving dashed line and some arrows. In the Properties panel on the left, underneath Custom Properties, you will see the two properties you previously added to the tileset. They will appear in a gray font, indicating that the current values are the default values for the tileset. Click to the right of the property named *message*, in the value column, and enter some new text (Collect all the Starfish, for example), then press Enter. Repeat this process for your other sign and enter some different text. If you click on the first sign again, you will notice that the row for the custom property called *message* now appears in a black font, indicating that you have changed the value from the default.

Finally, you will add some additional custom data to the object layer using rectangles, rather than tiles. In theory, all object data could be specified using rectangles, but being able to see the images makes the level design easier to visualize. The final piece of data that will be included in this map is a start location for the turtle object. Press R to activate the *Insert Rectangle* tool (or click the icon featuring a rectangle with a thick blue outline), and on the tilemap click and drag the mouse pointer to draw a rectangle around the grid square where you would like the turtle to start. As soon as you are finished drawing, while the rectangle you drew is still selected, click on the plus icon at the bottom of the Properties panel to add a new custom property. As before, enter name in the window that appears, and in the value column for this property, enter Start. In this case, Start does not refer to a class to be created; it is just a name we will use to reference this rectangle later.

When you are finished, save your file and close the Tiled map-editor program. In the next section, you will write a class that can be used to parse the data in the tilemap file and integrate it into the *Starfish Collector* project.

Creating the TilemapActor Class

In this section, you will write a class that merges the Tiled map file-parsing capabilities provided by LibGDX with the BaseActor class framework that you developed in the first part of this book. The class you create will be used for the games revisited in this chapter, as well as for the games covered in the next two chapters (platformer games and adventure games). This class will extend the LibGDX Actor class, rather than the BaseActor class, since it will not make use of any of the BaseActor functionality. This requires you to write two methods, act and draw. The draw method will make use of an OrthographicCamera object—which will be aligned with the Camera from the main stage—to render the image layers and tile layers from the map. Object layers are not rendered to the screen; instead, you will write methods that extract a list of objects (tiles or rectangles) that contain a custom property called name with a particular value, very similar to the getList method of the BaseActor class. You can then use that data to create instances of the corresponding classes in your game.

To begin, open the Starfish Collector Ch 10 project (if it isn't already open). Create a new class named TilemapActor with the following code, which will be explained further in a moment:

```
import com.badlogic.gdx.scenes.scene2d.Actor;
import com.badlogic.gdx.scenes.scene2d.Stage;
import com.badlogic.gdx.graphics.Camera;
import com.badlogic.gdx.graphics.OrthographicCamera;
import com.badlogic.gdx.graphics.g2d.Batch;
import com.badlogic.gdx.maps.MapLayer;
import com.badlogic.gdx.maps.MapObject;
import com.badlogic.gdx.maps.MapProperties;
import com.badlogic.gdx.maps.objects.RectangleMapObject;
import com.badlogic.gdx.maps.tiled.TiledMap;
import com.badlogic.gdx.maps.tiled.TmxMapLoader;
import com.badlogic.gdx.maps.tiled.TiledMapTile;
import com.badlogic.gdx.maps.tiled.objects.TiledMapTileMapObject;
import com.badlogic.gdx.maps.tiled.renderers.OrthoCachedTiledMapRenderer;
import java.util.ArrayList;
import java.util.Iterator;

public class TilemapActor extends Actor
{
    // window dimensions
    public static int windowWidth  = 800;
    public static int windowHeight = 600;

    private TiledMap tiledMap;
    private OrthographicCamera tiledCamera;
    private OrthoCachedTiledMapRenderer tiledMapRenderer;
```

```java
    public TilemapActor(String filename, Stage theStage)
    {
        // set up tile map, renderer, and camera
        tiledMap = new TmxMapLoader().load(filename);

        int tileWidth         = (int)tiledMap.getProperties().get("tilewidth");
        int tileHeight        = (int)tiledMap.getProperties().get("tileheight");
        int numTilesHorizontal = (int)tiledMap.getProperties().get("width");
        int numTilesVertical  = (int)tiledMap.getProperties().get("height");
        int mapWidth  = tileWidth  * numTilesHorizontal;
        int mapHeight = tileHeight * numTilesVertical;

        BaseActor.setWorldBounds(mapWidth, mapHeight);

        tiledMapRenderer = new OrthoCachedTiledMapRenderer(tiledMap);
        tiledMapRenderer.setBlending(true);
        tiledCamera = new OrthographicCamera();
        tiledCamera.setToOrtho(false, windowWidth, windowHeight);
        tiledCamera.update();

        theStage.addActor(this);
    }

    public void act(float dt)
    {
        super.act( dt );
    }

    public void draw(Batch batch, float parentAlpha)
    {
        // adjust tilemap camera to stay in sync with main camera
        Camera mainCamera = getStage().getCamera();
        tiledCamera.position.x = mainCamera.position.x;
        tiledCamera.position.y = mainCamera.position.y;
        tiledCamera.update();
        tiledMapRenderer.setView(tiledCamera);

        // need the following code to force batch order,
        //  otherwise it is batched and rendered last
        batch.end();
        tiledMapRenderer.render();
        batch.begin();
    }
}
```

The TilemapActor class constructor requires two inputs: the name of the tilemap file to open and the Stage to which this actor should be added. The constructor then begins by loading the tilemap file into a TiledMap object. After this, the properties of the map can be accessed. Once the number of tiles and the tile size are determined, the dimensions of the game world can be calculated and the boundary of the world is set using the BaseActor method setWorldBounds. Then, a few more objects are initialized: a camera and a renderer, which are used when drawing the tilemap. The draw method keeps the tilemap's camera in the same position as the stage's camera and then renders the tilemap. The strange calls to the Batch class methods end and begin are necessary to force the map to be rendered immediately before queueing additional actors to be rendered, otherwise the map may (incorrectly) appear on top of other objects on the stage.

Next, you will write the methods needed to retrieve the lists of objects stored in the TiledMap object. Just as is the case with the Tiled map-editor program, it contains a list of layers (represented by the MapLayer class), each of which contains a list of objects (represented by the MapObject class). Each of the following methods will iterate over these lists, checking whether each object is of a certain type (either RectangleMapObject or TiledMapTileMapObject). If so, the set of properties (represented by the MapProperties class) will be analyzed further. You can check if a custom property with a certain name exists in this set via the containsKey method, and you can retrieve its value via the get method (although this method has return type Object, and the results will often need to be cast to the intended class). To begin, you will write the simpler of the two methods, getRectangleList, which checks for rectangles that contain a custom property called name with a particular value (stored in the variable propertyName). In the TilemapActor class, add the following method:

```
public ArrayList<MapObject> getRectangleList(String propertyName)
{
    ArrayList<MapObject> list = new ArrayList<MapObject>();

    for ( MapLayer layer : tiledMap.getLayers() )
    {
        for ( MapObject obj : layer.getObjects() )
        {
            if ( !(obj instanceof RectangleMapObject) )
                continue;

            MapProperties props = obj.getProperties();

            if ( props.containsKey("name") && props.get("name").equals(propertyName) )
                list.add(obj);
        }
    }
    return list;
}
```

Next, you will write a similar method, getTileList, which performs a similar check on tile objects. This process is slightly more complicated, since a tile object has two associated MapProperty objects: the default values, which are specified in the associated tile, and the non-default values, which are accessed as seen earlier in the getRectangleList method. To get the set of properties containing default values, the map object must be cast into a TiledMapTileMapObject. Then, the original tile can be accessed via the getTile method, and then its properties can be accessed via the getProperties method as seen before. The class name is stored in the tile's property set. If the name field exists and matches the value in the propertyName variable, then the object is added to the list. However, one additional step remains: any of the properties in the tileset that do not exist in the map object's property set must be copied over (which can be implemented with a while loop). The code for this method is as follows:

```java
public ArrayList<MapObject> getTileList(String propertyName)
{
    ArrayList<MapObject> list = new ArrayList<MapObject>();

    for ( MapLayer layer : tiledMap.getLayers() )
    {
        for ( MapObject obj : layer.getObjects() )
        {
            if ( !(obj instanceof TiledMapTileMapObject) )
                continue;

            MapProperties props = obj.getProperties();

            // Default MapProperties are stored within associated Tile object
            // Instance-specific overrides are stored in MapObject

            TiledMapTileMapObject tmtmo = (TiledMapTileMapObject)obj;
            TiledMapTile t = tmtmo.getTile();
            MapProperties defaultProps = t.getProperties();

            if ( defaultProps.containsKey("name") &&
                 defaultProps.get("name").equals(propertyName) )
                    list.add(obj);

            // get list of default property keys
            Iterator<String> propertyKeys = defaultProps.getKeys();

            // iterate over keys; copy default values into props if needed
            while ( propertyKeys.hasNext() )
            {
                String key = propertyKeys.next();

                // check if value already exists; if not, create property with default value
                if ( props.containsKey(key) )
                {
                    continue;
                }
                else
                {
                    Object value = defaultProps.get(key);
                    props.put( key, value );
                }
            }
        }
    }
    return list;
}
```

With this addition, the TilemapActor class is complete and is ready to be integrated into your project!

Project Integration

As mentioned at the beginning of this chapter, the gameplay for your projects will not be changed at all when adding tilemaps; only a few changes need to be made when initializing the screen. To begin, in the LevelScreen class, locate the initialize method and *delete* the following code that was used to initialize the background and all the game entities:

```
BaseActor ocean = new BaseActor(0,0, mainStage);
ocean.loadTexture( "assets/water-border.jpg" );
ocean.setSize(1200,900);
BaseActor.setWorldBounds(ocean);

new Starfish(400,400, mainStage);
new Starfish(500,100, mainStage);
new Starfish(100,450, mainStage);
new Starfish(200,250, mainStage);

new Rock(200,150, mainStage);
new Rock(100,300, mainStage);
new Rock(300,350, mainStage);
new Rock(450,200, mainStage);

turtle = new Turtle(20,20, mainStage);

Sign sign1 = new Sign(20,400, mainStage);
sign1.setText("West Starfish Bay");

Sign sign2 = new Sign(600,300, mainStage);
sign2.setText("East Starfish Bay");
```

Next, to initialize the tilemap actor, at the beginning of the initialize method, add the following code:

```
TilemapActor tma = new TilemapActor("assets/map.tmx", mainStage);
```

To initialize the various objects, you will use the methods previously implemented to get lists of objects with particular names. When iterating over these lists, you will need to get the object's properties, especially the specific properties you need (at a minimum, the *x* and *y* coordinates of the object, which are required by the BaseActor class constructor). To begin, add the following import statements to the LevelScreen class:

```
import com.badlogic.gdx.maps.MapObject;
import com.badlogic.gdx.maps.MapProperties;
```

Next, in the initialize method, after the tilemap actor is initialized, add the following code to create the Starfish, Rock, and Sign objects. Note that when creating the signs, you also need to get the message property (and cast it to a String).

```
for (MapObject obj : tma.getTileList("Starfish") )
{
    MapProperties props = obj.getProperties();
    new Starfish( (float)props.get("x"), (float)props.get("y"), mainStage );
}
```

```
for (MapObject obj : tma.getTileList("Rock") )
{
    MapProperties props = obj.getProperties();
    new Rock( (float)props.get("x"), (float)props.get("y"), mainStage );
}

for (MapObject obj : tma.getTileList("Sign") )
{
    MapProperties props = obj.getProperties();
    Sign s = new Sign( (float)props.get("x"), (float)props.get("y"), mainStage );
    s.setText( (String)props.get("message") );
}
```

Before you initialize the turtle, you need to retrieve the rectangle object named Start to determine its position. Due to the way the data was stored (using a rectangle object), you will use the getRectangleList method here. However, since this list will only contain one object, you don't need to use a loop; you can simply get the one and only object in the list, which has index 0. To do this, add the following code to the initialize method:

```
MapObject startPoint = tma.getRectangleList("start").get(0);
MapProperties props = startPoint.getProperties();
turtle = new Turtle( (float)props.get("x"), (float)props.get("y"), mainStage);
```

At this point, if you run your game, you should see the tilemap you created displayed in your game.

Rectangle Destroyer Revisited

To practice the skills and implementation you have learned in redesigning the *Starfish Collector* level, you will also redesign the layout of and add colors to the Brick objects in the *Rectangle Destroyer* game. Using a tilemap will also simplify the placement and size of the walls and starting position of the paddle.

To begin, make a copy of the Rectangle Destroyer project from Chapter 8 and change the name of the folder (and thus the project) to Rectangle Destroyer Ch 10. In addition, copy the TilemapActor.java file from the Starfish Collector Ch 10 project folder into this folder. Download the source code files for this chapter and copy the contents of the assets folder from the downloaded project into the assets folder of your new project; new files include a larger version of the background image, named large-space.png, that is 832 by 640 pixels; an image called wall-square.png that is 32 by 32 pixels; and a spritesheet called brick-colors.png that is a 2 by 4 grid of colored bricks, each of which is 64 by 32 pixels (resulting in an image that is 128 by 128 pixels overall). As before, these sizes were chosen to align with the tilemap that will be created.

Creating the Tilemap

To begin, run the Tiled map-editor program. Once it starts, from the File menu, select *New*, then *New Map*, and the general map settings window will appear. In the area labeled *Map size*, change the *Width* to 26 tiles and the *Height* to 20 tiles, and change the Tile size *Width* and *Height* settings to 32 px. This will create a tilemap that is 832 by 640 pixels; later on, you will change the size of the window to match. Click on the button labeled *Save As . . .* and navigate to your project's assets directory; save the file with the name map.tmx. The tilemap will be initialized, and an empty grid of squares will appear in the center of the screen, with the Properties panel to the left, the Layers panel to the upper-right, and the Tileset panel to the lower-right.

From the Layer menu, add a new image layer, then add a new object layer. For this project, the default tile layer will not be needed, so you can right-click *Tile Layer 1* in the list of layers and select *Remove Layer*.

To add the background image, select *Image Layer 1* in the list of layers. In the Properties panel, in the row with the property named *Image*, click on the area to the right in the value column, and a button labeled "..." will appear. Click this button and select the image large-space.png from your assets directory. When you are finished, the image will be displayed in the central area. However, since the background image is dark, it is difficult to see the grid of squares. To increase the visibility of the grid squares, you can decrease the opacity of the image using the slider near the top of the Layers panel. (However, this also affects how the image appears in the actual game, so you will want to increase the opacity back to 100 percent after you are finished with the tilemap.)

Next, you will need to create two tilesets (one for walls, one for bricks) for use in the object layer. In the Tileset panel area, click on the icon to create a new tileset. In the New Tileset window that appears, click *Browse*, select the image wall-square.png from the assets directory, change both the tile width and tile height values to 32 px, check the box for "Embed in map," and click the *OK* button. Then, in the Tileset panel, click on the icon to edit the tileset properties. In the new tab that appears, click on the gray square to select it. At the bottom of the Properties panel, click the plus icon to add a new custom property; enter name for the property name, and enter Wall in the value column. When you are finished, click on the tab labeled map.tmx to return to the tilemap.

Next, you will create the brick tileset, which is slightly more involved, as the tiles contain additional data. Create a new tileset as before, this time using the image file brick-colors.png and changing the tile width to 64 px and tile height to 32 px. Click the icon to edit the tileset properties. Click on one of the brick tiles to select it, then hold down the Ctrl key and click on each of the remaining brick tiles so that they are all selected, allowing you to enter properties for all of them at once. Click on the plus icon to add a new custom property; enter name for the property name, and enter Brick in the value column. Then, click on the plus icon again to add a new custom property called color; do not enter any values yet. Instead, click on the red brick tile so that it is the only tile selected, and in the value column next to color, enter red. Repeat this process to enter values for each of the remaining bricks; the code that follows in the next section assumes you will assign the values orange, yellow, green, blue, purple, white, and gray to the bricks of the corresponding color.

Now, you are ready to return to the tilemap. First, make sure that *Object Layer 1* is selected in the Layers panel. Select the wall-square tileset and click on the single tile from that set. Press T to activate the *Insert Tile* tool and then click on the top-left grid square in the tilemap area. To change the size of this object, press the S key to activate the *Select Objects* tool. If the object tile were already selected, double-sided arrows would appear by the edges and corners of the tile; if the object tile were not already selected, if you clicked on it these arrows would appear. Clicking and dragging an arrow will change the size of the object; resize this tile until it covers the top two rows of the tilemap. Press T to switch to the *Insert Tile* tool again and place a wall-square tile in the bottom-left corner. Press S to switch to the *Select Objects* tool and increase the height of the tile until it reaches the previously added tile, thus forming the left wall for the game. Repeat this process to form the right wall for the game. When you are finished, the walls should appear similar to Figure 10-11.

Figure 10-11. *Adding walls to the tilemap*

Next, you will design and arrange the bricks for the level. Switch to the brick-colors tileset, press T to activate the *Insert Tile* tool, and add bricks to the tilemap any way you like (remembering to leave space near the bottom edge of the tilemap for the paddle). One possible such arrangement is shown in Figure 10-12.

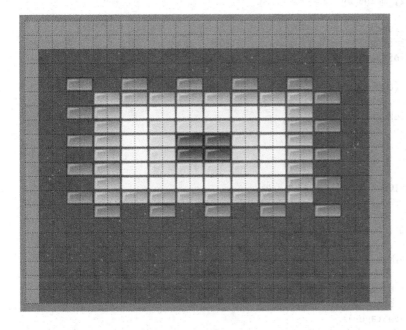

Figure 10-12. *Adding bricks to the tilemap*

You will use a rectangle object to specify the starting position of the paddle. Press R to activate the *Insert Rectangle* tool and draw a small rectangle near the center-bottom of the screen. While this rectangle is selected, click the plus icon in the Properties panel to add a custom property called name with value Start. Finally, if you changed the opacity of the image layer previously, change it back to 100 percent. Save your work and close the Tiled map-editor program.

Project Integration

Integrating the tilemap data into the *Rectangle Destroyer* game is similar to what you've seen before in the *Starfish Collector* game. Open the Rectangle Destroyer Ch 10 project in BlueJ. Since the size of the tilemap is slightly larger than the previous version of this game, the window size needs to be changed to match. In the Launcher class, change the last line of code in the main method to the following:

```
LwjglApplication launcher = new LwjglApplication( myGame, "Rectangle Destroyer", 832, 640 );
```

In the LevelScreen class, add the following two import statements:

```
import com.badlogic.gdx.maps.MapObject;
import com.badlogic.gdx.maps.MapProperties;
```

Next, in the initialize method, *delete* the following code that was used to initialize the background, walls, bricks, and paddle:

```
BaseActor background = new BaseActor(0,0, mainStage);
background.loadTexture("assets/space.png");
BaseActor.setWorldBounds(background);

paddle = new Paddle(320, 32, mainStage);

new Wall(0,0, 20,600, mainStage);
new Wall(780,0, 20,600, mainStage);
new Wall(0,550, 800,50, mainStage);

Brick tempBrick = new Brick(0,0,mainStage);
float brickWidth = tempBrick.getWidth();
float brickHeight = tempBrick.getHeight();
tempBrick.remove();

int totalRows = 10;
int totalCols = 10;
float marginX = (800 - totalCols * brickWidth) / 2;
float marginY = (600 - totalRows * brickHeight) - 120;

for (int rowNum = 0; rowNum < totalRows; rowNum++)
{
    for (int colNum = 0; colNum < totalCols; colNum++)
    {
        float x = marginX + brickWidth  * colNum;
        float y = marginY + brickHeight * rowNum;
        new Brick( x, y, mainStage );
    }
}
```

Next, add the following code at the beginning of the initialize method to create the TilemapActor:

```
TilemapActor tma = new TilemapActor("assets/map.tmx", mainStage);
```

To create the Wall objects, you will use the getTileList method as you did earlier in this chapter. Since the Wall class constructor also requires the width and height of the wall, you will also get those properties from the map object. Add the following code after the TilemapActor is initialized:

```
for (MapObject obj : tma.getTileList("Wall") )
{
    MapProperties props = obj.getProperties();
    new Wall( (float)props.get("x"),      (float)props.get("y"),
            (float)props.get("width"), (float)props.get("height"),
             mainStage );
}
```

To create the Brick objects, once again you will make use of the getTileList method. Since the tiles you used in the Tiled map editor were a slightly different size than the brick image in the assets folder, you can retrieve the width and height properties of the tile object to resize the brick object. In addition, you will retrieve the color property from the tile object, and you will set the color of the brick accordingly. To accomplish these tasks, add the following code:

```
for (MapObject obj : tma.getTileList("Brick") )
{
    MapProperties props = obj.getProperties();
    Brick b = new Brick( (float)props.get("x"), (float)props.get("y"), mainStage );
    b.setSize( (float)props.get("width"), (float)props.get("height") );
    b.setBoundaryRectangle();

    String colorName = (String)props.get("color");
    if ( colorName.equals("red") )
        b.setColor(Color.RED);
    else if ( colorName.equals("orange") )
        b.setColor(Color.ORANGE);
    else if ( colorName.equals("yellow") )
        b.setColor(Color.YELLOW);
    else if ( colorName.equals("green") )
        b.setColor(Color.GREEN);
    else if ( colorName.equals("blue") )
        b.setColor(Color.BLUE);
    else if ( colorName.equals("purple") )
        b.setColor(Color.PURPLE);
    else if ( colorName.equals("white") )
        b.setColor(Color.WHITE);
    else if ( colorName.equals("gray") )
        b.setColor(Color.GRAY);
}
```

Finally, just as you set the starting position of the turtle in *Starfish Collector*, you set the starting position of the paddle by adding the following code:

```
MapObject startPoint = tma.getRectangleList("start").get(0);
MapProperties props = startPoint.getProperties();
paddle = new Paddle( (float)props.get("x"), (float)props.get("y"), mainStage);
```

At this point, the modifications to the *Rectangle Destroyer* project are complete. Test out your game and enjoy your newly designed level!

Summary and Next Steps

In this chapter, you learned how to use Tiled, a general-purpose map-editing program that can be used to streamline level development. You learned how to set up maps, add tilesets with custom properties, and work with different types of map layers (image, tile, and object). You also learned how to integrate the built-in functionality of LibGDX to work with Tiled map data files in the process of creating the TiledMapActor class. This knowledge was put to practical use to improve the level design of two earlier game projects: *Starfish Collector* and *Rectangle Destroyer*.

In the following two chapters, you will continue to use your newly developed design skills and the TilemapActor class as you create a platformer game and a sword-fighting adventure game.

CHAPTER 11

![bullets]

Platform Games

In this chapter, you will learn how to create the platform game *Jumping Jack*, shown in Figure 11-1, inspired by arcade and console games such as *Donkey Kong* and *Super Mario Bros.* New concepts introduced in this chapter include actors with multiple animations, platform physics, using extra actors as "sensors" to monitor the area around an actor for overlap and collision, jump-through platforms, and key-and-lock mechanics.

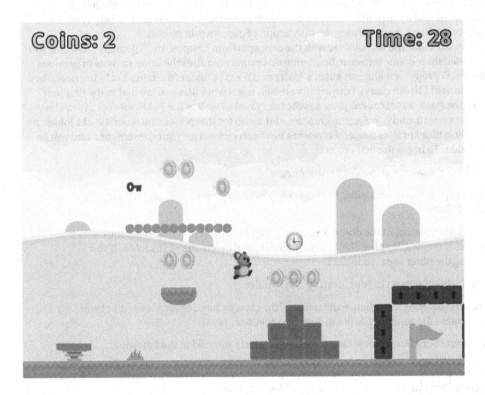

Figure 11-1. *The platform game Jumping Jack*

© Lee Stemkoski 2018
L. Stemkoski, *Java Game Development with LibGDX*, https://doi.org/10.1007/978-1-4842-3324-5_11

Game Project: Jumping Jack

Jumping Jack is an action game where the character, Jack the Koala, jumps around a level collecting as many coins as possible; he must reach the goal flag before time runs out. Collecting timer objects gives the koala more time to explore. Some of the surfaces in the game are *jump-through platforms*, which behave like solid objects except that the koala can jump up through them from below and land on top, or fall down through the platforms from above. There are also springboard objects, which launch the koala high into the sky if he lands on them from above. Finally, there are lock blocks, which may come in many colors and are impassable until the koala collects the key of the same color.

The player uses the left and right arrow keys to walk back and forth and the spacebar key to jump (when the koala is standing on a solid object). The koala will automatically jump up through a platform from below, but to fall down through a platform, the player must hold the down arrow key while pressing the key to jump. The user interface displays the number of coins collected in the upper-left corner of the screen and the amount of time remaining in the upper-right. When any keys are collected, an image of a key with the corresponding color will appear in the top-center area of the screen. If the player reaches the goal flag or runs out of time, a message will appear in the center of the screen stating "You Win!" or "Time Up—Game Over," respectively.

The game uses a vibrant, colorful, cartoonish art style. Most objects with which the player can interact involve either an image-based or a value-based animation to draw the player's attention. Suggestions for additional special effects and audio will be discussed in the final section of this chapter to help establish the mood, provide player feedback, and enhance the interaction of game-world objects.

The chapter assumes that you are familiar with the concepts from Chapter 10, "Tilemaps," and that you have installed the Tiled map-editor software. Beginning this project requires the same steps as in previous projects: creating a new project, creating an assets folder and a +libs folder (the latter not being necessary if you have set up the userlib directory), copying the custom framework files you created in the first part of this book (BaseGame.java, BaseScreen.java, BaseActor.java) as well as the TilemapActor.java class you developed in Chapter 10, and copying the graphics and audio for this project into your assets folder. As described previously, a BlueJ project named Framework has been created for your convenience and will be used as a starting point. To begin the first project:

- Download the source code files for this chapter.

- Make a copy of the downloaded Framework folder (and its contents) and rename it to Jumping Jack.

- Copy all the contents of the downloaded Jumping Jack project assets folder into your newly created Jumping Jack assets folder (and delete the +libs folder if you are using the BlueJ userlib folder).

- Open the BlueJ project in your Jumping Jack folder.

- In the CustomGame class, change the name of the class to JumpingJackGame (BlueJ will then rename the source code file to JumpingJackGame.java).

- In the Launcher class, change the contents of the main method to the following:

```
Game my Game = new JumpingJackGame ();
LwjglApplication launcher = new LwjglApplication(
        myGame, "Jumping Jack", 800, 640 )
```

Starting the Level

To begin, start the Tiled map-editor software. Create a new map with a map size that has width of 50 tiles and height of 20 tiles, and a tile size with the width and height both set to 32 pixels. The resulting map will be 1600 pixels by 640 pixels. Click the *Save As . . .* button and save the file to your assets directory with the filename map.tmx.

Next, add an image layer and an object layer to your map and reorder the layers so that the tile layer appears in the middle of the list. In the Layers panel, select *Image Layer 1*, and in the Properties panel, set the image to background.png (whose dimensions match the size of the tilemap). Then, in the Tileset panel, add a new tileset using the image platform-tileset.png (shown on the left side of Figure 11-2), setting the tile size to 32 by 32 and checking the box to embed the tileset in the map. Add another new tileset to the map, this time using the image object-tileset.png (shown on the right side of Figure 11-2), in the same way. Since the object tiles will be used to indicate where game-world objects should be spawned, you will need to specify the corresponding Java classes (which you will create later). In the Tileset panel, select *object-tileset* and click on the icon to edit the tileset. In the tab that appears, you will need to click on each tile (one at a time) and add a new custom property to each. The property should be called name; the corresponding values for the tiles (from left to right) are Coin, Flag, Timer, Springboard, Platform, Key, and Lock. In addition, for the key and lock object tiles, add a second custom property called color with the value red. (This default color can be overridden for specific instances later on in the tilemap editor).

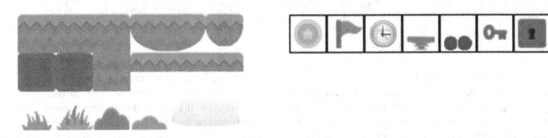

Figure 11-2. *Tilesets for the tile layer (left) and object layer (right)*

Return to the tab featuring the tilemap. In the Layers panel, select *Tile Layer 1*. In the Tileset panel, select *platform-tileset* and then press the B key to activate the *Stamp Brush* tool. Add tiles across the bottom row of the map, as well as some tiles representing solids to jump on, as well as some scenery. Note that the cloud graphic occupies two tiles, so you should add these tiles in adjacent pairs. One possible arrangement is shown in Figure 11-3 (which only displays part of the map, for clarity).

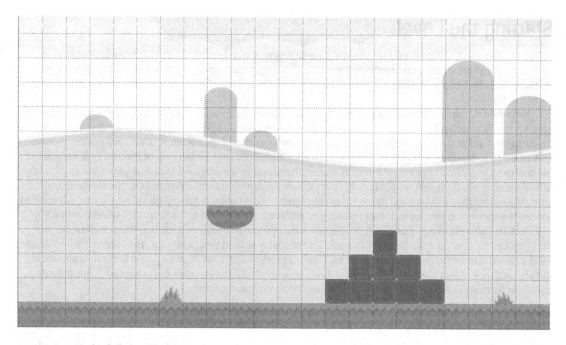

Figure 11-3. *Additions to the tile layer*

It is important to note that the tile layer is being used only to simplify creating an image from tilesets; none of these tiles are returned when using the getTileList method in the TilemapActor class. Instead, for the regions covered by tiles that represent solid objects (in contrast to the tiles that represent scenery), you will add rectangles in the object layer to store the data corresponding to those regions. In the Layers panel, select *Object Layer 1* and press R to activate the *Rectangle* tool. Draw rectangles around all the regions containing solid tiles; for simplicity, rectangles can be drawn that surround multiple tiles at once. To align rectangles with the grid, you may want to activate the *Snap to Grid* setting in the View menu if it isn't already activated. For the design shown in Figure 11-3, you would add rectangles around the ground, the floating platform, and the staircase made out of boxes, but not the two tiles with pictures of grass. Each time you add one of these rectangles, you must also add a custom property called name with the value Solid (which will be used to initialize corresponding actors later), or you can create them all and then use the *Select* tool to give them all the same property at once. Finally, add a rectangle at the position where the koala should start the level and add a custom property called name with the value Start. Applying this process to the design shown in Figure 11-3 produces the result shown in Figure 11-4, where the rectangles are drawn with a gray border. Now would also be a good time to save your tilemap file!

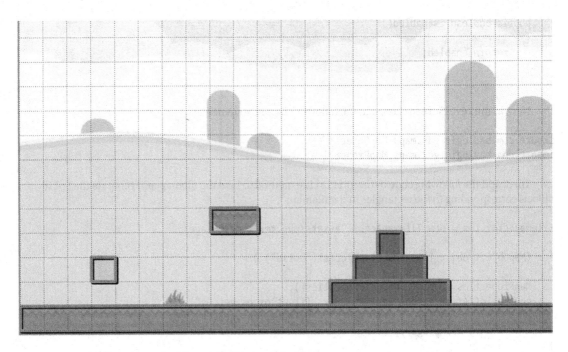

Figure 11-4. *Adding rectangle objects to indicate solid objects*

Next, open the Jumping Jack project in BlueJ. You need a way to represent regions corresponding to solid objects. To this end, create a new class named Solid that contains the following code. Since no graphics are used for this object (the tilemap determines the graphics that will be appear in these areas), the size and boundary shape for these objects must be set directly, and the width and height values are passed in via the constructor. Note that this class also contains functionality to enable and disable the solid status of the object; this will be needed by the platform and lock objects introduced later on in this chapter.

```
import com.badlogic.gdx.scenes.scene2d.Stage;

public class Solid extends BaseActor
{
    private boolean enabled;

    public Solid(float x, float y, float width, float height, Stage s)
    {
        super(x,y,s);
        setSize(width,height);
        setBoundaryRectangle();
        enabled = true;
    }

    public void setEnabled(boolean b)
    {
        enabled = b;
    }
```

```
    public boolean isEnabled()
    {
        return enabled;
    }
}
```

Next, in the LevelScreen class, add the following import statements:

```
import com.badlogic.gdx.maps.MapObject;
import com.badlogic.gdx.maps.MapProperties;
```

Then, add the following code to the initialize method to load the tilemap and generate the Solid objects corresponding to the rectangles in the tilemap:

```
TilemapActor tma = new TilemapActor("assets/map.tmx", mainStage);

for (MapObject obj : tma.getRectangleList("Solid") )
{
    MapProperties props = obj.getProperties();
    new Solid( (float)props.get("x"),      (float)props.get("y"),
               (float)props.get("width"), (float)props.get("height"),
                mainStage );
}
```

At this point, you can test your project, although you will only see the leftmost part of the level. In the next section, you will add the player's character (Jack the Koala), which will enable you to move around and see the rest of your level.

Platform Character Setup

In this section, you will create a class for the main character (the koala) that is controlled by the player. One new feature of this class is that it will contain multiple animations corresponding to different types of movement (standing, walking, and jumping). Due to the complexity of platform character movement, the physics-related methods in the BaseActor class are insufficient for a game of this type. For example, platform characters typically have different maximum speeds for horizontal movement (walking) and vertical movement (jumping/falling). For this reason, the character's act method will contain custom code for implementing physics-based movements. Before continuing, you may want to review the "Physics and Movement" section from Chapter 3, which contains an extensive discussion of physics-related concepts and calculations that will be revisited here.

To begin, create a new class called Koala containing the following code, which initializes two animations: stand, which consists of a single image, and walk, which contains multiple images.

```
import com.badlogic.gdx.scenes.scene2d.Stage;
import com.badlogic.gdx.graphics.g2d.Animation;

public class Koala extends BaseActor
{
    private Animation stand;
    private Animation walk;
```

```
    public Koala(float x, float y, Stage s)
    {
        super(x,y,s);

        stand = loadTexture( "assets/koala/stand.png" );

        String[] walkFileNames =
            {"assets/koala/walk-1.png", "assets/koala/walk-2.png",
                "assets/koala/walk-3.png", "assets/koala/walk-2.png"};

        walk = loadAnimationFromFiles(walkFileNames, 0.2f, true);
    }
}
```

Next, you will begin to implement the custom physics. First, in the BaseActor class, change the access modifier of the variables accelerationVec and velocityVec from private to protected so that the Koala class can access these variables directly. Return to the Koala class and add the following import statements:

```
import com.badlogic.gdx.Gdx;
import com.badlogic.gdx.Input.Keys;
import com.badlogic.gdx.math.MathUtils;
import com.badlogic.gdx.math.Vector2;
```

Next, you need to add variables to store physics-related constants: acceleration and deceleration rates for walking, the maximum horizontal (walking) speed, the magnitude of the force of gravity that pulls the character downward, and the maximum possible vertical (jumping/falling) speed. To this end, add the following variable declarations to the Koala class:

```
private float walkAcceleration;
private float walkDeceleration;
private float maxHorizontalSpeed;
private float gravity;
private float maxVerticalSpeed;
```

In the constructor method, add the following code to set the values of these variables:

```
maxHorizontalSpeed = 100;
walkAcceleration   = 200;
walkDeceleration   = 200;
gravity            = 700;
maxVerticalSpeed   = 1000;
```

Now, you will turn your attention to implementing platformer physics. First, in the Koala class, add the following method:

```
public void act(float dt)
{
    super.act( dt );
}
```

All the code that follows is to be added to the act method until stated otherwise. The first order of business is to check for keyboard input. If the player is pressing the left arrow key or the right arrow key, then the acceleration vector is updated. Then, the effect of gravity is taken into account, and the acceleration vector is used to update the velocity vector. To do so, add the following code:

```
if (Gdx.input.isKeyPressed(Keys.LEFT))
    accelerationVec.add( -walkAcceleration, 0 );

if (Gdx.input.isKeyPressed(Keys.RIGHT))
    accelerationVec.add( walkAcceleration, 0 );

accelerationVec.add(0, -gravity);

velocityVec.add( accelerationVec.x * dt, accelerationVec.y * dt );
```

Next, if the character is not accelerating (which happens when the player is not pressing left or right), then deceleration takes place. First, the amount of deceleration is calculated (which depends on dt, the amount of time that has elapsed). The walking direction (positive indicating right, negative indicating left) and the walking speed (the absolute value of the velocity) are stored in variables. The walk speed is decreased by the deceleration amount, and if the value becomes negative, it is set to 0. After these adjustments, the velocity x value is recalculated from the walk speed and direction. See the following:

```
if ( !Gdx.input.isKeyPressed(Keys.RIGHT) && !Gdx.input.isKeyPressed(Keys.LEFT) )
{
    float decelerationAmount = walkDeceleration * dt;

    float walkDirection;

    if ( velocityVec.x > 0 )
        walkDirection = 1;
    else
        walkDirection = -1;

    float walkSpeed = Math.abs( velocityVec.x );

    walkSpeed -= decelerationAmount;

    if (walkSpeed < 0)
        walkSpeed = 0;
    velocityVec.x = walkSpeed * walkDirection;
}
```

In addition to the effects of deceleration, the velocity in the x and y directions needs to stay within the bounds established by the variables that store the maximum speed in these directions. This can be accomplished by using the MathUtils class clamp method as follows:

```
velocityVec.x = MathUtils.clamp( velocityVec.x, -maxHorizontalSpeed, maxHorizontalSpeed );
velocityVec.y = MathUtils.clamp( velocityVec.y, -maxVerticalSpeed,   maxVerticalSpeed );
```

Now that the final adjustments to the velocity have been performed, the velocity values are used to adjust the position, and the acceleration vector is reset to (0,0), via the following code:

```
moveBy( velocityVec.x * dt, velocityVec.y * dt );
accelerationVec.set(0,0);
```

You also want to make sure that the camera stays aligned with the koala, and that the koala stays on the screen at all times. To do this, add the following lines of code:

```
alignCamera();
boundToWorld();
```

Finally, you need to switch between the animations according to the velocity in the *x* direction; a velocity of 0 indicates the koala is standing still and should use the corresponding animation. Furthermore, if the koala is moving to the left, you want to use the mirror image of the textures so that the koala appears to be facing to the left. Reversing the image can be easily accomplished by setting the scale in the *x* direction to -1, and the image can be restored by setting the scale back to 1. To do so, add the following code.

```
if ( velocityVec.x == 0 )
    setAnimation(stand);
else
    setAnimation(walk);

if ( velocityVec.x > 0 ) // face right
    setScaleX(1);
if ( velocityVec.x < 0 ) // face left
    setScaleX(-1);
```

At this point, sufficiently many features have been added to the Koala class for you to be ready to add the koala to the game. In the LevelScreen class, add the following import statement:

```
import com.badlogic.gdx.math.Vector2;
```

Also add the following variable declaration to the class:

```
Koala jack;
```

In the initialize method, add the following code to retrieve the start position specified in the tilemap, then initialize the Koala object at that position.

```
MapObject startPoint = tma.getRectangleList("start").get(0);
MapProperties startProps = startPoint.getProperties();
jack = new Koala( (float)startProps.get("x"), (float)startProps.get("y"), mainStage);
```

Next, collisions with solid objects (represented by the Solid class) are handled. The preventOverlap method is used to stop the koala from passing through any solid objects. A subtle issue that needs to be addressed is how the koala's speed should be adjusted when this occurs. Not adjusting the speed at all can lead to glitchy behavior; for example, if the koala falls and collides with the ground and the vertical speed is not set to zero, then gravity will cause the speed to build up, and eventually the koala will pass through the solid object in a single frame, causing it to seemingly disappear from the game. If the velocity vector is set to (0,0) on all collisions, however, this also leads to problems: for example, if the koala were to hit the side of a wall while falling, the koala would appear to stop for an instant, and if the player were to hold down an arrow key that moved the koala against a solid (such as a wall) while it was falling, the koala would appear to slowly float down the side of the wall. To avoid problems such as these, the direction of the impact must be taken into account. You encountered a similar issue when creating the *Rectangle Destroyer* game in Chapter 8, in that you needed to know the side of an object that was hit. As before, you can resolve this issue by analyzing the displacement vector returned by the preventOverlap method to determine the direction in which collision occurred and then setting the velocity in that direction to 0. To implement all of this, in the update method, add the following code:

```
for (BaseActor actor : BaseActor.getList(mainStage, "Solid"))
{
    Solid solid = (Solid)actor;

    if ( jack.overlaps(solid) && solid.isEnabled() )
    {
        Vector2 offset = jack.preventOverlap(solid);

        if (offset != null)
        {
            // collided in X direction
            if ( Math.abs(offset.x) > Math.abs(offset.y) )
                jack.velocityVec.x = 0;
            else // collided in Y direction
                jack.velocityVec.y = 0;
        }
    }
}
```

Finally, you will add the ability to jump to the Koala class. The most difficult part of this process is determining when the koala is on the ground and therefore able to jump. Checking if the velocity in the *y* direction equals 0 is insufficient, as this is also true at the instant when the koala is at the maximum height of a jump. The approach that will be used here is to create a small auxiliary object (named belowSensor) positioned directly below the koala at all times, as shown in Figure 11-5. If this object overlaps a solid object, then the koala will be able to jump. In the final version of the game, this sensor will be invisible, but for testing purposes, the box will be colored green or red, depending on whether the koala is on a solid or not.

Figure 11-5. *The koala and the sensor box below to detect if the koala is standing on a solid object or not*

To begin, add the following import statement to the Koala class:

```
import com.badlogic.gdx.graphics.Color;
```

Next, add the following variables to the class:

```
private Animation jump;
private float jumpSpeed;
private BaseActor belowSensor;
```

These objects are set up in the constructor (along with the collision polygon) by adding the following code. Note that belowSensor is slightly less wide than the koala in accordance with the collision polygon that is being used:

```
jump = loadTexture( "assets/koala/jump.png");
jumpSpeed = 450;
setBoundaryPolygon(6);
belowSensor = new BaseActor(0,0, s);
belowSensor.loadTexture("assets/white.png");
belowSensor.setSize( this.getWidth() - 8, 8 );
belowSensor.setBoundaryRectangle();
belowSensor.setVisible(true);
```

To keep belowSensor in the correct position, in the act method, add the following code after the acceleration has been reset:

```
belowSensor.setPosition( getX() + 4, getY() - 8 );
```

To check if the koala is standing on a solid object, add the following pair of methods to the Koala class:

```
public boolean belowOverlaps(BaseActor actor)
{
    return belowSensor.overlaps(actor);
}

public boolean isOnSolid()
{
    for (BaseActor actor : BaseActor.getList( getStage(), "Solid" ))
    {
        Solid solid = (Solid)actor;
        if ( belowOverlaps(solid) && solid.isEnabled() )
            return true;
    }
    return false;
}
```

Jumping will be handled by the following method, which should also be added to the Koala class:

```
public void jump()
{
    velocityVec.y = jumpSpeed;
}
```

Since jumping is a discrete action, it will be called from the LevelScreen class (similar to the shooting action in the *Space Rocks* game). To this end, in the LevelScreen class, add the following import statement:

```
import com.badlogic.gdx.Input.Keys;
```

Then, add the following method to the LevelScreen class:

```
public boolean keyDown(int keyCode)
{
    if (keyCode == Keys.SPACE)
    {
        if ( jack.isOnSolid() )
        {
            jack.jump();
        }
    }
    return false;
}
```

Finally, returning to the Koala class, in the act method, replace the if-else statement used to set the animation with the following improved code, which determines which of the three animations (stand, walk, or jump) should be used, as well as sets the color of belowSensor, for testing and visualization purposes:

```
if ( this.isOnSolid() )
{
    belowSensor.setColor( Color.GREEN );
    if ( velocityVec.x == 0 )
        setAnimation(stand);
    else
        setAnimation(walk);
}
else
{
    belowSensor.setColor( Color.RED );
    setAnimation(jump);
}
```

You are now ready to test your game again. Press the spacebar key (while the koala is on the ground) to jump and watch the color of the belowSensor rectangle change accordingly. Try pressing the spacebar key while the koala is in the air to verify that the koala cannot jump in this situation. Depending on how you designed your level in the Tiled map editor, you may find that you want to change the jump strength of the koala or adjust your level design. At this point, you have implemented the most difficult part of the platformer game. When you are finished testing, in the Koala class, set the visibility of belowSensor to false. In the following section, you will add a variety of objects for the koala to interact with (other than the ground).

Game-World Objects

Now, you will turn your attention to level design. Open your map.tmx file in the Tiled map-editor program. In the Layers panel, select *Object Layer 1*, and in the Tileset panel, select the *object-tileset* tab. Press T to activate the *Insert Tile* tool. Figure 11-6 illustrates a minimal level that features all the different object tiles; Figure 11-7 shows how your program would render that particular map. In the level portrayed, the goal flag is enclosed by red lock blocks, which require the player to obtain the red key. The key can be accessed either by jumping on the springboard to the left or by jumping onto the grassy tiles and then through the platform. Along the way, there are coins for the player to collect and a timer that can be collected to add extra time to reach the goal. Note that the springboard and flag objects will be larger than a single tile, and so the object tile indicates the lower-left corner of where the object will appear. Don't forget to save your tilemap file regularly so that the changes you make are incorporated into your game project.

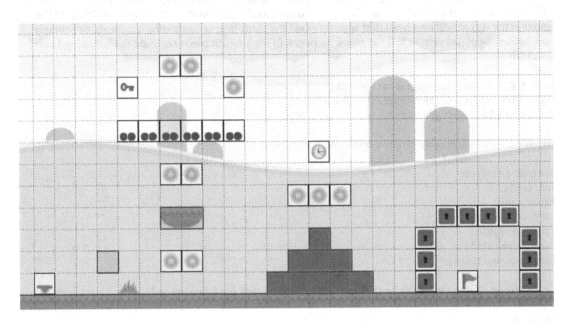

Figure 11-6. *Level design in the Tiled map editor*

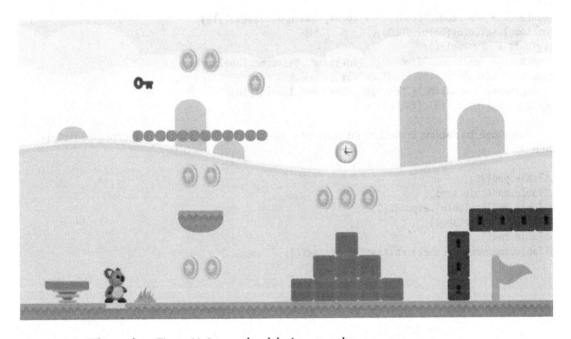

Figure 11-7. *Tilemap from Figure 11-6 as rendered during gameplay*

User Interface

Before adding the code for the game-specific objects, you will set up the user interface. As described in the beginning of this chapter, across the top of the screen will be a label to display the number of coins collected, a table that contains images for collected keys, and a label to show the time remaining. In the center of the screen will be a label that appears when the game is over containing a message dependent on whether the player won or lost the game. To begin, in the LevelScreen class, add the following import statements:

```
import com.badlogic.gdx.graphics.Color;
import com.badlogic.gdx.scenes.scene2d.ui.Label;
import com.badlogic.gdx.scenes.scene2d.ui.Table;
```

Next, add the following variable declarations to the class:

```
boolean gameOver;
int coins;
float time;
Label coinLabel;
Table keyTable;
Label timeLabel;
Label messageLabel;
```

To set up all these variables, in the initialize method, add the following code:

```
gameOver = false;
coins = 0;
time = 60;
coinLabel = new Label("Coins: " + coins, BaseGame.labelStyle);
coinLabel.setColor(Color.GOLD);
keyTable = new Table();
timeLabel = new Label("Time: " + (int)time, BaseGame.labelStyle);
timeLabel.setColor(Color.LIGHT_GRAY);
messageLabel = new Label("Message", BaseGame.labelStyle);
messageLabel.setVisible(false);
```

To arrange the displays in the user-interface table, add the following code to the end of the initialize method:

```
uiTable.pad(20);
uiTable.add(coinLabel);
uiTable.add(keyTable).expandX();
uiTable.add(timeLabel);
uiTable.row();
uiTable.add(messageLabel).colspan(3).expandY();
```

The Goal: Reach the Flag

The first code you will add corresponds to the flag, which is fundamental to the gameplay, as it provides a goal for the player: a location in the level that the koala must reach. To begin, create a new class named Flag that contains the following code:

```
import com.badlogic.gdx.scenes.scene2d.Stage;

public class Flag extends BaseActor
{
    public Flag(float x, float y, Stage s)
    {
        super(x,y,s);
        loadAnimationFromSheet("assets/items/flag.png", 1, 2, 0.2f, true);
    }
}
```

Next, to create an instance of the flag based on the tilemap data, in the LevelScreen class, add the following code to the initialize method:

```
for (MapObject obj : tma.getTileList("Flag") )
{
    MapProperties props = obj.getProperties();
    new Flag( (float)props.get("x"), (float)props.get("y"), mainStage );
}
```

Finally, to handle what happens when Jack the Koala reaches the flag (ending the game, displaying the message, and removing the koala), at the *beginning* of the update method, add the following code:

```
if ( gameOver )
    return;

for (BaseActor flag : BaseActor.getList(mainStage, "Flag"))
{
    if ( jack.overlaps(flag) )
    {
        messageLabel.setText("You Win!");
        messageLabel.setColor(Color.LIME);
        messageLabel.setVisible(true);
        jack.remove();
        gameOver = true;
    }
}
```

At this point, even if you surrounded your goal flag with lock blocks, as seen in Figure 11-6, you could test out the goal-flag mechanic, since the lock blocks have not yet been implemented.

Coins

Next, you will implement the code for the coins, which provide an immediate sense of accomplishment and a measure of progress for the player, and many players will self-impose a secondary goal of collecting as many coins as possible (and, preferably, all the coins). To begin, create a new class called `Coin` that contains the following code:

```
import com.badlogic.gdx.scenes.scene2d.Stage;

public class Coin extends BaseActor
{
    public Coin(float x, float y, Stage s)
    {
        super(x,y,s);
        loadAnimationFromSheet("assets/items/coin.png", 1, 6, 0.1f, true);
    }
}
```

Next, to create instances of the coin based on the tilemap data, in the `LevelScreen` class, add the following code to the `initialize` method:

```
for (MapObject obj : tma.getTileList("Coin") )
{
    MapProperties props = obj.getProperties();
    new Coin( (float)props.get("x"), (float)props.get("y"), mainStage );
}
```

Finally, to handle what happens when Jack the Koala collects a coin (increasing the coin variable, updating the display, and removing the coin from the level), in the `update` method (after the conditional statement that checks if the game is over), add the following code:

```
for (BaseActor coin : BaseActor.getList(mainStage, "Coin"))
{
    if ( jack.overlaps(coin) )
    {
        coins++;
        coinLabel.setText("Coins: " + coins);
        coin.remove();
    }
}
```

At this point, you can test your game and verify that coin collecting works as intended, although depending on your level design, the koala might not be able to reach some of the coins yet.

Time and Timers

Next, you will add the time-based functionality, which provides a sense of urgency and tension in the game, depending on the amount of time available to the player. The timer objects will add a sense of relief to the player by increasing the amount of time available. Timer objects can also be used to create a set of forced checkpoints: if it is impossible for the player to reach the goal flag in the amount of time initially given, they will be forced to collect the timer objects along the way. If you opt for this design, don't forget to test your level to make sure that it is possible to reach the goal! To begin, create a new class called Timer with the following code. Note that since there is no image-based animation, a value-based animation (a pulsing action) is added to draw the player's attention and indicate that this object is interactive.

```
import com.badlogic.gdx.scenes.scene2d.Stage;
import com.badlogic.gdx.scenes.scene2d.Action;
import com.badlogic.gdx.scenes.scene2d.actions.Actions;

public class Timer extends BaseActor
{
    public Timer(float x, float y, Stage s)
    {
        super(x,y,s);
        loadTexture("assets/items/timer.png");

        Action pulse = Actions.sequence(
                Actions.scaleTo(1.1f, 1.1f, 0.5f),
                Actions.scaleTo(1.0f, 1.0f, 0.5f) );

        addAction( Actions.forever(pulse) );
    }
}
```

Next, to create instances of timers based on the tilemap data, in the LevelScreen class, add the following code to the initialize method:

```
for (MapObject obj : tma.getTileList("Timer") )
{
    MapProperties props = obj.getProperties();
    new Timer( (float)props.get("x"), (float)props.get("y"), mainStage );
}
```

Finally, you need to automatically decrement the time variable, update the display, increase the time remaining when a timer is collected, and end the game when the time runs out. To do so, add the following code to the update method:

```
time -= dt;
timeLabel.setText("Time: " + (int)time);

for (BaseActor timer : BaseActor.getList(mainStage, "Timer"))
{
    if ( jack.overlaps(timer) )
    {

        time += 20;
        timer.remove();
    }
}
```

```
if (time <= 0)
{
    messageLabel.setText("Time Up - Game Over");
    messageLabel.setColor(Color.RED);
    messageLabel.setVisible(true);
    jack.remove();
    gameOver = true;
}
```

Once again, feel free to test your code to verify that the time-related functionality works as expected.

Springboards

Jumping is an integral part of any platformer game. However, the player's character is typically unable to reach the top of the screen from the bottom with a single jump. To reach these higher locations, you could add a staircase-like series of solid tiles or, as an alternative, an object that launches the character high into the air (higher than a normal jump). In this spirit, this game features springboard objects, which appear to the player as bouncy platforms. If the koala lands on top of one, he will be launched high into the air. (Simply walking past the object will not trigger this effect, so as to give the player more agency in determining whether they want to make use of the springboard or not.) First, you need to create a class to represent this object. Create a new class called Springboard as follows:

```
import com.badlogic.gdx.scenes.scene2d.Stage;

public class Springboard extends BaseActor
{
    public Springboard(float x, float y, Stage s)
    {
        super(x,y,s);
        loadAnimationFromSheet("assets/items/springboard.png", 1, 3, 0.2f, true);
    }
}
```

Next, in the Koala class, add the following methods, which will be used to determine if the koala is falling and then, if so, launch the koala into the air (similar to the jump method):

```
public boolean isFalling()
{
    return (velocityVec.y < 0);
}

public void spring()
{
    velocityVec.y = 1.5f * jumpSpeed;
}
```

Next, to set up the springboards, in the LevelScreen class, add the following code to the initialize method. Also note the use of the toFront method, which will cause the koala to appear in front of the springboards (rather than behind) when walking by them.

```
for (MapObject obj : tma.getTileList("Springboard") )
{
    MapProperties props = obj.getProperties();
    new Springboard( (float)props.get("x"), (float)props.get("y"), mainStage );
}

jack.toFront();
```

Finally, as usual, you need specify what happens when Jack interacts with a springboard, which also includes the additional conditions just described. In the update method, add the following code:

```
for (BaseActor springboard : BaseActor.getList(mainStage, "Springboard"))
{
    if ( jack.belowOverlaps(springboard) && jack.isFalling() )
    {
        jack.spring();
    }
}
```

Feel free to test your project and watch the koala fly high into the air!

Platforms

Next, you will add the jump-through platforms. These provide a way for a player to reach higher parts of the level (other than jumping on a springboard or jumping up a series of solid tiles). Creating a vertical arrangement of platform objects provides ladder-like functionality. The Platform class will be one of two classes that extend the Solid class, and the jump-through functionality is one of the reasons that the Solid class was designed with the enabled property built in. To begin, create a new class called Platform with the following code:

```
import com.badlogic.gdx.scenes.scene2d.Stage;

public class Platform extends Solid
{
    public Platform(float x, float y, Stage s)
    {
        super(x,y,32,16,s);
        loadTexture("assets/items/platform.png");
    }
}
```

Next, in the Koala class, add the following method, which will be used to determine if the koala is jumping:

```
public boolean isJumping()
{
    return (velocityVec.y > 0);
}
```

Creating the platform objects is a straightforward process. As before, in the `initialize` method of the `LevelScreen` class, add the following code:

```
for (MapObject obj : tma.getTileList("Platform") )
{
    MapProperties props = obj.getProperties();
    new Platform( (float)props.get("x"), (float)props.get("y"), mainStage );
}
```

Typically, platforms function the same as solid objects, with two exceptions: the solid functionality is disabled when jumping up through the platform from below, or when jumping down through the platform from above. In both of these scenarios, the solid functionality of the platform in question must be re-enabled after the koala has passed through it. To begin, in the `update` method, locate the block of code that iterates over the list of `Solid` objects. Since the `Platform` class extends the `Solid` class, platform objects are included in the list. Directly after the line of code that casts the actor to the `Solid` class, add the following code, which completely handles the case where the koala jumps up through a platform:

```
if ( solid instanceof Platform )
{
    if ( jack.isJumping() && jack.overlaps(solid) )
        solid.setEnabled(false);

    if ( jack.isJumping() && !jack.overlaps(solid) )
        solid.setEnabled(true);
}
```

Jumping down through a solid is slightly more complicated. The idea is this: when the player presses the spacebar to jump (which is handled by the keyDown method), if the player is also currently pressing the down arrow key, then any platforms underneath the koala (those which overlap the below sensor) should have their solid functionality disabled. Then, once the koala has completely fallen through the platform (which can be checked in the `update` method), the solid functionality will be re-enabled. To accomplish this, in the `LevelScreen` class, add the following import statement:

```
import com.badlogic.gdx.Gdx;
```

Then, change the keyDown method to the following:

```
public boolean keyDown(int keyCode)
{
    if (gameOver)
        return false;

    if (keyCode == Keys.SPACE)
    {
        if ( Gdx.input.isKeyPressed(Keys.DOWN) )
        {
            for (BaseActor actor : BaseActor.getList(mainStage, "Platform"))
            {
```

```
                Platform platform = (Platform)actor;
                if ( jack.belowOverlaps(platform) )
                {
                    platform.setEnabled(false);
                }
            }
        }
        else if ( jack.isOnSolid() )
        {
            jack.jump();
        }
    }
    return false;
}
```

This change takes care of disabling the solid functionality when jumping down. To re-enable it, in the update method, in the block of code you recently added (that checks for instances of platforms), add the following code:

```
if ( jack.isFalling() && !jack.overlaps(solid) && !jack.belowOverlaps(solid) )
    solid.setEnabled(true);
```

With these additions, jump-through functionality is complete.

Keys and Locks

This final addition to the *Jumping Jack* game involves key and lock objects. The locks are solid blocks that the koala cannot pass through until he collects a key with the same color. Locks can be used to surround the goal flag, wall off collections of coins, or block access to a shortcut or further progress in the level. Keys and locks and a puzzle-like element can be used to encourage backtracking and level exploration. In the tilemap, the object tiles representing the keys and locks have a custom property called color that can be set to any value desired; when reading in the data from the tilemap, this data can be used and the actor color set accordingly.

To begin, create a new class called Key with the following code. Since there is no image-based animation (as was also the case for the Timer object), a value-based animation is added to this object to make the key rotate back and forth by a small amount.

```
import com.badlogic.gdx.scenes.scene2d.Stage;
import com.badlogic.gdx.scenes.scene2d.Action;
import com.badlogic.gdx.scenes.scene2d.actions.Actions;

public class Key extends BaseActor
{
    public Key(float x, float y, Stage s)
    {
        super(x,y,s);
        loadTexture("assets/items/key.png");

        rotateBy(10);
```

```
        Action tilt = Actions.sequence(
                Actions.rotateBy(-20, 0.5f),
                Actions.rotateBy(20, 0.5f) );

        addAction( Actions.forever(tilt) );
    }
}
```

Next, create a new class called Lock with the following code. Since locks are solid, this class extends the Solid class (as was also the case for the Platform class).

```
import com.badlogic.gdx.scenes.scene2d.Stage;

public class Lock extends Solid
{
    public Lock(float x, float y, Stage s)
    {
        super(x,y,32,32,s);
        loadTexture("assets/items/lock.png");
    }
}
```

Whenever a key is collected, this is indicated by adding a corresponding-color key icon to the user interface. To keep track of the data (the colors of the keys that have been collected), an ArrayList will be used. When the koala comes into contact with a lock and has collected the corresponding-color key, the lock will fade out and then be removed from the game. To begin, in the LevelScreen class, add the following import statements:

```
import java.util.ArrayList;
import com.badlogic.gdx.scenes.scene2d.actions.Actions;
```

Then, add the following variable declaration to the class:

```
ArrayList<Color> keyList;
```

In the initialize method, initialize the list as follows:

```
keyList = new ArrayList<Color>();
```

To set up the keys and locks based on the tilemap data, add the following code. Note that in both cases, the value of the custom property named color needs to be determined, and according to that value, the color of the actor needs to be set.

```
for (MapObject obj : tma.getTileList("Key") )
{
    MapProperties props = obj.getProperties();
    Key key = new Key( (float)props.get("x"), (float)props.get("y"), mainStage );
    String color = (String)props.get("color");
    if ( color.equals("red") )
        key.setColor(Color.RED);
```

```
        else // default color
            key.setColor(Color.WHITE);
}

for (MapObject obj : tma.getTileList("Lock") )
{
    MapProperties props = obj.getProperties();
    Lock lock = new Lock( (float)props.get("x"), (float)props.get("y"), mainStage );
    String color = (String)props.get("color");
    if ( color.equals("red") )
        lock.setColor(Color.RED);
    else // default color
        lock.setColor(Color.WHITE);
}
```

Then, in the update method, to handle the collecting of the keys, add the following code:

```
for (BaseActor key : BaseActor.getList(mainStage, "Key"))
{
    if ( jack.overlaps(key) )
    {
        Color keyColor = key.getColor();
        key.remove();
        BaseActor keyIcon =  new BaseActor(0,0,uiStage);
        keyIcon.loadTexture("assets/key-icon.png");
        keyIcon.setColor(keyColor);
        keyTable.add(keyIcon);
        keyList.add(keyColor);
    }
}
```

Also in the update method, locate the for loop that iterates over the list of Solid objects. Since the Lock class extends the Solid class, the locks are included in this list as well. Directly after the block of code corresponding to the conditional statement that checks if the solid is an instance of the Platform class, add the following code. This code checks if the solid is an instance of the Lock class, and, if so, disables and removes the lock if its color has previously been added to the keyList.

```
if ( solid instanceof Lock && jack.overlaps(solid) )
{
    Color lockColor = solid.getColor();
    if ( keyList.contains(lockColor) )
    {
        solid.setEnabled(false);
        solid.addAction( Actions.fadeOut(0.5f) );
        solid.addAction( Actions.after( Actions.removeActor() ) );
    }
}
```

With this addition, the key-and-lock game mechanic is complete. Test your project to verify that the locks are initially solid. Then, collect the corresponding key, check that a key icon appears in the user interface, and then make sure that the locks disappear when you come into contact with them thereafter.

At this point, you have finished implementing all the game mechanics described at the beginning of this chapter. Congratulations, and enjoy your game!

Summary and Next Steps

In this chapter, you learned how to create a platform game, including a main character that had animations for each of its actions (standing, walking, jumping), custom physics, and a "sensor" to determine when it was standing on a solid object and was therefore able to jump. You created a variety of objects for your character to interact with, including a flag to represent the goal, coins to collect, a timer to increase time remaining to complete the level, a springboard that launches the character into the air, platforms to jump through, and keys to remove locks that block the path ahead.

As always, there are more features you should add to the game. The largest omissions are a title screen and instructions screen, as well as audio. Background music should be included to set the mood. Sound effects should be added that correspond with player inputs (such as jumping), as well as game-object interaction (such as collecting an object, bouncing off a springboard, when a lock fades away, or when the game ends, either by reaching the goal flag or by running out of time). You may want to add a secondary obstacle, such as spikes, that penalize the player for coming into contact with them. The penalty could be that the player loses a life (perhaps starting with three lives) and has to restart the level, losing the game after all lives are lost. Alternatively, the player could lose a "health point" and continue on from that point, losing the game after all health points are lost. This alternative approach can be more complicated, however, as you will need to add an "invincibility" period after the character is damaged to give them an opportunity to move away from and escape the danger, otherwise all the character's health points will be drained immediately.

In the next chapter, you will continue using your tilemap-based design skills by creating a top-down swordfighting adventure game called *Treasure Quest*.

CHAPTER 12

■ ■ ■

Adventure Games

This chapter features the most ambitious game project in the entire book: a combat-based adventure game named *Treasure Quest*, inspired by classic console games such as *The Legend of Zelda*. This game uses new features, such as enemy combat with two different types of weapons (a sword and an arrow), non-player characters (NPCs) with messages that depend on the state of the game (such as the number of enemies remaining), and an item-shop mechanic. Figures 12-1 and 12-2 feature screenshots of in-game combat and the item shop, respectively.

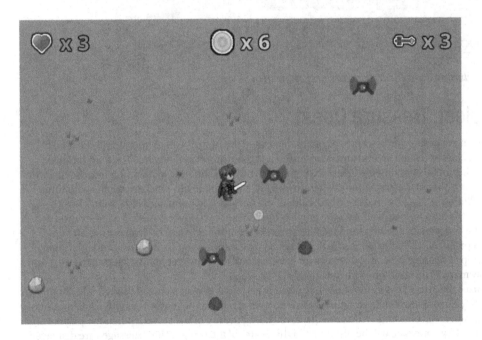

Figure 12-1. Swordfighting the Flyer enemies

© Lee Stemkoski 2018
L. Stemkoski, *Java Game Development with LibGDX*, https://doi.org/10.1007/978-1-4842-3324-5_12

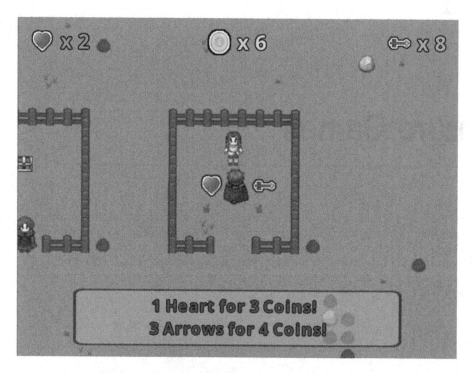

Figure 12-2. *Purchasing items (hearts and arrows) at the Item Shop*

Game Project: Treasure Quest

Treasure Quest is an adventure game where the character, called the hero, is called upon to rid the land of flying bat-like creatures (called Flyers) and is promised a treasure chest as a reward. The hero has two methods of attacking and destroying the Flyers: swinging a sword and shooting arrows (the hero begins with three). Contact with either of these weapons will destroy a Flyer in a single hit. The hero begins with three health points. Colliding with a Flyer reduces the health of the hero by one point, and if the hero's health reaches zero, then the hero is destroyed, and the game is over. When each Flyer is destroyed, they drop a coin, which can be collected by the hero and used to purchase additional health or arrows from an item shop. There are a pair of NPCs in the game: the Shopkeeper, who informs you of the prices and quantities of items in the shop (1 health for 3 coins, 3 arrows for 4 coins), and the Gatekeeper, who guards the treasure and tells you how many Flyers remain to be defeated.

The player uses the arrow keys to move the hero, and the S and A keys to swing the sword and shoot arrows, respectively. Arrows travel in a straight line in whatever direction the player is facing. The amount of health and the numbers of coins and arrows are displayed along the top of the screen. When the player wins or loses the game, a large message will be displayed in the center of the screen. NPC messages are displayed automatically on the bottom of the screen (as seen in Figure 12-2) when the hero is within four pixels of the NPC and automatically disappear when the hero moves away.

The graphics for this game are colorful and cartoonish. Only a few animations are implemented in this project: the hero walking, the sword swinging, the enemies flying, and fading smoke that appears when an enemy is destroyed. Adding additional animations and sound effects to enhance the interaction with game-world objects would be an important and worthwhile addition to this project.

This chapter assumes that you are familiar with the material on tilemaps from Chapters 10 and 11, and that you have installed the Tiled map-editor software. In addition, you will need to be familiar with the material on dialog boxes and sign mechanics from Chapter 5, which is necessary to set up interactions with the NPCs.

Beginning this project requires the same steps as in previous projects: creating a new project, creating an assets folder and a +libs folder (the latter not being necessary if you have set up the userlib directory), copying the custom framework files you created in the first part of this book (BaseGame.java, BaseScreen.java, BaseActor.java), as well as the TilemapActor.java class you developed in Chapter 10 and the DialogBox.java class you developed in Chapter 5, and copying the graphics and audio for this project into your assets folder. As described previously, a BlueJ project named Framework has been created for your convenience and contains the necessary source code files to provide a convenient starting point. To begin the first project:

- Download the source code files for this chapter.

- Make a copy of the downloaded Framework folder (and its contents) and rename it to Treasure Quest.

- Copy all the contents of the downloaded Treasure Quest project assets folder into your newly created Treasure Quest assets folder.

- Open the BlueJ project in your Treasure Quest folder.

- In the CustomGame class, change the name of the class to TreasureQuestGame (BlueJ will then rename the source code file to TreasureQuestGame.java).

- In the Launcher class, change the contents of the main method to the following:

```
Game myGame = new TreasureQuestGame ();
LwjglApplication launcher = new LwjglApplication(
        myGame, "Treasure Quest", 800, 600 );
```

Level Setup

To begin, start the Tiled map-editor software. Create a new map with a map size that has a width of 40 tiles and a height of 40 tiles, and a tile size with the width and height both set to 32 pixels. The resulting map will be 1280 by 1280 pixels. Click the *Save As . . .* button and save the file to your assets directory with the filename map.tmx.

Next, add an object layer to your map. Then, in the Tileset panel, add a new tileset using the image adventure-tiles.png (shown on the left side of Figure 12-3), set the tile size to 32 by 32, and check the box to embed the tileset in the map. Add another new tileset to the map, this time using the image object-tiles. png (shown on the right side of Figure 12-3), in the same way. Since the object tiles will be used to indicate where game-world objects should be spawned, you will need to specify the corresponding Java classes (which you will create later). In the Tileset panel, select *object-tiles* and click on the icon to edit the tileset. In the tab that appears, you will need to click on each tile (one at a time) and add a new custom property to each. The property should be called name; the corresponding values for the tiles (from left to right) are Bush, Rock, Coin, Treasure, Flyer, NPC, ShopHeart, and ShopArrow. In addition, for the NPC tile, add a second custom property called id with a value of default, and a third custom property called text with a value of Hello, World!. (These default values will be overridden for specific instances later on in the tilemap editor).

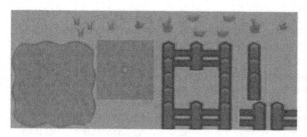

Figure 12-3. *Tilesets for the tile layer (left) and object layer (right)*

Return to the tab featuring the tilemap. In the Layers panel, select *Tile Layer 1*. In the Tileset panel, select *adventure-tiles*, and then press the B key to activate the *Stamp Brush* tool. Add grass tiles across the entire map (which can be greatly accelerated using the *Bucket Fill* tool), then add the wooden fence tiles along the edges. Also, add two large fenced-in areas near the center of the map, each with a two-tile-wide entrance so that the hero can move through; the bottom half of the tilemap is shown in Figure 12-4.

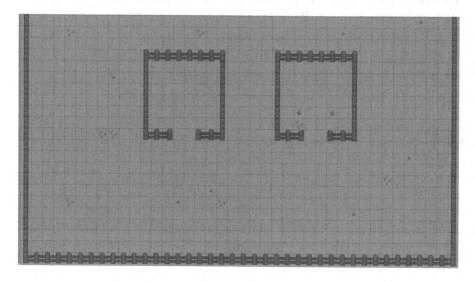

Figure 12-4. *Adding grass and fence tiles to the tile layer*

As was mentioned in the previous chapter, the tile layer is being used only to simplify creating an image from a tileset. The fence tiles should be solid barriers in the actual game, and so you will add rectangles in the object layer to store the data corresponding to those regions. In the Layers panel, select *Object Layer 1* and press R to activate the *Rectangle* tool. Draw rectangles around all the regions containing solid tiles; for simplicity, rectangles can be drawn that surround multiple tiles at once. Each time you add one of these rectangles, you must also add a custom property called name with a value of Solid (which will be used to initialize corresponding actors later). To accelerate this process, when a rectangle is selected and the *Select Object* tool is active, you can use the shortcut key combination Ctrl+D to duplicate the object (including the custom property) and simply reposition and resize the new object (which appears directly on top of the original object). Once you have added rectangles corresponding to all the regions containing solid tiles, add one final rectangle in the bottom center of the map to indicate the starting position of the hero; add the custom property name with a value of Start.

Next, you will add the game objects, aiming for a design similar to that seen in Figure 12-5. Press T to activate the *Insert Tile* tool. Add Bush and Rock tiles (from the *object-tiles* tileset) to wall off a region that includes the hero's starting position and the entrances to the two fenced-in areas you created earlier; this will be used to block enemies from reaching the hero until the player decides they are ready and uses the sword to remove the bushes. In the left fenced area, place a Treasure tile in the center and an NPC tile in the middle of the entrance. It may be useful during this process to hold down the Ctrl key while positioning a tile, which allows a tile to be placed in-between grid squares. For that NPC tile, temporarily switch to the *Select* tool and change the custom property id value to Gatekeeper. (The text that this NPC will display will be set via code later, and so you do not need to change this property.) In the right fenced area, add an NPC tile in the top center, changing id to Shopkeeper and text to 1 heart for 3 coins! 3 arrows for 4 coins! (This will produce the message seen in Figure 12-2.) Also add a ShopHeart tile and a ShopArrow tile in the middle, at least one grid square apart from each other. Add a Coin tile somewhere in this area for later testing purposes. Finally, outside of the closed-in area you created, add a bunch of Flyer tiles and some more scattered Bush and Rock tiles.

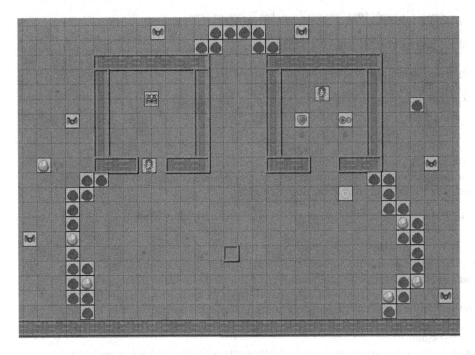

Figure 12-5. *Adding object tiles to the object layer*

When you are finished, save the tilemap, close the Tiled map editor if you wish, and open the Treasure Quest project in BlueJ (if it isn't already open). First, to represent the solid objects with which the hero and other game entities will collide, similar to the process from Chapter 11, create a class named Solid containing the following code:

```
import com.badlogic.gdx.scenes.scene2d.Stage;
public class Solid extends BaseActor
{
    public Solid(float x, float y, float width, float height, Stage s)
```

```
    {
        super(x,y,s);
        setSize(width, height);
        setBoundaryRectangle();
    }
}
```

Next, in the LevelScreen class, add the following import statements:

```
import com.badlogic.gdx.maps.MapObject;
import com.badlogic.gdx.maps.MapProperties;
```

Then, add the following code to the initialize method to load the tilemap and generate the Solid objects corresponding to the rectangles in the tilemap:

```
TilemapActor tma = new TilemapActor("assets/map.tmx", mainStage);

for (MapObject obj : tma.getRectangleList("Solid") )
{
    MapProperties props = obj.getProperties();
    new Solid( (float)props.get("x"),     (float)props.get("y"),
               (float)props.get("width"), (float)props.get("height"),
               mainStage );
}
```

At this point, you can test your project, although you will only see a small part of the level, and you have yet to write the code that creates the game entities represented by the object tiles. Your first task will be to add the hero character, as will be explained in the next section.

The Hero

In this section, you will create the code for the hero character. Since this game features a top-down perspective, the hero will have four different animations corresponding to walking in each of the four compass directions (north, south, east, and west). The main responsibilities of this class are to initialize the animations and display the correct animation depending on the actual angle of motion. It will also be important for this class to be able to determine the angle at which the character is currently facing (which will be a multiple of 90 degrees).

For adventure games or role-playing games, many spritesheets containing top-down character-walking animations typically contain the animation frames for all four directions in a single spritesheet, one direction per row, as illustrated in Figure 12-6. This layout standard has been popularized in particular by the game engine software RPG Maker. To extract the animation frames from the individual rows and create the corresponding animation will require the use of the TextureRegion class split method, as you will see.

Figure 12-6. *A single spritesheet containing walking animations for four directions*

To begin, create a class called Hero with the following code:

```
import com.badlogic.gdx.scenes.scene2d.Stage;
import com.badlogic.gdx.Gdx;
import com.badlogic.gdx.graphics.Texture;
import com.badlogic.gdx.graphics.g2d.TextureRegion;
import com.badlogic.gdx.graphics.g2d.Animation;
import com.badlogic.gdx.utils.Array;

public class Hero extends BaseActor
{
    Animation north;
    Animation south;
    Animation east;
    Animation west;
    float facingAngle;

    public Hero(float x, float y, Stage s)
    {
        super(x,y,s);

        String fileName = "assets/hero.png";
        int rows = 4;
        int cols = 4;
        Texture texture = new Texture(Gdx.files.internal(fileName), true);
        int frameWidth  = texture.getWidth()  / cols;
        int frameHeight = texture.getHeight() / rows;
        float frameDuration = 0.2f;

        TextureRegion[][] temp = TextureRegion.split(texture, frameWidth, frameHeight);
```

```
        Array<TextureRegion> textureArray = new Array<TextureRegion>();
        for (int c = 0; c < cols; c++)
            textureArray.add( temp[0][c] );
        south = new Animation(frameDuration, textureArray, Animation.PlayMode.LOOP_PINGPONG);

        textureArray.clear();
        for (int c = 0; c < cols; c++)
            textureArray.add( temp[1][c] );
        west = new Animation(frameDuration, textureArray, Animation.PlayMode.LOOP_PINGPONG);

        textureArray.clear();
        for (int c = 0; c < cols; c++)
            textureArray.add( temp[2][c] );
        east = new Animation(frameDuration, textureArray, Animation.PlayMode.LOOP_PINGPONG);

        textureArray.clear();
        for (int c = 0; c < cols; c++)
            textureArray.add( temp[3][c] );
        north = new Animation(frameDuration, textureArray, Animation.PlayMode.LOOP_PINGPONG);

        setAnimation(south);
        facingAngle = 270;

        setBoundaryPolygon(8);
        setAcceleration(400);
        setMaxSpeed(100);
        setDeceleration(400);
    }
}
```

Next, you need to select the correct animation according to the direction of movement. This is a straightforward calculation, as visualized in Figure 12-7. For example, if the angle of motion is between 45 and 135 degrees, then the player's movement is mainly to the north, and the hero is facing in the 90-degree direction. The eastern direction is slightly more complicated, as it corresponds to an angle that is either between 0 and 45 degrees or between 315 and 360 degrees, and so this case is left until last in the corresponding set of if-else statements.

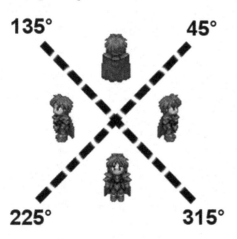

135°   **45°**

225°   **315°**

Figure 12-7. *Ranges for the angle of motion and the corresponding animation*

To implement this functionality—to handle activating the correct animation according to the direction of movement, as well as setting and retrieving the angle at which hero is currently facing—add the following two methods to the Hero class:

```
public void act(float dt)
{
    super.act(dt);
    // pause animation when character not moving
    if ( getSpeed() == 0 )
        setAnimationPaused(true);
    else
    {
        setAnimationPaused(false);

        // set direction animation
        float angle = getMotionAngle();
        if (angle >= 45 && angle <= 135)
        {
            facingAngle = 90;
            setAnimation(north);
        }
        else if (angle > 135 && angle < 225)
        {
            facingAngle = 180;
            setAnimation(west);
        }
        else if (angle >= 225 && angle <= 315)
        {
            facingAngle = 270;
            setAnimation(south);
        }
        else
        {
            facingAngle = 0;
            setAnimation(east);
        }
    }

    alignCamera();
    boundToWorld();
    applyPhysics(dt);
}

public float getFacingAngle()
{
    return facingAngle;
}
```

Next, you will add the hero to the game as well as keyboard controls for moving the hero.

In the LevelScreen class, add the following import statements:

```
import com.badlogic.gdx.Gdx;
import com.badlogic.gdx.Input.Keys;
```

Then, add the following variable declaration:

```
Hero hero;
```

In the initialize method, add the following code, which determines the starting position of the hero from the tilemap data and initializes the object:

```
MapObject startPoint = tma.getRectangleList("start").get(0);
MapProperties startProps = startPoint.getProperties();
hero = new Hero( (float)startProps.get("x"), (float)startProps.get("y"), mainStage);
```

Finally, in the update method, to move the hero with the arrow keys and stop the hero from moving through solid objects, add the following:

```
// hero movement controls
if (Gdx.input.isKeyPressed(Keys.LEFT))
        hero.accelerateAtAngle(180);
if (Gdx.input.isKeyPressed(Keys.RIGHT))
        hero.accelerateAtAngle(0);
if (Gdx.input.isKeyPressed(Keys.UP))
        hero.accelerateAtAngle(90);
if (Gdx.input.isKeyPressed(Keys.DOWN))
        hero.accelerateAtAngle(270);

for (BaseActor solid : BaseActor.getList(mainStage, "Solid"))
{
    hero.preventOverlap(solid);
}
```

This is a good point at which to test your project to make sure that the hero moves as intended.

The Sword

Next, you will add a sword to the game; pressing the S key will make the sword appear. The hero will appear to swing the sword in an arc, and then the sword will disappear. The first challenge in this process is making the sword appear in the correct location, consistent with the animation currently being displayed. In this game, you will assume the hero is right handed, and so the hilt of the sword should appear at the location of the hero's right hand, as shown in Figure 12-8. This position, relative to the bottom-left corner of the hero image, will be stored as a percentage of the width and height of the hero graphic.

Figure 12-8. *The position of the hero's right hand, marked with an X, in each directional image*

In addition, once the sword has been placed correctly, it will be swung through a 90-degree arc, as illustrated in Figure 12-9. This can be accomplished by setting the initial rotation to 45 degrees less than the angle at which the hero is facing, then using an action to rotate the sword by 90 degrees (counter-clockwise). Since the sword should rotate around its hilt (not the center), the *x*-coordinate of the origin should be set to 0.

Figure 12-9. *Arc of rotation used when swinging the sword*

Finally, instead of spawning a new sword object every time the player presses the S key, there will be a single instance of the sword object, visible only when the hero is swinging the sword. In addition, while swinging the sword, the hero will stop moving, and the sword cannot be swung a second time until the first swing is completed (indicated by the sword becoming invisible again). To implement all these features, begin by creating a new class named Sword with the following code:

```
import com.badlogic.gdx.scenes.scene2d.Stage;

public class Sword extends BaseActor
{
    public Sword(float x, float y, Stage s)
    {
        super(x,y,s);
        loadTexture("assets/sword.png");
    }
}
```

Next, in the LevelScreen class, add the following import statements:

```
import com.badlogic.gdx.math.Vector2;
import com.badlogic.gdx.scenes.scene2d.actions.Actions;
```

Then, add the following variable declaration:

```
Sword sword;
```

In the initialize method, set up the sword as follows:

```
sword = new Sword(0,0, mainStage);
sword.setVisible(false);
```

In the update method, to stop the hero from moving during a sword swing, locate the if statements corresponding to hero acceleration and enclose them in a conditional statement as follows:

```
if ( !sword.isVisible() )
{
    // hero movement controls
    // (code omitted below)
}
```

To handle the actual swinging of the sword, add the following method to the LevelScreen class:

```
public void swingSword()
{
    // visibility determines if sword is currently swinging
    if ( sword.isVisible() )
        return;

    hero.setSpeed(0);

    float facingAngle = hero.getFacingAngle();

    Vector2 offset = new Vector2();
    if (facingAngle == 0)
        offset.set( 0.50f, 0.20f );
    else if (facingAngle == 90)
        offset.set( 0.65f, 0.50f );
    else if (facingAngle == 180)
        offset.set( 0.40f, 0.20f );
    else // facingAngle == 270
        offset.set( 0.25f, 0.20f );

    sword.setPosition( hero.getX(), hero.getY() );
    sword.moveBy( offset.x * hero.getWidth(), offset.y * hero.getHeight() );
```

```
    float swordArc = 90;
    sword.setRotation(facingAngle - swordArc/2);
    sword.setOriginX(0);

    sword.setVisible(true);
    sword.addAction( Actions.rotateBy(swordArc, 0.25f) );
    sword.addAction( Actions.after( Actions.visible(false) ) );

    // hero should appear in front of sword when facing north or west
    if (facingAngle == 90 || facingAngle == 180)
        hero.toFront();
    else
        sword.toFront();
}
```

Finally, to enable the player to swing the sword, as this is a discrete action, you need to add a keyDown method to the LevelScreen class:

```
public boolean keyDown(int keycode)
{
    if (keycode == Keys.S)
        swingSword();

    return false;
}
```

At this point, your code is ready to test again. Walk around the screen and try swinging the sword in each direction. However, there is nothing to swing at yet; this will be remedied in the next section.

Bushes and Rocks

At this point, you will add the code to create the bush and rock objects that you entered in the tilemap earlier. Bushes and rocks will be solid objects, and therefore their classes will extend the Solid class. The bushes will be destroyed when hit by the sword, while the rocks will not. The rocks are being implemented as their own object (rather than as a tile) so that a non-square boundary polygon can be set.

To begin, create a class named Bush with the following code:

```
import com.badlogic.gdx.scenes.scene2d.Stage;

public class Bush extends Solid
{
    public Bush(float x, float y, Stage s)
    {
        super(x,y,32,32,s);
        loadTexture("assets/bush.png");
        setBoundaryPolygon(8);
    }
}
```

Then, create a class named Rock with the following code:

```
import com.badlogic.gdx.scenes.scene2d.Stage;

public class Rock extends Solid
{
    public Rock(float x, float y, Stage s)
    {
        super(x,y,32,32,s);
        loadTexture("assets/rock.png");
        setBoundaryPolygon(8);
    }
}
```

To create these objects from the tilemap data, in the LevelScreen class, add the following code to the initialize method:

```
for (MapObject obj : tma.getTileList("Bush") )
{
    MapProperties props = obj.getProperties();
    new Bush( (float)props.get("x"), (float)props.get("y"), mainStage );
}

for (MapObject obj : tma.getTileList("Rock") )
{
    MapProperties props = obj.getProperties();
    new Rock( (float)props.get("x"), (float)props.get("y"), mainStage );
}
```

Since the Bush and Rock classes extend the Solid class, overlap with these objects is already prevented in the update method by the for loop that iterates over the list of Solid objects. For the sword to destroy the bushes, add the following code to the update method:

```
if ( sword.isVisible() )
{
    for (BaseActor bush : BaseActor.getList(mainStage, "Bush"))
    {
        if (sword.overlaps(bush))
            bush.remove();
    }
}
```

At this point, you can test your code again, slashing bushes with the hero's sword to your heart's content.

User Interface

Next, you will set up the user interface, which displays the amount of health remaining and the number of coins and arrows currently being held by the player. To keep the interface simple and minimal, images will be used rather than words, as shown in Figure 12-10. The user interface will also contain a label that displays a "Game Over" message when appropriate, as well as a dialog box for discussions with NPCs (although this will not be used until later).

Figure 12-10. *Images used in the user interface to represent health, coins, and arrows*

To begin, add the following import statements to the LevelScreen class:

```
import com.badlogic.gdx.graphics.Color;
import com.badlogic.gdx.scenes.scene2d.ui.Label;
```

Then, add the following variables to the class:

```
int health;
int coins;
int arrows;
boolean gameOver;
Label healthLabel;
Label coinLabel;
Label arrowLabel;
Label messageLabel;
DialogBox dialogBox;
```

Next, to set up all these variables, add the following code to the initialize method:

```
health = 3;
coins = 5;
arrows = 3;
gameOver = false;

healthLabel = new Label(" x " + health, BaseGame.labelStyle);
healthLabel.setColor(Color.PINK);
coinLabel  = new Label(" x " + coins,  BaseGame.labelStyle);
coinLabel.setColor(Color.GOLD);
arrowLabel = new Label(" x " + arrows, BaseGame.labelStyle);
arrowLabel.setColor(Color.TAN);
messageLabel = new Label("...", BaseGame.labelStyle);
messageLabel.setVisible(false);

dialogBox = new DialogBox(0,0, uiStage);
dialogBox.setBackgroundColor( Color.TAN );
dialogBox.setFontColor( Color.BROWN );
dialogBox.setDialogSize(600, 100);
dialogBox.setFontScale(0.80f);
dialogBox.alignCenter();
dialogBox.setVisible(false);
```

To create the icons used in the interface, add these statements:

```
BaseActor healthIcon = new BaseActor(0,0,uiStage);
healthIcon.loadTexture("assets/heart-icon.png");
BaseActor coinIcon = new BaseActor(0,0,uiStage);
coinIcon.loadTexture("assets/coin-icon.png");
BaseActor arrowIcon = new BaseActor(0,0,uiStage);
arrowIcon.loadTexture("assets/arrow-icon.png");
```

To arrange all these items in the uiTable, add the following code as well:

```
uiTable.pad(20);
uiTable.add(healthIcon);
uiTable.add(healthLabel);
uiTable.add().expandX();
uiTable.add(coinIcon);
uiTable.add(coinLabel);
uiTable.add().expandX();
uiTable.add(arrowIcon);
uiTable.add(arrowLabel);
uiTable.row();
uiTable.add(messageLabel).colspan(8).expandX().expandY();
uiTable.row();
uiTable.add(dialogBox).colspan(8);
```

To keep the labels updated with the correct values of the variables, add the following code to the update method:

```
healthLabel.setText(" x " + health);
coinLabel.setText(" x " + coins);
arrowLabel.setText(" x " + arrows);
```

In addition, when the game is over, you will no longer want to move the player or swing the sword, so add the following code at the *beginning* of the update method:

```
if ( gameOver )
    return;
```

Similarly, at the beginning of the keyDown method, add the following:

```
if ( gameOver )
    return false;
```

This is a good point at which to add a few more game objects: the coins that can be collected and the treasure chest that you find to win the game. First, create a new class named Coin with the following code:

```
import com.badlogic.gdx.scenes.scene2d.Stage;

public class Coin extends BaseActor
{
    public Coin(float x, float y, Stage s)
```

```
    {
        super(x,y,s);
        loadTexture("assets/coin.png");
    }
}
```

Then, create a class named Treasure with the following code:

```
import com.badlogic.gdx.scenes.scene2d.Stage;

public class Treasure extends BaseActor
{
    public Treasure(float x, float y, Stage s)
    {
        super(x,y,s);
        loadTexture("assets/treasure-chest.png");
    }
}
```

Since there will only ever be one treasure object in the game, for simplicity in the code that will follow, add the following variable declaration to the LevelScreen class:

```
Treasure treasure;
```

To create the objects from the map data, add the following to the initialize method:

```
for (MapObject obj : tma.getTileList("Coin") )
{
    MapProperties props = obj.getProperties();
    new Coin( (float)props.get("x"), (float)props.get("y"), mainStage );
}
MapObject treasureTile = tma.getTileList("Treasure").get(0);
MapProperties treasureProps = treasureTile.getProperties();
treasure = new Treasure( (float)treasureProps.get("x"), (float)treasureProps.get("y"),
    mainStage );
```

To handle overlap with these objects, in the update method, add the following code:

```
for ( BaseActor coin : BaseActor.getList(mainStage, "Coin") )
{
    if ( hero.overlaps(coin) )
    {
        coin.remove();
        coins++;
    }
}

if ( hero.overlaps(treasure) )
{
    messageLabel.setText("You win!");
    messageLabel.setColor(Color.LIME);
    messageLabel.setFontScale(2);
    messageLabel.setVisible(true);
```

287

```
        treasure.remove();
        gameOver = true;
}
```

In addition, this is a good time to add the code that handles losing the game, which happens when the hero runs out of health (even though this is not possible yet), so also add the following:

```
if ( health <= 0 )
{
    messageLabel.setText("Game over...");
    messageLabel.setColor(Color.RED);
    messageLabel.setFontScale(2);
    messageLabel.setVisible(true);
    hero.remove();
    gameOver = true;
}
```

Once again, you are ready to test your game. Collect coins (if you have added any) and collect the treasure to see the "You win!" message appear on the screen.

Enemies

Every game should have an obstacle that makes it difficult to reach or achieve the goal. In *Treasure Quest*, you must use your weapons to destroy the enemies that fly around the screen, which are named *Flyers*. Flyers are somewhat random: each has a random speed, and at random times they change their direction of motion to a random angle. Create a new class called Flyer that contains the following code:

```
import com.badlogic.gdx.scenes.scene2d.Stage;
import com.badlogic.gdx.math.MathUtils;

public class Flyer extends BaseActor
{
    public Flyer(float x, float y, Stage s)
    {
        super(x,y,s);
        loadAnimationFromSheet( "assets/enemy-flyer.png", 1, 4, 0.05f, true);
        setSize(48,48);
        setBoundaryPolygon(6);

        setSpeed( MathUtils.random(50,80) );
        setMotionAngle( MathUtils.random(0,360) );
    }
    public void act(float dt)
    {
        super.act(dt);
        if ( MathUtils.random(1,120) == 1 )
            setMotionAngle( MathUtils.random(0,360) );

        applyPhysics(dt);
        boundToWorld();
    }
}
```

When a Flyer is destroyed, it will disappear in a puff of smoke. To this end, create a new class called Smoke that contains the following code, which creates an image that fades out and then removes itself from the game:

```java
import com.badlogic.gdx.scenes.scene2d.Stage;
import com.badlogic.gdx.scenes.scene2d.actions.Actions;

public class Smoke extends BaseActor
{
    public Smoke(float x, float y, Stage s)
    {
        super(x,y,s);
        loadTexture("assets/smoke.png");
        addAction( Actions.fadeOut(0.5f) );
        addAction( Actions.after( Actions.removeActor() ) );
    }
}
```

As usual, you need to create these new objects in the LevelScreen class initialize method, as follows:

```java
for (MapObject obj : tma.getTileList("Flyer") )
{
    MapProperties props = obj.getProperties();
    new Flyer( (float)props.get("x"), (float)props.get("y"), mainStage );
}
```

Flyers will also be blocked by solid objects and change their direction on collision, so in the update method, locate the for loop that iterates over the Solid objects and in the corresponding block of code add the following:

```java
for (BaseActor flyer : BaseActor.getList(mainStage, "Flyer"))
{
    if (flyer.overlaps(solid))
    {
        flyer.preventOverlap(solid);
        flyer.setMotionAngle( flyer.getMotionAngle() + 180 );
    }
}
```

The sword can destroy enemies when it is visible (which indicates it is in the process of being swung). In this case, if the sword overlaps an enemy, smoke will be created and a coin will be spawned (rewarding the player for their victory). In the update method, locate the conditional statement that checks if the sword is visible, and in the corresponding block of code add the following:

```java
for (BaseActor flyer : BaseActor.getList(mainStage, "Flyer"))
{
    if (sword.overlaps(flyer))
    {
        flyer.remove();
        Coin coin = new Coin(0,0, mainStage);
        coin.centerAtActor(flyer);
```

```
        Smoke smoke = new Smoke(0,0, mainStage);
        smoke.centerAtActor(flyer);
    }
}
```

Finally, the hero should lose health when he comes into contact with a Flyer. Checking for overlap is straightforward, but there is a subtle point that needs to be addressed: the hero and the Flyer should be "pushed apart" as much as possible because otherwise the hero could overlap the Flyer multiple times in rapid succession, and the player would quickly lose the game. Therefore, after a collision occurs, the Flyer will start moving in the opposite direction, and the hero will be pushed away from the enemy, which is also sometimes called *knockback*. To calculate the angle of motion, you calculate the vector from the hero to the Flyer by subtracting their positions and then use the angle method of the Vector2 class. To implement these features, add the following code to the update method:

```
for (BaseActor flyer : BaseActor.getList(mainStage, "Flyer"))
{
    if ( hero.overlaps(flyer) )
    {
        hero.preventOverlap(flyer);
        flyer.setMotionAngle( flyer.getMotionAngle() + 180 );
        Vector2 heroPosition  = new Vector2( hero.getX(),  hero.getY() );
        Vector2 flyerPosition = new Vector2( flyer.getX(), flyer.getY() );
        Vector2 hitVector = heroPosition.sub( flyerPosition );
        hero.setMotionAngle( hitVector.angle() );
        hero.setSpeed(100);
        health--;
    }
}
```

At this point, you have finished implementing the Flyer enemies. Test your project, slash the enemies with your sword, and collect the coins they drop.

Arrows

Many combat-centric games feature multiple weapons to appeal to multiple styles of gameplay. You will now add an arrow weapon to this game, which allows you to attack enemies from a distance. To make sure the player doesn't rely on this weapon exclusively, the number of arrows is limited (although additional arrows may be purchased at the item shop that will be created near the end of this chapter). The player can shoot an arrow by pressing the A key, and if the hero has any arrows remaining, an arrow will be spawned and travel in the direction the hero is facing. If the arrow hits an enemy, the enemy will be destroyed; if the arrow hits a solid object, then the arrow will stop moving and fade out. To begin, create a new class called Arrow with the following code:

```
import com.badlogic.gdx.scenes.scene2d.Stage;

public class Arrow extends BaseActor
{
    public Arrow(float x, float y, Stage s)
    {
        super(x,y,s);
```

```
        loadTexture("assets/arrow.png");
        setSpeed(400);
    }

    public void act(float dt)
    {
        super.act(dt);
        applyPhysics(dt);
    }
}
```

Shooting arrows will be handled by the following method, which should be added to the LevelScreen class:

```
public void shootArrow()
{
    if ( arrows <= 0 )
        return;

    arrows--;

    Arrow arrow = new Arrow(0,0, mainStage);
    arrow.centerAtActor(hero);
    arrow.setRotation( hero.getFacingAngle() );
    arrow.setMotionAngle( hero.getFacingAngle() );
}
```

In the keyDown method, add the following code after the code that causes the hero to swing their sword:

```
if (keycode == Keys.A)
    shootArrow();
```

Finally, to specify how the arrows interact with the Flyers and with solid objects, add the following code to the update method:

```
for (BaseActor arrow : BaseActor.getList(mainStage, "Arrow"))
{
    for (BaseActor flyer : BaseActor.getList(mainStage, "Flyer"))
    {
        if (arrow.overlaps(flyer))
        {
            flyer.remove();
            arrow.remove();
            Coin coin = new Coin(0,0, mainStage);
            coin.centerAtActor(flyer);
            Smoke smoke = new Smoke(0,0, mainStage);
            smoke.centerAtActor(flyer);
        }
    }
```

```
    for (BaseActor solid : BaseActor.getList(mainStage, "Solid"))
    {
        if (arrow.overlaps(solid))
        {
            arrow.preventOverlap(solid);
            arrow.setSpeed(0);
            arrow.addAction( Actions.fadeOut(0.5f) );
            arrow.addAction( Actions.after( Actions.removeActor() ) );
        }
    }
}
```

This completes the arrow-shooting mechanic. Test your game and make sure that arrows destroy Flyer enemies, arrows stop when colliding with a solid, the number of arrows decreases when they are shot, and once the number of arrows reaches 0, no more arrows can be shot.

Non-Player Characters

The next feature you will implement is the addition of non-player characters (NPCs). They are very closely related to the sign objects introduced in Chapter 5; you may want to reread the corresponding section before continuing. Similar to signs, approaching an NPC causes the dialog box in the user interface to display an associated message. Unlike signs, however, each NPC will have a distinct appearance, using the identification (id) data set in the tilemap. In addition, each NPC's ID will be checked before displaying the associated message, which gives you the opportunity to display different messages depending on the state of the game. In particular, the game designed in this chapter features two NPCs, one called the Gatekeeper, the other called the Shopkeeper. The Gatekeeper initially blocks access to the treasure, provides instructions to the player (destroy all the Flyers to get the treasure!), informs you how many Flyers remain, and fades out and disappears once you have destroyed them all, thus enabling you to collect the treasure. The Shopkeeper does not feature dynamic text; they simply inform the hero of the prices and quantities of items available for sale in the item shop (which will be created in the next section).

To begin, create a new class called NPC with the following code. Note that the image for the character is not set in the constructor; rather, it is set when the ID is set.

```
import com.badlogic.gdx.scenes.scene2d.Stage;

public class NPC extends BaseActor
{
    // the text to be displayed
    private String text;

    // used to determine if dialog box text is currently being displayed
    private boolean viewing;

    // ID used for specific graphics
    //    and identifying NPCs with dynamic messages
    private String ID;
```

```
    public NPC(float x, float y, Stage s)
    {
        super(x,y,s);
        text = " ";
        viewing = false;
    }

    public void setText(String t)
    {   text = t;   }

    public String getText()
    {   return text;   }

    public void setViewing(boolean v)
    {   viewing = v;   }

    public boolean isViewing()
    {   return viewing;   }

    public void setID(String id)
    {
        ID = id;

        if ( ID.equals("Gatekeeper") )
            loadTexture("assets/npc-1.png");
        else if (ID.equals("Shopkeeper"))
            loadTexture("assets/npc-2.png");
        else // default image
            loadTexture("assets/npc-3.png");
    }

    public String getID()
    {   return ID;   }
}
```

To set up the NPCs, in the initialize method of the LevelScreen class, add the following code; note that you need to also retrieve the properties named id and text that you created when designing the tilemap. Note that the NPC position will be slightly offset from where it was placed in the Tiled map editor, because the NPC size is larger than the icon used to represent it in the tileset. You may find that you wish to adjust the NPC positions in Tiled later.

```
for (MapObject obj : tma.getTileList("NPC") )
{
    MapProperties props = obj.getProperties();
    NPC s = new NPC( (float)props.get("x"), (float)props.get("y"), mainStage );
    s.setID( (String)props.get("id") );
    s.setText( (String)props.get("text") );
}
```

Finally, in the update method, add the following code. If the hero is within four pixels of an NPC, the hero is considered to be nearby, and the corresponding message will be displayed. Once the hero is no longer near the NPC whose message is being viewed, the dialog box will disappear. The majority of the following code is used to create the dynamic messages for the Gatekeeper NPC, which depend on the number of Flyers remaining in the game. Once all the Flyers are destroyed, the Gatekeeper will slowly fade out and then move off-screen, thus enabling the hero to reach the treasure.

```java
for ( BaseActor npcActor : BaseActor.getList(mainStage, "NPC") )
{
    NPC npc = (NPC)npcActor;
    hero.preventOverlap(npc);
    boolean nearby = hero.isWithinDistance(4, npc);

    if ( nearby && !npc.isViewing() )
    {
        // check NPC ID for dynamic text
        if ( npc.getID().equals("Gatekeeper") )
        {
            int flyerCount = BaseActor.count(mainStage, "Flyer");
            String message = "Destroy the Flyers and you can have the treasure. ";
            if ( flyerCount > 1 )
                message += "There are " + flyerCount + " left.";
            else if ( flyerCount == 1 )
                message += "There is " + flyerCount + " left.";
            else // flyerCount == 0
            {
                message += "It is yours!";
                npc.addAction( Actions.fadeOut(5.0f) );
                npc.addAction( Actions.after( Actions.moveBy(-10000, -10000) ) );
            }

            dialogBox.setText(message);
        }
        else
        {
            dialogBox.setText( npc.getText() );
        }

        dialogBox.setVisible( true );
        npc.setViewing( true );
    }

    if (npc.isViewing() && !nearby)
    {
        dialogBox.setText( " " );
        dialogBox.setVisible( false );
        npc.setViewing( false );
    }
}
```

At this point, the NPCs are fully functional. Test your game and talk to each of the NPCs. Try to destroy the Flyers, and then make sure that the Gatekeeper vanishes as expected.

Item Shop

The final mechanic you will implement in the *Treasure Quest* game is the item shop, which consists of two tiles that the hero can stand on, and if the player presses the B key (to buy) and has enough coins, the player will receive the quantity of items stated by the Shopkeeper. This gives value to the coins collected by the player, rather than their just being an abstract number of points or measure of progress. To begin, create a new class named ShopHeart with the following code:

```
import com.badlogic.gdx.scenes.scene2d.Stage;

public class ShopHeart extends BaseActor
{
    public ShopHeart(float x, float y, Stage s)
    {
        super(x,y,s);
        loadTexture("assets/heart-icon.png");
    }
}
```

Also create a class named ShopArrow as follows:

```
import com.badlogic.gdx.scenes.scene2d.Stage;

public class ShopArrow extends BaseActor
{
    public ShopArrow(float x, float y, Stage s)
    {
        super(x,y,s);
        loadTexture("assets/arrow-icon.png");
    }
}
```

Since there will only be one instance of each of these objects, in the LevelScreen class, add the following variables:

```
ShopHeart shopHeart;
ShopArrow shopArrow;
```

To create these objects, add the following to the initialize method:

```
MapObject shopHeartTile = tma.getTileList("ShopHeart").get(0);
MapProperties shopHeartProps = shopHeartTile.getProperties();
shopHeart = new ShopHeart( (float)shopHeartProps.get("x"), (float)shopHeartProps.get("y"),
    mainStage );

MapObject shopArrowTile = tma.getTileList("ShopArrow").get(0);
MapProperties shopArrowProps = shopArrowTile.getProperties();
shopArrow = new ShopArrow( (float)shopArrowProps.get("x"), (float)shopArrowProps.get("y"),
    mainStage );
```

Since buying items is a discrete action, add the following code to the keyDown method after the code that activates the weapons:

```
if (keycode == Keys.B)
{
    if (hero.overlaps(shopHeart) && coins >= 3)
    {
        coins -= 3;
        health += 1;
    }

    if (hero.overlaps(shopArrow) && coins >= 4)
    {
        coins -= 4;
        arrows += 3;
    }
}
```

That's all there is to it! Try out your game again, destroy some Flyers, and spend your hard-earned coins.

Once you have reached this point, congratulations are in order, as you have completed the longest project in this book!

Summary and Next Steps

In this chapter, you created the game *Treasure Quest*, a combat-based adventure game, which included new features such as combat with multiple types of weapons, NPCs with dynamic text, and an item shop. While implementing these features, you also handled subtle details such as sword placement, the interaction of enemies and arrows with solid objects, and knockback resulting from hero-enemy collisions.

As always, you should add features such as menus and sounds. If you wish, you could add new types of weapons, such as bombs, that create explosions that destroy both rocks and enemies. Bombs would likely be a limited resource, similar to arrows, and could perhaps be purchased at the item shop as well. Additionally, you could create a new kind of enemy that follows the player for added difficulty. You could change the goal of the game: instead of destroying Flyers, perhaps you have to collect a certain number of coins to proceed. You could remove the sword from the game, or even remove weapons entirely, making the game about dodging and avoiding enemies. The possibilities are endless!

At this point, you have completed the second part of the book. The final part of this book contains advanced techniques and algorithms that explain how to use gamepad controllers, advanced graphics, and more, which can be used to improve all of the games you have worked on up to this point.

PART III

■ ■ ■

Advanced Topics

This final part of the book contains some additional optional features that can be added to many of the previous projects, such as gamepad controller input and special effects made with particle systems (an efficient method for creating unique, non-repeating animated effects). Some game projects involving advanced algorithms and 3D graphics are also included in this part.

Chapter 13: Alternative Sources of User Input

This chapter will explore two alternative sources of user input: gamepad controllers and touch-screen controls. In particular, you will add these alternative sources of user input to the *Starfish Collector* game that has been featured in previous chapters.

Chapter 14: Maze Games

In this chapter, you will learn how to create the maze-based game *Maze Runman*, which is inspired by arcade games such as *Pac-Man* and the early console game *Maze Craze*. The main new concepts in this chapter are algorithms for generating and solving mazes.

Chapter 15: Advanced 2D Graphics

In this chapter, you will learn two techniques for incorporating sophisticated graphics into your projects. The first technique is particle systems, which can create special effects such as explosions; this will be incorporated into the *Space Rocks* game in place of spritesheet-based animations. The second technique is shader programming, which manipulates the pixels of a rendered image to create effects such as blurring or glowing; this will be incorporated into the *Starfish Collector* game.

Chapter 16: Introduction to 3D Graphics and Games

This chapter will introduce some of the 3D graphics capabilities of LibGDX and the concepts and classes necessary to describe and render a three-dimensional scene. To simplify and streamline this process, you'll adapt some old classes and write some new classes to accomplish the various tasks involved. Finally, you'll create the game *Starfish Collector 3D*, a three-dimensional version of the *Starfish Collector* game introduced at the beginning of the book.

Chapter 17: The Journey Continues

This final chapter will present a variety of steps to consider as you continue on in game development. Among these, you'll explore working on additional projects, learning skills in related areas, and bringing your games to a wider audience. Along the way, the chapter will present lists of resources of all types, as well as general advice for many situations.

CHAPTER 13

▪▪▪

Alternative Sources of User Input

In previous chapters, your games have been controlled with traditional desktop computer hardware: a keyboard and a mouse. In this chapter, you'll explore two alternative sources of user input: gamepad controllers and touchscreen controls. In particular, you will add these alternative sources of user input to the *Starfish Collector* game that has been featured in previous chapters. If you do not have access to a gamepad with a USB connector (as discussed later in this chapter), you can still follow along; the code will still compile, and you'll leave keyboard controls as a fallback (a good practice to consider in general for the convenience of your game's players). Similarly, even if you don't have access to a device that's touchscreen capable, learning about the associated design considerations is still worthwhile. Furthermore, touch events and mouse events are handled by the same methods in LibGDX; you can simulate single-touch input (but not multitouch input) with the mouse. On the other hand, if neither gamepad nor touch-based input is of interest to you, this entire chapter may be omitted without loss of continuity.

Gamepad Controllers

Gamepad controllers are specialized hardware devices that make it easier for the player to enter game-related input. They have been in existence as long as game consoles have, and have included various configurations of components such as joysticks, buttons, directional pads, dials, triggers, and touch pads. With the increase in console-style gaming available on desktop computers, many gamepads that can be connected via USB ports are now available. In this section, you'll develop controls for an Xbox 360 gamepad, or one of the many alternative products that emulate it, such as the Logitech F310 gamepad, shown in Figure 13-1.

Figure 13-1. Xbox 360 and Logitech F310 gamepad controllers

© Lee Stemkoski 2018
L. Stemkoski, *Java Game Development with LibGDX*, https://doi.org/10.1007/978-1-4842-3324-5_13

Support for gamepad input is provided by the Controller and Controllers classes. These are not part of the core LibGDX libraries, and thus their code is contained in different JAR files, which must be included in your project. To begin, make a copy of your Starfish Collector project from Chapter 5 and rename the copied project folder to Starfish Collector Gamepad. Download the source code for this chapter and copy the contents of the downloaded gamepad project's +libs folder into your project's +libs folder (or into the BlueJ userlib directory if you chose to set it up at the beginning of the book). In particular, there are three new JAR files required to integrate gamepad controllers in desktop games: gdx-controllers.jar, gdx-controllers-desktop.jar, and gdx-controllers-desktop-natives.jar.

Recall that there are two types of input, *continuous* and *discrete*, which are processed using different techniques. For continuous input (corresponding to actions such as walking), you poll the state of the hardware device in the update method, which typically runs 60 times per second. Later, you will see that this process is analogous to polling for keyboard input: keyboard polling uses methods of the Gdx.input object, such as isKeyPressed, while gamepad polling uses methods of a Controller object, such as getAxis and getButton. For discrete input (corresponding to actions such as jumping), you previously implemented the methods in the InputProcessor interface. Those methods are automatically activated when certain inputs are received (such as when a key is initially pressed down). Similarly, you will implement the methods of an interface named ControllerListener, which are activated in response to discrete gamepad events, such as when a gamepad button is initially pressed down. You will write the code for both continuous and discrete gamepad input over the course of the next two sections.

Continuous Input

In this section, you will modify the Turtle class so that the joystick of a gamepad can be used to move the turtle. In particular, this will allow you to precisely control both the speed and the angle of motion of the turtle, which is not possible when using keyboard controls alone. This process will require you to retrieve the instance of the active Controller object. The Controllers class provides the static utility method getControllers, which will help you with this process. Once the Controller has been obtained, you can poll for the state of joysticks, buttons, directional pads, and trigger buttons by using one of four provided get-style methods. Many of these require a single parameter: a constant value that corresponds to a component of the gamepad. These values are gamepad specific, and a particular gamepad might even have different values for different operating systems. The most robust method for determining these values is to allow the player to configure the gamepad mapping at runtime by looping through the different actions required by the game, asking the player to press the corresponding button, and storing the values for later use. For simplicity, you will assume that the player will use an Xbox 360–style controller (which includes those such as the Logitech F310 controller mentioned earlier), and you will create a class to store the constant values corresponding to the various gamepad components for this model. Open the Starfish Collector Gamepad project in BlueJ and create a new class named XBoxGamepad with the following code:

```
import com.badlogic.gdx.controllers.PovDirection;

public class XBoxGamepad
{
    /** button codes */
    public static final int BUTTON_A               = 0;
    public static final int BUTTON_B               = 1;
    public static final int BUTTON_X               = 2;
    public static final int BUTTON_Y               = 3;
    public static final int BUTTON_LEFT_SHOULDER   = 4;
    public static final int BUTTON_RIGHT_SHOULDER  = 5;
    public static final int BUTTON_BACK            = 6;
    public static final int BUTTON_START           = 7;
```

```
public static final int BUTTON_LEFT_STICK    = 8;
public static final int BUTTON_RIGHT_STICK   = 9;

/** directional pad codes */
public static final PovDirection DPAD_UP    = PovDirection.north;
public static final PovDirection DPAD_DOWN  = PovDirection.south;
public static final PovDirection DPAD_RIGHT = PovDirection.east;
public static final PovDirection DPAD_LEFT  = PovDirection.west;

/** joystick axis codes */
// X-axis: -1 = left, +1 = right
// Y-axis: -1 = up  , +1 = down
public static final int AXIS_LEFT_X  = 1;
public static final int AXIS_LEFT_Y  = 0;
public static final int AXIS_RIGHT_X = 3;
public static final int AXIS_RIGHT_Y = 2;

/** trigger codes */
// Left & Right Trigger buttons treated as a single axis; same ID value
// Values - Left trigger: 0 to +1.  Right trigger: 0 to -1.
// Note: values are additive; they can cancel each other if both are pressed.
public static final int AXIS_LEFT_TRIGGER  = 4;
public static final int AXIS_RIGHT_TRIGGER = 4;
}
```

The following Controller class methods are available to poll the state of a gamepad component:

- To poll the state of the joystick, use getAxis(code), where code is an integer corresponding to either the left or right joystick, and either the *x* or *y* direction. The value returned is a float in the range from –1 to 1. On the *x* axis, –1 corresponds to left and +1 corresponds to right, while on the *y* axis, –1 corresponds to up and +1 corresponds to down. For example, consider the following line of code: float x = gamepad.getAxis(XBoxGamepad.AXIS_LEFT_X); If the value of x equals 0.5, then that means the left joystick of the gamepad is being pressed halfway to the right. It is important to remember that the orientation of the *y* axis used by most controllers (negative values correspond to the "up" direction) is the opposite orientation assumed by the LibGDX libraries (positive values correspond to the "up" direction). This will be important when processing input later.

- To poll the state of the triggers, you also use getAxis(code). On Xbox 360-style controllers, the left and right triggers are treated as a single axis. Pressing the left trigger generates the values in the range from 0 (not pressed) to +1 (fully pressed), while pressing the right trigger generates values in the range from 0 (not pressed) to –1 (fully pressed). If both triggers are pressed at once, the getAxis method will return the sum of their values; in particular, if both triggers are fully pressed, getAxis will return 0.

- To check the state of the gamepad buttons, use getButton(code), where code is an integer corresponding to a gamepad button. The value returned is a Boolean that indicates whether the corresponding button is currently being pressed down.

- To determine which direction is being pressed on the directional pad,[1] use getPov(num), where num is the index of the directional pad (typically 0). Directional pads are interesting in that they yield return values more complex than a button (a Boolean value) but less complex than a joystick axis (a float value). This "middle ground" level of input is handled by returning an enumerated type (an enum) defined in the imported PovDirection class. However, for convenience, the XBoxGamepad class defines a set of alternative names that may be more familiar to modern gamers.

To begin incorporating this new functionality into your project, in the Turtle class, add the following import statements:

```
import com.badlogic.gdx.controllers.Controller;
import com.badlogic.gdx.controllers.Controllers;
import com.badlogic.gdx.math.Vector2;
```

Next, you will modify some of the code in the act method, which is where the continuous input is processed. In the following code, you check to see whether a controller is connected by testing whether the Array of controllers (retrieved by the getControllers method) contains at least one element; if not, the else block contains the keyboard controls you previously created as a fallback. If a single gamepad is connected, you retrieve it by getting the zeroth element of the array. Then, you determine the amount that the left analog joystick is being pressed in the *x* and *y* directions (remembering to negate the *y* value as mentioned previously), using the constants defined in the XBoxGamepad class you created earlier. Those values are then used to create a Vector2 object, which represents the direction in which the joystick is being pressed. You then need to check whether the joystick has moved passed a certain threshold (called the *deadzone*, used to compensate for controller sensitivity, typically set to a value between 10 and 20 percent), which can be determined by checking the length of the vector. If it passes this test, then you set the speed of the turtle to a fraction of its maximum speed (using the length of the direction vector as the percentage) and set the angle of motion of the turtle to the angle in which the direction vector is pointing. To accomplish these tasks, add the following code to the act method of the Turtle class, noting that the code corresponding to processing keyboard input should be moved into the else block:

```
if (Controllers.getControllers().size > 0)
{
    Controller gamepad = Controllers.getControllers().get(0);
    float xAxis =  gamepad.getAxis(XBoxGamepad.AXIS_LEFT_X);
    float yAxis = -gamepad.getAxis(XBoxGamepad.AXIS_LEFT_Y);
    Vector2 direction = new Vector2(xAxis, yAxis);

    float length = direction.len();
    float deadZone = 0.10f;
    if (length > deadZone)
    {
        setSpeed( length * 100 );
        setMotionAngle( direction.angle() );
    }
}
```

---

[1]The control element typically referred to as a directional pad was referred to as a *point-of-view* control in traditional flight simulators, which explains the use of the POV acronym in the LibGDX source code.

```
else
{
    if (Gdx.input.isKeyPressed(Keys.LEFT))
        accelerateAtAngle(180);
    if (Gdx.input.isKeyPressed(Keys.RIGHT))
        accelerateAtAngle(0);
    if (Gdx.input.isKeyPressed(Keys.UP))
        accelerateAtAngle(90);
    if (Gdx.input.isKeyPressed(Keys.DOWN))
        accelerateAtAngle(270);
}
```

If you have an XBox 360–style gamepad available, you can test the code at this point.

Discrete Input

Next, you will write the code necessary to process discrete gamepad input events. To avoid modifying your existing BaseScreen class, you will create an extension of this class that implements the ControllerListener interface with default versions of all the necessary methods, which can then be overridden as needed. (In practice, you will probably only make use of the buttonDown method.) Any class that uses gamepad input can then extend this new class instead of the original BaseScreen class. To begin, create a new class named BaseGamepadScreen with the following code:

```
import com.badlogic.gdx.controllers.ControllerListener;
import com.badlogic.gdx.controllers.Controller;
import com.badlogic.gdx.controllers.Controllers;
import com.badlogic.gdx.controllers.PovDirection;
import com.badlogic.gdx.math.Vector3;

public abstract class BaseGamepadScreen extends BaseScreen implements ControllerListener
{
    public BaseGamepadScreen()
    {
        super();
        Controllers.clearListeners();
        Controllers.addListener(this);
    }

    // methods required by ControllerListener interface
    //   enable discrete input processing

    public void connected(Controller controller)
    {  }

    public void disconnected(Controller controller)
    {  }

    public boolean xSliderMoved(Controller controller, int sliderCode, boolean value)
    {  return false;  }

    public boolean ySliderMoved(Controller controller, int sliderCode, boolean value)
    {  return false;  }
```

```
    public boolean accelerometerMoved(Controller controller, int accelerometerCode,
                                      Vector3 value)
    {   return false;   }

    public boolean povMoved(Controller controller, int povCode, PovDirection value)
    {   return false;   }

    public boolean axisMoved(Controller controller, int axisCode, float value)
    {   return false;   }

    public boolean buttonDown(Controller controller, int buttonCode)
    {   return false;   }

    public boolean buttonUp(Controller controller, int buttonCode)
    {   return false;   }
}
```

Note that this class must be declared as abstract because it does not implement the initialize or update methods from the BaseScreen class. Also note that the listener is "activated" by adding the currently active Screen to the set of listeners managed by the Controllers class. At the same time, you must also remove (via the clearListeners method) any previously added ControllerListener objects; you don't want other Screen objects that may be inactive (but still reside in memory) to respond to input, because this could cause unexpected problems. (For example, if pressing the Start button on a gamepad were used to begin a new game from the menu screen, after switching to the game screen you would no longer want this action to occur when pressing the gamepad Start button; therefore, you must stop the menu screen from "listening" and responding to these events.)

Next, you want to modify the LevelScreen class so that pressing the Back key on the gamepad will restart the level (similar to clicking on the Restart button in the top-right corner of the user interface). This requires three steps. First, in the LevelScreen class, add the following import statement:

```
import com.badlogic.gdx.controllers.Controller;
```

Next, change the class declaration so that it extends the BaseGamepadScreen class rather than the BaseScreen class, as follows:

```
public class LevelScreen extends BaseGamepadScreen
```

Finally, you need to add a buttonDown method to this class to process discrete gamepad button presses (analogous to how the keyDown method processes discrete keyboard key presses). Add the following method to the LevelScreen class:

```
public boolean buttonDown(Controller controller, int buttonCode)
{
    if (buttonCode == XBoxGamepad.BUTTON_BACK)
        StarfishGame.setActiveScreen( new LevelScreen() );

    return false;
}
```

That's all there is to it! Feel free to test out your project once again; move the turtle and collect some starfish, and then press the Back button on the gamepad to reset the level, thus enabling you to enjoy collecting the starfish all over again.

Touchscreen Controls

In this section, you'll learn how to implement gamepad-inspired onscreen touch controls. Again, as mentioned in the beginning of this chapter, access to a touchscreen device is not needed to test the code for this section, as LibGDX handles mouse events and touch events with the same methods; single-touch input is simulated by the mouse. Since you already learned about the Button class in Chapter 5, you are well on your way. In what follows, you'll learn about another user-interface control provided by the LibGDX library, the Touchpad class, which was created to simulate a traditional arcade joystick. Figure 13-2 shows an example of a traditional arcade-style joystick and a touchpad control that can be created with LibGDX, which is rendered in a top-down perspective of the arcade-style joystick.

Figure 13-2. *A traditional arcade-style joystick and a touchpad control created in LibGDX*

The biggest challenge to successfully using these controls is not the creation of the object, but rather a design challenge: how should these elements be arranged and placed on the screen? One option is to overlay the elements on top of the game world itself, as you have with various Label objects in previous chapters. However, you rapidly discover the problem that the controls—which must typically be much larger than labels, for easy operation—can obscure the game world to the extent that it interferes with game play. If poorly placed, a touchpad could completely obscure the main character. Figure 13-3 illustrates this possible situation by placing the touchpad in the lower-left corner of the game screen. Notice how it could cover the turtle partially, or even completely!

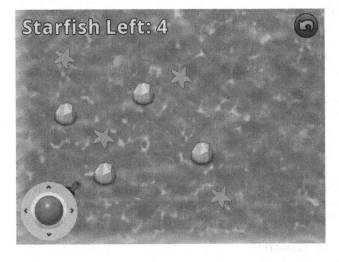

Figure 13-3. *A poorly placed touchpad control obscuring the turtle*

Some games attempt to address this issue by making the controls on the user interface translucent, yet the core difficulty remains because the player's fingers will often be positioned over the region where the controls are, thus still obscuring the view of the game world. An alternative approach that you will implement in this section is to reserve a particular region of the screen for the controls and render the game world in the remaining area, as illustrated in Figure 13-4.

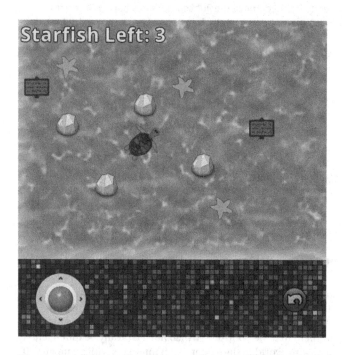

Figure 13-4. *Placing the game controls in a dedicated region below the game world*

Redesigning the Window Layout

To begin, make another copy of your Starfish Collector project from Chapter 5 and rename this one to Starfish Collector Touchscreen. Download the source code for this project from the book's website and copy the contents of the downloaded project's assets folder into your new project's assets folder. In particular, there are three new images, corresponding to the additions seen in Figure 13-4. (You do not need to copy the contents of the +libs folder; unlike the gamepad project from the first half of this chapter, there are no new JAR files required.)

Your first goal will be to reconfigure where the stages will be displayed on the screen and to add a new stage and table to contain the touch controls. You will need to resize the LevelScreen window to 800 by 800 pixels, reserving the lower 800 by 200 pixels for the touch controls, but to minimize the number of changes you need to make, you will keep the other screens at their original size. In addition, you will want to render the game world in an 800 by 600 region, with its lower-left corner starting at the point (0, 200); this rendering area can be set using a method called glViewport, as you will see later. As a first step, in the BaseScreen class, you need to set the size of the main and user interface stages using a FitViewport object, for otherwise they will default to the size of the entire window (which has been acceptable for previous projects, but will not be for this project). In the BaseScreen class, add the following import statement:

```
import com.badlogic.gdx.utils.viewport.FitViewport;
```

In the BaseScreen constructor, change the lines of code that initialize the mainStage and uiStage objects to the following:

```
mainStage = new Stage( new FitViewport(800,600) );
uiStage = new Stage( new FitViewport(800,600) );
```

Next, you need to create the stage and table for the controls and determine where everything will be rendered. As in the previous project, you will create an extension of the BaseScreen class, called BaseTouchScreen, which incorporates these new elements and overrides the render method. Unlike the BaseScreen class, however, you will *not* initialize the stage and table in the BaseTouchScreen constructor method. This is because the BaseTouchScreen constructor immediately and automatically calls the BaseScreen constructor, which in turn calls the initialize method (which is where you will add components to the stage and table), and only after this does the program flow return to execute the rest of the code in the BaseTouchScreen constructor. Due to this unavoidable order of execution, you will create a separate method called initializeControlArea that sets up the stage and table that will contain the controls, and you will call this method from the initialize method in the LevelScreen class. You also need to make sure that the new stage is able to process discrete input by adding it to and removing it from the game's InputMultiplexer at the appropriate times, which takes place in the show and hide methods. In addition, to avoid the complexity of translating touch/mouse coordinates to viewport coordinates, the stage containing the controls will be the same height as the window, even though only the lower 200 pixels will be used. To implement these features, create a new class called BaseTouchScreen with the following code:

```
import com.badlogic.gdx.Gdx;
import com.badlogic.gdx.graphics.GL20;
import com.badlogic.gdx.scenes.scene2d.Stage;
import com.badlogic.gdx.scenes.scene2d.ui.Table;
import com.badlogic.gdx.InputMultiplexer;
import com.badlogic.gdx.utils.viewport.FitViewport;

public abstract class BaseTouchScreen extends BaseScreen
{
    protected Stage controlStage;
    protected Table controlTable;

    public BaseTouchScreen()
    {
        super();
    }

    // run this method during initialize
    public void initializeControlArea()
    {
        controlStage = new Stage( new FitViewport(800,800) );
        controlTable = new Table();
        controlTable.setFillParent(true);
        controlStage.addActor(controlTable);
    }
```

```
public void show()
{
    super.show();
    InputMultiplexer im = (InputMultiplexer)Gdx.input.getInputProcessor();
    im.addProcessor(controlStage);
}

public void hide()
{
    super.hide();
    InputMultiplexer im = (InputMultiplexer)Gdx.input.getInputProcessor();
    im.removeProcessor(controlStage);
}

public void render(float dt)
{
    // act methods
    uiStage.act(dt);
    mainStage.act(dt);
    controlStage.act(dt);

    // defined by user
    update(dt);

    // clear the screen
    Gdx.gl.glClearColor(0,0,0,1);
    Gdx.gl.glClear(GL20.GL_COLOR_BUFFER_BIT);

    // set the drawing regions and draw the graphics
    Gdx.gl.glViewport(0,200, 800,600);
    mainStage.draw();
    uiStage.draw();

    Gdx.gl.glViewport(0,0, 800,800);
    controlStage.draw();
}
}
```

The next steps are to add a joystick-like control, represented by the Touchpad class, and move the Reset button to controlStage, which is covered in the following section.

Working with a Touchpad

Touchpad objects are rendered using two images: one representing the background, and the other representing the knob. The user can touch (or click) the knob and drag it off-center; its movement is constrained to a circular area contained within the rectangular region defined by the background image.

These objects require two parameters to be initialized. First, you supply a value for the deadzone radius—the minimal distance (in pixels) the knob must be dragged in order for any change to register. (This is the same deadzone concept as was discussed earlier in the gamepad section of this chapter.) This is useful for situations when the player wants to leave a finger on the touchpad but also wants the character to remain still. Without a deadzone setting, the controls would be too sensitive for this to be possible. It is unlikely that the average player would have pixel-perfect finger positioning to keep the knob exactly centered, and the result would be unwanted (and possibly player-frustrating) drift of the character being controlled.

Second, the images used in a Touchpad object are stored in a TouchpadStyle object, which contains two images, both stored as Drawable objects, as is standard for UI elements in LibGDX; you encountered this situation before when creating the image for the Restart button object. As before, you will load each image into a Texture object then convert it to a TextureRegion and then a TextureRegionDrawable.

To begin these additions, in the LevelScreen class, change the class declaration so that it extends your newly created BaseTouchScreen class instead of BaseScreen as follows:

```
public class LevelScreen extends BaseTouchScreen
```

Then, add the following import statements:

```
import com.badlogic.gdx.scenes.scene2d.ui.Touchpad;
import com.badlogic.gdx.scenes.scene2d.ui.Touchpad.TouchpadStyle;
import com.badlogic.gdx.math.Vector2;
```

Also, add the following variable declaration:

```
private Touchpad touchpad;
```

Then, in the initialize method, add the following code to change the size of the window, activate the function that sets up the control stage and table, and add a background image:

```
Gdx.graphics.setWindowedMode(800,800);
initializeControlArea();
BaseActor controlBackground = new BaseActor(0,0, controlStage);
controlBackground.loadTexture("assets/pixels.jpg");
```

After this, add the following code to set up the Touchpad object, with a deadzone radius of 5 pixels:

```
TouchpadStyle touchStyle = new TouchpadStyle();

Texture padKnobTex = new Texture(Gdx.files.internal("assets/joystick-knob.png"));
TextureRegion padKnobReg = new TextureRegion(padKnobTex);
touchStyle.knob = new TextureRegionDrawable(padKnobReg);

Texture padBackTex = new Texture(Gdx.files.internal("assets/joystick-background.png"));
TextureRegion padBackReg = new TextureRegion(padBackTex);
touchStyle.background = new TextureRegionDrawable(padBackReg);

touchpad = new Touchpad(5, touchStyle);
```

Next, add the touchpad and the Restart button to controlTable as follows. Note the addition of an empty row with height 600, which is used to keep the controls in the lower 200 pixels of the window (which has height 800).

```
controlTable.toFront();
controlTable.pad(50);
controlTable.add().colspan(3).height(600);
```

```
controlTable.row();
controlTable.add(touchpad);
controlTable.add().expandX();
controlTable.add(restartButton);
```

Now, in order to make use of the touchpad data, in the update method, add the following code, which stores the touchpad knob displacement data in a vector, using the length of the vector to set the turtle's speed to a percentage of its maximum speed (100 pixels/second) and the angle of the vector to set the turtle's direction of motion. This code is similar to the code from the earlier section on gamepad controllers, except that the Touchpad class itself handles the deadzone calculation, so it does not appear in the comparison here:

```
Vector2 direction = new Vector2( touchpad.getKnobPercentX(), touchpad.getKnobPercentY() );
float length = direction.len();
if ( length > 0 )
{
    turtle.setSpeed( 100 * length );
    turtle.setMotionAngle( direction.angle() );
}
```

Finally, since you are using the touchpad to control the turtle's motion, you can delete the lines of code in the Turtle class act method that check for keyboard input and set the acceleration of the turtle. At this point, the *Starfish Collector* game should now render as shown in Figure 13-4, and you are ready to test your program, using the mouse to control the touchpad that now moves the turtle.

Summary and Next Steps

In this chapter, you added two new ways for the player to interact with the *Starfish Collector* game. First, you added gamepad-controller support to the base game by using the controller extensions for the LibGDX libraries. This required the inclusion of some new JAR files in your project, as well as the creation of an extension of the BaseScreen class and a class dedicated to storing the values corresponding to each of the joysticks, buttons, directional pads, and triggers on your particular gamepad. You learned how to poll for continuous input, as well as how to implement an interface that responds to discrete input. Following this, you learned how to add touchscreen-style support, creating another extension of the BaseScreen class and using a Touchpad object. This chapter also discussed the design issues that arise when adding onscreen controls and showed one way to alleviate these issues—by repositioning the rendering locations of the stages using the glViewport method.

At this point, to practice and refine your newfound skills, you can return to earlier game projects and implement gamepad or touchscreen controls for them as well. When you are satisfied with your progress, the next chapter will introduce another advanced topic: procedural content generation in the context of creating maze-based games.

■ ■ ■

CHAPTER 14

Maze Games

In this chapter, you will learn how to create the maze-based game *Maze Runman*, shown in Figure 14-1, inspired by arcade games such as *Pac-Man* and the Atari 2600 console game *Maze Craze: A Game of Cops 'n Robbers*. The main new concepts in this chapter are algorithms for generating and solving mazes.

Figure 14-1. *The* Maze Runman *game*

Game Project: Maze Runman

Maze Runman is an action game in which the main character, referred to as the hero, races through a maze attempting to collect all the coins before being captured by a ghost. The ghost is somewhat slower than the hero but always follows the shortest path to reach the player, even if that requires suddenly changing directions as the hero moves about the maze. Each time the player starts the game, a new maze is generated, and some maze layouts may be more difficult than others: there may be long, dead-end corridors that the hero needs to navigate. One strategy for dealing with situations like this is for the hero to lead the ghost to the opposite end of the maze to give themselves enough time to make it in and out of the corridor before being trapped or cornered by the ghost. If the ghost makes contact with the hero, the player instantly loses, but if the hero collects all the coins, the ghost disappears and the player wins.

The game features a top-down perspective, and the player uses the arrow keys to walk north, south, east, and west. By holding down multiple arrow keys, it is possible for the hero to move diagonally, which may provide a small advantage depending on the layout of the maze. The user interface consists of a label across the top of the screen (above the maze area) that displays the number of coins remaining, as well as a large text message that appears in the middle of the screen when the game ends, displaying a message that depends on whether the player won or lost the game.

The game uses simple graphics for the game world, four-directional walking animations for the hero (similar to those used in the *Treasure Quest* game in Chapter 12), and a translucent animation for the ghost. When a coin is collected, a sound effect plays. In addition, there is a quiet ambient wind sound that plays in the background that gets louder as the ghost gets closer to the hero.

Beginning this project requires similar steps as in previous projects. In BlueJ, create a new project called Maze Runman. In the project folder, create an assets folder and a +libs folder containing the LibGDX JAR files (the latter not being necessary if you have set up the userlib directory). Add the custom framework files you created in the first part of this book (BaseGame.java, BaseScreen.java, BaseActor.java). In addition, you should download the source files for this chapter and copy the contents of the downloaded assets folder into your project's assets folder.

Maze Generation

The first and most important task in this project is to create the maze that the hero and the ghost will navigate. While in theory you could create a maze using level-design software such as the Tiled map editor, in this chapter you will instead write an algorithm that generates a new maze every time the player starts the game. One benefit to this approach is that it greatly adds to the replay value of the game; each new play session will be a brand-new experience. Techniques such as this fall under the category of procedural content generation: the creation of structured game content with algorithms. It can also incorporate techniques such as creating entire textures from code (rather than loading them from image files), but typically does not include techniques such as randomly initializing game-character parameters (such as enemy size or speed) or background scenery elements that have no effect on gameplay.

The overall process you will use for maze generation is as follows: first, you will create a rectangular grid of rooms (each 64 by 64 pixels large), where walls are placed on each of the edges. Second, you will remove walls between rooms in such a way as to create a maze: starting from any room in the maze, there should be a path the player can follow to reach any other room. Third, you will remove some additional walls at random to create multiple paths between rooms.

To implement the first step in this process, you will create a Wall class, followed by a Room class (which will contain four Wall objects and store references to the adjacent Room objects), and then a Maze class that will create the grid of rooms. To test it out, you will then create a LevelScreen class that extends BaseScreen, a MazeGame class that extents BaseGame, and a Launcher class to run the game.

To begin, create a new class named Wall with the following code. Note that the constructor also takes the width and the height of the wall as parameters; this will be useful, as in each room the north and south walls will have a greater width, while the east and west walls will have a greater height.

```
import com.badlogic.gdx.scenes.scene2d.Stage;

public class Wall extends BaseActor
{
    public Wall(float x, float y, float w, float h, Stage s)
    {
        super(x,y,s);
```

```
        loadTexture("assets/square.jpg");
        setSize(w,h);
        setBoundaryRectangle();
    }
}
```

Next, create a class called Room as follows. Note that there are arrays to store the walls and references to adjacent rooms (called neighbors), as well as a set of named constants to more easily identify which direction each array index represents. There are also methods for accessing and altering the data in these arrays.

```
import com.badlogic.gdx.scenes.scene2d.Stage;
import java.util.ArrayList;

public class Room extends BaseActor
{
    public static final int NORTH = 0;
    public static final int SOUTH = 1;
    public static final int EAST  = 2;
    public static final int WEST  = 3;
    public static int[] directionArray = {NORTH, SOUTH, EAST, WEST};

    private Wall[] wallArray;
    private Room[] neighborArray;

    public Room(float x, float y, Stage s)
    {
        super(x,y,s);
        loadTexture("assets/dirt.png");

        float w = getWidth();
        float h = getHeight();

        // t = wall thickness in pixels
        float t = 6;

        wallArray = new Wall[4];
        wallArray[SOUTH] = new Wall(x,y, w,t, s);
        wallArray[WEST]  = new Wall(x,y, t,h, s);
        wallArray[NORTH] = new Wall(x,y+h-t, w,t, s);
        wallArray[EAST]  = new Wall(x+w-t,y, t,h, s);

        neighborArray = new Room[4];
        // contents of this array will be initialized by Maze class
    }

    public void setNeighbor(int direction, Room neighbor)
    {  neighborArray[direction] = neighbor;  }

    public boolean hasNeighbor(int direction)
    {  return neighborArray[direction] != null;  }
```

```
    public Room getNeighbor(int direction)
    {   return neighborArray[direction];   }

    // check if wall in this direction still exists (has not been removed from stage)
    public boolean hasWall(int direction)
    {   return wallArray[direction].getStage() != null;   }

    public void removeWalls(int direction)
    {   removeWallsBetween(neighborArray[direction]);   }

    public void removeWallsBetween(Room other)
    {
        if (other == neighborArray[NORTH])
        {
            this.wallArray[NORTH].remove();
            other.wallArray[SOUTH].remove();
        }
        else if (other == neighborArray[SOUTH])
        {
            this.wallArray[SOUTH].remove();
            other.wallArray[NORTH].remove();
        }
        else if (other == neighborArray[EAST])
        {
            this.wallArray[EAST].remove();
            other.wallArray[WEST].remove();
        }
        else // (other == neighborArray[WEST])
        {
            this.wallArray[WEST].remove();
            other.wallArray[EAST].remove();
        }
    }
}
```

Next, you will set up a class that will construct the maze, although at this point it will only set up the grid of rooms and set the neighbor data for each room in each direction, when one exists (rooms along the edges of the grid will only have three neighbors, while rooms at the corners of the grid only have two neighbors). Create a new class called Maze with the following code:

```
import com.badlogic.gdx.scenes.scene2d.Stage;
import java.util.ArrayList;

public class Maze
{
    private Room[][] roomGrid;

    // maze size constants
    private final int roomCountX = 12;
    private final int roomCountY = 10;
    private final int roomWidth  = 64;
    private final int roomHeight = 64;
```

```java
    public Maze(Stage s)
    {
        roomGrid = new Room[roomCountX][roomCountY];

        for (int gridY = 0; gridY < roomCountY; gridY++)
        {
            for (int gridX = 0; gridX < roomCountX; gridX++)
            {
                float pixelX = gridX * roomWidth;
                float pixelY = gridY * roomHeight;
                Room room = new Room( pixelX, pixelY, s );
                roomGrid[gridX][gridY] = room;
            }
        }

        // neighbor relations
        for (int gridY = 0; gridY < roomCountY; gridY++)
        {
            for (int gridX = 0; gridX < roomCountX; gridX++)
            {
                Room room = roomGrid[gridX][gridY];
                if (gridY > 0)
                    room.setNeighbor( Room.SOUTH, roomGrid[gridX][gridY-1] );
                if (gridY < roomCountY - 1)
                    room.setNeighbor( Room.NORTH, roomGrid[gridX][gridY+1] );
                if (gridX > 0)
                    room.setNeighbor( Room.WEST, roomGrid[gridX-1][gridY] );
                if (gridX < roomCountX - 1)
                    room.setNeighbor( Room.EAST, roomGrid[gridX+1][gridY] );
            }
        }
    }

    public Room getRoom(int gridX, int gridY)
    {   return roomGrid[gridX][gridY];   }
}
```

Next, you will extend the BaseScreen class to set up the screen that displays the game. The size of the background image is derived from the size of the maze, with an additional area on the top where the number of coins left will be displayed. Since the rooms are 64 by 64 pixels, and the maze is 12 rooms horizontally and 10 rooms vertically, this accounts for a region that is 768 by 640 pixels; an additional 60 pixels of height will be saved for the user interface. In addition, you will add the ability for the player to restart the game (by pressing the R key), which will be useful later on when the player wants to generate a new maze, or if the game ends and the player wants to try again. Create a class called LevelScreen as follows:

```java
import com.badlogic.gdx.graphics.Color;
import com.badlogic.gdx.Input.Keys;

public class LevelScreen extends BaseScreen
{
    Maze maze;
```

```
    public void initialize()
    {
        BaseActor background = new BaseActor(0,0,mainStage);
        background.loadTexture("assets/white.png");
        background.setColor(Color.GRAY);
        background.setSize(768, 700);

        maze = new Maze(mainStage);
    }

    public void update(float dt)
    {    }

    public boolean keyDown(int keyCode)
    {
        if ( keyCode == Keys.R )
            BaseGame.setActiveScreen( new LevelScreen() );

        return false;
    }

}
```

Next, you need an extension of the BaseGame class to load this screen. Create a new class called MazeGame as follows:

```
public class MazeGame extends BaseGame
{
    public void create()
    {
        super.create();
        setActiveScreen( new LevelScreen() );
    }
}
```

Finally, to run the game, you need a launcher-style class. Recalling the size of the background object from the LevelScreen class, create a new class named Launcher with the following code:

```
import com.badlogic.gdx.Game;
import com.badlogic.gdx.backends.lwjgl.LwjglApplication;

public class Launcher
{
    public static void main (String[] args)
    {
        Game myGame = new MazeGame();
        LwjglApplication launcher = new LwjglApplication( myGame, "Maze Runman", 768, 700 );
    }
}
```

At this point, your project is ready to test. Run the main function in the Launcher class, and you should see the screen displayed in Figure 14-2.

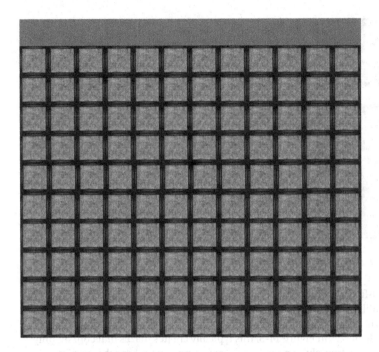

Figure 14-2. *Initializing a grid of rooms with walls*

The second step will be to remove a sequence of walls so that you can reach any room from any other room. One algorithm that can be used is called *depth-first search*. In this algorithm, one room is chosen as a starting location, and a room is called *connected* when it there is a path from the starting location to that room. The algorithm also maintains a list of connected rooms that have neighboring rooms that are *not* connected. The algorithm, in pseudocode, is as follows:

- Select a room as a starting location; mark it as connected and add it to the list.

- While there are still rooms remaining in the list:

  - Let currentRoom be the most recently added room from the list.

  - If currentRoom has any unconnected neighbors,

    - let nextRoom be a random unconnected neighbor of currentRoom;

    - remove the walls between currentRoom and nextRoom;

    - mark nextRoom as connected; and

    - add nextRoom to the end of the list.

  - If currentRoom does not have any unconnected neighbors, remove it from the list.

When this algorithm finishes, there are no more connected rooms with unconnected neighbors; all the rooms are connected! This algorithm produces mazes such as those shown in Figure 14-3.

Figure 14-3. *Sample mazes generated with a depth-first algorithm*

As the name indicates, the depth-first algorithm creates paths that move randomly throughout the grid for as long (or as deep) as possible until the path reaches a dead end (a room with no adjacent unconnected rooms). At that point, another path will be generated, branching off from the room most recently added to the list. As you can see from the sample mazes in Figure 14-3, this typically creates mazes that contain only a few paths that are very long and have few branching points. In order to create more branching points, you could change the first line in the `while` loop to `let currentRoom be a random room in the list`. This will have the opposite effect: instead of only a few long paths, mazes will be produced that have very many short paths and lots of dead ends; some examples are shown in Figure 14-4.

Figure 14-4. *Sample mazes generated by always selecting random rooms for branching paths*

The approach you will use in this chapter is a hybrid of these two methods: with probability 0.50, the algorithm will return to a random earlier room in the list. This generates mazes with medium-length corridors and more branching paths than the depth-first algorithm. Some sample mazes generated using this technique are shown in Figure 14-5.

Figure 14-5. *Sample mazes generated using the hybrid approach*

To implement this algorithm, in the Room class, add the following variable declaration:

```
private boolean connected;
```

In the constructor, initialize this variable to false:

```
connected = false;
```

Then, add the following methods, which will be used to set and check the value of connected, determine if any neighboring rooms are connected, and randomly select one of the neighboring unconnected rooms:

```
public void setConnected(boolean b)
{  connected = b;  }

public boolean isConnected()
{  return connected;  }

public boolean hasUnconnectedNeighbor()
{
    for (int direction : directionArray)
    {
        if ( hasNeighbor(direction) && !getNeighbor(direction).isConnected() )
            return true;
    }
    return false;
}
```

```java
public Room getRandomUnconnectedNeighbor()
{
    ArrayList<Integer> directionList = new ArrayList<Integer>();

    for (int direction : directionArray)
    {
        if ( hasNeighbor(direction) && !getNeighbor(direction).isConnected() )
            directionList.add(direction);
    }

    int directionIndex = (int)Math.floor( Math.random() * directionList.size() );
    int direction = directionList.get(directionIndex);
    return getNeighbor(direction);
}
```

Next, these methods will be used when creating the maze. In the constructor of the Maze class, after the code that sets the neighbor data for each room, add the following:

```java
ArrayList<Room> activeRoomList = new ArrayList<Room>();

Room currentRoom = roomGrid[0][0];
currentRoom.setConnected(true);
activeRoomList.add(0, currentRoom);

// chance of returning to a random connected room
//   to create a branching path from that room
float branchProbability = 0.5f;

while (activeRoomList.size() > 0)
{
    if (Math.random() < branchProbability)
    {
        // get random previously visited room
        int roomIndex = (int)(Math.random() * activeRoomList.size());
        currentRoom = activeRoomList.get(roomIndex);
    }
    else
    {
        // get the most recently visited room
        currentRoom = activeRoomList.get(activeRoomList.size() - 1);
    }

    if ( currentRoom.hasUnconnectedNeighbor() )
    {
        Room nextRoom = currentRoom.getRandomUnconnectedNeighbor();
        currentRoom.removeWallsBetween(nextRoom);
        nextRoom.setConnected( true );
        activeRoomList.add(0, nextRoom);
    }
```

```
    else
    {
        // this room has no more adjacent unconnected rooms
        //   so there is no reason to keep it in the list
        activeRoomList.remove( currentRoom );
    }
}
```

The final addition you will make to the maze-generation algorithm is the removal of a random number of walls. This is important to create looping paths, which will give the player multiple options to maneuver the hero around the maze and avoid the ghost that is constantly approaching. The results will be similar to the mazes pictured in Figure 14-6.

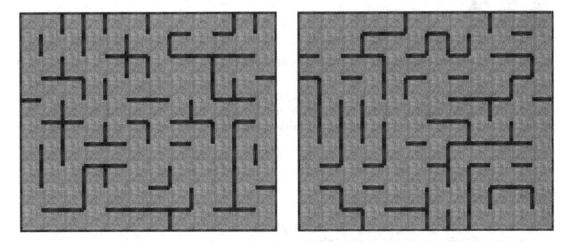

Figure 14-6. *Mazes with additional walls removed at random to create multiple paths between locations*

To accomplish this task, at the end of the constructor method in the Maze class, add the following code. The value of wallsToRemove may be adjusted as you wish.

```
int wallsToRemove = 24;
while (wallsToRemove > 0)
{
    int gridX = (int)Math.floor( Math.random() * roomCountX );
    int gridY = (int)Math.floor( Math.random() * roomCountY );
    int direction = (int)Math.floor( Math.random() * 4 );
    Room room = roomGrid[gridX][gridY];

    if ( room.hasNeighbor(direction) && room.hasWall(direction) )
    {
        room.removeWalls(direction);
        wallsToRemove--;
    }
}
```

At this point, the maze generation is complete, and you are ready to add the hero: the character controlled by the player.

321

The Hero

The next addition to the *Maze Runman* game is the hero character, who will navigate the maze. The character will feature walking animations in each of the four compass directions (north, south, east, and west), seen in the spritesheet shown in Figure 14-7.[1]

Figure 14-7. *Spritesheet used for four-directional hero animation*

The code for setting up the animations and the logic for determining which animation should be used (based on the angle of motion) is identical to the code from the *Treasure Quest* game in Chapter 12. For further details, you can review the explanations in the corresponding section. Create a new class named Hero as follows:

```
import com.badlogic.gdx.scenes.scene2d.Stage;
import com.badlogic.gdx.Gdx;
import com.badlogic.gdx.Input.Keys;
import com.badlogic.gdx.graphics.Texture;
import com.badlogic.gdx.graphics.g2d.TextureRegion;
import com.badlogic.gdx.graphics.g2d.Animation;
import com.badlogic.gdx.utils.Array;

public class Hero extends BaseActor
{
    Animation north;
    Animation south;
    Animation east;
    Animation west;

    public Hero(float x, float y, Stage s)
    {
        super(x,y,s);

        String fileName = "assets/hero.png";
        int rows = 4;
        int cols = 3;
        Texture texture = new Texture(Gdx.files.internal(fileName), true);
        int frameWidth = texture.getWidth() / cols;
```

---

[1]Spritesheet character created by Andrew Viola and used with permission.

```
    int frameHeight = texture.getHeight() / rows;
    float frameDuration = 0.2f;

    TextureRegion[][] temp = TextureRegion.split(texture, frameWidth, frameHeight);

    Array<TextureRegion> textureArray = new Array<TextureRegion>();
    for (int c = 0; c < cols; c++)
        textureArray.add( temp[0][c] );
    south = new Animation(frameDuration, textureArray, Animation.PlayMode.LOOP_PINGPONG);

    textureArray.clear();
    for (int c = 0; c < cols; c++)
        textureArray.add( temp[1][c] );
    west = new Animation(frameDuration, textureArray, Animation.PlayMode.LOOP_PINGPONG);

    textureArray.clear();
    for (int c = 0; c < cols; c++)
        textureArray.add( temp[2][c] );
    east = new Animation(frameDuration, textureArray, Animation.PlayMode.LOOP_PINGPONG);

    textureArray.clear();
    for (int c = 0; c < cols; c++)
        textureArray.add( temp[3][c] );
    north = new Animation(frameDuration, textureArray, Animation.PlayMode.LOOP_PINGPONG);

    setAnimation(south);

    // set after animation established
    setBoundaryPolygon(8);

    setAcceleration(800);
    setMaxSpeed(100);
    setDeceleration(800);
}

public void act(float dt)
{
    super.act(dt);

    // hero movement controls
    if (Gdx.input.isKeyPressed(Keys.LEFT))
        accelerateAtAngle(180);
    if (Gdx.input.isKeyPressed(Keys.RIGHT))
        accelerateAtAngle(0);
    if (Gdx.input.isKeyPressed(Keys.UP))
        accelerateAtAngle(90);
    if (Gdx.input.isKeyPressed(Keys.DOWN))
        accelerateAtAngle(270);
```

323

```
        // pause animation when character not moving
        if ( getSpeed() == 0 )
        {
            setAnimationPaused(true);
        }
        else
        {
            setAnimationPaused(false);
            // set direction animation
            float angle = getMotionAngle();
            if (angle >= 45 && angle <= 135)
                setAnimation(north);
            else if (angle > 135 && angle < 225)
                setAnimation(west);
            else if (angle >= 225 && angle <= 315)
                setAnimation(south);
            else
                setAnimation(east);
        }

        applyPhysics(dt);
    }
}
```

Then, to incorporate the hero into the game, in the LevelScreen class, add the following variable declaration:

```
Hero hero;
```

To set up and place the hero in the lower-left corner of the maze, add the following to the initialize method:

```
hero = new Hero(0,0,mainStage);
hero.centerAtActor( maze.getRoom(0,0) );
```

Finally, to add collision detection between the hero and the walls, in the update method, add the following:

```
for (BaseActor wall : BaseActor.getList(mainStage, "Wall"))
{
    hero.preventOverlap(wall);
}
```

At this point, you can test the program and press the arrow keys to move the hero throughout the maze.

The Ghost

Next, you will create a ghost character that will chase the hero around the maze. The key feature of the algorithm used to determine the path the ghost will follow is that it is the shortest path between the room occupied by the ghost (called startRoom) and the room occupied by the hero (called targetRoom). In this algorithm, the order in which the rooms are visited is very important: rooms closer to startRoom should be considered before rooms that are farther away. All the rooms that are one square away from startRoom will be checked first, followed by all the rooms that are two squares away from startRoom, then all those that are three squares away, and so forth. An algorithm that considers rooms in this order is called a *breadth-first search algorithm*, in contrast to the approach used for initially generating the maze, which used a depth-first algorithm. There are two additional practical considerations to take into account when searching for the path. First, since there are looping paths in the maze, you will need to keep track of which rooms have already been considered by the algorithm to avoid needlessly considering them additional times. This will be tracked by a Boolean variable called visited. Second, you will need to keep track of the sequence in which the rooms are considered when searching for a path: each of the rooms that are $n+1$ squares away from startRoom were arrived at after considering a room that was n squares away from startRoom. This information will be stored in a Room variable named previousRoom. This algorithm, in pseudocode, is as follows:

- Identify startRoom and targetRoom.

- Set currentRoom equal to startRoom.

- Mark currentRoom as visited, set its previous room to null, and add currentRoom to a list.

- While the list is not empty, do the following:

  - Set currentRoom to the first element in the list and remove it from the list.

  - For each unvisited neighbor (called nextRoom) of currentRoom,

    - set nextRoom's previous room to currentRoom;

    - end the algorithm if nextRoom is targetRoom; and

    - if nextRoom is not targetRoom, then mark nextRoom as visited and add nextRoom to the end of the list.

Once this algorithm finishes, the path can be retrieved as follows: set currentRoom to targetRoom and add it to a new list of rooms. Then, set currentRoom to its previous room and add this to the front of the list. Repeat this process until currentRoom has no previous room (previousRoom is null; this will only be true for startRoom). At this point, the list contains a sequence of rooms that form a shortest path from startRoom to targetRoom.

An example of this algorithm in practice is illustrated in Figure 14-8. The upper-right corner room, occupied by the ghost, is startRoom, and the room near the lower-left corner, occupied by the hero, is targetRoom. The rooms are labeled with numbers indicating the order in which they are visited by the algorithm and with arrows illustrating the previous room of each room. In the illustration, rooms 1 and 2 are one room away from the ghost, rooms 3 and 4 are two rooms away, 5 and 6 are three rooms away, 7 and 8 are four rooms away, 9, 10, 11, and 12 are five rooms away, and 13, 14, and targetRoom are six rooms away. Once the target room is located, following the sequence of previous rooms yields the path consisting of startRoom, 1, 3, 5, 7, 10, targetRoom—this is one of the shortest possible paths to the hero.

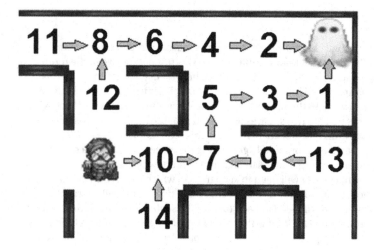

Figure 14-8. *Order in which rooms are visited to find the shortest path from the ghost to the hero*

To implement this algorithm, each room needs to keep track of whether it has been visited in the algorithm and what the previously visited room was. To this end, in the Room class, add the following variables:

```
private boolean visited;
private Room previousRoom;
```

Initialize visited to false in the constructor method:

```
visited = false;
```

Next, you need some methods to get and set these new variables, as well as to retrieve all the adjacent neighbors of a room that have not yet been visited. This is accomplished with the following code, which should also be added to the Room class:

```
public void setVisited(boolean b)
{  visited = b;  }

public boolean isVisited()
{  return visited;  }
public void setPreviousRoom(Room r)
{  previousRoom = r;  }

public Room getPreviousRoom()
{  return previousRoom;  }

// Used in pathfinding: locate accessible neighbors that have not yet been visited
public ArrayList<Room> unvisitedPathList()
{
    ArrayList<Room> list = new ArrayList<Room>();
```

```
    for (int direction : directionArray)
    {
        if ( hasNeighbor(direction) && !hasWall(direction) &&
                !getNeighbor(direction).isVisited() )
            list.add( getNeighbor(direction) );
    }

    return list;
}
```

It is helpful to have a method that identifies the rooms in which the ghost and hero are located and resets the visited and previousRoom variables of each room, which is necessary before searching for a new path. In the Maze class, add the following methods to perform these tasks:

```
public Room getRoom(BaseActor actor)
{
    int gridX = (int)Math.round(actor.getX() / roomWidth);
    int gridY = (int)Math.round(actor.getY() / roomHeight);
    return getRoom(gridX, gridY);
}

public void resetRooms()
{
    for (int gridY = 0; gridY < roomCountY; gridY++)
    {
        for (int gridX = 0; gridX < roomCountX; gridX++)
        {
            roomGrid[gridX][gridY].setVisited( false );
            roomGrid[gridX][gridY].setPreviousRoom( null );
        }
    }
}
```

Next, you will create the Ghost class, which includes a method named findPath that implements the breadth-first search algorithm previously described. The method adds a sequence of actions to the actor to move it along the first few rooms of the path. The ghost does not follow the path all the way to the end, because by then the hero will have moved on to a different location. Instead, each time the ghost completes its current set of movement actions, the path to the hero is recalculated, and a new set of movement actions along this path is added to the ghost. Create a new class called Ghost with code as follows:

```
import com.badlogic.gdx.scenes.scene2d.Stage;
import com.badlogic.gdx.scenes.scene2d.Action;
import com.badlogic.gdx.scenes.scene2d.actions.Actions;
import java.util.ArrayList;

public class Ghost extends BaseActor
{
    public float speed = 60; // pixels per second

    public Ghost(float x, float y, Stage s)
    {
```

```
        super(x,y,s);
        loadAnimationFromSheet("assets/ghost.png", 1,3, 0.2f, true);
        setOpacity(0.8f);
    }

    public void findPath(Room startRoom, Room targetRoom)
    {
        Room currentRoom = startRoom;

        ArrayList<Room> roomList = new ArrayList<Room>();
        currentRoom.setPreviousRoom( null );
        currentRoom.setVisited( true );
        roomList.add(currentRoom);

        while (roomList.size() > 0)
        {
            currentRoom = roomList.remove(0);
            for (Room nextRoom : currentRoom.unvisitedPathList())
            {
                nextRoom.setPreviousRoom( currentRoom );
                if (nextRoom == targetRoom)
                {
                    // target found!
                    roomList.clear();
                    break;
                }
                else
                {
                    nextRoom.setVisited( true );
                    roomList.add(nextRoom);
                }
            }
        }

        // create list of rooms corresponding to shortest path
        ArrayList<Room> pathRoomList = new ArrayList<Room>();
        currentRoom = targetRoom;
        while (currentRoom != null)
        {
            // add current room to beginning of list
            pathRoomList.add( 0, currentRoom );
            currentRoom = currentRoom.getPreviousRoom();
        }

        // only move along a few steps of the path;
        //    path will be recalculated when these actions are complete.
        int maxStepCount = 2;

        // to remove the pause between steps, start loop index at 1
        //    but make ghost speed slower to compensate
        for (int i = 0; i < pathRoomList.size(); i++)
        {
```

```
        if (i == maxStepCount)
            break;
        Room nextRoom = pathRoomList.get(i);
        Action move = Actions.moveTo( nextRoom.getX(), nextRoom.getY(), 64/speed );
        addAction( move );
    }
  }
}
```

To integrate the ghost into the game, in the LevelScreen class, add the following variable declaration:

```
Ghost ghost;
```

Set it up by adding the following code to the initialize method:

```
ghost = new Ghost(0,0,mainStage);
ghost.centerAtActor( maze.getRoom(11,9) );
```

In the update method, check whether the ghost has finished its movements (when the ghost contains no more actions), in which case you activate its findPath method with the following code:

```
if (ghost.getActions().size == 0)
{
    maze.resetRooms();
    ghost.findPath( maze.getRoom(ghost), maze.getRoom(hero) );
}
```

At this point, you can once again test your project and watch as the ghost moves around the maze, always moving closer to the hero.

Winning and Losing the Game

Now that the maze is set up, along with a player-controller character and an intelligently programmed adversary, it is time to add a goal for the player, as well as win and lose conditions. As described at the beginning of the chapter, there will be coins for the hero to collect. If the hero collects them all, the player wins the game, but if the ghost reaches the hero first, the player loses the game. The first step will be to create the coins. Create a new class called Coin with the following code:

```
import com.badlogic.gdx.scenes.scene2d.Stage;

public class Coin extends BaseActor
{
    public Coin(float x, float y, Stage s)
    {
        super(x,y,s);
        loadTexture("assets/coin.png");
        setBoundaryPolygon(6);
    }
}
```

Next, you will add coins to the level, placing one in the center of each room. At the same time, you will set up a label to display the number of coins remaining, and while you're at it, add a label to display a message at the end of the game. The positioning of the labels is illustrated in Figure 14-9, which shows what the screen will look like when the player loses the game.

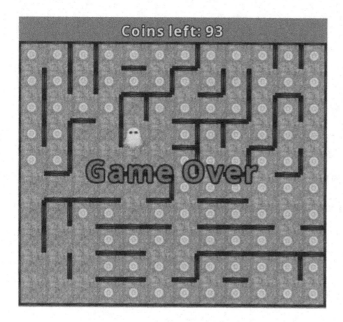

Figure 14-9. *The Maze* Runman *game after the hero is caught by the ghost*

To implement these additions, first add the following `import` statements to the `LevelScreen` class:

```
import com.badlogic.gdx.scenes.scene2d.ui.Label;
import com.badlogic.gdx.graphics.Color;
import com.badlogic.gdx.scenes.scene2d.Action;
import com.badlogic.gdx.scenes.scene2d.actions.Actions;
```

Next, add the following variable declarations:

```
Label coinsLabel;
Label messageLabel;
```

In the `initialize` method, you will create a `Coin` object centered on each of the `Room` objects, set up the labels, and arrange them in the user interface table by adding the following code. Note the use of the `toFront` method so that the ghost renders above the coins, rather than below.

```
for (BaseActor room : BaseActor.getList(mainStage, "Room"))
{
    Coin coin = new Coin(0,0,mainStage);
    coin.centerAtActor(room);
}
```

```
ghost.toFront();

coinsLabel = new Label("Coins left:", BaseGame.labelStyle);
coinsLabel.setColor( Color.GOLD );
messageLabel = new Label("...", BaseGame.labelStyle);
messageLabel.setFontScale(2);
messageLabel.setVisible(false);

uiTable.pad(10);
uiTable.add(coinsLabel);
uiTable.row();
uiTable.add(messageLabel).expandY();
```

Next, in the update method, you need to check whether the hero overlaps any coins as well as update the label that displays the number of coins remaining. If the ghost overlaps the hero, then the player loses the game, and if there are no coins remaining, then the player wins the game. In either case, a corresponding message will be displayed. In the case of a loss, the player is removed from the stage. In the case of a win, the ghost is removed from the stage, and an infinitely-repeating delay action is added to the ghost so that its findPath method will not be invoked.

```
for (BaseActor coin : BaseActor.getList(mainStage, "Coin"))
{
    if (hero.overlaps(coin))
    {
        coin.remove();
    }
}

int coins = BaseActor.count(mainStage, "Coin");
coinsLabel.setText("Coins left: " + coins);

if (coins == 0)
{
    ghost.remove();
    ghost.setPosition(-1000, -1000);
    ghost.clearActions();
    ghost.addAction( Actions.forever( Actions.delay(1) ) );
    messageLabel.setText("You win!");
    messageLabel.setColor(Color.GREEN);
    messageLabel.setVisible(true);
}

if (hero.overlaps(ghost))
{
    hero.remove();
    hero.setPosition(-1000, -1000);
    ghost.clearActions();
    ghost.addAction( Actions.forever( Actions.delay(1) ) );
    messageLabel.setText("Game Over");
    messageLabel.setColor(Color.RED);
    messageLabel.setVisible(true);
}
```

331

At this point, you have finished implementing all the game mechanics. Test out the game and see if you are able to win. You may find that you want to adjust the speed of the ghost or change the number of extra walls that are removed when the maze is generated in order to make the game easier or more difficult.

Audio

In this section, you will add some polish to your game in the form of sound effects. The first effect will be a quiet jingle sound that plays each time a coin is collected. Instead of background music, an ambient sound of rushing wind will play, and the volume will increase as the ghost approaches the hero to subtly build a sense of tension. To begin, in the LevelScreen class, add the following import statements. (The math-related classes being imported will be used when calculating the distance from the ghost to the hero.)

```
import com.badlogic.gdx.Gdx;
import com.badlogic.gdx.audio.Sound;
import com.badlogic.gdx.audio.Music;
import com.badlogic.gdx.math.MathUtils;
import com.badlogic.gdx.math.Vector2;
```

Next, add the following variables:

```
Sound coinSound;
Music windMusic;
```

In the initialize method, load and start the audio as follows:

```
coinSound  = Gdx.audio.newSound(Gdx.files.internal("assets/coin.wav"));
windMusic = Gdx.audio.newMusic(Gdx.files.internal("assets/wind.mp3"));
windMusic.setLooping(true);
windMusic.setVolume(0.1f);
windMusic.play();
```

In the update method, locate the block of code corresponding to when the hero overlaps a coin and add the following line directly after the coin is removed:

```
coinSound.play(0.10f);
```

Also in the update method, you will adjust the volume of the wind sound. To calculate the distance from the ghost to the hero, you calculate the length of a Vector2 object from the ghost's coordinates to the hero's coordinates. When this distance is 64 pixels (which is as close as the ghost can get without overlapping the hero), the volume should equal 1. When the distance is 300 pixels, the volume should equal 0. Using some algebra, you can calculate a linear equation that converts distance to volume based on these values, as you will see in the code that follows. However, you also will clamp the volume level to a number between 0.10 and 1 so that the sound is always somewhat audible and never goes above the maximum possible value of 1. Finally, the audio should only be adjusted while the game is in progress, which is indicated when the message label is not visible. To accomplish these tasks, add the following code:

```
if ( !messageLabel.isVisible() )
{
    float distance = new Vector2(hero.getX() - ghost.getX(), hero.getY() - ghost.getY()).len();
    float volume = -(distance - 64)/(300 - 64) + 1;
```

```
    volume = MathUtils.clamp(volume, 0.10f, 1.00f);
    windMusic.setVolume(volume);
}
```

With this addition, you are ready to test the project once more to verify that the audio plays as expected. Congratulations on finishing the project!

Summary and Next Steps

In this chapter, you developed the maze-based game, *Maze Runman*, where the hero tries to collect all the coins while avoiding a ghost. You learned how to use a depth-first algorithm to generate mazes and a breadth-first algorithm to search for the shortest path between two points in a maze. You once again created a main character that uses four walking animations, one for each direction. You also added a special audio effect that increases in volume as the ghost approaches the hero.

In addition to the usual suggestions (adding a title screen, instructions screen, and visual and audio special effects), there are many refinements and additions you could make in this project. You could have larger mazes that are not entirely visible on screen to add to the challenge. You could add more ghosts to chase the hero, or have the ghost increase its speed as time passes (although the ghost speed should never be greater than the hero's speed). To compensate for these additional challenges, you might want to introduce health points or extra lives, which would allow the player to be hit multiple times. You could also display a timer in the user interface so that, as a secondary goal, the player tries to collect all the coins in the shortest amount of time; this provides a more exact way for players to measure their skill and compare performance.

In the next chapter, you will shift your focus from advanced algorithms for content generation to advanced 2D graphics. In particular, you will add particle effects and image shaders and filters to improve the visuals in some of your earlier game projects.

■ ■ ■

CHAPTER 15

Advanced 2D Graphics

In this chapter, rather than create a new game, you will learn two techniques for incorporating sophisticated graphics into your projects. The first section will introduce particle systems, which can create special effects such as explosions, which will be incorporated into the *Space Rocks* game in place of the spritesheet-based animation. The second section will introduce shader programs, which manipulate the pixels of the rendered image to create effects such as blurring or glowing, which will be incorporated into the *Starfish Collector* game.

Particle Systems

A *particle system* is a collection of many small images that can be used to create a variety of graphical special effects. Some effects that can be replicated by this technique include fire, smoke, explosions, fireworks, electric sparks, water fountains, rain, snow, and star fields. Each of the small images in a particle system is called a *particle*. Every particle has many properties (such as velocity, size, color, and transparency) that can be initialized to a random value within a given range, and these property values may be configured to change over time. Particles are produced at a set rate by an object called an *emitter*, which may be configured to spawn particles either for a limited time or continuously, depending on the visual effect being created.

LibGDX provides classes that support the display of particle systems. Furthermore, the Particle Editor tool provided with LibGDX can be used to design and preview particle effects and then to export them to a file format that can be easily imported within the LibGDX framework.

The LibGDX Particle Editor

The LibGDX Particle Editor can be run directly from the source code, as explained on the LibGDX wiki.[1] However, for simplicity, you can use the executable JAR file `ParticleEditor.jar`, available in the `Particle Editor` folder in the source code directory for this chapter. Figure 15-1 shows this program when it is first started.

---

[1]`https://github.com/libgdx/libgdx/wiki/2D-Particle-Editor`

© Lee Stemkoski 2018

L. Stemkoski, *Java Game Development with LibGDX*, https://doi.org/10.1007/978-1-4842-3324-5_15

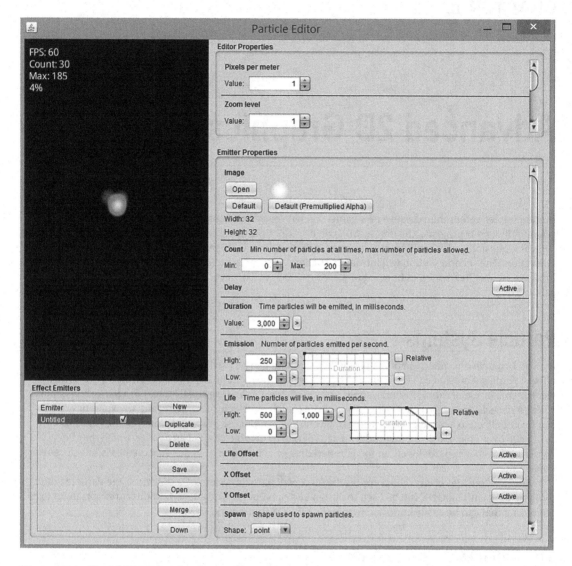

Figure 15-1. *The LibGDX Particle Editor program at startup*

A fire effect appears in the preview region in the upper-left panel of the Particle Editor window. The parameters that produce this effect are shown in the Emitter Properties panel that occupies the majority of the right-hand side of the window. This panel has so many properties, each with corresponding values and graphs, that it can be somewhat overwhelming at first. This section will discuss only the emitter properties that have the greatest impact on the final visual effect; for more thorough coverage, please consult the LibGDX wiki (previously referenced) for details.

- *Image*: From this area, you can select the image to use for each particle. Particles are often tinted with a color; grayscale images work best for this purpose.

- *Count*: This area can be used to set the minimum and maximum number of particles that should appear onscreen at any time.

- *Duration*: This is how long the emitter will produce particles. (When creating a continuous effect, this value will be ignored.)

- *Emission*: This is how many particles will be emitted per second.

- *Life*: This is how long each particle will be active in the particle system.

- *Size*: This is the size of the image, in pixels.

- *Velocity*: This is the particle speed, in pixels per second.

- *Angle*: This is the particle direction, in degrees.

- *Tint*: This displays the color(s) used to tint the particle image.

- *Transparency*: This controls the transparency of the particles over time.

- *Additive*: When active, this blends colors by adding together the color components, resulting in brighter areas where many particles are present.

- *Continuous*: When active, this causes the emitters to continue emitting particles (ignoring the preceding Duration value).

Next to some of the parameters, you'll see text boxes and a graph, as shown in Figure 15-2, which can be used for fine-tuning the initial values and changes in values over time. (For some parameters, you will need to click the *Active* button to the right of the parameter name to make these elements appear.)

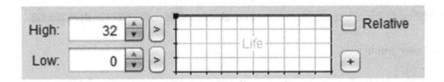

Figure 15-2. *Particle Editor interface for fine-tuning parameter values*

The numeric values in the boxes labeled High and Low refer to the values of the top and bottom edges on the graph to the right. The blue line on the graph indicates how the parameter value will change during the lifetime of the particle. In the graph pictured in Figure 15-2, the dark blue line remains straight across the top, indicating that the parameter value will remain constant at the High value. Figure 15-3 illustrates two more possible graphs; the graph on the left represents a continuous decrease from the High value to the Low value, while the graph on the right represents a parameter that remains at the High value for the majority of the lifetime of the particle and then suddenly decreases to the Low value. These two graphs will be referred to as the "Gradual Decrease" and the "Sudden Decrease" graphs later in this section.

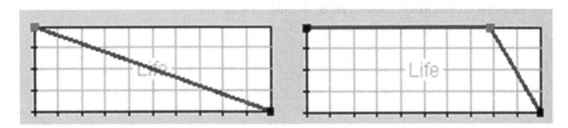

Figure 15-3. *Variations on the parameter change graph*

To modify one of these graphs, you can click anywhere to add a point, click and drag to move a point around, and double-click a point to remove it.

In addition, next to the High and Low values are small buttons labeled with > or <; these can be used to toggle between one or two values appearing in the corresponding row. When two values are displayed, they represent a range of values from which the High or Low values will be randomly selected for each particle. This can be used to great effect, as you will see later.

Finally, it is useful to understand how to set the parameters for the Tint property. If desired, the color of a particle can change over time; the progression of the color is displayed from the left to the right in the topmost rectangle. For example, Figure 15-4 represents a particle that will begin tinted red, shift to blue, and finally end tinted green. As with the parameter-change graphs discussed previously, additional points (represented by triangles) can be added by clicking within the rectangle. Triangles can be selected by clicking them, and their colors can be adjusted by using the sliders underneath, which control the hue, saturation, and brightness of the color. The triangles can be moved by clicking and dragging, and they can be deleted by double-clicking.

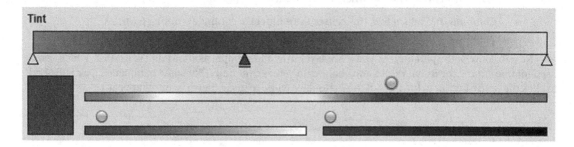

Figure 15-4. *The tint parameter graph*

With this knowledge of the user interface of the Particle Editor, you'll work through examples that show how to create particle-based versions of the effects from the game *Space Rocks*. Creating lots of effects, more than anything, is what will ultimately give you a feel for the role each parameter plays in crafting a particle-based effect.

You need a location to save your final effects, so at this time, create a copy of your Space Rocks project from Chapter 4 and rename the copy to Space Rocks Particles. You will store the effect files created with the LibGDX Particle Editor in the assets folder of this directory. Also, download the source files for this chapter, and from the assets folder of the downloaded Space Rocks Particles project, copy the image file particle.png into the assets folder of your Space Rocks Particles project.

Rocket-Thruster Effect

Your first goal is to create a rocket-thruster effect, pictured in Figure 15-5.

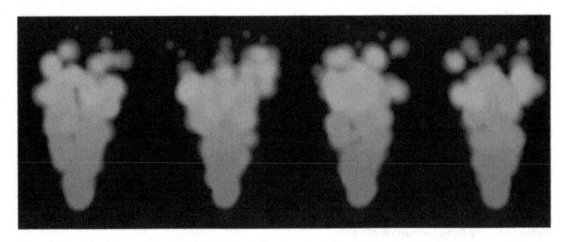

Figure 15-5. *The rocket-thruster particle effect*

After starting the Particle Editor program, in the Effect Emitters panel in the lower left, click the *New* button and rename the newly created list entry thruster (double-click its name to rename it). Click the list item named Untitled (which corresponds to the default fire-like example) and click the *Delete* button to remove it.

In the set of options at the bottom of the Emitter Properties panel, deselect the "Additive" checkbox and select the "Continuous" checkbox. You should now see a single red dot in the middle of the preview panel.

First, you will adjust the number of particles that will be active at any given moment. Change the Count property's Max value to 100. To achieve this amount, you also must change the Emission property's High value to 200. (Changing this value to 100 would be insufficient, as each particle lasts for only 0.5 seconds, since 500 milliseconds is the default value for the Life property. An emission rate of 100 would result in only 50 active particles at any given time.)

Next, click the *Active* buttons next to the Velocity and Angle properties. For Velocity, click the > button next to High and enter the values 300 and 400. For Angle, again click the > button next to High and enter the values 70 and 110. You should now see red particles spraying upward in a wobbly, cone-shaped pattern.

Now, change the Tint parameter graph so that the tint color changes from red at the start to orange in the middle and yellow at the end. After completing this step, the particles in the preview panel should appear red at the base of the emitter and gradually change colors until they become yellow at the top.

Finally, the particles should shrink and fade out of existence at the end of their lifetime. To accomplish this, modify the parameter-change graphs for both Size and Transparency so that they both resemble the Sudden Decrease graph from Figure 15-3.

When this step is finished, click the *Save* button and save your file to your project assets directory using the filename thruster.pfx. Although the particle-effect data is stored in a text file, you will use the extension pfx as a mnemonic to indicate the type of data in the file. In addition, you will need to copy the image file particle.png from the Particle Editor directory to your local project's assets directory as well, if you haven't previously, for the effect to load correctly in LibGDX.

Explosion Effect

A classic effect that you will now create is an explosion, as illustrated in Figure 15-6. This effect is composed of two emitters, one controlling the fire that appears initially, and the other controlling the smoke that appears afterward.

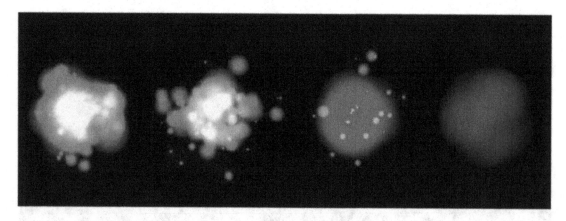

Figure 15-6. *The explosion particle effect*

Restart the Particle Editor. As before, create a new emitter. Name it `fire` and then delete the default emitter. You'll keep the default option settings: the "Additive" checkbox should be selected, and the "Continuous" checkbox should not be.

Adjust the Count property's Max value to 100. Change the Duration value to 250. To attain the maximum number of particles, change the Emission property's High value to 400. Set the Size property's High value to range from 0 to 100, and modify the graph so that it resembles the Gradual Decrease graph. Set the Velocity property to Active, set its High value to range from 0 to 160, and modify its graph so that it resembles the Sudden Decrease graph. Set the Angle property to Active and set its High value to range from 0 to 360. Finally, set the Tint property so that the color changes from red to orange over the course of the particle lifetime.

At this point, the Preview panel should be displaying the following effect repeatedly: a globule shape appears, red at the borders and yellow in the center, which then expels fragments that shrink as they move away from the center.

Once you are pleased with this effect, create another emitter and name it `smoke`. (Do *not* delete the fire emitter!) Select the smoke emitter from the list and click the *Up* button; this moves it higher up in the rendering order. Make sure that the checkbox next to the emitter is checked for it to be seen. This is important because you want the smoke particles to appear behind the fire particles, and so the smoke particles must be rendered first. Before continuing, make sure that in the emitter list, the smoke emitter is both checked (so it is visible) and highlighted (so that the parameters that will be changed are those of the smoke emitter).

The next step is to change the smoke emitter properties. Set the Count Max value to 20, the Duration value to 200, and the Emission High value to 100. Set the Delay property to Active and set its value to 400; this will cause the smoke emitter to begin 400 milliseconds after the fire emitter has started. Next, change the Size High value to 64. Activate the Velocity property, set the High value to 100, and modify the graph so that it is gradually decreasing. Also, activate the Angle property and set the High value to range from 0 to 360. Change the Tint color to a medium shade of gray by dragging the knob on the lower-left color slider all the way to the right and then dragging the knob on the lower-right color slider to the middle. Modify the Transparency graph so that it is slowly decreasing. Last of all, uncheck the "Additive" option.

This completes the explosion effect! Save your file to the `assets` directory with the filename `explosion.pfx`.

The ParticleActor Class

At this point, you are ready to integrate particle effects into the *Space Rocks* game. You will first create an extension of the `Actor` class, called `ParticleActor`. This class stores a `ParticleEffect` object, which is used to update and draw the effect. Most of the methods in this class simply activate the methods of the corresponding ParticleEffect object, with somewhat more intuitive names. However, one feature missing from the ParticleEffect class is that its draw method is not designed to take into account rotation or scaling factors. To address this situation, you will create an inner class called ParticleRenderer that renders the particle effect, make the ParticleActor class extend the Group class instead of the Actor class, and add an instance of the ParticleRenderer to the ParticleActor. In this way, calling the ParticleActor draw method will apply the geometric transformation data to the attached object before it is drawn, which is the desired outcome.

The update and draw methods of the ParticleEffect class will be activated by the standard act and draw methods common to all Actor objects, and a clone method will be included for convenience. Open BlueJ, then open the Space Rocks Particles project you created earlier. The code for the ParticleActor class is as follows:

```
import com.badlogic.gdx.Gdx;
import com.badlogic.gdx.scenes.scene2d.Actor;
import com.badlogic.gdx.scenes.scene2d.Group;
import com.badlogic.gdx.graphics.g2d.Batch;
import com.badlogic.gdx.graphics.g2d.ParticleEffect;
import com.badlogic.gdx.graphics.g2d.ParticleEmitter;

public class ParticleActor extends Group
{
    private ParticleEffect   effect;
    private ParticleRenderer renderingActor;

    private class ParticleRenderer extends Actor
    {
        private ParticleEffect effect;

        ParticleRenderer(ParticleEffect e)
        {  effect = e;  }

        public void draw(Batch batch, float parentAlpha)
        {  effect.draw(batch);  }
    }

    public ParticleActor(String pfxFile, String imageDirectory)
    {
        super();
        effect = new ParticleEffect();
        effect.load(Gdx.files.internal(pfxFile), Gdx.files.internal(imageDirectory));
        renderingActor = new ParticleRenderer(effect);
        this.addActor( renderingActor );
    }

    public void start()
    {  effect.start();  }

    // pauses continuous emitters
    public void stop()
    {  effect.allowCompletion();  }
```

```
    public boolean isRunning()
    {   return !effect.isComplete();   }

    public void centerAtActor(Actor other)
    {
        setPosition( other.getX() + other.getWidth()/2 , other.getY() + other.getHeight()/2 );
    }

    public void act(float dt)
    {
        super.act( dt );
        effect.update( dt );

        if ( effect.isComplete() && !effect.getEmitters().first().isContinuous() )
        {
            effect.dispose();
            this.remove();
        }
    }

    public void draw(Batch batch, float parentAlpha)
    {
        super.draw( batch, parentAlpha );
    }
}
```

With this class ready for action, you can use it, together with the particle effects you recently generated, in the *Space Rocks* game.

Integrating Particle Effects into Gameplay

The next step is to replace the explosion effects and the thruster fire with the corresponding particle effects, as seen in Figure 15-7.

Figure 15-7. *The* Space Rocks *game with particle effects added*

To begin, you will extend the ParticleActor class to create these effects. Create a new class called ExplosionEffect with the following code:

```
public class ExplosionEffect extends ParticleActor
{
    public ExplosionEffect()
    {
        super("assets/explosion.pfx", "assets/");
    }
}
```

There are three times when explosion effects should be created: when a laser collides with a rock, when a rock collides with the shields, and when a rock collides with the spaceship. First, in the update method of the LevelScreen class, locate the block of code where the spaceship is removed from the game and replace these two lines of code

```
Explosion boom = new Explosion(0,0, mainStage);
boom.centerAtActor(spaceship);
```

with the following:

```
ExplosionEffect boom = new ExplosionEffect();
boom.centerAtActor( spaceship );
boom.start();
mainStage.addActor(boom);
```

Next, locate the two blocks of code where a rock is removed from the game (when colliding with the shields or with a laser) and, in both cases, replace these two lines of code

```
Explosion boom = new Explosion(0,0, mainStage);
boom.centerAtActor(rockActor);
```

with the following:

```
ExplosionEffect boom = new ExplosionEffect();
boom.centerAtActor( rockActor );
boom.start();
mainStage.addActor(boom);
```

To integrate the thruster effect, create a new class called ThrusterEffect with the following code:

```
public class ThrusterEffect extends ParticleActor
{
    public ThrusterEffect()
    {
        super("assets/thruster.pfx", "assets/");
    }
}
```

Then, in the Spaceship class, remove all code containing a reference to the thrusters object: the class variable declaration, the code in the constructor used to initialize it, and the two lines of code in the act method that set the visibility of the thrusters. Then, add the following variable declaration:

```
private ThrusterEffect thrusterEffect;
```

In the constructor method, add the following code to set up and correctly position the effect:

```
thrusterEffect = new ThrusterEffect();
thrusterEffect.setPosition(0,32);
thrusterEffect.setRotation(90);
thrusterEffect.setScale(0.25f);
addActor(thrusterEffect);
```

Finally, in the act method, change the if-else statement that checks if the up arrow key is pressed to the following:

```
if (Gdx.input.isKeyPressed(Keys.UP))
{
    accelerateAtAngle( getRotation() );
    thrusterEffect.start();
}
else
{
    thrusterEffect.stop();
}
```

With this addition, the modifications to the *Space Rocks* game are complete. Test out your project; the gameplay should be the same as before, with improved special effects! In the next section, you will learn another technique for creating different types of special effects and try them out in the *Starfish Collector* game.

Shader Programming

In this section, you will learn about *shaders*: programs designed to run on a graphics processing unit (GPU) that can be used to create sophisticated visual effects. Similar to the central processing unit in a computer, a GPU is specialized circuitry designed for accelerated image processing and rendering. All modern video games and multimedia software use shaders to leverage the power of the GPU, which uses a parallel architecture with thousands of cores running tasks simultaneously. LibGDX (more specifically, the SpriteBatch class) creates and uses shader programs in the background to render graphics efficiently. Shader programs use OpenGL (Open Graphics Library), a cross-platform application-programming interface for drawing 2D and 3D graphics that uses a syntax similar to the C programming language.

Rendering graphics involves processing lots of data, which is grouped into a data structure called a *vertex*. Informally, you can think of a vertex as a point in space with some associated information. A vertex stores the coordinates of its position and additional data as needed, such as an associated color or *texture coordinates*, which are used to determine a corresponding location on an image. When rendering an object (such as a square that displays an image), the vertex data is sent to buffers on the GPU for high-speed access, which is processed through the following set of stages, known as the *graphics pipeline*:[2]

- Vertex Processing: runs a program called the *vertex shader*, which can perform geometric transformations (translation, rotation, and scaling) on each vertex (typically using matrix multiplication) and sends any needed data along the pipeline.

- Rasterizing: groups vertices into sets (such as triangles) and converts the corresponding area into *fragments*, data structures that correspond to pixels on the display. Each fragment interpolates and stores data from the vertex shader. For example, the color stored in a fragment that corresponds to the point in the exact center of a triangle will be the average of the colors stored in the three vertices of the triangle. All the fragments are sent to the next stage of the pipeline.

- Fragment Processing: runs a program called the *fragment shader* to determine the color of the associated pixel that will be displayed. This can take into account associated colors, textures, and transparency. Image filters and effects can be created here, such as color tinting, blurring, or glowing effects.

After these stages are complete, the final image data is available for the display. In the sections that follow, you will learn about the default shader programs provided by LibGDX, and how to create your own fragment shaders and incorporate them in the *Starfish Collector* game. In particular, you will create a grayscale filter, a colored border around an image, blurred images, a glowing effect, and an animated wave-like distortion.

---

[2]Technically, there are additional stages available in the graphics pipeline than those listed here, but for brevity only the fundamental and required stages are described here.

Default Shaders

Before diving into the actual code of the default vertex and fragment shaders used by LibGDX, a brief overview of the relevant syntax and language will be provided. This is in no way meant to be a comprehensive introduction; such an undertaking is worthy of an entire book in its own right!

Many of the variable types available in OpenGL have similar counterparts in Java:

- `float`, `int`, and `bool` refer to floating-point numbers, integers, and Boolean values (one-bit integers), respectively.

- `vec2`, `vec3`, and `vec4` refer to vectors with two, three, and four components. These are usually used to store position coordinates, although `vec4` is also used to store color values (red, green, blue, and alpha/transparency). In addition, the arithmetic operators (`+`, `-`, `*`, `/`) can all be used on instances of these types.

- `mat4` refers to a 4-by-4 matrix, which typically encodes geometric transformations (which are automatically generated for you by the LibGDX libraries).

- `sampler2D` refers to a two-dimensional grid of values, usually the color data associated with an image.

Many of the keywords and commands are also used in OpenGL, such as `if`-`else` statements, `for` and `while` loops, and logical operators (`&&` for "and," `||` for "or," `!` for "not"). There are also many mathematical functions available, such as `sqrt`, `pow`, `sin`, `cos`, `abs`, `round`, `floor`, `max`, and `min`, each of which corresponds directly to a function in the Java `Math` class. One special OpenGL function that you will see repeatedly is called `texture2D`, which takes a `sampler2D` and a `vec2` as input and returns the data from the sample (the color from the image) at the position specified by the vector; if the vector does not correspond to an exact pixel from the image, then the color will be interpolated from the colors of nearby pixels.

Both the vertex shader and the fragment shader must contain a single function called `main` with a `void` return type. (You can write additional "helper" functions with non-`void` return values if you wish, but that topic will not be covered here.) The vertex shader must assign a `vec4` value to the variable `gl_Position`, which represents the final position of the vertex. The fragment shader must assign a `vec4` value to the variable `gl_FragColor`, which represents the final color of the associated pixel.

You will also see variables declared externally to the main function that, in addition to having a specific data type, have one of three additional qualifiers specified:

- `attribute`: refers to a property of an individual vertex and may only appear in a vertex shader program. For example, the position of a vertex must be qualified as an attribute, since this data will be different for each vertex.

- `varying`: used for data that is sent from the vertex shader to the fragment shader. Any varying variable declaration in the vertex shader should also appear in the associated fragment shader. Values must be assigned to these variables in the vertex shader, and these variables are read-only (may not be modified) in the fragment shader. The fragment shader will interpolate the values of these variables from the values assigned to the vertices.

- `uniform`: refers to global values that are the same for each vertex of an object. For example, the texture data associated with an object should be qualified as uniform, since this data is the same for all vertices of an object. Similarly, geometric-transformation matrices are uniform variables, as all vertices in an object will be translated, rotated, or scaled in the same way or by the same amounts. Uniform variables can appear in either the vertex shader or the fragment shader, as necessary.

With this background, you are ready to examine the default shaders provided by LibGDX. First is the code for the default vertex shader. In this code, three attribute vectors are set up to access the position, color, and texture coordinates of each vertex. A uniform matrix stores the geometric transformation data, as this is the same for all vertices. Two varying variables are created to forward particular data (the color and texture coordinates) along to the fragment shader, where it will be needed to determine pixel colors. Note the variable naming convention used by LibGDX: attribute variables are prefaced by a_, uniform variables by u_, and varying variables by v_. (This convention will be used throughout the chapter.) Finally, note that the main function assigns values to the varying variables and calculates gl_Position by multiplying the transformation matrix by the original position of the vertex.

```
attribute vec4 a_position;
attribute vec4 a_color;
attribute vec2 a_texCoord0;

uniform mat4 u_projTrans;

varying vec4 v_color;
varying vec2 v_texCoords;

void main()
{
    v_color = a_color;
    v_texCoords = a_texCoord0;
    gl_Position = u_projTrans * a_position;
}
```

Next is the code for the default fragment shader. In this code, there are two varying variables, which correspond to the varying variables in the vertex shader. There is also a uniform variable that stores the texture data. In the main function, the texture2D function (described earlier) is used to obtain color data from the associated texture. This is multiplied by the color passed from the vertex shader, which has the effect of tinting the image by whatever color was assigned to the actor via the setColor method. (The default color associated with an actor is white, and since the red, green, and blue components of white are all equal to 1.0, multiplying by this color results in no change to the original image.) The result is assigned to the gl_FragColor variable, which will be the final color of the associated pixel.

```
varying vec4 v_color;
varying vec2 v_texCoords;

uniform sampler2D u_texture;

void main()
{
    gl_FragColor = v_color * texture2D(u_texture, v_texCoords);
}
```

Now that you know what the default shader programs are, you will see how to incorporate them into your game projects.

Using Shaders in LibGDX

In this section, you will learn how to add shaders to the actors in the *Starfish Collector* game. To begin, make a copy of the Starfish Collector project from Chapter 5 and rename the copy to Starfish Collector Shaders. In the assets folder of this project, make a new folder named shaders; this is where you will add text files containing the code for vertex and fragment shader programs. Using a text-editor program of your choice, create a new text file containing the code from the default vertex shader previously presented; save the file in the shaders folder with the filename default.vs (the extension vs is a mnemonic for *vertex shader*). Similarly, create a text file with the default fragment shader code and save it to the shaders folder with the filename default.fs (fs for *fragment shader*). In what follows, you will read the contents of these files into a String in the process of creating shader programs.

Open the Starfish Collector Shaders project. To begin, in the Turtle class, add the following import statements:

```
import com.badlogic.gdx.Gdx;
import com.badlogic.gdx.graphics.glutils.ShaderProgram;
import com.badlogic.gdx.graphics.g2d.Batch;
```

Then, add the following variable declarations to the same class:

```
String vertexShaderCode;
String fragmentShaderCode;
ShaderProgram shaderProgram;
```

To initialize the shader program, you need the code for both a vertex shader and a fragment shader. This can be obtained via the FileHandle class readString method, which returns the entire contents of a text file as a single String. With this code, you can initialize the ShaderProgram object, which automatically sends the code to the GPU and compiles it. You also need to check manually for errors after compiling the shader programs. To accomplish these tasks, add the following code to the Turtle class constructor method:

```
vertexShaderCode   = Gdx.files.internal("assets/shaders/default.vs").readString();
fragmentShaderCode = Gdx.files.internal("assets/shaders/default.fs").readString();
shaderProgram = new ShaderProgram(vertexShaderCode, fragmentShaderCode);
if (!shaderProgram.isCompiled())
    System.out.println( "Shader compile error: " + shaderProgram.getLog() );
```

Finally, to actually render the turtle using your custom ShaderProgram object rather than the default, you need to override the draw method from the BaseActor class and set the shader using the Batch class setShader method. When you are finished rendering the turtle, passing null as an argument to the setShader method causes the Batch class to return to using the built-in default shader provided by LibGDX. Add the following method to the Turtle class:

```
public void draw(Batch batch, float parentAlpha)
{
    batch.setShader(shaderProgram);
    super.draw( batch, parentAlpha );
    batch.setShader(null);
}
```

At this point, you can test your program. It should appear exactly as it did before you added the shader, which is to be expected, since all you did was reconstruct the default shaders. However, the framework you have set up will be quite useful, as you will be able to rapidly test out a series of shaders you will write in the following sections.

Grayscale Shader

Here, you will write a fragment shader that renders a texture in grayscale. When the red, green, and blue components of a color are all equal, the resulting color is a shade of gray. Therefore, to convert a color to gray, you can calculate the average of its red, green, and blue values and set all the components of the new color equal to this average. The alpha value should remain unchanged, however. The red, green, blue, and alpha values of a color c (stored as a vec4) can be accessed via c.r, c.g, c.b, and c.a, respectively. In a text-editor program, create a file named grayscale.fs (in the shaders directory, as before) with the following code:

```
varying vec4 v_color;
varying vec2 v_texCoords;

uniform sampler2D u_texture;

void main()
{
    vec4 color = texture2D(u_texture, v_texCoords);
    float average = (color.r + color.g + color.b) / 3.0;
    gl_FragColor = vec4(average, average, average, color.a);
}
```

In your BlueJ project, in the Turtle class, locate the line of code in the constructor method that sets fragmentShaderCode and change it to the following:

```
fragmentShaderCode = Gdx.files.internal("assets/shaders/grayscale.fs").readString();
```

That's all there is to it; run your project, and the turtle should be displayed in grayscale!

Custom Uniform Values

Next, you will write a shader that causes a change in the appearance of an image over time. In particular, your next fragment shader will cause the turtle to smoothly change between rendering in its original color and in grayscale. To do this requires the use of a value that oscillates over time. To this end, you will create a fragment shader that contains a new uniform variable, called u_time. The Turtle class will contain a corresponding variable called time, updated in its act method, and the value of time will be sent to the shader and stored in the variable u_time. The first step is to use your text-editor program to create a file in the shaders folder named grayscale-pulse.fs that contains the following:

```
varying vec4 v_color;
varying vec2 v_texCoords;

uniform sampler2D u_texture;
uniform float u_time;
```

```
void main()
{
    vec4 color = texture2D(u_texture, v_texCoords);

    float average = (color.r + color.g + color.b) / 3.0;
    vec4 grayscale = vec4(average, average, average, color.a);

    float value = (sin(6.28 * u_time) + 1.0) * 0.5;

    gl_FragColor = value * color + (1.0 - value) * grayscale;
}
```

Note that the variable value is based on a sine function, and it will oscillate between 0 and 1 once per second. In turn, gl_FragColor is set equal to grayscale when value equals 0, gl_FragColor is set equal to color when value equals 1, and gl_FragColor is an intermediate color when value is between 0 and 1.

Next, in BlueJ, in the Turtle class, add the following variable declaration:

```
float time;
```

In the constructor method, set the initial value of time to 0:

```
time = 0;
```

Also, change the line of code that sets fragmentShaderCode to the following:

```
fragmentShaderCode = Gdx.files.internal("assets/shaders/grayscale-pulse.fs").readString();
```

In the act method, increment time by the elapsed time dt:

```
time += dt;
```

Finally, change the draw method so that it contains the following code:

```
batch.setShader(shaderProgram);
shaderProgram.setUniformf("u_time", time);
super.draw( batch, parentAlpha );
batch.setShader(null);
```

Note that the preceding new line of code sends the value of time to the shader variable whose name is the String "u_time", and it must be included after the shader program is set, but before the call to super. draw. (This will be the case whenever you need to set the value of a uniform variable.) At this point, you are ready to test your program and watch the turtle image shift from full color to grayscale and back.

Border Shader

Here, you will create a shader that draws a border around the turtle, as shown in Figure 15-8. The color and thickness of the border will be easily set using uniform variables.

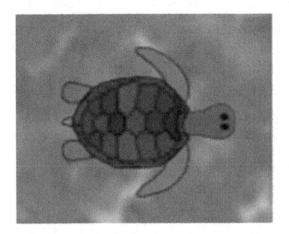 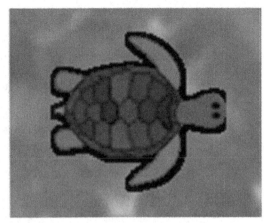

Figure 15-8. Turtle rendered with default shader (left) and border shader (right)

Conceptually, the trickiest part of writing this shader is determining which pixels correspond to the border of the visible part of the image. The approach used here is as follows: for any pixel, check all the pixels that are "nearby" (as specified by the border-size parameter). If all of them have alpha values greater than 0.5, then the original pixel is in a mostly opaque area and will be considered an interior point. If all the nearby pixels have alpha values that are less than 0.5, then the original pixel is in a mostly transparent area and will be considered an exterior point. If the original pixel is neither an interior point nor an exterior point, then the nearby pixels are both opaque and transparent, and so the original pixel will be considered as "on the border." Border pixels on translucent areas will be rendered using the specified border color; all other pixels will be rendered using the original color specified by the texture. Note that if opaque areas are adjacent to the edge of the texture, then the border may appear cut off at that point, as seen on the right side of the bordered image in Figure 15-8.

There is a second, subtle complexity in writing this shader: texture coordinates are specified as percentages; the x and y texture coordinates each range from 0 to 1. Since the border size is specified in terms of pixels, you will need to convert texture units to pixel units and back. The texture coordinates (1,1) correspond to pixel coordinates (w,h), where w and h are the width and height of the image. Therefore, the relationship between texture coordinates (tx, ty) and pixel coordinates (px, py) can be expressed as (px, py) = (tx * w, ty * h) or as (tx, ty) = (px / w, py / h).

With this understanding, you are ready to write the shader. In your text-editor program, create a file in the shaders folder named border.fs that contains the following:

```
varying vec4 v_color;
varying vec2 v_texCoords;

uniform sampler2D u_texture;

uniform vec2  u_imageSize;
uniform vec4  u_borderColor;
uniform float u_borderSize;

void main()
{
    vec4 color = texture2D(u_texture, v_texCoords);
    vec2 pixelToTextureCoords = 1 / u_imageSize;
```

```
    bool isInteriorPoint = true;
    bool isExteriorPoint = true;

    for (float dx = -u_borderSize; dx < u_borderSize; dx++)
    {
        for (float dy = -u_borderSize; dy < u_borderSize; dy++)
        {
            vec2 point = v_texCoords + vec2(dx,dy) * pixelToTextureCoords;
            float alpha = texture2D(u_texture, point).a;

            if ( alpha < 0.5 )
                isInteriorPoint = false;
            if ( alpha > 0.5 )
                isExteriorPoint = false;
        }
    }

    if (!isInteriorPoint && !isExteriorPoint && color.a < 0.5)
        gl_FragColor = u_borderColor;
    else
        gl_FragColor = v_color * color;
}
```

Next, in the Turtle class, add the following import statements, which correspond to the data types you will be passing into the shader:

```
import com.badlogic.gdx.graphics.Color;
import com.badlogic.gdx.math.Vector2;
```

Change the line of code that sets fragmentShaderCode to the following:

```
fragmentShaderCode = Gdx.files.internal("assets/shaders/border.fs").readString();
```

Finally, change the draw method so that it contains the following code. Note that the line of code from the previous example that set the value of "u_time", has been removed, as it is not used by this shader.

```
batch.setShader(shaderProgram);
shaderProgram.setUniformf( "u_imageSize", new Vector2(getWidth(), getHeight()) );
shaderProgram.setUniformf( "u_borderColor", Color.BLACK );
shaderProgram.setUniformf( "u_borderSize", 3 );
super.draw( batch, parentAlpha );
batch.setShader(null);
```

With these changes, the border shader is complete. Test out the program and verify that the border appears as expected.

Blur Shader

Here, you will create a shader that blurs the turtle image, as shown in Figure 15-9. The amount of blur will be set using a uniform variable.

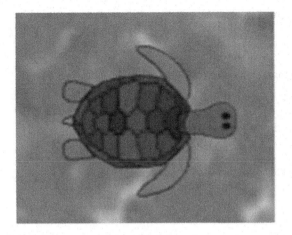 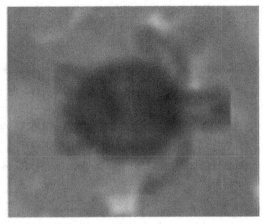

Figure 15-9. *Turtle rendered with default shader (left) and blur shader (right)*

The blur shader has a similar structure to the border shader from the previous example. For each pixel, a nested for loop is used to iterate over a square region of pixels centered on the original pixel. The average color of the pixels in this region is calculated by adding together the color vectors for each pixel and dividing by the total number of pixels in the square region;[3] this is the final value used for gl_FragColor. In your text-editor program, create a file in the shaders folder named blur.fs that contains the following:

```
varying vec4 v_color;
varying vec2 v_texCoords;

uniform sampler2D u_texture;

uniform vec2  u_imageSize;
uniform int   u_blurRadius;

void main()
{
    vec4 color = texture2D(u_texture, v_texCoords);
    vec2 pixelToTextureCoords = 1 / u_imageSize;

    vec4 averageColor = vec4(0.0, 0.0, 0.0, 0.0);

    for (int dx = -u_blurRadius; dx <= u_blurRadius; dx++)
    {
        for (int dy = -u_blurRadius; dy <= u_blurRadius; dy++)
        {
            vec2 point = v_texCoords + vec2(dx,dy) * pixelToTextureCoords;
            averageColor += texture2D(u_texture, point);
        }
    }
```

---

[3]More sophisticated blur algorithms will instead calculate a weighted average of the pixel colors, where the closer a pixel is to the center, the larger the influence it has when computing the final color.

```
    averageColor /= pow(2.0 * u_blurRadius + 1.0, 2.0);
    gl_FragColor = v_color * averageColor;
}
```

Next, in the Turtle class, change the line of code that sets fragmentShaderCode to the following:

```
fragmentShaderCode = Gdx.files.internal("assets/shaders/blur.fs").readString();
```

Finally, change the draw method so that it contains the following code:

```
batch.setShader(shaderProgram);
shaderProgram.setUniformf( "u_imageSize", new Vector2(getWidth(), getHeight()) );
shaderProgram.setUniformf( "u_blurRadius", 5 );
super.draw( batch, parentAlpha );
batch.setShader(null);
```

With these changes, the blur shader is complete. Test out the program and verify that the blur appears as expected.

Glow Shader

Once you understand how the blur shader works, you can create a glowing effect by adding the original image color to the blurred color at each pixel, which lightens the image and blends the colors together slightly. For a fancy visual effect, in this shader you will also add a pulsing effect (similar to your earlier work with the grayscale shader) that causes the turtle to smoothly change between rendering in its original color and with the glow effect, which will cause the turtle to appear to pulse with an inner light. In your text-editor program, create a file in the shaders folder named glow-pulse.fs that contains the following:

```
varying vec4 v_color;
varying vec2 v_texCoords;

uniform sampler2D u_texture;

uniform float u_time;
uniform vec2  u_imageSize;
uniform int   u_glowRadius;

void main()
{
    vec4 color = texture2D(u_texture, v_texCoords);
    vec2 pixelToTextureCoords = 1 / u_imageSize;

    vec4 averageColor = vec4(0.0, 0.0, 0.0, 0.0);

    for (int dx = -u_glowRadius; dx <= u_glowRadius; dx++)
    {
        for (int dy = -u_glowRadius; dy <= u_glowRadius; dy++)
        {
            vec2 point = v_texCoords + vec2(dx,dy) * pixelToTextureCoords;
            averageColor += texture2D(u_texture, point);
        }
    }
```

354

```
averageColor /= pow(2.0 * u_glowRadius + 1.0, 2.0);

float amount = (sin(6.0 * u_time) + 1.0) * 0.5;
// extra factor of 2.0 intensifies glow effect
vec4 glowFactor = vec4( 2.0 * averageColor.rgb, averageColor.a );

gl_FragColor = v_color * (color + amount * glowFactor);
}
```

Next, in the Turtle class, change the line of code that sets fragmentShaderCode to the following:

```
fragmentShaderCode = Gdx.files.internal("assets/shaders/glow-pulse.fs").readString();
```

Finally, change the draw method so that it contains the following code:

```
batch.setShader(shaderProgram);
shaderProgram.setUniformf( "u_time", time );
shaderProgram.setUniformf( "u_imageSize", new Vector2(getWidth(), getHeight()) );
shaderProgram.setUniformf( "u_glowRadius", 5 );
super.draw( batch, parentAlpha );
batch.setShader(null);
```

With these changes, the pulsing glow shader is complete. Test out the program and verify that the effect appears as expected.

Wave-Distortion Shader

For the final shader in this chapter, instead of altering pixel colors, you will distort the image itself in a wave pattern using sine functions, some examples of which appear in Figure 15-10. The distortion may be animated if desired, to produce a rippling effect.

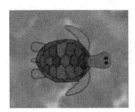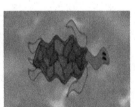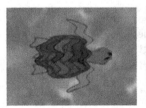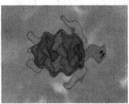

Figure 15-10. *Turtle rendered with default shader, horizontal wave distortion, vertical wave distortion, and wave distortion in both directions*

To create this effect, you will add an offset to the texture coordinates; this offset is calculated using a sine function. In order to customize the effect to your liking, you will include uniform parameters that adjust the wavelength and amplitude of the sine wave, quantities illustrated in Figure 15-11. You will also be able to set the velocity of the sine wave, which will be the rate (in pixels/second) at which the distortion moves across the texture; setting this value to 0 will cause the distortion to be stationary. Since there will be both horizontally and vertically oriented sine waves distorting the texture, each of these parameters will come in pairs, one value for each of the directions (along the x and y axes). Setting the amplitude of the sine wave to 0 in a given direction will cause there to be no distortion at all.

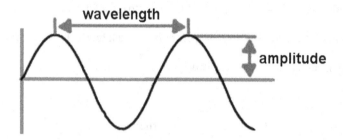

Figure 15-11. *The wavelength and amplitude of a sine wave.*

The formula that produces the sine wave with amplitude A, wavelength W, and moving with velocity V along the x-axis is given by the formula $y = A * sin(6.283/W * (x + t * V))$, while the sine wave along the y-axis is given by the formula $x = A * sin(6.28/W * (y + t * V))$. Implementing these formulas in a shader is straightforward. You must also remember to convert texture coordinates to pixel coordinates and back, since the amplitude, wavelength, and velocity that are used in the calculation are all expressed in terms of pixels. In your text-editor program, create a file in the shaders folder named wave.fs that contains the following:

```
varying vec4 v_color;
varying vec2 v_texCoords;

uniform float u_time;
uniform vec2 u_imageSize;
uniform vec2 u_amplitude;
uniform vec2 u_wavelength;
uniform vec2 u_velocity;

uniform sampler2D u_texture;

void main()
{
    vec2 pixelCoords = v_texCoords * u_imageSize;
    vec2 offset = u_amplitude * sin(6.283/u_wavelength * (pixelCoords.yx - u_velocity *
    u_time));
    vec2 texCoords = v_texCoords + offset / u_imageSize;
    gl_FragColor = v_color * texture2D(u_texture, texCoords);
}
```

Next, in the Turtle class, change the line of code that sets fragmentShaderCode to the following:

```
fragmentShaderCode = Gdx.files.internal("assets/shaders/wave.fs").readString();
```

Finally, change the draw method so that it contains the following code:

```
batch.setShader(shaderProgram);
shaderProgram.setUniformf( "u_time", time );
shaderProgram.setUniformf( "u_imageSize", new Vector2(getWidth(), getHeight()) );
shaderProgram.setUniformf("u_amplitude",  new Vector2( 2,  3) );
shaderProgram.setUniformf("u_wavelength", new Vector2(17, 19) );
shaderProgram.setUniformf("u_velocity",   new Vector2(10, 11) );
super.draw( batch, parentAlpha );
batch.setShader(null);
```

With these changes, the wave-distortion shader is complete. Test out the program and verify that the effect appears as expected, then experiment with the uniform values to get a sense of the range of possibilities.

Summary and Next Steps

In this chapter, you learned two advanced and powerful approaches to improving the graphics in your game-development projects. First, you learned how to create particle systems with the LibGDX Particle Editor, which can be used to simulate a variety of effects, such as the thruster and explosion effects you created. You then designed a class called ParticleActor, which enabled you to integrate these effects into the *Space Rocks* game. Second, you learned how to write shader programs, which leverage the power of the GPU to create effects such as blur, glow, and distortion. You then learned how to use the ShaderProgram class to use the shader programs when drawing actors in the *Starfish Collector* game.

At this point, you can solidify your knowledge by incorporating more special effects into your games. For example, try creating a particle effect that looks like water droplets splashing out of a puddle, and use this effect in the *Starfish Collector* game to replace the Whirlpool object. You could also add shader programs to objects other than the turtle in *Starfish Collector*; for example, you could add the glow-pulse effect to the Starfish class. You could even create a new class called Water to replace the BaseActor containing the background image and apply the wave-distortion shader in its draw method. Alternatively, in the *Space Rocks* game, you could add the glow-pulse effect to the Laser class and add the wave-distortion effect to the Warp class.

In the next chapter, you will continue learning about advanced graphics, but in the context of 3D games, concluding with a 3D version of the game that started it all in this book: *Starfish Collector*.

CHAPTER 16

▪ ▪ ▪

Introduction to 3D Graphics and Games

This chapter will introduce some of the 3D graphics capabilities of LibGDX. Along the way, you'll learn about the concepts and classes necessary to describe and render a three-dimensional scene. To simplify and streamline this process, you'll both adapt some old classes and write some new classes to accomplish the various tasks involved. Next, to understand 3D movement, you'll create a simple interactive demo that enables players to control both an object within the scene and the camera viewing the scene. Finally, you'll create the game *Starfish Collector 3D*, shown in Figure 16-1, which once again features a turtle on a quest to collect all the starfish that it can. For simplicity, this game will actually use 2.5D techniques: the game will render three-dimensional graphics, while the underlying gameplay (movement and collisions) will occur in two dimensions.

Figure 16-1. *The* Starfish Collector *3D game*

Exploring 3D Concepts and Classes

As it turns out, all of the previously created games in this book exist in a three-dimensional space. You may have noticed that, for example, when setting the position of a camera object (in the `alignCamera` method of the `BaseActor` class), you have *x*, *y*, and *z* components to set. If the *x*-axis and the *y*-axis represent the horizontal and vertical directions on the screen, respectively, then the *z*-axis corresponds to a straight line pointing toward the viewer, perpendicular to the *xy plane*—the plane containing the *x* and *y* axes. The camera can be thought of as being positioned on the *z* axis, pointing straight toward the *xy* plane; all of the game entities have implicitly had their *z* coordinate set to 0. This configuration is illustrated in Figure 16-2, which shows roughly how the camera sees the *Starfish Collector* game from previous chapters.

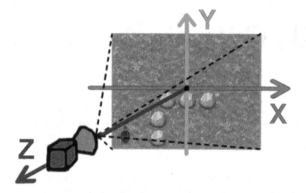

Figure 16-2. *A camera looking down the z axis at the* Starfish Collector *game*

Your previous projects have relied heavily on the Stage class, which manages the Camera and a Batch object (for rendering purposes). To create 3D scenes, you need the "3D versions" of these objects, provided by the PerspectiveCamera and ModelBatch classes, which will be covered in detail next. However, there is no corresponding stage-like object to manage them, and so you will create your own manager class (called Stage3D) in a later section.

To render a scene, you can use one of two types of cameras: an orthographic camera or a perspective camera. (The Stage class uses an OrthographicCamera object for rendering.) The difference between these two is in how they represent, or project, a 3D scene onto a 2D surface such as a computer screen. To illustrate the difference, consider one of the simplest 3D shapes: a cube. Figure 16-3 shows an orthographic projection and a perspective projection of a cube. In an orthogonal projection, if the edges of an object have the same length, then they will be drawn as having the same length in the projection, regardless of their distance from the viewer. This is in contrast to a perspective projection, in which objects with two edges of the same length may appear different in the projection; an edge that is farther away from the viewer will appear shorter. This also has the side effect that, if two edges of an object are parallel, then they remain parallel in an orthographic projection, but they appear to converge in a perspective projection. (In a perspective drawing, the point at which all such edges appear to converge is called the *vanishing point.*)

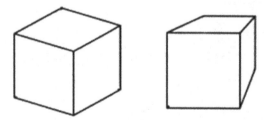

Figure 16-3. *A cube drawn using orthographic projection (left) and perspective projection (right)*

When initializing a `PerspectiveCamera` object, you have to define the region visible to the camera, which has the shape of a truncated pyramid, or frustum (illustrated in Figure 16-4). This is specified by five parameters: the field of view (an angle that represents how far the camera can see to either side), the width and height of the rectangle onto which the scene is being projected (determined by a `Viewport` object in LibGDX), and the near and far values (which represent the closest and farthest distances that the camera will include while rendering).

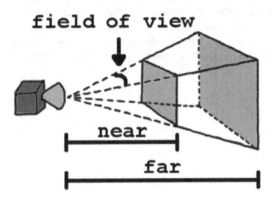

Figure 16-4. *A region visible to a perspective camera; near and far distances are indicated by shaded planes*

The next new class is `ModelBatch`. Just as a `SpriteBatch` object can be used to render two-dimensional `Texture` objects, `ModelBatch` is used to render three-dimensional objects. The data needed to describe the appearance of a three-dimensional object is contained in a `Model` object, which consists of two major components: `Mesh` and `Material`. A *mesh* is a collection of vertices, edges, and triangular faces that define the shape of an object. A *material* contains color or texture data that is applied to the mesh; the material defines the appearance of the mesh while rendering. Figure 16-5 contains two images of a teapot: a wireframe representation of the mesh, and its appearance after applying a material. This particular teapot is a classic model called the *Utah teapot*, created by the computer scientist Martin Newell in 1975. Models can be loaded from standard 3D object file formats.

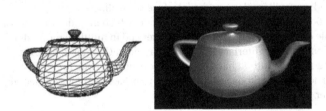

Figure 16-5. *The Utah teapot, rendered in wireframe (left) and with material applied (right)*

Models can be created in two ways in LibGDX. Using the `ModelLoader` class, a model can be loaded from standard 3D object file formats (such as the Wavefront format, typically indicated by the `.obj` file extension), which may also contain references to image files used by the accompanying material. Alternatively, some basic shapes (such as spheres and boxes) can be generated at runtime using the `ModelBuilder` class. You will see examples of both of these approaches over the course of this chapter.

Finally, in order to give 3D models a realistic appearance, the effects of light sources need to be considered. In fact, if lights are not added to a scene, you will not be able to see anything at all! Lights are managed by the Environment class. The two types of lighting effects you will use are ambient light and directional light. *Ambient light* provides overall illumination and shines equally from all directions. Typically, it is important to include ambient light in a scene so that even the sides facing away from a light source will be somewhat visible (although this amount may vary depending on the type of location you are simulating). A *directional light* is used to simulate light shining throughout the scene in a particular direction. This helps provide a sense of depth in a scene, in particular allowing you to distinguish between different faces when an object's material consists of just a single color. Figure 16-6 illustrates these effects with two renderings of a cube. In the image on the left, the scene contains only ambient light, which makes it difficult to see all the edges of the cube. The image on the right has a directional light, primarily aimed toward the left (and thus the right side of the cube appears brightest).

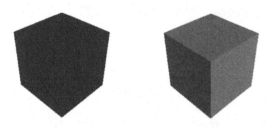

Figure 16-6. *A cube illuminated with ambient light only (left) and directional light added (right)*

Creating a Minimal 3D Demo

You are now ready to create a minimal code example that renders a cube in LibGDX using the previously mentioned classes. The result is a single blue box, oriented and shaded as on the right side of Figure 16-6. To begin, create a new project in BlueJ called Project3D, copy the +libs folder (if not using the BlueJ userlib folder) and its contents from a previous project into this new project's directory, and restart BlueJ so that the JAR files are loaded correctly. You don't need to copy any classes or assets to this project at this time. Rather than starting with the Game class as usual (which implements the ApplicationListener interface methods), this example will be self-contained; you will implement the interface yourself.

To begin, create a new class called CubeDemo that contains the following code, which includes the core of a 3D application: import statements, variable declarations (those that are referenced in multiple methods), and the methods required by the ApplicationListener interface. As was explained in Chapter 2, the create method is used to initialize objects, while the render method handles the game loop; the code for each of these methods is presented in detail later. (The other methods required by the interface aren't fundamental to this example and so are not discussed later.)

```
import com.badlogic.gdx.ApplicationListener;
import com.badlogic.gdx.Gdx;
import com.badlogic.gdx.graphics.GL20;
import com.badlogic.gdx.graphics.Color;
import com.badlogic.gdx.graphics.PerspectiveCamera;
import com.badlogic.gdx.graphics.VertexAttributes.Usage;
import com.badlogic.gdx.graphics.g3d.Environment;
import com.badlogic.gdx.graphics.g3d.attributes.ColorAttribute;
import com.badlogic.gdx.graphics.g3d.environment.DirectionalLight;
import com.badlogic.gdx.graphics.g3d.utils.ModelBuilder;
```

```java
import com.badlogic.gdx.graphics.g3d.Model;
import com.badlogic.gdx.graphics.g3d.ModelBatch;
import com.badlogic.gdx.graphics.g3d.ModelInstance;
import com.badlogic.gdx.graphics.g3d.Material;
import com.badlogic.gdx.math.Vector3;

public class CubeDemo implements ApplicationListener
{
        public Environment environment;
        public PerspectiveCamera camera;
        public ModelBatch modelBatch;
        public ModelInstance boxInstance;

        public void create() {  }

        public void render() {  }

        public void dispose() {  }

        public void resize(int width, int height) {  }

        public void pause() {  }

        public void resume() {  }
}
```

The create method begins with initializing the Environment and adding a parameter (a subclass of the Attribute class) that defines the color of the ambient light in the scene. In general, shades of gray are used for lights (rather than, say, colors such as yellow or blue) so that your scene will not be tinted with unexpected colors. Then, an instance of a DirectionalLight is created using a brighter shade of gray, and its direction is specified (using a Vector3 object) to be primarily to the left and downward; after configuring its parameters, the light is added to the environment. A PerspectiveCamera is then initialized, with a field of view of 67 degrees and with near and far visibility set to 0.1 and 1000, respectively (these values have been chosen to guarantee that the view area contains the object you will add to the scene). The camera's position is set, and the location it should initially be looking toward is specified via the lookAt method. Finally, a ModelBatch object is initialized, which will be used later when rendering. These steps "set the scene" and are accomplished by adding the following code to the create method:

```java
environment = new Environment();
environment.set( new ColorAttribute(ColorAttribute.AmbientLight, 0.4f, 0.4f, 0.4f, 1f) );

DirectionalLight dLight = new DirectionalLight();
Color     lightColor = new Color(0.75f, 0.75f, 0.75f, 1);
Vector3  lightVector = new Vector3(-1.0f, -0.75f, -0.25f);
dLight.set( lightColor, lightVector );
environment.add( dLight ) ;

camera = new PerspectiveCamera(67, Gdx.graphics.getWidth(), Gdx.graphics.getHeight());
camera.near = 0.1f;
camera.far  = 1000f;
```

```
camera.position.set(10f, 10f, 10f);
camera.lookAt(0,0,0);
camera.update();

modelBatch = new ModelBatch();
```

The next task is to create instances of models to add to your scene. For the sake of simplicity in this example, you will use the createBox method of the ModelBuilder class to construct a cube. You must also create a Material to give the cube its appearance on screen; here, a solid blue diffuse color is used. (The *diffuse color* of an object is the apparent color of the object when illuminated by pure white light.)

You must also determine what types of data each vertex of the model should contain: in every case, vertices should store a position, but for this example, they also store color data and a vector (called the *normal vector*) that is used to determine how light reflects off an object, thus providing shading effects. Each of these attributes has a corresponding constant value defined in the Usage class; position data corresponds to Usage.Position, color data corresponds to Usage.ColorPacked, normal vector data corresponds to Usage.Normal, and so forth. When a combination of this data is needed, a value is generated by adding together the constant values for each of the desired attributes. The resulting value is passed as a parameter to the createBox method.

You also need to decide on the dimensions of the box itself. Because of the scale used by many modeling programs, these values are often in the range from 1 to 10, and so you should use similar ranges of values when creating objects with the ModelBuilder class. After creating the Model (which you can think of as a template object), a ModelInstance is initialized. This object contains a copy of the information from the model, as well as a transformation matrix that stores position, rotation, and scaling data for this particular instance. The following code performs all these tasks and should be added to the create method:

```
ModelBuilder modelBuilder = new ModelBuilder();

Material boxMaterial = new Material();
boxMaterial.set( ColorAttribute.createDiffuse(Color.BLUE) );

int usageCode = Usage.Position + Usage.ColorPacked + Usage.Normal;

Model boxModel = modelBuilder.createBox( 5, 5, 5, boxMaterial, usageCode );
boxInstance = new ModelInstance(boxModel);
```

Finally, the render method is given, which is where all the phases of the game loop happen. In this case, the program consists of a static scene, so there is no user input to process nor updating tasks to be done—just rendering to perform. The code for this method should appear relatively familiar. One difference is that the glClear function also needs to erase the depth information generated during the previous render, since the distance from the camera to each object in the scene may change if the camera moves around, in which case the depth values will need to be recalculated. Another difference is that the ModelBatch takes the PerspectiveCamera as input in its begin method. The corresponding code to add to the render method is as follows:

```
Gdx.gl.glClearColor(1,1,1,1);
Gdx.gl.glViewport(0, 0, Gdx.graphics.getWidth(), Gdx.graphics.getHeight());
Gdx.gl.glClear( GL20.GL_COLOR_BUFFER_BIT | GL20.GL_DEPTH_BUFFER_BIT );

modelBatch.begin(camera);
modelBatch.render( boxInstance, environment );
modelBatch.end();
```

As usual, you'll also need a launcher-style class, as shown here:

```
import com.badlogic.gdx.backends.lwjgl.LwjglApplication;
public class Launcher1
{
    public static void main ()
    {
        CubeDemo myProgram = new CubeDemo();
        LwjglApplication launcher = new LwjglApplication( myProgram, "Cube Demo", 800, 600 );
    }
}
```

At this point, you should try out the code. Feel free to make some modifications and rerun the code to see the effects of your changes. For example, you could alter the color of the cube, the direction of the light source, or the location of the camera.

Recreating the Actor/Stage Framework

To facilitate and accelerate the development of future projects, in this section you'll write some classes that function similarly to the BaseActor and Stage classes, but instead store data structures and methods useful for three-dimensional graphics. For convenience, you'll continue adding code to the previously created project, which was called Project3D.

The BaseActor3D Class

To begin, recall that the Actor class stored transformation data (position, rotation, and scale) and methods to get, set, and change these values. All Actor objects contained an act method, which could be used to update their internal state, and a draw method, which the actor could use to render itself with a given Batch object. You then wrote an extension of the Actor class, called the BaseActor class, which additionally stored a Texture, a Polygon for collision detection, and related methods. Here, the BaseActor3D class will be presented, which will provide similar functionality in a 3D setting.

Some of the most complicated underlying concepts in 3D graphics are the mathematical structures used to store the transformation data. The technical details will not be covered in depth here,[1] but to understand the code for this example, it's important to know what the objects are and how to use their associated methods.

The transformation data for a ModelInstance object is stored in its transform field as a Matrix4 object: a four-by-four grid of numbers. From this object, you can extract a Vector3 that contains the position of the object. You can also extract another Vector3 that contains the scaling factor in each direction (initialized to 1 in all directions, which results in no change in the default size). The transformation also stores the orientation of the model, which *cannot* be stored with a single number (in contrast to the rotation value of an Actor), because an object in three-dimensional space can be rotated any amount around any combination of the *x*, *y*, and *z* axes. For many technical reasons (such as computation, performance,

---

[1]For additional information, two excellent books about the mathematical details of 3D graphics are *3D Math Primer for Graphics and Game Development* by Fletcher Dunn and Ian Parberry (A K Peters/CRC Press, 2011) and *Mathematics for 3D Game Programming and Computer Graphics* by Eric Lengyel (Cengage Learning PTR, 2011).

and avoiding a phenomena known as *gimbal lock*[2]), an object called a Quaternion (corresponding to a mathematical object of the same name) is used to store orientation data. For convenience, rather than work with the Matrix4 directly, you'll maintain separate objects to store the position, rotation, and scale data for each BaseActor3D object and combine them into a Matrix4 that will be stored in the ModelInstance when needed.

Next, create a new class named BaseActor3D that contains the following code, which includes import statements, variable declarations, and the fundamental methods. This first set of methods includes the constructor; a method to set the ModelInstance for this actor; the calculateTransform method to combine the position, rotation, and scale data into a Matrix4; methods to set the Color and load a Texture used by the associated Material; the act method to update the transformation data of the model instance; and the draw method to render the model instance using the supplied ModelBatch and Environment.

```
import com.badlogic.gdx.graphics.g3d.Environment;
import com.badlogic.gdx.graphics.g3d.ModelBatch;
import com.badlogic.gdx.graphics.g3d.ModelInstance;
import com.badlogic.gdx.graphics.g3d.Material;
import com.badlogic.gdx.graphics.g3d.attributes.ColorAttribute;
import com.badlogic.gdx.Gdx;
import com.badlogic.gdx.graphics.g3d.attributes.TextureAttribute;
import com.badlogic.gdx.graphics.Color;
import com.badlogic.gdx.graphics.Texture;
import com.badlogic.gdx.graphics.Texture.TextureFilter;
import com.badlogic.gdx.math.Vector3;
import com.badlogic.gdx.math.Quaternion;
import com.badlogic.gdx.math.Matrix4;

public class BaseActor3D
{
    private ModelInstance modelData;
    private final Vector3 position;
    private final Quaternion rotation;
    private final Vector3 scale;

    public BaseActor3D(float x, float y, float z)
    {
        modelData = null;
        position = new Vector3(x,y,z);
        rotation = new Quaternion();
        scale    = new Vector3(1,1,1);
    }

    public void setModelInstance(ModelInstance m)
    {   modelData = m;   }

    public Matrix4 calculateTransform()
    {   return new Matrix4(position, rotation, scale);   }
```

---

[2]When using three values to represent the rotations of an object around three axes, *gimbal lock* refers to the problem that occurs when an object is in one of a few particular orientations and two axes of rotation line up, making it impossible for the object to rotate in certain ways while in the given orientation.

```
    public void setColor(Color c)
    {
        for (Material m : modelData.materials)
            m.set( ColorAttribute.createDiffuse(c) );
    }

    public void loadTexture(String fileName)
    {
        Texture tex = new Texture(Gdx.files.internal(fileName), true);
        tex.setFilter( TextureFilter.Linear, TextureFilter.Linear );

        for (Material m : modelData.materials)
            m.set( TextureAttribute.createDiffuse(tex) );
    }

    public void act(float dt)
    { modelData.transform.set( calculateTransform() ); }

    public void draw(ModelBatch batch, Environment env)
    { batch.render(modelData, env); }

}
```

Next are a variety of methods related to the position variable: get and set methods and methods to add values to the current position coordinates. For convenience, this code includes overloaded variations of the methods; the variations allow either a Vector3 or individual float inputs to be used.

```
public Vector3 getPosition()
{ return position; }

public void setPosition(Vector3 v)
{ position.set(v); }

public void setPosition(float x, float y, float z)
{ position.set(x,y,z); }

public void moveBy(Vector3 v)
{ position.add(v); }

public void moveBy(float x, float y, float z)
{ moveBy( new Vector3(x,y,z) ); }
```

The next functionality you will incorporate is the ability to rotate. While in theory a three-dimensional object can rotate around the x-axis, y-axis, or z-axis, for simplicity you will limit the actor to "turning" left and right, which corresponds to rotating around the y-axis, which points upward in this 3D world, as illustrated in Figure 8-2.[3] The amount of rotation around the y-axis will be referred to as the *turn angle*.[4] There will be methods to get, set, and adjust this value, each of which is implemented using methods from the Quaternion class; add these methods to the BaseActor3D class as well.

```
public float getTurnAngle()
{  return rotation.getAngleAround(0,-1,0);  }

public void setTurnAngle(float degrees)
{  rotation.set( new Quaternion(Vector3.Y,degrees) );  }

public void turn(float degrees)
{  rotation.mul( new Quaternion(Vector3.Y,-degrees) );  }
```

Also, methods must be written that enable an actor to move in directions relative to its current orientation. When a BaseActor3D is first initialized, it will be assumed that the forward direction is represented by the vector (0, 0, –1), since the initial position of the camera will have a positive z coordinate and the actor will be facing away from the camera. Similarly, the initial upward direction is the vector (0, 1, 0), and the rightward direction is the vector (1, 0, 0). After the actor has been rotated, the relative forward, upward, and rightward directions can be determined by transforming these original vectors by the actor's current rotation. Then, to move a given distance in one of these relative directions, you can scale the corresponding vector by the desired distance and add the result to the current position. The methods that enable the actor to move in these ways are given here:

```
public void moveForward(float dist)
{  moveBy( rotation.transform( new Vector3(0,0,-1) ).scl( dist ) );  }

public void moveUp(float dist)
{  moveBy( rotation.transform( new Vector3(0,1,0) ).scl( dist ) );  }

public void moveRight(float dist)
{  moveBy( rotation.transform( new Vector3(1,0,0) ).scl( dist ) );  }
```

Finally, a method will be added to set the scale of the object, which is useful for resizing a model:

```
public void setScale(float x, float y, float z)
{  scale.set(x,y,z);  }
```

This completes a large portion of the BaseActor3D class. A later section will discuss and present code for collision-detection and list-management methods (similar to the overlaps and getList methods from the BaseActor class). Next, you will create a complementary class that will be used to manage all these actors: the Stage3D class.

---

[3]In theory, this choice of the y-axis as the "up" direction is somewhat arbitrary, as you could orient yourself in the game world so that any axis corresponds to the up direction.

[4]The amount of rotation around the upward-pointing axis is also called the *yaw* angle. Similarly, the rotation around the sideways-pointing axis (the motion from tilting your head up and down) is called the *pitch* angle, and the rotation around the forward-pointing axis (the motion from tilting your head to the left and to the right) is called the *roll* angle.

The Stage3D Class

Recall that the LibGDX Stage object handles rendering tasks (using its internal Camera and Batch objects) and manages a list of Actor objects. There are also act and draw methods in the Stage class, which call the act and draw methods of all attached actors. You will create similar functionality with the Stage3D class. To begin, create a new class named Stage3D with the following code. This includes a set of import statements, the variables required for rendering (Environment, PerspectiveCamera, and ModelBatch), and an ArrayList to store the BaseActor3D objects. These variables are initialized in the constructor, with nearly identical code to the previous example.

```
import com.badlogic.gdx.Gdx;
import com.badlogic.gdx.graphics.Color;
import com.badlogic.gdx.math.Vector3;
import com.badlogic.gdx.graphics.PerspectiveCamera;
import com.badlogic.gdx.graphics.g3d.Environment;
import com.badlogic.gdx.graphics.g3d.ModelBatch;
import com.badlogic.gdx.graphics.g3d.attributes.ColorAttribute;
import com.badlogic.gdx.graphics.g3d.environment.DirectionalLight;
import java.util.ArrayList;

public class Stage3D
{
    private Environment environment;
    private PerspectiveCamera camera;
    private final ModelBatch modelBatch;
    private ArrayList<BaseActor3D> actorList;

    public Stage3D()
    {
        environment = new Environment();
        environment.set(new ColorAttribute(ColorAttribute.AmbientLight, 0.7f, 0.7f, 0.7f, 1));

        DirectionalLight dLight = new DirectionalLight();
        Color lightColor = new Color(0.9f, 0.9f, 0.9f, 1);
        Vector3 lightVector = new Vector3(-1.0f, -0.75f, -0.25f);
        dLight.set( lightColor, lightVector );
        environment.add( dLight ) ;

        camera = new PerspectiveCamera(67, Gdx.graphics.getWidth(), Gdx.graphics.getHeight());
        camera.position.set(10f, 10f, 10f);
        camera.lookAt(0,0,0);
        camera.near = 0.01f;
        camera.far = 1000f;
        camera.update();

        modelBatch = new ModelBatch();

        actorList = new ArrayList<BaseActor3D>();
    }
}
```

Next, are the act and draw methods, which invoke the corresponding methods on all the BaseActor3D objects contained in the ArrayList. In addition, the camera is updated in the act method.

```
public void act(float dt)
{
    camera.update();
    for (BaseActor3D ba : actorList)
        ba.act(dt);
}

public void draw()
{
    modelBatch.begin(camera);
    for (BaseActor3D ba : actorList)
        ba.draw(modelBatch, environment);
    modelBatch.end();
}
```

There are methods to add and remove actors and retrieve the list, given by the following code:

```
public void addActor(BaseActor3D ba)
{   actorList.add( ba );   }

public void removeActor(BaseActor3D ba)
{   actorList.remove( ba );   }

public ArrayList<BaseActor3D> getActors()
{   return actorList;   }
```

The final part of this class is an extensive set of methods to adjust the camera, which is a much more involved process than in a 2D game. First are the methods to set the camera position and to move the camera by a given amount; these values may be specified by either a Vector3 object or three float values:

```
public void setCameraPosition(float x, float y, float z)
{   camera.position.set(x,y,z);   }

public void setCameraPosition(Vector3 v)
{   camera.position.set(v);   }

public void moveCamera(float x, float y, float z)
{   camera.position.add(x,y,z);   }

public void moveCamera(Vector3 v)
{   camera.position.add(v);   }
```

Next, building on these methods are additional methods that move the camera relative to its current position. A Camera object stores two internal Vector3 objects: direction, which determines where the camera is currently facing, and up, which determines the direction that should be oriented toward the top of the screen. When moving the camera forward and backward in this program, the camera should maintain a constant height (even if the camera is tilted at an angle), and so the y component of the vector direction can be set to 0 in order to yield a vector that moves you forward in this way. Once the vector has been determined, it needs to be scaled by the distance you want the camera to travel, and then the vector should be added to the camera's current position via the moveCamera function. For moving to the left and right, you will similarly discard the *y* component of the vector; to transform the direction vector into a vector pointing to the right, interchange the *x* and *z* values and negate the *z* value, as illustrated by the example in Figure 16-7. In this picture, keep in mind that the values displayed refer to the change in direction represented by each of the vectors.

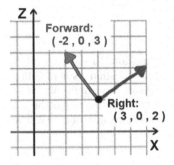

Figure 16-7. *Converting a forward-facing vector to a rightward-facing vector*

Moving the camera upward is a straightforward task. In this case, movement will always be in the direction of the *y*-axis and *not* the camera's up vector, since when the camera is tilted, its up vector will no longer be pointing in the same orientation as the *y*-axis. The methods for moving the camera in these ways are as follows:

```
public void moveCameraForward(float dist)
{
    Vector3 forward = new Vector3(camera.direction.x, 0, camera.direction.z).nor();
    moveCamera( forward.scl( dist ) );
}

public void moveCameraRight(float dist)
{
    Vector3 right = new Vector3(camera.direction.z, 0, -camera.direction.x).nor();
    moveCamera( right.scl( dist ) );
}

public void moveCameraUp(float dist)
{  moveCamera( 0,dist,0 );  }
```

Functionality should also be provided for rotating the camera, and, once again, restricting the types of possible camera movement will make the navigation easier for the user to visualize. As with BaseActor3D objects, the camera will be able to turn to the left and right, which corresponds to rotating it around the *y*-axis. In addition, it would be convenient to be able to tilt the camera up and down to look higher and lower. This can be done by determining the vector that points to the right, as before, and then rotating the direction vector of the camera around the vector pointing to the right. These two methods, turnCamera and tiltCamera, are given here:

```
public void turnCamera(float angle)
{  camera.rotate( Vector3.Y, -angle );  }

public void tiltCamera(float angle)
{
    Vector3 right = new Vector3(camera.direction.z, 0, -camera.direction.x);
    camera.direction.rotate(right, angle);
}
```

Finally, it is important to be able to orient the camera to look at a particular position. This is accomplished with a camera method called lookAt, but this method may have the undesired result of tilting the camera to the left or right, making the horizon no longer level, which can be disorienting to the player. So, after calling the camera's lookAt method, the camera's up axis needs to be reset to the direction of the y-axis to correct this problem; this method will be called setCameraDirection. As before, this method will be overloaded to take either a Vector3 or three float values as input.

```
public void setCameraDirection(Vector3 v)
{
    camera.lookAt(v);
    camera.up.set(0,1,0);
}

public void setCameraDirection(float x, float y, float z)
{  setCameraDirection( new Vector3(x,y,z) );  }
```

This is all the functionality you'll need for the Stage3D class. Now that you are finished writing this class, you can return to the BaseActor3D class to add some stage-related functionality. You will modify the constructor by adding a Stage3D parameter to which the actor will be added when it is created, and which will store a reference to the stage, which will be convenient later. In the BaseActor3D class, add the following variable declaration:

```
protected Stage3D stage;
```

Also, change the constructor of this class to the following:

```
public BaseActor3D(float x, float y, float z, Stage3D s)
    {
        modelData = null;
        position  = new Vector3(x,y,z);
        rotation  = new Quaternion();
        scale     = new Vector3(1,1,1);
        stage = s;
        s.addActor(this);
    }
```

You're now ready to move on to using these classes to create your first interactive 3D demo.

Creating an Interactive 3D Demo

This section presents an interactive demo inspired by Figure 16-2. This demo consists of a screenshot of the *Starfish Collector* game on a flattened box shape and cubes with colored crate textures to represent the origin of the scene and points on the *x*, *y*, and *z* axes. There is also a sphere that can be moved forward and backward, left and right, up and down, and turned to the left or right; the sphere is textured to help the user visualize these directions relative to the sphere. Finally, you will enable the user to turn, tilt, and move the camera in any direction. Figure 16-8 shows this demo in action.

Figure 16-8. *The 3D movement demo program*

Continuing with the Project3D project, you should first download the source code files for this chapter and copy the assets folder into your project, as it contains all the images you will need for this project. You will then create a simplified version of the BaseGame class that you have used in previous chapters. Create a new class called BaseGame with the following code:

```
import com.badlogic.gdx.Game;
import com.badlogic.gdx.Gdx;
import com.badlogic.gdx.InputMultiplexer;

public abstract class BaseGame extends Game
{
    private static BaseGame game;

    public BaseGame()
    {
        game = this;
    }

    public void create()
    {
        InputMultiplexer im = new InputMultiplexer();
        Gdx.input.setInputProcessor( im );
    }
```

```java
    public static void setActiveScreen(BaseScreen s)
    {
        game.setScreen(s);
    }
}
```

Next, you need a new version of the BaseScreen class that uses a Stage3D to contain the game entities, rather than a normal Stage object. However, a standard Stage object remains sufficient for the user interface, and most parts of this class should be familiar from earlier code development in this book, such as implementing the Screen and InputProcessor interfaces. Create a new class called BaseScreen with the following code:

```java
import com.badlogic.gdx.Screen;
import com.badlogic.gdx.InputProcessor;
import com.badlogic.gdx.Gdx;
import com.badlogic.gdx.graphics.GL20;
import com.badlogic.gdx.scenes.scene2d.Stage;
import com.badlogic.gdx.InputMultiplexer;
import com.badlogic.gdx.scenes.scene2d.ui.Table;

public abstract class BaseScreen implements Screen, InputProcessor
{
    protected Stage3D mainStage3D;
    protected Stage uiStage;
    protected Table uiTable;

    public BaseScreen()
    {
        mainStage3D = new Stage3D();
        uiStage    = new Stage();

        uiTable = new Table();
        uiTable.setFillParent(true);
        uiStage.addActor(uiTable);

        initialize();
    }

    public abstract void initialize();

    public abstract void update(float dt);

    // gameloop method
    public void render(float dt)
    {
        // limit amount of time that can pass while window is being dragged
        dt = Math.min(dt, 1/30f);

        // act methods
        uiStage.act(dt);
        mainStage3D.act(dt);
```

```java
    // defined by game-specific classes
    update(dt);

    // render
    Gdx.gl.glClearColor(0.5f,0.5f,0.5f,1);
    Gdx.gl.glClear(GL20.GL_COLOR_BUFFER_BIT + GL20.GL_DEPTH_BUFFER_BIT);

    // draw the graphics
    mainStage3D.draw();
    uiStage.draw();
}

// methods required by Screen interface
public void resize(int width, int height)
{   uiStage.getViewport().update(width, height, true);  }

public void pause()   {  }

public void resume()  {  }

public void dispose() {  }

public void show()
{
    InputMultiplexer im = (InputMultiplexer)Gdx.input.getInputProcessor();
    im.addProcessor(this);
    im.addProcessor(uiStage);
}

public void hide()
{
    InputMultiplexer im = (InputMultiplexer)Gdx.input.getInputProcessor();
    im.removeProcessor(this);
    im.removeProcessor(uiStage);
}

// methods required by InputProcessor interface
public boolean keyDown(int keycode)
{  return false;  }

public boolean keyUp(int keycode)
{  return false;  }

public boolean keyTyped(char c)
{  return false;  }

public boolean mouseMoved(int screenX, int screenY)
{  return false;  }

public boolean scrolled(int amount)
{  return false;  }
```

```java
public boolean touchDown(int screenX, int screenY, int pointer, int button)
{   return false;  }

public boolean touchDragged(int screenX, int screenY, int pointer)
{   return false;  }

public boolean touchUp(int screenX, int screenY, int pointer, int button)
{   return false;  }
}
```

Since this program—and potentially others—will use box and sphere shapes, you will next create some classes that extend the BaseActor3D class and create these shapes for you, using the functionality of the ModelBuilder class introduced previously. First, create a new class named Box with the following code:

```java
import com.badlogic.gdx.graphics.g3d.utils.ModelBuilder;
import com.badlogic.gdx.graphics.g3d.Material;
import com.badlogic.gdx.graphics.VertexAttributes.Usage;
import com.badlogic.gdx.graphics.g3d.Model;
import com.badlogic.gdx.graphics.g3d.ModelInstance;
import com.badlogic.gdx.math.Vector3;

public class Box extends BaseActor3D
{
    public Box(float x, float y, float z, Stage3D s)
    {
        super(x,y,z,s);
        ModelBuilder modelBuilder = new ModelBuilder();
        Material boxMaterial = new Material();

        int usageCode = Usage.Position + Usage.ColorPacked
                      + Usage.Normal    + Usage.TextureCoordinates;

        Model boxModel = modelBuilder.createBox(1,1,1, boxMaterial, usageCode);
        Vector3 position = new Vector3(0,0,0);
        setModelInstance( new ModelInstance(boxModel, position) );
    }
}
```

Next, you also need a class to create a sphere. The ModelBuilder class contains a method named createSphere, similar to createBox, which allows you to specify the radius of the sphere in the x, y, and z directions,[5] the resolution of the sphere in terms of the number of subdivisions in the latitudinal and longitudinal directions (for a smooth sphere, you'll set these both to 32), and the associated Material and usage code value. Create a new class called Sphere that contains the following code:

```java
import com.badlogic.gdx.graphics.g3d.utils.ModelBuilder;
import com.badlogic.gdx.graphics.g3d.Material;
import com.badlogic.gdx.graphics.VertexAttributes.Usage;
```

---

[5]Technically, a sphere has only one radius value; the figures created by the createSphere method are more accurately referred to as *ellipsoids*. However, in the class you are creating, all the radius values will be set to the same number, so it truly is a spherical object.

```
import com.badlogic.gdx.graphics.g3d.Model;
import com.badlogic.gdx.graphics.g3d.ModelInstance;
import com.badlogic.gdx.math.Vector3;

public class Sphere extends BaseActor3D
{
    public Sphere(float x, float y, float z, Stage3D s)
    {
        super(x,y,z,s);
        ModelBuilder modelBuilder = new ModelBuilder();
        Material mat = new Material();

        int usageCode = Usage.Position + Usage.ColorPacked
                      + Usage.Normal   + Usage.TextureCoordinates;
        int r = 1;
        Model mod = modelBuilder.createSphere(r,r,r, 32,32, mat, usageCode);
        Vector3 pos = new Vector3(0,0,0);
        setModelInstance( new ModelInstance(mod, pos) );
    }
}
```

Now you are ready to create the class that sets up the scene pictured in Figure 16-8. Create a new class named DemoScreen with the following code. The object named player will be controlled by the user.

```
import com.badlogic.gdx.Gdx;
import com.badlogic.gdx.Input.Keys;
import com.badlogic.gdx.graphics.Color;

public class DemoScreen extends BaseScreen
{
    BaseActor3D player;

    public void initialize()
    {   }

    public void update(float dt)
    {   }
}
```

Next, to set up the objects in the scene, you will create a flat box with the image of the *Starfish Collector* game as its texture, four cubical boxes with the same texture as each other but different colors, and a sphere that will be controlled by the user. You also need to set the starting position and direction of the camera. To accomplish these tasks, add the following code to the initialize method:

```
Box screen = new Box(0,0,0, mainStage3D);
screen.setScale(16, 12, 0.1f);
screen.loadTexture("assets/starfish-collector.png");

Box marker0 = new Box(0,0,0, mainStage3D);
marker0.setColor(Color.BROWN);
marker0.loadTexture("assets/crate.jpg");
```

```
Box markerX = new Box(5,0,0, mainStage3D);
markerX.setColor(Color.RED);
markerX.loadTexture("assets/crate.jpg");

Box markerY = new Box(0,5,0, mainStage3D);
markerY.setColor(Color.GREEN);
markerY.loadTexture("assets/crate.jpg");

Box markerZ = new Box(0,0,5, mainStage3D);
markerZ.setColor(Color.BLUE);
markerZ.loadTexture("assets/crate.jpg");

player = new Sphere(0,1,8, mainStage3D);
player.loadTexture("assets/sphere-pos-neg.png");

mainStage3D.setCameraPosition(3,4,10);
mainStage3D.setCameraDirection(0,0,0);
```

Finally, there is the update method to consider, which processes *lots* of potential player input. The player is controlled using the keyboard keys W/A/S/D, which correspond to moving forward/left/ backward/right, a standard configuration in many computer games. To this standard, you also add the R and F keys for moving up and down (which we think of as the Rise and Fall directions). You also use the Q and E keys to turn left and right (which also seems memorable because these keys are positioned above the keys for moving left and right). The camera can be controlled in the same way, using the same keys, when the Shift key is being pressed simultaneously. The camera can also be tilted upward and downward using the T and G keys (which you can remember with the mnemonic words *Top* and *Ground*). The following is the code that accomplishes all of these tasks, which, as mentioned previously, should be included in the update method:

```
float speed = 3.0f;
float rotateSpeed = 45.0f;

if ( !(Gdx.input.isKeyPressed(Keys.SHIFT_LEFT)
    || Gdx.input.isKeyPressed(Keys.SHIFT_RIGHT)) )
{
    if ( Gdx.input.isKeyPressed(Keys.W) )
        player.moveForward( speed * dt );
    if ( Gdx.input.isKeyPressed(Keys.S) )
        player.moveForward( -speed * dt );
    if ( Gdx.input.isKeyPressed(Keys.A) )
        player.moveRight( -speed * dt );
    if ( Gdx.input.isKeyPressed(Keys.D) )
        player.moveRight( speed * dt );

    if ( Gdx.input.isKeyPressed(Keys.Q) )
        player.turn( -rotateSpeed * dt );
    if ( Gdx.input.isKeyPressed(Keys.E) )
        player.turn( rotateSpeed * dt );

    if ( Gdx.input.isKeyPressed(Keys.R) )
        player.moveUp( speed * dt );
```

```
    if ( Gdx.input.isKeyPressed(Keys.F) )
        player.moveUp( -speed * dt );
}

if ( Gdx.input.isKeyPressed(Keys.SHIFT_LEFT)
    || Gdx.input.isKeyPressed(Keys.SHIFT_RIGHT) )
{
    if (Gdx.input.isKeyPressed(Keys.W))
        mainStage3D.moveCameraForward( speed * dt );
    if (Gdx.input.isKeyPressed(Keys.S))
        mainStage3D.moveCameraForward( -speed * dt );
    if (Gdx.input.isKeyPressed(Keys.A))
        mainStage3D.moveCameraRight( -speed * dt );
    if (Gdx.input.isKeyPressed(Keys.D))
        mainStage3D.moveCameraRight( speed * dt );

    if (Gdx.input.isKeyPressed(Keys.R))
        mainStage3D.moveCameraUp( speed * dt );
    if (Gdx.input.isKeyPressed(Keys.F))
        mainStage3D.moveCameraUp( -speed * dt );

    if (Gdx.input.isKeyPressed(Keys.Q))
        mainStage3D.turnCamera(-rotateSpeed * dt);
    if (Gdx.input.isKeyPressed(Keys.E))
        mainStage3D.turnCamera(rotateSpeed * dt);

    if (Gdx.input.isKeyPressed(Keys.T))
        mainStage3D.tiltCamera(rotateSpeed * dt);
    if (Gdx.input.isKeyPressed(Keys.G))
        mainStage3D.tiltCamera(-rotateSpeed * dt);
}
```

This completes the code for the update method. Before you can run this demo, you will need to write a launcher-style class and a class that extends BaseGame, as you have in previous projects. First, create a new class called MoveDemo with the following code:

```
public class MoveDemo extends BaseGame
{
    public void create()
    {
        super.create();
        setActiveScreen( new DemoScreen() );
    }
}
```

Next, create a class called Launcher2 that contains the following code:

```
import com.badlogic.gdx.backends.lwjgl.LwjglApplication;
public class Launcher2
{
    public static void main ()
```

```
    {
        MoveDemo myProgram = new MoveDemo();
        LwjglApplication launcher = new LwjglApplication(
            myProgram, "Movement Demo", 800, 600 );
    }
}
```

Now, try out the program and get a feel for moving around in three-dimensional space!

Game Project: Starfish Collector 3D

In this section, you'll create the game *Starfish Collector 3D*, which, as the name suggests, is a 3D version of the *Starfish Collector* game introduced at the beginning of this book; a side-by-side comparison of these games is shown in Figure 16-9. As you may expect, the goal in this new game will be to help the turtle collect all the starfish. You control the turtle using the arrow keys: pressing the up arrow key moves the turtle forward, while pressing the left and right arrow keys turns the turtle to the left and to the right. Most of the difficult groundwork has been laid in the previous section. The remaining topics include loading complex models from external files, displaying an image that surrounds the game world, and performing simplified collision detection. As before, you will continue adding code to Project3D, as it already contains many of the classes you will need (BaseGame, BaseScreen, BaseActor3D, and Stage3D).

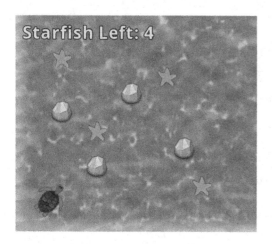

Figure 16-9. Starfish Collector in 2D (left) and 3D (right)

The first task, loading a model, is relatively straightforward. To do so, you need to use an extension of the ModelLoader class, called ObjLoader, which can import 3D models from files that use the Wavefront (*.obj) file format, and then you need to use ObjLoader class loadModel method, which takes a FileHandle as input and returns a Model. You can then use the model to create a ModelInstance that you use in a BaseActor3D object, as you did for the Box and Sphere classes. Since you will be importing multiple models in this game, it makes sense to make a new class that contains this functionality. Create a new class called ObjModel that contains the following code:

```
import com.badlogic.gdx.Gdx;
import com.badlogic.gdx.graphics.g3d.Model;
import com.badlogic.gdx.graphics.g3d.ModelInstance;
import com.badlogic.gdx.graphics.g3d.loader.ObjLoader;
```

```
public class ObjModel extends BaseActor3D
{
    public ObjModel(float x, float y, float z, Stage3D s)
    {
        super(x,y,z,s);
    }

    public void loadObjModel(String fileName)
    {
        ObjLoader loader = new ObjLoader();
        Model objModel = loader.loadModel(Gdx.files.internal(fileName), true);
        setModelInstance( new ModelInstance(objModel) );
    }
}
```

Next, you will need to surround your game world with an image so as to give the appearance of a sky in the background. In the previous 2D games in this book, you created a rectangular object that simply displayed image of the sky. Because you're in a 3D environment, here you'll create a spherical object that is significantly larger than and surrounds your game world, and then you will apply a texture to it, such as the one shown in Figure 16-10. This is often referred to as a *sky sphere* or a *sky dome*. You may notice that the image appears slightly stretched near the top (and it would on the bottom, too, were the bottom not simply a gray color). This is because the image has been spherically distorted: while it looks strange as a rectangle, when the image is applied to a sphere, everything will appear to have the correct proportions. This the same phenomena that occurs when trying to make a flat, rectangular map of the Earth, which is roughly spherical; the map will inevitably contain distorted areas corresponding to the regions near the poles. There is a second difficulty that will arise when trying to implement a sky dome: textures applied to the material of an object are typically only visible when viewed from the *outside* of the object. (This convention is to increase the efficiency of 3D programs; there is no need to render objects from a perspective that the user will not see.) Fortunately, you can perform a geometric trick to resolve this problem: after creating the sphere, you will scale the mesh by –1 in the z direction; this will cause the sphere to turn itself "inside-out," reversing the sides on which the image will be displayed.

Figure 16-10. A spherically distorted image of the sky

The third and final concept to discuss is collision detection. To keep the level of complexity manageable, the motion and placement of your three-dimensional objects will be restricted to a two-dimensional plane, thus allowing this project to reuse collision code from the original BaseActor class. This technique is well-known in game development. Games that use this approach (those that have 3D graphics but restrict game play to a 2D plane and have restricted camera movement) are called *2.5D games*. Figure 16-11 illustrates how the game will appear to the player, while on the right you can see the water represented by a grid and the collision polygons that will correspond to the pictured game entities (the two rocks and the turtle).

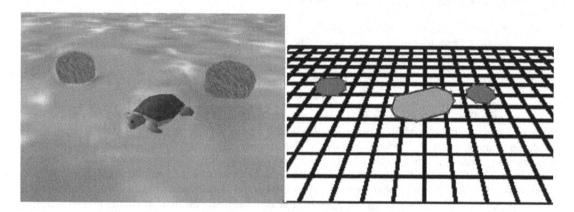

Figure 16-11. *The game world rendered in 3D, and the corresponding 2D collision polygons*

To incorporate collision into your project, you need to make some additions to the BaseActor3D class. First, add the following import statements:

```
import com.badlogic.gdx.math.collision.BoundingBox;
import com.badlogic.gdx.math.Polygon;
import com.badlogic.gdx.math.Intersector;
import com.badlogic.gdx.math.Intersector.MinimumTranslationVector;
```

Next, add the following variable declaration to the class:

```
private Polygon boundingPolygon;
```

Next are a pair of methods used to set the polygon to either a rectangular or an eight-sided polygon (octagon) shape. In both cases, you need to determine the dimensions of the object in the x and z dimensions; these quantities are analogous to the width and height in the two-dimensional case. These values can be determined by calculating the BoundingBox associated with the model, which is the smallest box that contains the entire model. A bounding box stores the dimensions of the model using two Vector3 objects, min and max, which store the values of the smallest and largest coordinates contained by the model, respectively. These values are used to create the array of vertices that is passed to the polygon object, as illustrated here:

```
public void setBaseRectangle ()
{
    BoundingBox modelBounds = modelData.calculateBoundingBox( new BoundingBox() );
    Vector3 max = modelBounds.max;
    Vector3 min = modelBounds.min;
```

```
    float[] vertices =
        {max.x, max.z, min.x, max.z, min.x, min.z, max.x, min.z};
    boundingPolygon = new Polygon(vertices);
    boundingPolygon.setOrigin(0,0);
}

public void setBasePolygon()
{
    BoundingBox modelBounds = modelData.calculateBoundingBox( new BoundingBox() );
    Vector3 max = modelBounds.max;
    Vector3 min = modelBounds.min;

    float a = 0.75f; // offset amount.
    float[] vertices =
        {max.x,0, a*max.x,a*max.z, 0,max.z, a*min.x,a*max.z,
         min.x,0, a*min.x,a*min.z, 0,min.z, a*max.x,a*min.z };
    boundingPolygon = new Polygon(vertices);
    boundingPolygon.setOrigin(0,0);
}
```

Once the polygon has been set up, you need a method that returns the boundary polygon that has been updated to take the position, rotation, and scale into account. Recall that because of the orientation of the coordinate axes, the horizontal plane contains the *x*-axis and the *z*-axis, and so these values will be used when updating the position and scale of the polygon, while the turn angle (the rotation around the *y*-axis) will be used to set its rotation. Add the following code to the BaseActor3D class:

```
public Polygon getBoundaryPolygon()
{
    boundingPolygon.setPosition( position.x, position.z );
    boundingPolygon.setRotation( getTurnAngle() );
    boundingPolygon.setScale( scale.x, scale.z );
    return boundingPolygon;
}
```

Next, you need methods to detect overlap (to check if the turtle has collected a starfish) and prevent overlap (so that the rocks behave as solids and the turtle cannot pass through them). These methods, which you also need to add to the BaseActor3D class, are identical to those from the BaseActor class, except that a BaseActor3D object must be passed in as a parameter. Add the following code:

```
public boolean overlaps(BaseActor3D other)
{
    Polygon poly1 = this.getBoundaryPolygon();
    Polygon poly2 = other.getBoundaryPolygon();

    if ( !poly1.getBoundingRectangle().overlaps(poly2.getBoundingRectangle()) )
        return false;

    MinimumTranslationVector mtv = new MinimumTranslationVector();

    return Intersector.overlapConvexPolygons(poly1, poly2, mtv);
}
```

```java
public void preventOverlap(BaseActor3D other)
{
    Polygon poly1 = this.getBoundaryPolygon();
    Polygon poly2 = other.getBoundaryPolygon();

    // initial test to improve performance
    if ( !poly1.getBoundingRectangle().overlaps(poly2.getBoundingRectangle()) )
        return;

    MinimumTranslationVector mtv = new MinimumTranslationVector();
    boolean polygonOverlap = Intersector.overlapConvexPolygons(poly1, poly2, mtv);

    if ( polygonOverlap )
        this.moveBy( mtv.normal.x * mtv.depth, 0, mtv.normal.y * mtv.depth );
}
```

Finally, you will recreate some methods from the Actor and BaseActor classes to work with lists: getList, count, and remove. First, add the following import statement to the BaseActor3D class:

```java
import java.util.ArrayList;
```

Then, add the following code to the BaseActor3D class:

```java
public static ArrayList<BaseActor3D> getList(Stage3D stage, String className)
{
    ArrayList<BaseActor3D> list = new ArrayList<BaseActor3D>();

    Class theClass = null;
    try
    {   theClass = Class.forName(className);   }
    catch (Exception error)
    {   error.printStackTrace();   }

    for (BaseActor3D ba3d : stage.getActors())
    {
        if ( theClass.isInstance( ba3d ) )
            list.add(ba3d);
    }

    return list;
}

public static int count(Stage3D stage, String className)
{
    return getList(stage, className).size();
}

public void remove()
{
    stage.removeActor(this);
}
```

At this point, the BaseActor3D class has all the core functionality you will need for the *Starfish Collector 3D* game. In this game, the water will be displayed using a Box object, the sky dome will be displayed using a Sphere object, and the turtle, starfish, and rocks will use imported model data from the ObjModel class. Create a new class called Turtle with the following code:

```
public class Turtle extends ObjModel
{
    public Turtle(float x, float y, float z, Stage3D s)
    {
        super(x,y,z,s);
        loadObjModel("assets/turtle.obj");
        setBasePolygon();
    }
}
```

Next, create a class called Starfish with the following code. Note that the act method is being used to make the starfish rotate.

```
public class Starfish extends ObjModel
{
    public Starfish(float x, float y, float z, Stage3D s)
    {
        super(x,y,z,s);
        loadObjModel("assets/star.obj");
        setScale(3,1,3);
        setBasePolygon();
    }

    public void act(float dt)
    {
        super.act(dt);
        turn( 90 * dt );
    }
}
```

Next, create a class called Rock with the following code:

```
public class Rock extends ObjModel
{
    public Rock(float x, float y, float z, Stage3D s)
    {
        super(x,y,z,s);
        loadObjModel("assets/rock.obj");
        setBasePolygon();
        setScale(3,3,3);
    }
}
```

To display the number of remaining starfish in a label, you will set up a LabelStyle object as you have done previously. In the BaseGame class, add the following import statements:

```
import com.badlogic.gdx.graphics.Color;
import com.badlogic.gdx.graphics.Texture;
import com.badlogic.gdx.graphics.Texture.TextureFilter;
import com.badlogic.gdx.graphics.g2d.BitmapFont;
import com.badlogic.gdx.graphics.g2d.freetype.FreeTypeFontGenerator;
import com.badlogic.gdx.graphics.g2d.freetype.FreeTypeFontGenerator.FreeTypeFontParameter;
import com.badlogic.gdx.scenes.scene2d.ui.Label.LabelStyle;
```

Then, add the following variable declaration:

```
public static LabelStyle labelStyle;
```

To initialize the labelStyle object, add the following code to the create method:

```
FreeTypeFontGenerator fontGenerator = new FreeTypeFontGenerator(Gdx.files.internal
("assets/OpenSans.ttf"));
FreeTypeFontParameter fontParameters = new FreeTypeFontParameter();
fontParameters.size = 36;
fontParameters.color = Color.WHITE;
fontParameters.borderWidth = 2;
fontParameters.borderColor = Color.BLACK;
fontParameters.borderStraight = true;
fontParameters.minFilter = TextureFilter.Linear;
fontParameters.magFilter = TextureFilter.Linear;

BitmapFont customFont = fontGenerator.generateFont(fontParameters);

labelStyle = new LabelStyle();
labelStyle.font = customFont;
```

Now you can set up the screen that contains the actual game. Begin by creating a new class called LevelScreen with the following code:

```
import com.badlogic.gdx.Gdx;
import com.badlogic.gdx.Input.Keys;
import com.badlogic.gdx.graphics.Color;
import com.badlogic.gdx.math.Vector3;
import com.badlogic.gdx.scenes.scene2d.ui.Label;

public class LevelScreen extends BaseScreen
{
    Turtle turtle;
    Label starfishLabel;
    Label messageLabel;
```

```
    public void initialize()
    {    }

    public void update(float dt)
    {    }
}
```

In the initialize method, you need to set up the floor and the sky dome, which will be scaled to a very large size. You also need to initialize the turtle, as well as a number of rocks and starfish. As before, you should also set the camera position and direction so that many of the objects you have added are in view when the game begins. Finally, you should initialize the labels and add them to the user-interface table. To accomplish these tasks, add the following code to the initialize method:

```
Box floor = new Box(0,0,0, mainStage3D);
floor.loadTexture( "assets/water.jpg" );
floor.setScale(500, 0.1f, 500);

Sphere skydome = new Sphere(0,0,0, mainStage3D);
skydome.loadTexture( "assets/sky-sphere.png" );
// when scaling, the negative z-value inverts the sphere
//    so that the texture is rendered on the inside
skydome.setScale(500,500,-500);

turtle = new Turtle(0, 0, 15, mainStage3D);
turtle.setTurnAngle(90);

new Rock(-15, 1,  0, mainStage3D);
new Rock(-15, 1, 15, mainStage3D);
new Rock(-15, 1, 30, mainStage3D);
new Rock(  0, 1,  0, mainStage3D);
new Rock(  0, 1, 30, mainStage3D);
new Rock( 15, 1,  0, mainStage3D);
new Rock( 15, 1, 15, mainStage3D);
new Rock( 15, 1, 30, mainStage3D);

new Starfish( 10, 0, 10, mainStage3D);
new Starfish( 10, 0, 20, mainStage3D);
new Starfish(-10, 0, 10, mainStage3D);
new Starfish(-10, 0, 20, mainStage3D);

mainStage3D.setCameraPosition(0,10,0);
mainStage3D.setCameraDirection( new Vector3(0,0,0) );

starfishLabel = new Label("Starfish left: 4", BaseGame.labelStyle);
starfishLabel.setColor( Color.CYAN );

messageLabel = new Label("You Win!", BaseGame.labelStyle);
messageLabel.setColor( Color.LIME );
messageLabel.setFontScale(2);
messageLabel.setVisible(false);
```

```
uiTable.pad(20);
uiTable.add(starfishLabel);
uiTable.row();
uiTable.add(messageLabel).expandY();
```

In the update method, you need to check for user input and move the turtle accordingly, keeping the camera directed toward the turtle. You also need to prevent overlap between the turtle and the rock objects, and if the turtle overlaps a starfish, the starfish should be "collected" and removed from the game. Finally, you need to update the label that displays the number of starfish left, and if there are none left, display the "You Win!" message. To implement all of this, add the following code to the update method:

```
float speed = 3.0f;
float rotateSpeed = 45.0f;

if ( Gdx.input.isKeyPressed(Keys.UP) )
    turtle.moveForward( speed * dt );
if ( Gdx.input.isKeyPressed(Keys.LEFT) )
    turtle.turn( -rotateSpeed * dt );
if ( Gdx.input.isKeyPressed(Keys.RIGHT) )
    turtle.turn( rotateSpeed * dt );

mainStage3D.setCameraDirection( turtle.getPosition() );

for ( BaseActor3D rock : BaseActor3D.getList( mainStage3D, "Rock") )
    turtle.preventOverlap(rock);

for ( BaseActor3D starfish : BaseActor3D.getList( mainStage3D, "Starfish") )
    if (turtle.overlaps(starfish) )
        starfish.remove();

int starfishCount = BaseActor3D.count(mainStage3D, "Starfish");
starfishLabel.setText( "Starfish left: " + starfishCount );

if (starfishCount == 0)
    messageLabel.setVisible(true);
```

At this point, the *Starfish Collector 3D* gameplay code is complete. To play this game, you need to create a new class called StarfishCollector3DGame as follows:

```
public class StarfishCollector3DGame extends BaseGame
{
    public void create()
    {
        super.create();
        setActiveScreen( new LevelScreen() );
    }
}
```

Also, create a new class called Launcher3 as follows:

```
import com.badlogic.gdx.Game;
import com.badlogic.gdx.backends.lwjgl.LwjglApplication;

public class Launcher3
{
    public static void main ()
    {
        Game myGame = new StarfishCollector3DGame();
        LwjglApplication launcher = new LwjglApplication(
                                    myGame, "Starfish Collector 3D", 800, 600 );
    }
}
```

Now, run your project, help the turtle collect all the starfish, and enjoy the 3D graphics as you play!

Summary and Next Steps

This chapter may have only scratched the surface of 3D game programming, but it's a topic that entails a lot of material. You explored the components of 3D scenes, perspective cameras, and lighting. You learned that 3D models contain meshes and materials, and that instances of models store transformation data (position, rotation, and scale) using matrices. You adapted and extended your custom game development framework to include 3D versions of actors and stages and learned the many ways you can move objects around in a three-dimensional world. Finally, you put your skills (and your code) to the test by creating a pair of interactive demo programs.

With the foundation laid in this chapter, you are now ready to create some games with 3D graphics (and 2.5D gameplay, for simplicity). A great place to start is recreating some of the earlier projects from this book. Games such as *Rectangle Destroyer* can be recreated simply using boxes and spheres. For other games, you will likely want to use pre-created model files (similar to the turtle, starfish, and rock). Some websites from which you can download model files (in a variety of formats) include the following:

- OpenGameArt: www.opengameart.org

- The Models Resource: www.models-resource.com

- TurboSquid: www.turbosquid.com
  (They have many free models available; this can be specified in their search options.)

Once you have downloaded a 3D model, and before loading it into LibGDX, you can view and modify it if desired using 3D graphics software such as Blender, which is freely available at www.blender.org, or, for the artistically inclined, Blender can even be used to create 3D models from scratch.

Once again, congratulations on finishing the final game project in this book! The next chapter concludes with some general advice and possible next steps in game development.

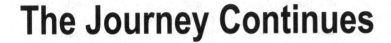

CHAPTER 17

The Journey Continues

This final chapter will present a variety of steps to consider as you continue on in game development. Among these, you'll explore working on additional projects, learning skills in related areas, and bringing your games to a wider audience. Along the way, the chapter will present lists of resources of all types, as well as general advice for many situations.

Continuing Developing

This section will cover how to refine your current projects and start working on new projects, either on your own or as part of a game jam event. The section will provide a list of online resources where you can obtain art assets to help you along the way, along with a healthy dose of advice for overcoming the inevitable obstacles that will arise.

Working on Projects

Hopefully, you've been working through all the project examples in this book. Many of the projects presented have concluded with a section titled "Summary and Next Steps." You should try to complete as many of the suggestions listed there as you can! This is vital because *you learn by doing*. No matter how much sense a topic makes when you read about it, you have truly understood a topic only when you can take the next steps of designing and writing code independently. After each of the projects is functional, you should always experiment with the code and try your own variations.

Make sure that you understand each program at all levels. At the local level, you should understand the effects of each line of code and also the purpose of each method and the design considerations that were taken into account when each was written. At the global level, you should know how all the classes fit together as a unified whole, the reasoning behind structuring the framework as it is, and the advantages and disadvantages to modifying the framework in different ways.

After you've extracted as much knowledge and experience from this book as you feel is possible, it's time to strike out on your own and start creating your own games. To start, try creating simple, minimalist examples that implement new game mechanics (that is, mechanics other than those featured in this book)— perhaps a shoot-em-up style game with enemies who periodically fire lasers at *you*, or a collectible card game where you randomly draw cards that represent magic spells or creatures that attack the enemy on your behalf, or a role-playing game with fetch quests and turn-based combat. In addition to the obvious benefits of knowing how to program even more mechanics, the process of figuring out how to do so is invaluable. Only by engaging in the acts of pondering, planning, writing code, testing, debugging, and rewriting code can you develop skills like inventiveness, organization, adaptability, and perseverance.

© Lee Stemkoski 2018
L. Stemkoski, *Java Game Development with LibGDX*, https://doi.org/10.1007/978-1-4842-3324-5_17

Once you become comfortable implementing game mechanics on your own, as a next step you could take a "cloning the classics" approach for learning purposes (but certainly not for publication!). Take a classic arcade or console game (particularly those from the 1980s) and attempt to re-create as many of its features as possible: implement the game mechanics, level design, artistic (graphics and audio) style, and user interface (menu screens and onscreen data displays).

In particular, you should create a physical list identifying and prioritizing the game-specific features that you'll be working on within each category, as described in Appendix A. Furthermore, you should prioritize the categories of the features themselves in the order presented in the previous paragraph. For example, if your main character is a winged archer, don't worry about the color of their belt until after the character is able to fly and shoot arrows. (In fact, it is common practice for developers to use simple colored polygon shapes during the game-mechanics phase of programming.) Don't worry if you're not an artist; many websites exist with freely available video game graphics, and many artists in the community are looking for collaborators. Finally, once you're comfortable with your skills and abilities, it's time to develop your own game or join a team working on a game and lend your programming skills.

Obtaining Art Resources

The typical reader of this book likely is mainly interested in the programming aspects of game development, but even so, every game still benefits from quality graphics and audio. I recommend the following websites for obtaining artistic resources. Most of these websites have both free and paid options, while others are driven by user donations:

- Kenney Game Assets: kenney.nl
  Created by Kenney Vleugels, this site features over 18,000 art assets that can be useful in many genres. In this book, assets from this site were featured in *Space Rocks*, *Plane Dodger*, *52 Card Pickup*, *Treasure Quest*, and the *Jumping Jack* series.

- GameArtGuppy: gameartguppy.com
  Created by Vicki Wenderlich, this site contains a collection of high-quality art crafted especially for independent game developers. In this book, the Koala character from the *Jumping Jack* games was obtained from this site.

- OpenGameArt: opengameart.org
  A repository for all types of media (2D and 3D graphics, as well as sound effects and music). Contributions are community driven. Licensing details and conditions are determined by the individual creators.

- The Spriters Resource: www.spriters-resource.com
  Features a nearly comprehensive set of game art assets from many game console systems throughout history. Due to copyright restrictions, however, these assets cannot be used in published or commercial games.

- Cool Text: cooltext.com
  A free text art graphics generator that can be useful for creating graphics for title screens as well as text and buttons for user interfaces.

- Textures.com: textures.com
  Offers images of many types of materials, both natural and constructed.

- Bfxr: bfxr.net
  Randomly generates a wide range of retro-style sound effects for use in games.

- Freesound: freesound.org
  A collaborative database of Creative Commons–licensed sounds, organized into packs and also grouped by tags.

- Incompetech: `incompetech.com`
  Created by Kevin MacLeod, this website features a collection of royalty-free
  original music compositions that can be searched by genre, tempo, feel, or
  instrumentation.

- Audionautix: `audionautix.com`
  Created by Jason Shaw, this website also features a collection of royalty-free
  original music that can be searched by genre, mood, or tempo.

Participating in Game Jams

One way to gain valuable game development experience is to participate in a game jam. A *game jam* is
a gathering of game developers for the challenge of designing and creating a game in a short timespan,
typically about 48 hours. Participants may be programmers, artists, writers, or others with related skills. Due
to the time limit, these events require rapid prototyping and development skills and encourage participants
to focus on creativity, core mechanics, and bringing a project to completion (or at least a playable state).
Individuals often take part in these events for the express purpose of increasing their skills in these areas. In
addition, many game jams select a theme that must be incorporated by all games developed at the event.
The themes are usually announced at the start of each event to discourage advanced planning and to
encourage creativity.

Although some game jams have panels of judges and declare one or more winners, these events are
typically informal and friendly, and they give participants the chance to connect with each other and provide
a sense of community. Some events may be held at one or more physical locations. Some events may have
no central location; developers work in areas of their own choosing (but are still held to the same time and
schedule restrictions). Some notable long-running game jam events are as follows:

- Global Game Jam: `globalgamejam.org`
  This is the largest game jam in the world—an international event that takes place
  once each year, typically at the end of January. This is *not* an online event; on-site
  participation is required, so there are typically hundreds of physical locations
  (jam sites) around the world where individuals can attend.

- Ludum Dare: `ludumdare.com`
  Major events are held three times a year, and minor (mini) events are held during
  the months when there is no major event. Some participants attend gatherings at
  various sites, but most developers work from their own locations.

- One Game a Month: `onegameamonth.com`
  As the name indicates, these game jams are held monthly. The rules are
  particularly relaxed, and each jam takes place over the course of the entire
  month so as to provide maximum flexibility to participants. The organizer is
  Christer Kaitila, who has also written a book called *The Game Jam Survival Guide*
  (Packt Publishing, 2012) that discusses these events in great detail and provides a
  plethora of advice on how to have a successful experience.

Overcoming Difficulties

On your journey as a game developer, you will stumble at times. Everyone does. Perhaps you can't figure out
how to implement a particular game mechanic. Perhaps your program has an error at runtime and you're
just not sure why. Perhaps your program compiles and runs, but your game entities are behaving in strange
and unexpected ways. Whatever your difficulty may be, don't give up! Spend some time wrestling with the
problem. Try different approaches—perhaps a different data structure, class, or algorithm is called for. Try to

reduce the complexity of your code, break a problem into simpler steps or methods, or implement a simpler version first and incrementally build up to your ultimate goal. Remember that the process of overcoming difficulties is part of being—and helps you grow as—a game developer.

However, also remember that balance is key in development (just as it is in games). Yes, it is valuable to learn how to debug and correct malfunctioning code, but if any particular problem persists for a long time, take a break before you become overly frustrated or discouraged. Keep things in perspective: it probably isn't worth spending five straight hours trying to figure out why your platformer character can't walk up a ramp. Spend some time away from your computer; take a walk, think about something else, and come back to your problem later with a refreshed outlook.

After making a sincere effort to resolve any difficulties yourself, if you are still stuck, don't despair: the vibrant and active community of fellow game developers and enthusiasts out there may be of assistance. The LibGDX forums (www.badlogicgames.com/forum) and Stack Overflow (www.stackoverflow.com) are two excellent places to ask for help. Start by searching these sites to see whether someone has asked the same or a similar question. If not, the next step is to read any recommended guidelines for posting questions.

Typically, you should describe your problem or goal fully and concisely and include details about what you have tried, what has worked, and what hasn't. Sometimes, you might even find that the process of phrasing the question carefully to an external audience will help clarify the problem and inspire you with a possible solution or an alternative approach. If your post includes code, do so in moderation, but make sure that all variables are defined or explained to the reader. Most of all, be polite and patient. The people who frequent these websites often have full-time jobs elsewhere, and voluntarily visit these forums and provide general assistance out of a sense of community. It's perfectly normal that a posted question might not generate a response for 48 hours or more. (In the meantime, be active in the community and see if anyone has posted any questions that *you* might be able to answer.)

Whenever someone responds to your question, be sure to acknowledge them; if they suggest a course of action, write a follow-up post as to whether it worked. And, finally, if you turn out to be the person to resolve your own question, or decide to proceed in a completely different direction to circumvent the problem altogether, you should post that information as well to provide future readers a sense of closure.

Broadening Your Horizons

In addition to increasing your depth of knowledge and programming proficiency, you should devote time to developing a breadth of knowledge in game-related areas, as this will have a positive impact on the quality of the games you produce. This section will briefly mention a few ways to work toward this goal.

Playing Different Games

Most game enthusiasts have a favorite genre. Some people spend most of their time playing first-person shooters, while others prefer to devote their time to role-playing games and so forth. As a game developer, you should consider playing games from as wide a range as you can: action, adventure, puzzle, strategy, role-playing, sports, simulation, storytelling, and so forth. At the same time, try games from various time periods (from classic to modern) and from different-size developers (from large professional companies to smaller studios to independent game makers and game jam competitors).

Even if you don't find a particular game or genre compelling, you will grow as a developer if you spend some time playing such games, especially when you do so with a developer's mindset. Try to understand why people like a given game. Examine each game's level progression, gameplay balance, narrative and character development, artistic style, and interface design. Keep an eye out for what makes each game innovative or unique. Try to mentally place yourself in the role of the original game developers who created the game and think about possible reasons why they might have made the decisions they did; ponder whether you might have done the same or branched out in a different direction.

Increasing Your Skill Set

While you continue to develop games, you should also consider broadening your overall skill set. A solid set of programming skills is highly desirable, but game developers (especially those working independently or in small studios) often need to be a jack-of-all-trades, especially in the areas of graphics and audio. To get started in these areas, I recommend the following software and tutorials:

- Inkscape: `inkscape.org`
  Software for creating vector graphics, freely available. This website contains a list of high-quality tutorials for all skill levels. Most relevant to our interests, however, is a set of game-art tutorials written by Chris Hildenbrand, available here:

  `http://2d-game-art-tutorials.zeef.com/chris.hildenbrand`.

- Ocenaudio: `ocenaudio.com`
  An easy, fast, and powerful audio editor great for simple audio-editing tasks.

- Audacity: `audacityteam.org`
  A multitrack audio editor and recorder, freely available. The Audacity manual contains an extensive list of tutorials that will teach you all sorts of useful recording and editing skills.

Recommended Reading

In addition to broadening your skill set, broadening your knowledge base is also worthwhile. A variety of books are available on topics related to game development that will help you do exactly that. Of course, there are far too many to list here, and no doubt I have omitted some high-quality titles. Nonetheless, this section lists a few representative samples from across a range of fields, a cross-section of topics, to give an indication of what's available out there: game design, literary aspects, history, and social impact:

- *Fundamentals of Game Design* (3rd edition), by Ernest Adams (published 2013; ISBN 0321929675)
  This book discusses a variety of topics: concept development, game-play design, core mechanics, user interfaces, storytelling, and balancing; exercises, worksheets, and case studies are also included.

- *The Ultimate Guide to Video Game Writing and Design* by Flint Dille and John Zuur Platten (published 2008; ISBN 9781580650663)
  Topics covered include integrating story elements into a game, writing a game script, creating design documentation, the creative process, team dynamics, and business considerations.

- *Vintage Games 2.0: An Insider Look at the Most Influential Games of All Time,* by Matt Barton (published 2016; ISBN 1138899135)
  This book explores the history of some of the most influential video games of all time, with a particular focus on their development, critical reception, and impact on the industry.

- *Reality Is Broken: Why Games Make Us Better and How They Can Change the World* by Jane McGonigal (published 2011; ISBN 9780143120612)
  In this book, the author discusses theories from psychology, cognitive science, sociology, and philosophy in the context of game playing and explains how games can make us more productive and change the world for the better.

It is also useful to stay abreast of current news and developments in the game industry, as well as to hear the opinions, approaches, struggles, and successes of your fellow game developers. For these purposes, there is no better alternative to following blogs. The following are some particularly substantial sites featuring regular blog postings (as well as additional useful information and resources):

- Gamasutra: `www.gamasutra.com`
  A website devoted to the art and business of making games that, among other resources, contains curated lists of blog postings that touch on all aspects of the industry.

- GameDev.net: `www.gamedev.net`
  A resource for developers of all fields and expertise, containing articles and tutorials on technical, creative, and business aspects of game development.

- HobbyGameDev: `www.hobbygamedev.com`
  Maintained by Chris DeLeon (a professional video game developer, author, and instructor), this regularly updated website contains articles, advice, tutorials, case studies, interviews, and more.

Disseminating Your Games

Once you have designed and created some games of your own, you should consider sharing them with others—after all, games are meant to be played! This process will require you to package your work in a playable format and find an audience of eager game enthusiasts

Packaging for Desktop Computers

The simplest way to share your games is to create executable JAR files.

1. To do so, verify that your launcher class contains a main method specified as follows (adjust the name and parameters of your method to match this if necessary):

   ```
   public static void main (String[] args)
   ```

2. Then, from the BlueJ menu bar, choose *Project* then *Create Jar File*; a small window appears. This window indicates that the JAR file you create will be executable if the main class is specified. That is exactly what you're hoping to do! From the "Main Class" drop-down list, select the name of your launcher class.

3. In addition, your executable JAR file will require copies of all the LibGDX JAR files used by BlueJ when developing your game. If you have been storing these files in a +libs folder in your project directory, you may skip ahead to the next paragraph. If you have been using an alternative approach, such as storing the LibGDX JAR files in the BlueJ userlibs directory, then the section of the window labeled "Include User Libraries" will include a list of names of JAR files, including those containing the LibGDX classes. In this case, be sure to select the checkboxes next to all of the LibGDX JAR files (the ones starting with "gdx") before continuing.

4. At this point, you can click the *Continue* button. A file directory appears, allowing you to select a folder and asking you to specify a name for the JAR file. It is normal to create the executable in a different location than the source code.

5. Enter the name of your game and then click the *Create* button. Since additional JAR files are required by your application, a directory is created in the location you specified, and in that directory you will find a file with the name of your game and the .jar extension; this directory should also contain all the LibGDX JAR files from your BlueJ project's +libs directory (or those from the BlueJ userlib directory, if you have been using that setup) or those that you selected from the Create Jar File window. All of these JAR files must be located in the same directory to be able to run your game. All the contents of the other folders contained in the BlueJ project directory (such as the assets folder) are stored within your game's JAR file.

To run your game, all you need to do is to double-click your game's JAR file, and your game will start.[1] You can easily share your game with others by sending them the set of files in this directory.[2] The one caveat is that in order to be able to run your game, potential users must have Java installed on their computers. For those who don't, you have two main options:

- You could inform users that they need to install Java and direct them to the Java website, www.java.com.

- You could use a third-party tool to convert your JAR files into native executable files for various operating systems; one such tool is called JWrapper and is available from www.jwrapper.com.

Compiling for Other Platforms

Compiling your project for other platforms (such as Android, iOS, and web browsers via HTML5/JavaScript) is one of the main strengths of LibGDX. However, to do so effectively requires the use of an advanced integrated development environment (IDE). This section only very briefly outlines the steps required to set up a LibGDX project for the Android Studio IDE; this process will take longer than it may appear from the length of this section. For further details concerning configuring the IDE setting, compiling, and exporting, you will need to consult the resources listed.

1. Android Studio[3] is an IDE based on the IntelliJ platform. After downloading and installing this software (the version bundled with the Android SDK), the installer will most likely download an updated set of packages.

2. After this process is complete, visit the LibGDX Wiki project setup site[4] and download gdx-tools.jar, which is an executable JAR file, from the link on the wiki page. Run this file, and you'll see a screen similar to Figure 17-1.

---

[1]If your project runs fine from within BlueJ but you encounter difficulties running the executable JAR file, the BlueJ website contains various suggestions and links to helpful resources at www.bluej.org/help/ask-help.html.
[2]To ensure that no files are forgotten when sending them to others, you may want to use a program such as 7-Zip (www.7-zip.org) to create a single file (called an archive or zip file) that contains all the JAR files needed for your game.
[3]Available at: http://developer.android.com/sdk/index.html.
[4]Available at: http://github.com/libgdx/libgdx/wiki/Project-Setup-Gradle.

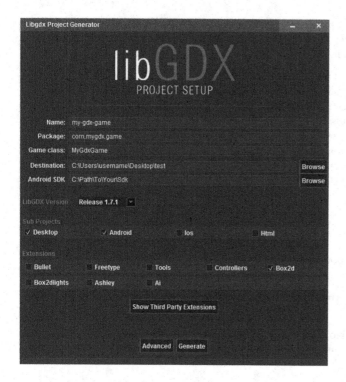

Figure 17-1. The LibGDX project setup tool

3. Here, you'll need to enter a name for your project, a package name (such as com.
    mygdx.spacerocks), the name of your Game class (or, in our extended framework,
    the class that extends BaseGame), the directory where you'd like to store the files,
    and the path where the Android SDK was installed when you installed Android
    Studio.

4. In the next series of checkboxes, you can specify which platforms you'll be
    developing for (for starters, I recommend selecting Android and Desktop). If
    your project requires any third-party libraries or extensions (such as Box2D or
    the game-pad controllers extension), you can specify that here.

5. Then, click the *Generate* button, and a set of project files will be created for you
    in the directory you specified during setup. This process can take a while the
    first time a project is generated, as the setup file will download a number of
    dependency files.

6. When it is all finished, restart Android Studio, select the *Import Project* option,
    and choose the file named build.gradle.

When your project opens, you'll notice a directory structure has been prepared for you, including
directories named core, android, and desktop. The latter two directories contain premade launcher files for
their corresponding platforms. The core directory is where you should place all your other classes. There are
many settings that you will need to configure for your project, such as editing the configuration to specify
a working directory where game assets are located. The LibGDX wiki, referenced earlier, contains details
that you will need to read through to help get your project up and running should you decide to pursue this
direction further.

Finding Distribution Outlets

One of the greatest joys of being a game developer is having others play your games. Even if a project is unfinished, having people play-test your game and provide feedback can help your creations reach even greater heights and attract an even larger audience. Many websites support independent game developers and provide forums for sharing your work with the community. Some of these websites (such as Indie DB and Game Jolt) will even provide you with the ability to upload your games onto their servers after you register for an account.

- `indiedb.com`

- `gamejolt.com`

- `itch.io`

- `gamedev.net`

- `tigsource.com` (The Independent Games Source)

- `forums.indiegamer.com` (The Indie Gamer Forums)

If you post a game to one of these sources, while you're waiting to hear people's opinions on your work, you should strive to be an active participant in their forums. Try out a few games and provide feedback to your fellow developers. We all benefit from a vibrant game development community, so be sure to join in and be a part of it!

With that final piece of advice, we come to the end of our journey together through this book. Hopefully, however, your journey as a game developer will continue. May you have good fortune in all your future endeavors!

APPENDIX A

■ ■ ■

Game Design Documentation

While you will learn many technical and practical aspects of game development as you work through the example projects in this book, it is equally important to have a solid foundation in the theoretical aspects of game design. The first effort to create a framework for these concepts is discussed in a paper published by Robin Hunicke, Marc LeBlanc, and Robert Zubek in 2004.[1] There, they proposed the Mechanics-Dynamics-Aesthetics (MDA) framework, which provides a useful way to categorize the components of a game. They defined *Mechanics* as the formal rules of the game, expressed at the level of data structures and algorithms, *Dynamics* as the interaction between the player and the game mechanics while the game is in progress, and *Aesthetics* as the emotional responses experienced by the player as they interact with the game. Since then, other frameworks have been proposed, each of which provides a different way of analyzing games. A popular example is Jesse Schell's *Elemental Tetrad*,[2] which consists of Mechanics, Story, Aesthetics, and Technology (where aesthetics is defined more broadly than in the original MDA framework). Frameworks such as these are a valuable tool to help people consistently and fully analyze games. Players can use frameworks to better understand and express what they enjoy about particular games. Developers can use the formal structure to help them create a more cohesive design and to organize and document the development process; explaining how to write such documentation is the goal of this appendix.

A *game design document* (GDD) serves as the blueprint or master plan for creating a game. It describes the overall vision of a game, as well as the details (often based on a game design framework such as MDA). Practical aspects are also included, such as a schedule that lists when certain features will be completed, a list of team members and responsibilities, and plans for testing and releasing the game. A GDD can provide clarity and focus while serving as a guide and a reference to the person or people working on the game. To be most effective, the GDD should be as complete as possible before the development process begins. Depending on the flexibility of the developers, a certain amount of modification may be permitted over the course of development, and various adjustments may need to be made after collecting feedback from gameplay testing.

There is no one standard format for game design documents; an internet search will provide many templates for a variety of development scenarios. GDD templates often contain a bulleted list of topics or questions for your consideration (when applicable). In this chapter, we present a similar list of questions for you to ponder as you design your own games, followed by a sample response for a more polished version of the *Space Rocks* game presented earlier in this book. The scope of these questions is particularly good for individuals or small teams working on game development projects. By recording detailed responses to the queries that follow, you will effectively create your own game design document to help guide you through the development process.

---

[1]Hunicke, LeBlanc, and Zubek. "MDA: a Formal Approach to Game Design and Research." *Proceedings of the Nineteenth National Conference on Artificial Intelligence*, 2004.
[2]Schell. *The Art of Game Design: A Book of Lenses*. CRC Press, 2008.

Game Design Documentation Questions

1. Overall Vision

    a. Write a short paragraph (3–6 sentences) explaining your game. (This is sometimes called the *elevator pitch*: a short summary used to quickly and simply describe an idea or product during a 30-second elevator ride.)

    b. How would you describe the genre(s)? Is it single-player or multi-player (and, if the latter, cooperative or competitive)?

    c. What is the target audience? Include demographics (the age, interests, and game experience of potential players), the game platform (desktop, console, or smartphone), and any special equipment required (such as gamepads).

    d. Why will people want to play this game? What features distinguish this game from similar titles? What is the hook that will get people interested at first, how will the game keep people interested, and what makes it fun?

2. Mechanics: the rules of the game world. (Note that the questions that follow are phrased in terms of the game's main character, as distinguished from the player, since the player is the focus of the section on dynamics. However, if no such character exists, the player can be considered as the character.)

    a. What are the character's goals? These may be divided into short-term, medium-term, and long-term goals.

    b. What abilities does the character have? This should include any action the character is capable of performing, such as moving, attacking, defending, collecting items, interacting with the environment, and so forth. Describe the abilities or actions in detail; for example, how high can the character jump? Can the character both walk and run?

    c. What obstacles or difficulties will the character face? Some obstacles are active (such as enemies, projectiles, or traps) and should be described in detail (how they affect the player, their location, movement patterns, and so forth). Other obstacles are passive (such as doors that need to be unlocked, mazes that need to be navigated, puzzles that need to be solved, or time limits that need to be to beat). How can the character overcome these obstacles (items, weapons, spells, quick reflexes)?

    d. What items can the character obtain? What are their effects, where are they obtained, and how frequently do they appear?

    e. What resources must be managed (such as health, money, energy, and experience)? How are these resources obtained and used? Are they limited?

    f. Describe the game-world environment. How large is the world (relative to the screen)? Are there multiple rooms or regions? Is the gameplay linear or open? In other words, is there a strictly linear progression of levels or tasks to complete, or can the character select levels, explore the world, and complete quests at will?

3. Dynamics: the interaction between the player and the game mechanics.

   a. What hardware is required by the game (keyboard, mouse, speakers, gamepad, touchscreen)? Which keys/buttons are used, and what are their effects? How is the player informed of the control scheme (a separate manual document, game menus, tutorials, or in-game signs)?

   b. What type of proficiency will the player need to develop to become proficient at the game? Are there any complex actions that can be created from combinations of basic game mechanics? Do the game mechanics or game-world environment directly or indirectly encourage the player to develop or discourage any particular play strategies? Does the player's performance affect the gameplay mechanics (as in feedback loops)?

   c. What gameplay data is displayed during the game (such as points, health, items collected, time remaining)? Where is this information displayed on the screen? How is the information conveyed (text, icons, charts, status bars)?

   d. What menus, screens, or overlays will there be (title screen, help/ instructions, credits, game over)? How does the player switch between screens, and which screens can be accessed from each other?

   e. How does the player interact with the game at the software level (pause, quit, restart, control volume)?

4. Aesthetics: the visual, audio, narrative, and psychological aspects of the game; these are the elements that most directly affect the player's experience.

   a. Describe the style and feel of the game. Does the game take place in a world that is rural, technological, or magical? Does the game world feel cluttered or sparse, ordered or chaotic, geometric or organic? Is the mood lighthearted or serious? Is the pace relaxing or frenetic? All the aesthetic elements discussed here should work together and contribute to create a coherent and cohesive theme.

   b. Does the game use pixel art, line art, or realistic graphics? Are the colors bright or dark, varied or monochromatic, shiny or dull? Will there be value-based or image-based animations? Are there any special effects? Create a list of graphics you will need.

   c. What style of background music or ambient sounds will the game use? What sound effects will be used for character actions, or for interactions with enemies, objects, and the environment? Will there be sound effects corresponding to interactions with the user interface? List all the music and sounds you will need.

   d. What is the relevant backstory for the game? What is the character's motivation for pursuing their goal? Will there be a plot or storyline that unfolds as the player progresses through the game?

   e. What emotional state(s) does the game try to provoke: happiness, excitement, calm, surprise, pride, sadness, tension, fear, frustration?

f. What makes the game "fun"? Some players may enjoy the graphics, music, story, or emotions evoked by the game. Other features players might enjoy include

i. fantasy (simulating experiences one doesn't have in real life)

ii. role-playing (identifying with a character)

iii. competition (against other players or against records previously set by oneself)

iv. cooperation (working with others toward a common goal)

v. compassion (providing assistance or rescuing others)

vi. discovery (finding objects or exploring a world)

vii. overcoming challenges (such as defeating enemies or solving puzzles)

viii. collection (including game items or badges/trophies for achievements)

ix. social aspects (both within the game and the communities that form around the game).

5. Development

a. If working with a group: list the team members and their roles (game designer, programmer, illustrator, animator, composer, sound editor, writer, manager, etc.), responsibilities, and skills.

b. What equipment will you need for this project? Include both hardware and software that will be needed for content creation (graphics and audio), game development, and playtesting.

c. What are the tasks that need to be accomplished to create this game? Estimate the time required for each task and note the estimated completion date, the team member responsible, and the priority of each feature (in case some features need to be eliminated due to time constraints or unexpected circumstances).

d. What points in the development process are suitable for playtesting? How will you find people to playtest your game? What specific kinds of feedback are you interested in gathering? (For example, you could ask how clear the goals are, how easy or intuitive the controls are, how balanced the difficulty level is, and which parts of the game were most or least enjoyable.) Finally, how will you collect this information (such as a questionnaire or a brief discussion)?

e. What are your plans for dissemination? Do you have plans to promote this game through social media, forum postings, gameplay videos, or advertisements?

Case Study: Space Rocks

This section features a sample set of responses to the game design documentation questions for a significantly more complete version of the *Space Rocks* game from Chapter 4.

1. Overall Vision

    a. *Space Rocks* is a space-themed shoot-em-up game. The player controls a spaceship whose goal is to shoot lasers and destroy rocks that are flying around the screen, earning points along the way. Once each screen is cleared, the player earns bonus points depending on the time needed to complete the level, then moves onto a similar but slightly more difficult level. The ultimate goal is to attain the highest score possible.

    b. This is a single-player action game.

    c. This game is appropriate for all ages and is simple enough to be enjoyed by casual gamers. The target platform is desktop computers, and the game is controlled with the keyboard; gamepad controller support is also possible (only the directional pad and buttons are needed).

    d. This game is fast-paced, and average gameplay sessions will be only a few minutes long, encouraging players to try repeatedly to achieve the highest score they can. A variety of background images and special effects will be used for visual interest.

2. Mechanics

    a. The short-term goal is to avoid being hit by rocks in order to survive. The medium-term goals are to destroy the rocks flying around the screen and to do so quickly to maximize the score for that level. The long-term goal is to earn the highest score possible.

    b. Abilities:

    i. The spaceship moves by rotating left and right and accelerating forward in the direction it is facing. There is no deceleration; to stop or reverse direction, the spaceship must rotate and accelerate in the opposite direction.

    ii. The spaceship is able to shoot lasers (one per second), which travel in a straight line for one second, then fade out and disappear from the game if they haven't collided with a rock. If a laser hits a rock, the rock and the laser are both destroyed.

    iii. The spaceship is surrounded by a shield. If the spaceship is hit by a rock while the shields are active, the rock is destroyed and the shields lose power. After shield power is reduced to 0, the shields disappear, and being hit by a rock destroys the spaceship and ends the game.

    iv. The spaceship also has the ability to instantly, randomly teleport to a new location on the screen. While this can be used for quick escapes from an imminent collision, there is the possibility of teleporting onto a rock, and so the player may choose to use this ability sparingly (only in case of imminent destruction) or perhaps not at all.

c. The only active obstacles are the rocks that the spaceship must avoid and shoot; they have random initial directions and speeds within a given range. The time required to finish each screen affects the player's score, but does not have a direct effect on the spaceship in any way. In each subsequent level, the challenge increases by one or more of the following factors: increasing the number of rocks, increasing the overall speed of the rocks, or decreasing the size of the rocks.

d. When an asteroid is destroyed, there is a 10 percent chance that it will leave behind a small energy capsule, which is an item that can be collected by the player to recharge the shields to 100 percent. Similarly, there is a 10 percent chance that sparkling golden fragments will be left behind, which awards more points to the player. Each item vanishes four seconds after appearing, so the player must be quick if they wish to collect them. (Thus, there is a 20 percent chance overall that a special item will appear, which will be an energy capsule half the time, and gold half the time.)

e. The number of lasers the player can fire are unlimited; the only resource the player needs to be aware of is the remaining shield power, which can be recharged by collecting energy capsule items.

f. The game world is a single screen, but features wraparound: after an object (spaceship, rock, or laser) moves past one edge of the screen, it reappears on the opposite edge. This design makes the game world feel larger (by not having a boundary) while still allowing the player to see all objects in the game world at the same time.

3. Dynamics

a. To play this game, a desktop computer is required. Navigating the menus requires a mouse to click on various buttons. The spaceship is controlled entirely by the keyboard: left/right arrow keys rotate the ship, up arrow activates the thrusters and accelerates the ship forward, spacebar shoots lasers, and the X key teleports the spaceship to a random location. Gamepad controls are provided but are optional: directional pad left/right rotates the ship, and three buttons (such as A, B, and X on an XBox 360-style gamepad) are used for acceleration, lasers, and teleportation, respectively. The controls are listed in an instructions menu.

b. To be proficient at this game, the player will need to be able to precisely control the movement of the spaceship and predict the position of the rocks to line up shots from a distance. Maintaining a large distance between the spaceship and the rocks minimizes the chance that the shields will be damaged, but also makes it more difficult to obtain the items that can be dropped.

c. The amount of power remaining in the shields is indicated visually by the shield graphic. A number indicating the points earned by the player is displayed in the top-center of the screen; the user interface is kept simple to avoid overlapping game-world elements as much as possible. When each level is complete, a congratulations message appears on the screen, as well as the number of seconds it took to clear the screen and the corresponding point bonus; the player presses a key to continue on to the next level.

    d. The menu system is navigated by using the mouse. There will be a start menu that displays a title graphic, the highest score earned, and buttons that allow the player to go to an instructions menu or begin the game right away (for experienced players). The instructions menu displays the backstory, lists the controls (keyboard and gamepad) for the game, and has a button that allows the player to return to the main menu. When the player loses the game, a "Game Over" message appears, along with another message if the player has earned a high score, followed by a button that allows the player to return to the start menu.

    e. There is no in-game pause or volume-control functionality. The player can quit the game at any time by clicking on the standard window controls located in the top-right corner of the window.

4. Aesthetics

    a. The game is set in outer space and has many technological elements. The game world feels increasingly cluttered and chaotic due to the increasingly large number of rocks drifting around at random angles. As the rocks are destroyed in each level, the pace becomes more relaxed.

    b. The graphics are colorful and cartoonish. There will be a variety of background images used to make the levels feel different. The basic graphics required will be the spaceship, lasers, and rocks. There will be visual special effects corresponding to player actions and interactions between game-world objects:

        i. A particle effect simulating thruster fire will appear whenever the player accelerates the spaceship.

        ii. The shields will have a slow rotation and pulse effect to make them appear more dynamic, and their opacity will change according to the remaining shield power.

        iii. Lasers will fade out before they disappear.

        iv. When teleporting, a wormhole-like animation will appear at the original and the new locations of the spaceship.

        v. Whenever a rock is destroyed (from laser or shield collision), the rock will disappear and an explosion will appear in its place.

        vi. Items will feature a pulsing effect to draw the player's attention and will fade out before they disappear. If they are collected, a small sparkling effect will appear.

c. The menus will feature a quiet, ambient technological humming or droning sound, as one might imagine in the background of a spaceship. A small beep will play when navigation buttons are pressed. The game itself will feature exciting, driving background music to reinforce the mood of the game. Analogous to the visual effects described previously, there will be sound effects corresponding to player actions and interactions between game-world objects:

    i. A continuous rocket exhaust sound will play as long as the player is accelerating the spaceship.

    ii. When a rock collides with the shields, an electric shock–like sound will play.

    iii. A laser fire sound will play when each laser is shot.

    iv. When teleporting, a deep whoosh-like sound will play.

    v. Whenever a rock is destroyed, a rumbling explosion sound will be heard.

    vi. If an item is collected, a quiet chime sound will play.

d. The backstory for the game is: "You are a spaceship pilot tasked with clearing out the interstellar debris that makes deep-space voyages dangerous for less-experienced pilots. With the aid of your advanced laser, shield, and teleportation technology, destroy as many rocks as you can before your own ship is destroyed and you are teleported back to your home base."

e. This game creates a feeling of excitement and tension.

f. The fun aspect of this game comes from competition with oneself and with others to achieve the highest score possible. (Each player will have to keep track of their own high scores.)

5. Development

a. This project will completed individually; graphics and audio will be obtained from third-party websites that make their assets available under the Creative Commons license, and so the main task will be programming.

b. A desktop computer (with keyboard, mouse, and speakers), a gamepad controller, and internet access will be necessary to complete this project. Playtesting can be performed on-site or remotely.

c. The main sequence of steps to complete this project is as follows:

    i. Obtain graphics.

    ii. Program ship movement and abilities (laser fire, teleportation, shields).

    iii. Program rock movement and laser-rock interaction.

    iv. Implement user interface (point system and high-score storage) and game-over screen.

      v.   Add items (shield recharge and bonus points).

      vi.   Add visual effects, music, and sound effects.

      vii. Load new level with increased difficulty when screen is cleared.

      viii. Menu system (start and instructions screens)

      ix.   Gamepad support

d.   The main points for playtesting are after the user interface is finished, after the new level feature is added, and after all the preceding steps have been completed. The questions that will be asked are:

      i.   How do the spaceship controls feel: too slow/sluggish, too fast, or just right?

      ii.   Is the gameplay too hard or too easy, too short or too long?

      iii. Does the difficulty level increase at a slow, moderate, or fast pace?

      iv. Do you have any suggestions to improve this game?

e.   This game will be disseminated for free as an executable file through various indie game-portal websites, and gameplay images and video will be posted via social media.

APPENDIX B

Review of Java Fundamentals

This appendix will briefly review the core Java concepts that you should be familiar with to understand the material presented in this book. This is not a complete introduction to Java programming, so if any of the topics are unfamiliar, you may want to consult a textbook or tutorial series on Java[1] to learn more about the corresponding material.

Data Types and Operators

Let's begin by listing some of the basic, or *primitive*, data types available in Java:

- int: Integers (numbers with no decimal part)

- float: Decimal values

- double: Decimal values, stored with twice the precision of a float

- char: A single character (a letter, number, or symbol)

- boolean: The value true or false

Another commonly used data type is String, which represents text: a set of characters. Technically, this is not a primitive data type, but it can be initialized in a similar way.

Java also uses the common binary arithmetic operators: addition, subtraction, multiplication, division (or quotient, in the case of integers), and remainder, represented by the symbols +, -, *, /, and %, respectively. When used with two values of the same type, the result will also be of the same type. For example, the value of 5.0/2.0 is 2.5, whereas the value of 5/2 is 2. The results are different because in the first example the values have type double, and in the second example the values have type int.

When performing arithmetic involving two types of values, the values will be converted, or *cast*, to the more complex type. For instance, 5.0/2 yields a value of 2.5. If desired, a numeric value of one type can be manually cast to another type by prefacing it with the name of the desired type in parentheses. For example, (double)2 produces a value of 2.0, whereas (int)2.5 produces the value 2. (When casting to an int, the value is always rounded down to the nearest integer value.)

Primitive variables can be declared and initialized with a single line of code, with the following syntax:

```
variableType variableName = initialValue;
```

---

[1]The official Java tutorials, maintained by the Oracle corporation, are available online at http://docs.oracle.com/javase/tutorial/java/index.html.

© Lee Stemkoski 2018
L. Stemkoski, *Java Game Development with LibGDX*, https://doi.org/10.1007/978-1-4842-3324-5

Alternatively, these tasks can be carried out in separate statements:

```
variableType variableName;
variableName = initialValue;
```

In addition to using = to assign values to variables, Java provides *assignment operators* (for brevity), which modify the value of a variable by a constant amount. For example, the statement x = x + 5 can be replaced with the statement x += 5. Each of the other arithmetic operations has a corresponding assignment operator: -=, *=, /=, and %=.

Numeric values can be compared with the conditional operators: == for equality, != for inequality, < for less than, <= for less than or equal to, > for greater than, and >= for greater than or equal to. The result of a comparison is a Boolean value—true or false—and can be stored in a Boolean variable if desired. Boolean values can be combined with the Boolean operators: && for "and," || for "or," and ! for "not."

An *array* is an object that contains a fixed number of values of the same type. The length of the array is set when the array is created. The values in an array can be initialized when it is created (and the size will be inferred). For example, the following creates an array that contains five characters:

```
char[] letters = { 'g' , 'a' , 'm' , 'e' , 's' } ;
```

Alternatively, an array can be created with only the length specified, shown here for an array that will contain ten integers (and the values can be set at a later time):

```
int[] values = new int[10];
```

The items in an array are accessed by their position, or index, which begins with the number 0. For example, given the preceding array named letters, the expression letters[0] produces the value 'g', letters[1] produces 'a', and so forth, up to letters[4], which produces 's'. Note that the array has length 5, but the positions are numbered 0 through 4. (This is true in general; an array with length *n* will have indices numbered 0 through *n* – 1.) Note that once an array is created, its size cannot be changed; trying to store a value in an array at a nonexistent index value will result in an error when the program is running.

Control Structures

The statements within a Java program are typically run one after the other in sequence. Control structures can change the order of execution, either by running some statements only when certain conditions are met or by repeating a given set of statements.

Conditional Statements

An if statement is used to specify that a certain set of statements should be run only when a certain condition (or combination of conditions or a Boolean expression) evaluates to true. For example, the following code will add 100 to the variable bonus only if the value of time is greater than 60; if the value of time is *not* greater than 60, the code contained within the braces will not be executed.

```
if (time > 60)
{
    bonus += 100;
}
```

Any number of statements may be contained within the braces. However, if only one statement is contained within the braces, the braces may be omitted, and the code will have the same results, as follows:

```
if (time > 60)
    bonus += 100;
```

An if-else statement is used when you need to provide an alternative set of statements that will be executed when the associated condition evaluates to false. The following code builds on the previous example, adding the behavior that if the value of time is not greater than 60, then the value of bonus will be incremented by 50 instead.

```
if (time > 60)
{
    bonus += 100;
}
else
{
    bonus += 50;
}
```

On occasion, you may want to test a variable for equality against a set of values and execute a different set of statements in each case. For example, consider the following code, which prints a message depending on whether the value of itemCount is equal to 0, 1, 2, or anything else.

```
if (itemCount == 0)
    System.out.print("You have no items.");
else if (itemCount == 1)
    System.out.print("You have a single item.");
else if (itemCount == 2)
    System.out.print("You have two items.");
else
    System.out.print("You have many items!");
```

A switch statement presents an alternative way to write this type of code (which is often easier to read). The following code features a switch statement that has exactly the same effect as the if-else statements presented previously. Each of the value comparisons in the if-else statements correspond to an occurrence of the case keyword within the switch code block, while the final else statement corresponds to the default keyword. After listing the set of statements to be executed for a given case, a break statement must be included (otherwise, the statements corresponding to the following cases will also be executed, regardless of whether the variable is equal to the value presented).

```
switch (itemCount)
{
    case 0:
        System.out.print("You have no items.");
        break;
    case 1:
        System.out.print("You have a single item.");
        break;
```

```java
case 2:
    System.out.print("You have two items.");
    break;
default:
    System.out.print("You have many items!");
}
```

Repetition Statements

The while statement is used to repeat a set of statements as long as a given condition is true. For example, the following code will continue to add 5 to the variable score and subtract 1 from the value of stars as long as the value of stars is greater than 0:

```java
while (stars > 0)
{
    score += 5;
    stars -= 1;
}
```

A while statement is particularly useful when a set of statements needs to be repeated an unknown number of times. You must be careful when using a while statement, however, because if the associated condition always remains true, then the statements will continue to execute forever!

The for statement is used to repeat a set of statements a fixed number of times. In typical usage, a variable is set to an initial value, and as long as a condition involving the variable is true, a set of statements is executed. Afterward, the value of the variable is changed by a given amount, the condition is checked again, and so forth, until the given condition evaluates to false. The following example initially sets a variable n to 1, and as long as n is less than 10, adds 3 to points; the value of n is increased by 1 with each iteration of the loop. Note that the statement n++ has the same effect as n += 1.

```java
for (int n = 1; n < 10; n++)
{
    points += 3;
}
```

For loops are particularly useful in tasks involving arrays. As an example, the following code initializes an array named numbers to store five integers, and the for loop stores the value 10*n at each position n in the array. Note that the loop variable is initialized to 0 (as this is the first index in an array), and the condition is that the variable is less than the length (that is, the size or the capacity) of the array. (You must use the less-than comparison in the condition, since the largest index in an array is always equal to the length of the array minus 1.)

```java
int[] numbers = new int[5];
for (int index = 0; index < numbers.length; index++)
{
        numbers[index] = 10 * index;
}
```

A variation on the syntax of the `for` statement, called the enhanced for statement, is convenient for accessing the values of an array. As a motivating example, consider the following code, which takes each of the values from an array called grades and adds them all to a variable called `total`:

```java
for (int index = 0; index < grades.length; index++)
{
    int num = grades[index];
    total += num;
}
```

The exact same result can be achieved with less code using the following code, which automatically extracts the elements of an array (in order), and stores them into a variable before proceeding to the statements contained within the loop:

```java
for (int num : grades)
{
    total += num;
}
```

Methods

A *method* is a set of statements, grouped together, that can be called upon repeatedly to perform a task. Every method has an associated name, can take zero or more values as input, and may or may not return a value. Each method is contained within a structure called a *class*, which is covered in further detail later. The syntax for a method is presented here, and the various components are summarized immediately afterward:

```java
modifer returnType methodName ( variableType variableName , ... )
{
     // statements
}
```

- `modifier` is a keyword (such as `public` or `private`) that indicates where this method can be used in the program (see later in the appendix for more information).

- `returnType` indicates the type of data being returned and can be set to `void` if no data is returned by the method.

- `methodName` is the name of the method.

Within the parentheses, for each input that is to be provided, you must list the type of input (indicated by `variableType`) and the name by which it will be referred to in the statements that follow (indicated by `variableName`).

For example, the following public-access method called average takes two `float` values as input, calculates their average (which is also a `float`), and returns this value:

```java
public float average(float x, float y)
{
    return (x + y) / 2;
}
```

Methods can be called upon in two ways, depending on how they are written. Some methods may be called from the class that contains them. For example, the Math class contains a method named sqrt that calculates the square root of a number; to use this method to calculate the square root of 4, you would write Math.sqrt(4). Alternatively, some methods are called from a variable. As an example, every String variable contains a method named charAt that returns the character at a given position in the string. If you create a String named word that contains the text "games," then word.charAt(2) returns the character 'm'.

Objects and Classes

An *object* is a collection of related data and methods that operate on that data. A *class* is a set of code that is used as a prototype or a blueprint from which objects can be created. Some classes are automatically available in Java (such as the String, Math, and System classes). To use other classes in your program, you must indicate which of the many available classes should be loaded by using an import statement. For example, to be able to use the Random class in your program, which is part of the java.util package,[2] at the beginning of your program you must include this line:

```
import java.util.Random;
```

To create an object from this class (also called an *instance* of the class), you use the new operator, followed by a special method of the class called the *constructor*. The name of the constructor method will always be identical to the name of the corresponding class, and it may require input values to initialize the data that belongs to the class. For example, to create an instance of the Random class, you would use the following code:

```
Random rand = new Random();
```

Following this, you could then use the methods of the variable rand, such as nextInt (which returns a randomly generated integer), as follows:

```
int secret = rand.nextInt();
```

The previously mentioned String class is special in that it may be initialized in the same way as a primitive type variable (like int or float), but it may also be initialized using the new operator (which requires the text to be stored as input):

```
String name = new String("Lee");
```

One of the most powerful features of Java (or any object-oriented programming language) is the ability to define your own classes. As an example, the following class, called Fraction, stores the data used in a fractional number: a numerator and a denominator (both integers). There is a constructor to set these values, a method to create a String representation of the fraction, and a method to convert the fraction to a float value (by calculating the quotient).

```
class Fraction
{
    int numerator;
    int denominator;
```

---

[2]To find out the package that contains a particular class, you can consult the Java documentation or the documentation for the particular library you are using.

```
    // constructor
    Fraction(int n, int d)
    {
        numerator = n;
        denominator = d;
    }

    // creates a String representation
    public String toString()
    {
        return (numerator + "/" + denominator);
    }

    // convert to a float value
    public float convertToFloat()
    {
        return (float)numerator / denominator;
    }
}
```

Next is a sample class that uses the Fraction class as defined previously. In particular, it contains a method named main that you will run, which creates and initializes a Fraction object and then uses its methods and prints their results to the screen. A technical aside: you must declare the main method as static in order to be able to run the method directly from the class (with the code Sample.main( )) rather than from an instance of the class.

```
class Sample
{
    public static void main()
    {
        Fraction frac = new Fraction(3,4);
        String fracString = frac.toString();
        float  fracValue = frac.convertToFloat();
        System.out.println( "The value of " + fracString + " is " + fracValue );
    }
}
```

Sometimes, when you write a class, you'll want to control access to data, either to restrict the possible set of values that can be assigned or to prevent another part of the program from accidentally changing the data (possibly due to a mistake in the code). *Access modifiers* are used in such situations; they can be included to specify whether other classes can use a particular field or method. The two most common modifiers are public, which indicates that any class can access the corresponding variable or method, and private, which indicates that it may be accessed only within the class in which it is defined. There is a less frequently used modifier, protected, which allows access within the defining class and any subclasses of (that is, those that extend) the defining class.

As a practical example of when access modifiers are useful, let's return to our custom `Fraction` class. The denominator of a fraction should never be set equal to zero (because division by zero leads to contradictory mathematical results). You prevent this unwanted behavior by setting the class fields to `private` and rewriting the constructor (or any other relevant methods) to take action in this case, as demonstrated here:

```java
class Fraction
{

    private int numerator;
    private int denominator;

    // constructor
    Fraction(int n, int d)
    {
        numerator = n;
        if (d == 0)
        {
            System.err.println("Invalid denominator; changing value to 1.");
            denominator = 1;
        }
        else
        {
            denominator = d;
        }
    }

    // other methods remain the same as before
}
```

Summary

These topics—data types, operators, control structures, methods, and classes—are the foundations on which you will create your own programs. In real applications, your code will typically be much longer than the examples presented; your classes will no doubt contain multiple `import` statements, declare many variables of various types, and have an assortment of methods, each of which contains a significant number of statements. When working on your own projects, in addition to writing your own classes, your programs will probably use many predefined classes as well. For this reason, it is good to spend some time becoming familiar with the style and type of information that is presented in the Java documentation format, whether it be the official Java language reference[3] or the documentation for any Java libraries you include in your projects.

---

[3] http://docs.oracle.com/javase/8/docs/api/

■ ■ ■

Extended Framework Class Reference

In this book, you have developed multiple classes to extend the LibGDX framework. Each of these new classes in turn contains many fields and methods. For your convenience, this appendix contains a summary of the functionality of the most important classes that are used across multiple chapters: BaseScreen, BaseActor, and TilemapActor.

The BaseScreen Class

The BaseScreen class was introduced in Chapter 3 to support games that contain multiple screens and to simplify the implementation of the game loop. You extend this class in nearly every game project in this book. There are two abstract methods that extensions of this class must implement: initialize, which is where you set up game entities, and update, which processes continuous user input (such as a character that moves as long as a key is held down) and handles the game logic (such as interactions between game entities). This class also implements the InputProcessor interface, which enables extensions of this class to handle discrete input (such as a character that jumps one time when a key is pressed) by overriding methods such as keyDown.

Constructor

- BaseScreen()
  Initializes mainStage, uiStage, and uiTable

Fields

- protected Stage mainStage
  The stage to which all game entities should be added

- protected Stage uiStage
  The stage that contains the user-interface table

- protected Table uiTable
  A table used to organize user-interface elements

Methods

- `void dispose()`
  Called when this screen should release all resources

- `void hide()`
  Called when this is no longer the active screen in a game

- `abstract void initialize()`
  Used to initialize game objects and arrange user-interface elements.

- `boolean isTouchDownEvent(Event e)`
  Used for checking if an event is a touch-down event.

- `boolean keyDown(int keycode)`
  Called when a key is pressed. (This and other `InputProcessor` methods return
  true if input is processed and should not be handled by any other methods or
  `InputProcessor` objects.)

- `boolean keyTyped(char c)`
  Called when a key is typed

- `boolean keyUp(int keycode)`
  Called when a key is released

- `boolean mouseMoved(int screenX, int screenY)`
  Called when the mouse is moved without any buttons' being pressed

- `void pause()`
  Only called in Android applications when application is paused

- `void render(float dt)`
  Called when the screen should render itself

- `void resize(int width, int height)`
  Called when the application window is resized

- `void resume()`
  Only called in Android applications when application is resumed (after being
  paused)

- `boolean scrolled(int amount)`
  Called when the mouse wheel is scrolled

- `void show()`
  Called when this becomes the active screen in a game.

- `boolean touchDown(int screenX, int screenY, int pointer, int button)`
  Called when the screen is touched or a mouse button is pressed

- `boolean touchDragged(int screenX, int screenY, int pointer)`
  Called when a finger or the mouse is dragged

- `boolean touchUp(int screenX, int screenY, int pointer, int button)`
  Called when a finger is lifted or a mouse button is released

- `abstract void update(float dt)`
  Processes continuous input and updates game logic

The BaseActor Class

The BaseActor class was introduced in Chapter 3 to support many of the features needed for game entities: creating and rendering animations, implementing physics-based movement, and detecting and preventing collisions. A few methods were introduced in later chapters as necessary (such as wrapAroundWorld in Chapter 4 and isWithinDistance in Chapter 5). The BaseActor class also greatly simplifies retrieving lists of instances of a particular class with its getList method.

Constructor

- BaseActor(float x, float y, Stage s)
  Sets initial position of actor and adds to stage

Methods

- void accelerateAtAngle(float angle)
  Updates accelerate vector by angle and value stored in acceleration field

- void accelerateForward()
  Updates accelerate vector by current rotation angle and value stored in acceleration field

- void act(float dt)
  Processes all actions and related code for this object; automatically called by act method in Stage class

- void alignCamera()
  Center camera on this object while keeping camera's range of view (determined by screen size) completely within world bounds.

- void applyPhysics(float dt)
  Adjust velocity vector based on acceleration, deceleration, and maximum speed, then adjust position based on velocity vector.

- void boundToWorld()
  If an edge of an object moves past the world bounds, this adjusts its position to keep it completely on screen.

- void centerAtActor(BaseActor other)
  Repositions this BaseActor so its center is aligned with center of other BaseActor

- void centerAtPosition(float x, float y)
  Aligns center of actor at given position coordinates

- static int count(Stage, String className)
  Returns number of instances of a given class (that extends BaseActor)

- void draw(Batch batch, float parentAlpha)
  Draws current frame of animation; automatically called by draw method in Stage class

- Polygon getBoundaryPolygon()
  Returns bounding polygon for this BaseActor, adjusted by Actor's current position and rotation

- `static ArrayList<BaseActor> getList(Stage stage, String className)`
  Retrieves a list of all instances of the object from the given stage with the given class name or whose class extends the class with the given name

- `float getMotionAngle()`
  Gets the angle of motion (in degrees), calculated from the velocity vector

- `float getSpeed()`
  Calculates the speed of movement (in pixels/second)

- `static Rectangle getWorldBounds()`
  Gets world dimensions (width and height)

- `boolean isAnimationFinished()`
  Checks if animation is complete: if play mode is normal (not looping) and elapsed time is greater than time corresponding to last frame

- `boolean isMoving()`
  Determines if this object is moving (if speed is greater than zero)

- `boolean isWithinDistance(float distance, BaseActor other)`
  Determines if this BaseActor is near other BaseActor (according to collision polygons)

- `Animation<TextureRegion> loadAnimationFromFiles(String[] fileNames, float frameDuration, boolean loop)`
  Creates an animation from images stored in separate files.

- `Animation<TextureRegion> loadAnimationFromSheet(String fileName, int rows, int cols, float frameDuration, boolean loop)`
  Creates an animation from a spritesheet: a rectangular grid of images stored in a single file.

- `Animation<TextureRegion> loadTexture(String fileName)`
  Convenience method for creating a one-frame animation from a single texture.

- `boolean overlaps(BaseActor other)`
  Determine if this BaseActor overlaps other BaseActor (according to collision polygons)

- `Vector2 preventOverlap(BaseActor other)`
  Implement a "solid"-like behavior: when there is overlap, move this BaseActor away from other BaseActor along minimum translation vector until there is no overlap.

- `void setAcceleration(float acc)`
  Set acceleration of this object.

- `void setAnimation(Animation<TextureRegion> anim)`
  Sets the animation used when rendering this actor; also sets actor size.

- `void setAnimationPaused(boolean pause)`
  Sets the pause state of the animation.

- `void setBoundaryPolygon(int numSides)`
  Replaces default (rectangle) collision polygon with an *n*-sided polygon

- void setBoundaryRectangle()
  Sets rectangular-shaped collision polygon

- void setDeceleration(float dec)
  Sets deceleration of this object

- void setMaxSpeed(float ms)
  Sets maximum speed of this object

- void setMotionAngle(float angle)
  Sets the angle of motion (in degrees)

- void setOpacity(float opacity)
  Sets the opacity of this actor

- void setSpeed(float speed)
  Sets the speed of movement (in pixels/second) in current direction

- static void setWorldBounds(BaseActor ba)
  Sets world dimensions for use by methods alignCamera() and boundToWorld()

- static void setWorldBounds(float width, float height)
  Sets world dimensions for use by methods alignCamera() and boundToWorld().

- void wrapAroundWorld()
  If this object moves completely past the world bounds, adjust its position to the opposite side of the world.

The TilemapActor Class

The TilemapActor class is used to work with files created by the Tiled map editor program. It automatically renders any image layers or tile layers and can retrieve data stored as rectangles or tiles in an object layer. This class is first created in Chapter 10 and used extensively in Chapters 11 and 12.

Constructor

- TilemapActor(String filename, Stage theStage)
  Loads a Tiled map data file (*.tmx) with a given filename and adds it to a stage so that the tilemap automatically renders.

Fields

- static int windowHeight
  The width of the window where the tilemap will be rendered

- static int windowHeight
  The width of the window where the tilemap will be rendered

Methods

- `void act(float dt)`
  Automatically called by the Stage to which this actor is attached

- `void draw(Batch batch, float parentAlpha)`
  Automatically called by the Stage to which this actor is attached; keeps the map camera position in sync with the stage camera position and renders the map to the screen.

- `ArrayList<MapObject> getRectangleList(String propertyName)`
  Searches the map layers for Rectangle objects that contain a property (key) called "name" with associated value propertyName; typically used to store non-actor information such as spawn-point locations or dimensions of Solid objects.

- `ArrayList<MapObject> getTileList(String propertyName)`
  Searches the map layers for Tile Objects (tile-like elements of object layers) that contain a property (key) called "name" with associated value propertyName; typically used to store actor information and to create instances.

Index

A

Abstract class, 33
Adventure games, 271–296, *See also* Treasure
     Quest game
Ambient light, 362
Android Studio, 397–398
Animation
    image-based (*see* Image-based animations)
    value-based, 41–42
Anonymous inner class, 107
Anonymous instance, 107
Audacity, 395
Audio
    Rhythm Tappergame (*see* Rhythm
        Tapper game)
    sound and music, 143–147
Audionautix websites, 157, 393

B

BaseActor3D class
    create, 366
    enable actor, 368
    Matrix4 object, 365–366
    position variable, 367
    resizing model, 368
    rotating, 367
    turn angle, 368
BaseActor class
    constructor, 421
    game entities, 421
    methods, 421
BaseScreen class
    abstract methods, 419
    constructor, 419
    fields, 419
    InputProcessor interface, 419
    methods, 420
Bfxr websites, 392
Blip-like sound effect, 147

BlueJ, 3–4, 312, 396
    code editor, 6
    download options, 4
    features, 7
    installation, 4
    Open Editor selection, 6
    project window, 5
    text display, 7
Blur shader, 352–354
Border shader, 350–352
BounceOff method, 196–197
Breadth-first search algorithm, 325

C

52 Card Pickup, 207, 219–225, *See also* Solitaire
    card game
Cloning the classics approach, 392
Collectible card game, 391
Cool Text websites, 392
Crazy Eights game, 226
Cutscenes, 121
    BaseActor class, 124
    DelayAction, 124
    DialogBox, 123
    framework, 121
    SceneActions, 124
    Scene class act method, 125
    SceneSegment, 122
    SetTextAction, 123
    Starfish Collector game, 127
    static methods, 125
    StoryScreen class, 127–129

D

Default shaders
    attribute variables, 346–347
    fragment shader, 346
    keywords and commands, 346
    mathematical functions, 346

© Lee Stemkoski 2018
L. Stemkoski, *Java Game Development with LibGDX*, https://doi.org/10.1007/978-1-4842-3324-5

Get the eBook for only $5!

Why limit yourself?

With most of our titles available in both PDF and ePUB format, you can access your content wherever and however you wish—on your PC, phone, tablet, or reader.

Since you've purchased this print book, we are happy to offer you the eBook for just $5.

To learn more, go to http://www.apress.com/companion or contact support@apress.com.

Apress®

Printed in the United States
By Bookmasters